THE BLACK GEOGRAPHIC

THE BLACK

Camilla Hawthorne and
Jovan Scott Lewis, editors

GEOGRAPHIC

Praxis, Resistance, Futurity

DUKE UNIVERSITY PRESS
Durham and London
2023

© 2023 DUKE UNIVERSITY PRESS
Project Editor: Liz Smith
Designed by A. Mattson Gallagher
Typeset in Adobe Caslon Pro, Scala Sans Pro, and Martin
by Copperline Book Services

Library of Congress Cataloging-in-Publication Data
Names: Hawthorne, Camilla A., editor. | Lewis, Jovan Scott, editor.
Title: The Black geographic : praxis, resistance, futurity /
Camilla Hawthorne and Jovan Scott Lewis, editors.
Description: Durham : Duke University Press, 2023. |
Includes bibliographical references and index.
Identifiers: LCCN 2022061115 (print)
LCCN 2022061116 (ebook)
ISBN 9781478025153 (paperback)
ISBN 9781478020172 (hardcover)
ISBN 9781478027249 (ebook)
Subjects: LCSH: Black people—Race identity. | Black people—Study
and teaching. | Human geography. | African diaspora. | BISAC:
SOCIAL SCIENCE / Black Studies (Global) | SOCIAL SCIENCE /
Human Geography
Classification: LCC DT16.5 .G535 2023 (print) | LCC DT16.5 (ebook) |
DDC 305.8960071—dc23/eng/20230330
LC record available at https://lccn.loc.gov/2022061115
LC ebook record available at https://lccn.loc.gov/2022061116

Cover art: Sharita Towne, detail from *Black Life & Black Spatial
Imaginaries, Glimpses across Time & Space: A Visual Bibliography,
2018–2019.* Research and concept with Lisa K. Bates. Original
printed with Watershed Center for Fine Art Publishing and
Research. Image courtesy of the artist.

Duke University Press gratefully acknowledges the Ford Family
Foundation, which provided funds toward the publication of
this book.

CONTENTS

Black Geographies

Material Praxis of Black Life and Study

CAMILLA HAWTHORNE AND JOVAN SCOTT LEWIS

Our current moment is a deeply urgent one. The global resurgence of the far right; the increased visibility of anti-Black violence in the United States and beyond; and configurations of racism, nationalism, and xenophobia are but a few examples of the deadly entanglements of white supremacy, capitalism, settler colonialism, patriarchy, and heteronormativity that mark this historical conjuncture. In response to the need for new analytical tools and political imaginaries, scholars and activists alike have (re)turned to the history of the Black radical tradition; questioned the "human" and other taken-for-granted categories of liberalism; and engaged in challenging conversations about new social movements, including the possibilities and perils of solidarity and transversal alliance. Just as our current moment is an urgent one, so is the need for a critical intervention into the epistemological frameworks of differentiation that have formed it.

These formulas for shaping our world have long been the same in disciplinary pursuits to understand it.[1] The emergence of geography as a discipline was intertwined with colonialism, enslavement, and imperialism, and this history continues to shape the ways that mainstream geography has engaged with questions of racism and race.[2] Although racism—and "scientific racism" in particular—is commonly understood to be rooted in now-discredited understandings of biological or body-based difference, geography in the eighteenth and nineteenth centuries also contributed to the production of racial essentialisms based on *place*. Since the Enlightenment, race has been understood in spatial terms, through "sedentarist metaphysics."[3] This approach roots individuals and groups in bounded place, classifies them according to their geographic locations, and arranges them in a spatiotemporal hierarchy.[4] Geography is thus implicated in the elaboration of racial theories that continue to animate colonialism, fascism, and violent nationalisms.[5] To put it succinctly, the production of *space* is tied to the production of *difference*.

Until relatively recently, mainstream accounts of disciplinary geography have tended to sweep this history under the rug. Textbooks about the history of geography typically emphasize a sharp break between Eurocentric Enlightenment and Victorian geographies (or, at least, bracket the racism of geographers like Kant as inconsequential to their philosophical production) on the one hand, and the interventions of radical Marxist geographers studying inequality in the twentieth century on the other.[6] This latter work is undoubtedly important and also provided some of the earlier disciplinary engagements with racial inequality in geography; in fact, this scholarship is one component of the intellectual scaffolding of Black Geographies. Yet these interventions are all too frequently heralded as part of a redemptionist narrative that seeks to purge geography of its racist history. It is true that by the mid-twentieth century, mainstream geography no longer centered *race* as a unit of analysis, and geographers gradually abandoned environmental determinisms in favor of studying the economic structures that produced inequality. In practice, however, this meant that race was often studied as an ex post facto justification for colonial dispossession, exploitation, and a global division of labor—the ideological superstructure atop the clanking material gears of capital's totalizing reach.[7] But in this process, the discipline of geography failed to develop the sorts of sophisticated theoretical tools necessary to engage with the ongoing production of race and racisms via the production of space.[8] Laura Pulido has described this as the difference between research that documents racial differences and inequalities, and research that is fundamentally grounded in critical race theory.[9]

In this context, the field of Black Geographies has emerged as a rich site of both intellectual and political engagement. In *Black Geographies and the Politics of Place* (the first published anthology of Black Geographies scholarship), Katherine McKittrick and Clyde Woods identify three central areas of intervention in the study of Black Geographies:

1 "...the ways in which essentialism situates black subjects and their geopolitical concerns as being elsewhere (on the margin, the underside, outside the normal), a spatial practice that conveniently props up the mythical norm and erases or obscures the daily struggles of particular communities."

2 "...how the lives of these subjects demonstrate that 'common-sense' workings of modernity and citizenship are worked out, and normalized, though geographies of exclusion..."

3 "...the situated knowledge of these communities and their contributions to both real and imagined human geographies [as] significant political acts and expressions."[10]

This volume heeds the call of Woods and McKittrick, building on the profound intellectual labor of generations of scholars of Black Geographies to chart a path forward. As Black Geographies becomes a discipline and a broader process for studying, identifying, and analyzing Black life, this volume seeks to take the multitudinal spatial relations that Black Geographic analyses offer beyond the discipline of geography, as conventionally understood.

The chapters in this volume unpack the theoretical innovations of Black Geographies scholarship, which approach Blackness as neither singular nor universal but as always historically and geographically situated and produced through complex spatial processes and diasporic routes. They do this across many of the key sites of inquiry in Black Geographies—for instance, Black spatial imaginaries, modes of resistance to racial-spatial violence, the geographies of racial capitalism, and struggles over urban space. In their studies, the authors invoke a range of multidisciplinary methodologies that refuse any separation between the realms of the material and the poetic, drawing alternatively on practices such as ethnography, countercartography, creative forms of expression, and archival research (including Black feminist concerns with both archival presences *and* absences). These varied methodological approaches share a fundamental epistemological concern that cuts across the study of Black Geographies—specifically, that all knowing is geographically situated, and that the very spatiality of knowing and knowledge production is a powerful starting point from which to theorize. Finally, the chapters collected here also make note of new directions for future research in Black Geographies as the field continues to grow and expand—from the importance of thinking beyond the North American context, especially via anti-imperial oceanic routes that include but are also in excess of Black Atlantic geographies, to the spaces of intersection wherein emergent Black Geographic disciplinary formations meet Native and Latinx geographies.

Still, despite the continued growth of Black Geographies and its consolidation as a field of inquiry, we must resist the temptation to label Black Geographies something "new"—a new frontier for epistemic colonization or a new line of specialization to make CVs more desirable in a competitive academic job market. The characterization of Black Geographies as "surprising," "trendy," or "novel" simply reinforces the flawed claim that spatial theory only happens within geography departments. As McKittrick observes, this "element of surprise is contained in the material, political, and social landscape that presumes—and fundamentally requires—that subaltern populations have no relationship to the production of space."[11] While the discipline of geography has historically posed structural barriers to entry for Black scholars and excluded Black knowledge from the canon, Black Geographic thought has existed (often under other names) for centuries—across formal academic environments, political struggles, and everyday practices of Black space-making. It simply has not always been legible to the discipline of geography. At the same time, it is worth acknowledging that Black Geographies has received growing *institutional* recognition—indeed, this is the condition of possibility for the present volume.[12]

The Geography of Blackness

From W. E. B. Du Bois to Frantz Fanon to Stuart Hall and the theorists between and beyond, the question of Blackness's relationality has been a constant source of debate, troubling analysis, and unending inquiry. The question of the nature of Blackness—its origins, operation, and modality—has produced insights that not only respond to the question's concern but also have done much to illuminate the nature of the modern, especially

Western, world for which Blackness has been a, if not the, core impetus. Some of the early debates, often advanced by non-Black scholars, queried the definition of Blackness through the notion of retention, constantly holding the continent of Africa as the storehouse of that which defined Blackness while simultaneously asserting that Black cultural production in the Americas was either a "Creole" creation or simply an appropriation of white American cultural practices and ethical orientations, first adopted in the plantation.

All along, Blackness, recognized, as with all forms of racialization, as a myth used to categorize and "fix" bodies to labor or other modes of social functionality, has been the intimate, collectivist apparatus on which individual and collective identity were established. Inconstant, policed, and recalibrated even within the Black community, the "floating signifier" of Black identification has served as an anchoring to place and that place to belonging. The long-standing, everyday emplacement of Blackness has nevertheless not ceased the continued searching for Blackness's meaning. Contemporary scholarly debates pick up on the same traditions as of those of the past, being either concerned with the quotidian operation and experience of Blackness in relation to other sociological and cultural phenomena or occupied with the semiotic relationality of Blackness to its multiple instantiations across milieu. Contemporary studies of Blackness tend to privilege the cultural formulations of their subject, pursuing Black meaning and value as demonstrated through phenomenological articulations that often reinforce the subjugated, or vulnerable, form of Black subjectivity. Driving this focus is the necessary referent of the body to Blackness and the experiential circumstances and circuits in which the Black body sits. The body as a Black referent is a complicated, often tenuous situation of Blackness that elicits the need for contestation and contextual qualification of "culture."

Black Geographies, while not eschewing these approaches, argues that beyond the body, Blackness requires a framework of relationality to alternative, perhaps even more material processes and phenomena. The spatial, territorial, and geographic analysis of Blackness yields an understanding that more comprehensively positions Blackness as not just a subjectivity that experiences, that is impacted by external means of definition and manipulation, but instead a situating force, a place-making apparatus that in every geographic context makes its location more meaningful, more substantial, more human. By vigorously arguing for the deep intimacy between Blackness and place, Black Geographies repositions the myth of Blackness as a floating life of a sign that can only signal hardship or of life produced despite it. The geography of Blackness is a powerful frame of analysis that maps and charts the quality of Black life beyond, in an elsewhere that is proximate, co-generating meaning and purpose. Black Geographies therefore does not require a choice between the African continent and the multiple sites Blackness produced and continues to produce through multiple, "demonic" diasporic pathways.[13] It offers a capacious unframing by which disciplines have sought to understand but instead have constrained Blackness.

The Blackness of Geography

Black Geographies positions itself as an intervention not only into Black studies but also into the discipline of geography. But this does mean that Black Geographies is a liberal project of incorporating "Black" subjects and topics into the mainstream of geographic research, nor is it about "making visible" Black geographies and spaces that have been previously "hidden" or "overlooked." After all, traditional geography has long concerned itself with the empirical cataloging of Blackness—whether in the attempt to define and essentialize Blackness as a racial category through Enlightenment-era environmental determinisms, with the mapping and cataloging of African lands in conjunction with European imperial ventures, or—more recently—via "deficit-model" analyses of spatial segregation in urban Black communities.[14] In this sense, Blackness in traditional geography has been rendered both invisible (because Black practices of place-making are unacknowledged) or hypervisible (because Black spaces are deliberately or inadvertently represented as pathological, underserved, and otherwise *lacking*). Instead, Black Geographies foregrounds what Katherine McKittrick calls *a Black sense of place*: "a set of changing and differential perspectives that are illustrative of, and therefore remark upon, legacies of normalized racial violence that calcify, but do not guarantee, the denigration of black geographies and their inhabitants."[15] The sociospatial character of Black struggle, in other words, points to the mutual imbrication of race and the production of space.

If critical human geography is oriented around the relationship between space, place, and power and coheres disciplinarily around "a shared commitment to a broadly conceived emancipatory politics, progressive social change," then this must necessarily include a Black sense of place.[16] Marxian analyses of the relationship between capitalism and the production of space in particular are a mainstay of critical human geography. Black Geographies scholarship builds on these concerns by putting them into conversation with analyses of racial capitalism stemming from what Cedric Robinson famously called the Black radical tradition.[17] Gaye Theresa Johnson and Alex Lubin have described the Black radical tradition as "a tradition of resistance honed by the history of racialized, permanent, hereditary, and chattel slavery that formed the contours of civic and social life in the Americas, Europe, and Arica. Grounded in a Black resistance more than five centuries in the making, this practice produced an enduring vision of a shared future whose principal promise is the abolition of all forms of oppression."[18] Black Geographies shares critical human geography's emphasis on what is alternatively referred to as the "structural" or the "material"; however, it resituates this mode of analysis from a unidirectional teleology of capitalist diffusion out of Europe and into its peripheries, to a much more complex geographic "boomerang" in which racial domination, enslavement, and colonialism are central to the emergence and development of Western, capitalist modernity.[19] In *Development Arrested*, for instance, Woods subtly provincializes Karl Marx himself, describing him simply as "one observer of US capitalism during the 1850s" who happened to be preoccupied with the grafting of slavery onto capitalism.[20] Beginning with plantation slavery in this way troubles the very categories of labor, value, and property that are so central to classical Marxian analysis, revealing that the dynamics of capitalism are—and have always been—racial.

Black Geographies thus builds on the Black radical tradition by foregrounding the *spatialities* of racial capitalism—that the capitalist production of space is also the production of *racial difference*, and so struggles over space are also anticapitalist, abolitionist struggles for racial justice. As George Lipsitz argues, space is not merely an empty canvas on which the dynamics of racial capitalism unfold; rather, race is spatialized and space is racialized.[21] Race is central to the ways in which particular spaces (and, by extension, the bodies that have been "fixed" to or "contained" in those spaces) are constructed as empty, passive, immobile, or expendable or as exploitable sites of accumulation. We can see this, for instance, in Ruth Wilson Gilmore's understanding of the prison as a racialized "spatial fix" for the surpluses generated by capitalism's internal contradictions, in Bobby Wilson's exploration of the relationship between slavery and industrial capitalism in Birmingham, or in Woods's analysis of the centrality of racial domination to the plantation development bloc's hegemony in the Mississippi Delta.[22]

But why is *Blackness* specifically a particularly privileged location from which to develop such an analysis? After all, Robinson contended that "the Irish were negatively racialized, even before the Africans, in the European imagination. We were simply a lob to occupy a category already established."[23] He did suggest that the first racial subjects were located *inside* Europe.[24] Nevertheless, the transatlantic slave trade ultimately fixed Blackness as a central site of violent extraction and dispossession.[25] Thus, the construction of Blackness was integral to the consolidation of a white supremacist world order predicated on colonization, dispossession, and dehumanization. This is because Blackness, as Sarah Banet-Weiser, Roopali Mukherjee, and Herman Gray note, "anchors and signifies as a site of social excess, value extraction and threat."[26] In other words, it is not only the case that Black lives are inherently spatial but also that hegemonic notions of Blackness are integral to dominant modes of spatial organization. And precisely *because* the racialized and spatialized social hierarchies that characterize our world have been at least partly "recycled" from slavery, Blackness and Black struggles against geographies of domination constitute a point of revolutionary departure. As Johnson and Lubin put it, "Black freedom is freedom for all."[27]

Still, despite these common threads, there remains a rich multivocality in the emergent Black Geographies scholarship. One key point of debate, for instance, is how precisely to make sense of the afterlives of slavery, or "plantation futures."[28] To what extent (and in what specific ways) do the transatlantic slave trade and plantation capitalism produce a sociospatial template for Black life today? And what of spaces that fall outside the frame of the Middle Passage?[29] For instance, many Black communities in Europe understand their "origins and histories" through the epistemological frames of colonialism, migration, and—as Michelle Wright argues—the experiences of World War II.[30] If Black Geographies scholarship thus far has been primarily focused on North America, how can the legacies of the Black Atlantic be extended to other sites of Blackness without simply imposing a new set of abstract universalisms? Robinson argued, for instance, that the Mediterranean Sea was actually a laboratory within which technologies of plantation production and unfree labor were developed before they were subsequently exported across the Atlantic.[31] In that case, how might an analysis of the relationship between Blackness and racial capitalism be transformed if, for instance, we were to reorient our analyses on a Black *Mediterranean*?[32] This sort of approach refuses any linear or totalizing logics for theorizing Blackness on a global scale; instead, it points to the importance of attending to differently sedimented histories, as well as their multifarious global, world-historical interconnections and articulations.

Black Geographies, Racism, and Resistance

In "Life after Death," Woods issued a powerful and prescient warning that scholars of race and Blackness in geography not inadvertently become "academic coroners": "Have the tools of theory, method, instruction, and social responsibility become so rusted that they can only be used for autopsies? Does our research in any way reflect the experiences, viewpoints, and needs of the residents of these dying communities? On the other hand, is the patient really dead? What role are scholars playing in this social triage?"[33] Katherine McKittrick put it another way: racism "[shapes], but [does] not wholly define, Black worlds."[34] This is to say that Black Geographies is not merely the cataloging of the spatialities of anti-Black racial violence. And, when Black Geographies *is* concerned with spatial dimensions of racism, it does so with a particular theoretical conceptualization of racism itself—one that is oriented toward the conservation of Black resistance rather than the mere description of Black abjection. The work of retracing practices of racist spatial domination thus reveals opportunities for the undoing of this very same violence, through histories and practices of Black world-making. From Gilmore's understanding of the prison as a relational space through which radically coalitional abolition movements can unfold, to McKittrick's analysis of the auction block as a "site through which black women can sometimes radically disrupt an otherwise rigid site of racialization and sexualization," to Rashad Shabazz's description of urban gardens as sites for the ground-up transformation of carceral landscapes in Chicago, Black Geographies consistently foregrounds the "loopholes of retreat" through which geographies of domination and the imperial, cartographic gaze are subverted and challenged.[35] This approach is profoundly generative because rather than a closed system of domination, it shows that present colonial, anti-Black, capitalist, heterosexist spatial configurations are (to paraphrase Stuart Hall) "without guarantees."[36]

Any analysis of racism whose end point is merely the accumulation of evidence of spatial violence and violation against "Black bodies" actually risks reproducing the very same anti-Blackness it seeks to remedy, by positing Black geographies as already dead and dying.[37] Indeed, McKittrick's meditations on Édouard Glissant's spatial poetics and Sylvia Wynter's reconceptualization of the "human" point to the liberatory political possibilities of work that begins from a fundamental recognition of Black *livingness* and *humanness*.[38] This is why, rather than a simple binary of oppression and resistance, Black Geographies adopts a *relational* understanding of Blackness and space.[39] And it does this through a powerful respatialization of the metaphor of "margins": putatively marginal subjects and spaces, from Harriet Jacobs's garret to the modern prison as sites from which the workings of power writ large can be analyzed and denaturalized.[40] In other words, Blackness does not represent an incommensurable "outside" to systems of spatial domination.[41] Rather, because Blackness itself was so central to the articulation of racist, colonial spatial imaginaries and practices, it is also a privileged analytical location from which to challenge them and articulate different modes of living.

Black Geographic Praxis

A Black Geographic praxis is a means of holding in concert the political, intellectual, and lived potential of emplaced study of Blackness as well as the Black study of emplacement. Despite the disciplinary and methodological breadth of Black Geographies scholarship, the work shares a commitment to peeling back the layered histories embedded in place, challenging the allure of "transparent space"—of present spatial arrangements as natural, inevitable, and immediately discernible by the normatively white, masculinist cartographic gaze. As a conceptual foundation, then, we advance that Black Geographic praxes center the following commitments:

1 The nonsingularity and nonuniversality of Blackness;
2 Blackness as locally and globally produced and reproduced through processes (technologies, policies, theories) of circulation and diasporic routes;
3 Blackness as always historically and geographically situated;
4 The questioning of ontological claims and of *ontologizing* processes;
5 An attention to the interplay of material and poetic processes.

In understanding how Blackness is lived, constructed, and transformed, Black Geographies makes several important methodological interventions. Black Geographies is rooted in a practice of deep study that challenges arborescent understandings of intellectual lineage and looks instead to metaphors of queerings, rhizomes, undercommons, Sankofas, provincializations, and call-and-response.[42] These alternative and profoundly nonhierarchical modes of study necessarily entail an attentive and reparative citational politics that consciously privileges those thinkers who have been historically marginalized or deemed insufficiently scholarly.[43] They also cultivate powerful forms of what VéVé Clarke calls "diaspora literacy."[44] This involves a commitment to reading across national borders and engaging in the often messy work of translation (including linguistic translation and its relation to the translation of lived experience and political practices across geographically distinct yet interconnected diasporic contexts), taking seriously the commonalities and disjunctures across global Blacknesses.

Because of the extractivist and exploitative history of academic research in and on Black communities, the project of Black Geographies is also committed to questions of research ethics and, more important, justice. In other words, the theoretical and political interventions of Black Geographies are inseparable from the material *practice* of research itself. For instance, the politics of ethnographic research "about Blackness" is deeply fraught (prompting radical ethnographers, for instance, to envision the possibilities of an "abolitionist anthropology").[45] Some scholars of Black Geographies, though, have sought to address these concerns by undertaking various forms of community-engaged and/or participatory research.[46] Importantly, these projects do not rely on an idealized notion of a homogeneous or authentic Black community (or, alternatively, community representatives who are appointed as brokers, designated to "speak for" their constituents).[47] However, they do share an understanding that research undertaken in the name of racial-spatial justice must be held primarily accountable not merely to academic institutions, tenure committees, and research funders but to a much wider set of collaborators, stakeholders, and political communities.

But fieldwork does not constitute the only "archive" for Black Geographies research. Black Geographies also takes seriously alternative forms of knowledge production from outside the academy, embracing genres from poetry to speculative fiction to music. In this sense, Black Geographies is also influenced by insights from the Birmingham School of cultural analysis— and particularly the work of Stuart Hall and Paul Gilroy—for the way it expanded narrow definitions of the "political" to include culture as a potential site of struggle and political transformation. In the work of Clyde Woods, for instance, the blues was not only an aesthetic form but also an epistemology and ontology: a way of theorizing the world as it is and conveying images of an alternative future.[48] In other words, these various forms of Black poetics present alternative, multivocal narratives that push back against a "single story" of Blackness as represented by an accumulation of evidence of death, suffering, and violation.[49]

Ultimately, Black Geographies permits a multidirectional analysis where Blackness is not restricted to being merely the subject of analysis but also the means by which we understand a range of related phenomena. Yet, for this reason, there is often a productive tension in the emerging scholarship on Black Geographies between Blackness as an analytical frame and Blackness as subjectivity and lived geographic experience. After all, to borrow Gurminder Bhambra's critique of the study of race in sociology, Blackness is not only a matter of (individual or collective) *identity*; it is also a question of *system* and *structure*.[50] This raises the question of how these two approaches can and should be held together. Particularly in the context of a discipline that has had a fraught relationship to Blackness, as described earlier, scholars must ensure that Blackness is not rendered an "absented presence"— one visible only through the conspicuous absence of Black *people*—within Black Geographies itself.[51]

Organization of the Volume

The Black Geographic is organized around three main themes: praxis, resistance, and futurity. Part I, "Praxis," considers the epistemological challenges posed by Black Geographic thought to foundational categories such as space, scale, science, politics, and empire. But beyond elucidating and thinking past the limitations of those categories, the volume's attention to praxis offers newer considerations of methodological and theoretical practice that emerges from the complex process of Black life. In other words, by focusing on the poetic, the material, and the affective inputs and products of the Black lived experience, our contributors offer a means, a praxis, of exploring the geographic condition of Blackness, and the world that it shapes and occupies. Finally, chapters in this part consider the implications of Black Geographies' epistemological provocations in terms of both alternative research methodologies and transgressive forms of social action.

In "Call Us Alive Someplace: Du Boisian Methods and Living Black Geographies," Danielle Purifoy turns to W. E. B. Du Bois's research in Lowndes County, Alabama, as a model for interdisciplinary inquiry that weaves together narrative, art, and science. In the summer of 1906, Du Bois traveled to Lowndes County to study the political economy of Black labor in the Cotton Belt for the US Department of Agriculture; he was also commissioned to write a social novel based in that region. That novel, *The Quest of the Silver Fleece* (the only surviving text from his Lowndes research) employs rigorous scientific empiricism to craft a speculative fantasy of Black place-making in which land is no longer considered property and cotton symbolizes liberation. Purifoy, along with Black conceptual artist and abstract painter Torkwase Dyson, drew on Du Bois's epistemological framework in *Silver Fleece* (which weaves together social science, history, and fiction to craft alternative worlds) as the inspiration for their exhibition *In Conditions of Fresh Water*—a project that is similarly grounded in Lowndes County and weaves together social scientific and poetic approaches. Rather than rehearsing an inventory of Black death and deprivation, Purifoy and Dyson track the ways Black residents and community leaders in Lowndes continue to build their freedom dreams in the Black Belt, working toward the fulfillment of Du Bois's speculative fantasy of land, labor, and place even in the face of a global capitalist regime that accumulates through Black dispossession and death. Purifoy ultimately argues that Du Bois's undisciplined approach provides a model of a Black Geographic praxis that attends to both the political economic and the poetic to reject social death as the central feature of Black place-making.

Judith Madera's "Shaking the Basemap" shows how Black Geographic praxis mobilizes Black life across the movements of culture and capital through discursive narratives, memories, and projections. Madera focuses on three spheres of advocacy from the "long epoch of abolition": the development of critical literacies in Black women's civics, strategies against commodification from within colonial-capitalist systems, and the expression of Black political geographies through literature. In different ways, these Black abolitionist geographies questioned colonial basemaps (the supposedly stable spatial referents that undergird white supremacy) to reveal obscured agencies and fissures in systems of power that could become sites of struggle and resistance. Through these powerful examples, Madera makes two important claims about Black Geographic method. First, that archives—riddled with silences and structured by racist hierarchies—must be read against the grain to reveal the networks of Black social organization and resistance that exist at the edges of official history. And second, that Black literary texts and narrative-based cognitive maps are critical sites of geographic meaning-making, as they allow us to understand the relationship between the material organization of place and discursive practices in order to undo colonial-capitalist spatial epistemologies and chart alternative futures.

In "'My Bad Attitude toward the Pastoral': Race, Place, and Allusion in the Poetry of C. S. Giscombe," Chiyuma Elliott offers an exploration of the role played by race in shaping relationships to urban and rural spaces, through an analysis of C. S. Giscombe's long poem *Here*. Elliott argues that Giscombe's poem anticipates McKittrick's definition of a "black sense of place," as it articulates the ways "racial violences . . . shape, but do not wholly define, black worlds."[52] As such, it also offers a productive alternative to characterizations of the US South as an undifferentiated landscape of little more than unrelenting anti-Blackness. Giscombe's spatial poetic praxis is uniquely able to conjure the emotional or affective dimensions of living within a complex geographic landscape characterized by danger and ambiguity, as well as moments of quiet reprieve. Elliott's careful analysis of *Home* also provides a model of the kinds of close reading practices that can lead to a more systematic (rather than gestural) engagement with the geographic insights that can be derived from the language of songs and poetry.

Part II, "Resistances," highlights the processes and politics by which Black subjects engage with the resistances they encounter in navigating the circumstances that make up the contours of Black life, especially where structural adversity is the central experience. It also engages the modes of resistance that those subjects produce to mitigate those challenges. Moreover, those resistant practices become a modality for thinking and reasoning. As such, the idea of resistance becomes less of a narrative of reactive survival and more so a practice of strategic intellectualism. Therefore, when resistant lives of Black subjects are studied, their experiences offer themselves as theoretically core to Black Geographic thought.

In "Blackness Out of Place and In Between in the Sahara," Ampson Hagan considers the ways that West African migrants in the Maghreb subvert a "state-humanitarian" antimigration apparatus founded on white supremacist spatial logics. Colonial practices regulating and restricting Black mobility are today also being reproduced by majority-Black nation-states (in the case of Hagan's ethnography, Niger), in collaboration with the European Union and international nongovernmental organizations, against other Black migrants. In response, Black migrants have found creative ways to resist blocked movement and state surveillance—from the shadow mapping of countergeographies, to their own sousveillance of the state. These practices craft spaces of in-betweenness where unauthorized Black migrants live in the interstices of the state and the humanitarian migration apparatus. Hagan's contribution is also noteworthy for the way it complicates singular or universalizing portrayals of Blackness. He traces the ways Nigerien state officials invoke a range of markers beyond skin color (i.e., bodily movements, sartorial choices, hairstyles, or perceived physical differences) to identify "Blackness out of place"—a form of what Simone Browne calls "racializing surveillance" that, in this particular case, seeks to differentiate Nigeriens from unauthorized West African migrants.[53]

Diana Negrín considers another form of resistance in her chapter, "Words Re(en)visioned: Black and Indigenous Languages for Autonomy." Through a critical dialogue between Black Geographic thought and Mesoamerican Indigenous languages, she argues that language and orality are central to decolonial and autonomist possibilities. Drawing on theorists such as Katherine McKittrick, Clyde Woods, Sylvia Wynter, and Édouard Glissant, Negrín's work is part of a new wave of critical geographic scholarship that considers the political possibilities that exist at the convergence of Black and Indigenous scholarship. This convergence, she argues, has the potential to interrupt hegemonic and colonial structures of space and belonging. Language (in its spoken, written, and even sung forms) is significant because it can create spaces of cognitive autonomy, conjure cultural and political possibility, and craft new worlds that provide radical alternatives to the centuries of violence waged on Black and Indigenous geographies.

In "Blackness in the (Post)Colonial African City," Jordanna Matlon considers the various ways Blackness has been incorporated into the global racial capitalist system—from slave, to forced laborer, to interlocutor in colonial civilizing missions—and the different expressions of labor, race, and gender that have emerged in relation to these modalities. Matlon begins with the vestiges of the French empire and its *mission civilisatrice* (civilizing mission), which conflated culture with race, and race with space, to articulate a narrowly defined and racialized conception of the right to the city. Focusing on two sites—the colonial municipalities of the Four Communes in Senegal and the postcolonial city of Abidjan, Côte d'Ivoire—her chapter argues that urban belonging in the African city was and continues to be linked to deeply racialized notions of labor, consumption, and economic productivity—and, more broadly, differential insertion within the global capitalist economy. Matlon draws on urban theorist AbdouMaliq Simone's notion of "black urbanism" to chart Black African *extralives*—ambiguous practices of economic survival that exist in excess of the capitalist world system.[54] These precarious practices, she argues, seek to reject racialized dispossession and denigration in order to articulate alternative claims to the city.

Concluding part II, Solange Muñoz examines the spatiality of power and representation among Black and brown women in politics through an analysis of Marielle Franco's life, death, and legacy. Her chapter, "Marielle Franco and Black Spatial Imaginaries," uses the concepts of racialized spaces and imaginaries to examine the ways Black women occupy public positions of political power in the face of white supremacist violence by individuals and institutions that want to exclude them from these spaces and keep them "in their place." Muñoz asks why the presence of Black women in positions of political power is so often considered an aberration, and what potential spaces and collective subjectivities are produced by Black women when they occupy these positions. While focusing specifically on Franco, a queer Black woman and *favelada* who was assassinated after her election to the Rio de Janeiro city council, Muñoz's approach is explicitly transnational and hemispheric. She argues that analyses of racism, oppression, and white supremacy must extend beyond bounded local or national enframings and, in doing so, places Brazil in relation with the United States through interconnected histories of transatlantic slavery, fascist resurgence, and Black resistance.

"Futurity" is the thematic concern of part III. Black Geographies, this volume argues, is not simply a descriptive project, noting the how and where of Black life, but temporally ties the Black experience to a comprehensive notion and general quality of life and humanity, understood through intimate and meaningful material relationships. When considering the geographic relations of Blackness, the notions of the past and the present figure as dominant lenses, whether through an accounting of the locales of dispossession, or where Black people *have* been. Or, alternatively, how the experiential and structural determinant of that past shapes the current conjuncture of Blackness. And while the "Afro-futurism" turn in Black Studies has given much consideration to what the future of Blackness, as experience and condition, might look like, what is missed in these analyses are the (earthly) spatial dimensions of that Black life. Building on the work of Black Geographic envisioning of the future, such as the concepts of a "Black sense of place," or the blues model of development, and Black spatial imaginaries, contributors consider Black Geographic futures through questions of liberation and humanness as understood through the practices of planning, and through ideations of future spaces of belonging. The field of Black Geographies has had a strong orientation toward questions related to race, cities, and urban planning. As such, this part of the book focuses in particular on contestations over urban space and the racial politics of urban renewal to reveal how attention to Black geographies and a Black sense of place is central to crafting just and liberatory urban futures.

In an analysis of the West Oakland Specific Plan (WOSP), in Oakland, California, C.N.E. Corbin examines the visual dimensions of planning frameworks to understand how Oakland's future is envisioned as it transforms from a "chocolate city" into a green city. In "Rendering Gentrification and Erasing Race: Sustainable Development and the (Re)Visioning of Oakland, California, as a Green City," Corbin argues that the narratives and images contained in the WOSP, approved by the Oakland Planning Commission in 2014, depict a "green" and "sustainable" urban future for Oakland that relies on the displacement and removal of Black residents from a historically Black neighborhood. Drawing on environmental criticism, critical race theory, and visual media studies, this chapter shows that municipal planning documents like WOSP have become important tools of gentrification that envision and help to enact futures in which "undesirable" populations are removed from the landscape in the service of racialized, anti-Black environmentalisms.

In tracing the spatiality of leisure among Black millennials, Matthew Jordan-Miller Kenyatta, in his chapter "Need Black Joy? Mapping an Afro-techtonics of Gathering in Los Angeles," offers a transdisciplinary study of Black cultural and economic geographies in South Los Angeles that charts relationships between race, place, and taste to show how Blackness travels as a cultural identity that is embodied, commodified, consumed, and reproduced through interactions between digital technologies and physical spaces. Miller focuses in particular on cultural gatherings marketed toward Black millennials and digital natives in Los Angeles, through which he develops a theory of Black joy as urban practice. Black joyful space-making, he argues, is an oppositional practice of Black love in the face of systematic disregard for Black dreams and desires, one that subverts racialized capitalist economies and builds toward futures of cultural self-determination, economic justice, and the liberation of digital commons.

In "The San Francisco Blues," Lindsey Dillon invokes the legacy of Clyde Woods to argue that the West Coast blues provide a way to understand Black struggles over redevelopment in the Bayview–Hunters Point neighborhood of San Francisco, California. Clyde Woods famously argued that Black Americans in the Mississippi Delta region used the cultural form of the blues both to diagnose the racism and economic exploitation of the plantation system and to articulate alternative practices of just development. Dillon argues that the vision Black activists in the 1960s and

1970s articulated for a "new Hunters Point" by and for Black residents, with affordable homes designed by Black architects and built by Black workers, stems from a branch of the blues epistemology Woods identified in the delta. Reworked in relation to the racial politics and political-economic landscape of the US West, the San Francisco blues expressed a development theory and practice that contested a market economy that deploys racism to differentially devalue people and places. Dillon shows how these struggles, both cultural and material, constitute an important moment in the unfolding of Black San Francisco futures.

Finally, in "Today Like Yesterday, Tomorrow Like Today: Black Geographies in the Breaks of the Fourth Dimension," Anna Livia Brand considers the ways in which Black residents of post-Katrina New Orleans continue to counter Cartesian spatial epistemologies that displace Blackness, articulating alternative development agendas and geographic formations. Planning and design, Brand explains, are inherently future-oriented; however, they are also sites through which racial logics are naturalized and racial oppression is reproduced. Nonetheless, the alternative to the white supremacy of planning—especially as it pertains to post-Katrina redevelopment—is not merely an enumeration of all the ways planning produces Black death, displacement, and erasure. Rather, Brand argues that the practice of imagining abolitionist and liberatory futures entails attending to the *always present* and multiple ways Black residents of New Orleans have been destabilizing white spatial imaginaries.[55]

The volume concludes with "A Black Geographic Reverie & Reckoning in Ink and Form" by Sharita Towne, an artist who approaches art as a container for Black collective inquiry into relationships with land, air, and sky. Her mixed-process collage print *Black Life & Black Spatial Imaginaries, Glimpses across Time & Space: A Visual Bibliography, 2018–2019*; the corresponding book, *Alluvium*; and the digitized film *5th St. Imaginary: A Family, a Geography* all draw together intimate archiving, conversation, and art to map the everyday geographies of Black activists and families. In this way, Towne provides an inspiring example of art and experimental research as key modes of a Black Geographic praxis.

Taken together, these chapters—and their methodological, theoretical, historical, and geographic breadth—represent a powerful set of approaches for analyzing Blackness, apprehending the spatiality of power, and imagining abolitionist and liberatory futures.

Notes

1. Livingstone, *Geographical Tradition*; Kobayashi, "Dialectic of Race and the Discipline of Geography."
2. For a longer discussion of the evolution of Black Geographies scholarship in relation to the history of the discipline of geography, see Hawthorne, "Black Matters Are Spatial Matters"; on the connections between geography and slavery, colonialism, and imperialism, see Gilmore, "Fatal Couplings of Power and Difference"; and Pulido, "Reflections on a White Discipline."
3. Malkki, "National Geographic."
4. Massey, *For Space*.
5. Bassin, "Imperialism and the Nation State"; Godlewska and Smith, *Geography and Empire*.
6. Hawthorne and Meché, "Making Room for Black Feminist Praxis in Geography."
7. Chakrabarty, *Provincializing Europe*; Oswin, "Planetary Urbanization."
8. Domosh, "Why Is Our Geography Curriculum So White?"; Domosh, "Genealogies of Race, Gender, and Place."
9. Pulido, "Reflections on a White Discipline."
10. McKittrick and Woods, *Black Geographies and the Politics of Place*, 4.
11. McKittrick, *Demonic Grounds*, 92.
12. At the 2013 annual meeting of the American Association of Geographers, LaToya Eaves organized a panel entitled "Black Matters Are Spatial Matters," which would ultimately lay the groundwork for the institutionalization of Black Geographies. The Black Geographies Specialty Group of the AAG was formed in 2017 under the leadership of Dr. Eaves and Jovan Scott Lewis. Black Geographies was subsequently recognized as an official theme of the 2018 AAG annual meeting. The Berkeley Black Geographies Project, started by Jovan Scott Lewis in 2016, which led to the Berkeley Black Geographies Symposium held at UC Berkeley in 2017, represented a watershed moment for Black Geographies, gaining it national and ultimately international recognition. Over the next several years, the field will also see the publication of dozens of texts on Black Geographies and Black ecologies. The Duke University Press series Errantries (edited by Simone Browne, Deborah Cowen, and Katherine McKittrick) is another exciting locus of scholarly production focused on geographies of race.
13. McKittrick, *Demonic Grounds*.
14. For a critique of "deficit-model" analyses of Black spaces, see Reese, *Black Food Geographies*.
15. McKittrick, "On Plantations, Prisons, and a Black Sense of Place," 950.
16. Berg, "Critical Human Geography," 617.
17. Robinson, *Black Marxism*.
18. Johnson and Lubin, "Introduction," 10.

19 Arendt, *Imperialism*, 155; Chari, "The Blues and the Damned"; Bledsoe and Wright, "Anti-Blackness of Global Capital."

20 Woods, *Development Arrested*, 6.

21 Lipsitz, *How Racism Takes Place*, 6.

22 Gilmore, *Golden Gulag*; Wilson, *America's Johannesburg*; Woods, *Development Arrested*.

23 Robinson and Robinson, "Preface."

24 Kelley, "What Did Cedric Robinson Mean by Racial Capitalism?"; Kelley, "Foreword"; Robinson, *Black Marxism*.

25 Cedric Robinson's emphasis on the nondetermined character of racialization and racial subjection is significant because it challenges the idea that anti-Blackness is inevitable. As he wrote, "It became the impression that the category had always been ours, always been ours, exclusively. That simply isn't how human affairs have been conducted" (Robinson and Robinson, "Preface," 7).

26 Banet-Weiser, Mukherjee, and Gray, "Introduction," 12.

27 Banet-Weiser, Mukherjee, and Gray, "Introduction," 12; Johnson and Lubin, "Introduction," 13.

28 McKittrick, "Plantation Futures."

29 Wright, *Physics of Blackness*.

30 Wright, "Postwar Blackness and the World of Europe."

31 Robinson, *Black Marxism*, 16.

32 Kelley, "Foreword," xiv; Black Mediterranean Collective, *Black Mediterranean*.

33 Woods, "Life after Death," 63.

34 McKittrick, "On Plantations, Prisons, and a Black Sense of Place," 947.

35 Gilmore, *Golden Gulag*; McKittrick, *Demonic Grounds*, xxix; Shabazz, *Spatializing Blackness*. The expression "loopholes of retreat" is from McKittrick, *Demonic Grounds*, 37.

36 Hall, "Problem of Ideology."

37 McKittrick, "Diachronic Loops," 6.

38 McKittrick, "Commentary."

39 McKittrick, "Commentary," 4.

40 McKittrick, "Commentary," 4; Gilmore, *Golden Gulag*; McKittrick, "On Plantations, Prisons, and a Black Sense of Place," 958.

41 Hawthorne, "Black Matters Are Spatial Matters," 4.

42 For the undercommons, see Harney and Moten, *Undercommons*; for Sankofas, see Benjamin, *People's Science*; for call-and-response, see Hawthorne and Heitz, "A Seat at the Table?," 150.

43 See Lewis, "Releasing a Tradition."

44 Clark, "Developing Diaspora Literacy and Marasa Consciousness."

45 Shange, *Progressive Dystopia*.

46 Vasudevan, "Performance and Proximity." In their project "This Is a Black Spatial Imaginary," for instance, Lisa K. Bates and Sharita Towne brought together artists, scholars, and local residents to explore the possibilities of Black life in Portland, Oregon. In a similar vein, Romi Morrison and Treva Ellison used artistic, interactive maps in their project "Decoding Possibilities" to disrupt geographies of redlining and encourage participants to map their own experiences and subversions of racist landscapes.

47 For a powerful critique of "racial authenticity," see Jackson, *Real Black.*

48 In a continuation of this Woodsian legacy, Lynnée Denise has approached record stores in her work as archives, and she describes the practice of DJing as a way to narrate the diasporic roots and routes of transnational Black social movements (Denise, "Afro-Digital Migration"). Also, the untimely death of Prince in 2016 prompted scholars such as Rashad Shabazz to consider the geographies of his distinctive "Minneapolis sound" as the product of layered histories of race, displacement, and resistance (Shabazz, "How Prince Introduced Us to the 'Minneapolis Sound'"; #PurpleSyllabus website, accessed December 12, 2018, http://editions.lib.umn.edu/purplesyllabus/).

49 Adichie, "Danger of a Single Story"; McKittrick, "Diachronic Loops," 13, 15.

50 Bhambra, "Postcolonial Reflections on Sociology."

51 McKittrick, *Demonic Grounds*, 33.

52 McKittrick, "On Plantations, Prisons, and a Black Sense of Place," 947.

53 Browne, *Dark Matters*, 16.

54 Simone, *City Life from Jakarta to Dakar*, 307–8.

55 Lipsitz, *How Racism Takes Place.*

Bibliography

Adichie, Chimamanda Ngozi. "The Danger of a Single Story." TEDGlobal, 2009. Accessed January 16, 2023. https://www.ted.com/talks/chimamanda_adichie_the_danger_of_a_single_story.

Arendt, Hannah. *Imperialism: Part Two of the Origins of Totalitarianism.* 1948. San Diego: Harcourt Brace, 1968.

Banet-Weiser, Sarah, Roopali Mukherjee, and Herman Gray. "Introduction: Postrace Racial Projects." In *Racism Postrace*, edited by Roopali Mukherjee, Sarah Banet-Weiser, and Herman Gray, 1–18. Durham, NC: Duke University Press, 2019.

Bassin, Mark. "Imperialism and the Nation State in Friedrich Ratzel's Political Geography." *Progress in Human Geography* 11, no. 4 (1987): 473–95.

Bates, Lisa K., Sharita A. Towne, Christopher Paul Jordan, and Kitso Lynn Lelliott. "Race and Spatial Imaginary: Planning Otherwise." *Planning Theory and Practice* 19, no. 2 (2018): 254–88.

Benjamin, Ruha. *People's Science: Bodies and Rights on the Stem Cell Frontier.* Stanford, CA: Stanford University Press, 2013.

Berg, Lawrence D. "Critical Human Geography." In *Encyclopedia of Geography*, edited by Barney Warf, 617–21. Thousand Oaks, CA: Sage, 2010.

Bhambra, Gurminder. "Postcolonial Reflections on Sociology." *Sociology* 50, no. 5 (2016): 960–66.

Black Mediterranean Collective. *The Black Mediterranean: Bodies, Borders, and Citizenship in the Contemporary Migration Crisis*. London: Palgrave Macmillan, 2001.

Bledsoe, Adam. "Marronage as a Past and Present Geography in the Americas." *Southeastern Geographer* 57, no. 1 (2017): 30–50.

Bledsoe, Adam, and Willie Jamaal Wright. "The Anti-Blackness of Global Capital." *Environment and Planning D: Society and Space* 37, no. 1 (2019): 8–26.

Brahinsky, Rachel. "Leaning Into the Blues Epistemology." Antipode Foundation, April 30, 2012. https://antipodefoundation.org/2012/04/30/leaning-into-the -blues-epistemology/.

Browne, Simone. *Dark Matters: On the Surveillance of Blackness*. Durham, NC: Duke University Press, 2015.

Chakrabarty, Dipesh. *Provincializing Europe: Postcolonial Thought and Historical Difference*. Princeton, NJ: Princeton University Press, 2000.

Chari, Sharad. "The Blues and the Damned: (Black) Life-That-Survives Capital and Biopolitics." *Critical African Studies* 9, no. 2 (2017): 152–73.

Clark, VèVè A. "Developing Diaspora Literacy and Marasa Consciousness." *Theatre Survey* 50, no. 1 (2009): 9–18.

Denise, Lynée. "The Afro-Digital Migration: A DJ's Journey from Hip-Hop to House Music." *Girls Like Us* 6 (2014): 96–102.

Domosh, Mona. "Genealogies of Race, Gender, and Place." *Annals of the American Association of Geographers* 107, no. 3 (2017): 765–78.

Domosh, Mona. "Why Is Our Geography Curriculum So White?" American Association of Geographers President's Column, June 1, 2015. https://www.aag.org /author/mona-domosh/.

Du Bois, W. E. B. *Black Reconstruction in America, 1860–1880*. 1935. New York: Free Press, 1998.

Gilmore, Ruth Wilson. "Fatal Couplings of Power and Difference: Notes on Racism and Geography." *Professional Geographer* 54, no. 1 (2002): 15–24.

Gilmore, Ruth Wilson. *Golden Gulag: Prisons, Surplus, Crisis, and Opposition in Globalizing California*. Berkeley: University of California Press, 2007.

Godlewska, Anne, and Neil Smith, eds. *Geography and Empire*. Cambridge: Blackwell, 1994.

Hall, Stuart. "The Problem of Ideology—Marxism without Guarantees." *Journal of Communication Inquiry* 10, no. 2 (1986): 28–44.

Harney, Stefano, and Fred Moten. *The Undercommons: Fugitive Planning and Black Study*. Wivenhoe, UK: Minor Compositions, 2013.

Hawthorne, Camilla. "Black Matters Are Spatial Matters: Black Geographies for the Twenty-First Century." *Geography Compass* 13, no. 11 (2019): 1–13.

Hawthorne, Camilla, and Kaily Heitz. "A Seat at the Table? Reflections on Black Geographies and the Limits of Dialogue." *Dialogues in Human Geography* 8, no. 2 (2018): 148–51.

Hawthorne, Camilla, and Brittany Meché. "Making Room for Black Feminist Praxis in Geography." *Society and Space*, September 30, 2016. http://societyand space.org/2016/09/30/making-room-for-black-feminist-praxis-in-geography/.

Jackson, John L. *Real Black: Adventures in Racial Sincerity*. Chicago: University of Chicago Press, 2005.

Johnson, Gaye Theresa, and Alex Lubin. "Introduction." In *Futures of Black Radicalism*, edited by Gaye Theresa Johnson and Alex Lubin, 9–18. London: Verso Books, 2017.

Kelley, Robin D. G. "Foreword." In Cedric Robinson, *Black Marxism: The Making of the Black Radical Tradition*, xi–xxvi. Chapel Hill: University of North Carolina Press, 2005.

Kelley, Robin D. G. "What Did Cedric Robinson Mean by Racial Capitalism?" *Boston Review*, January 12, 2017. http://bostonreview.net/race/robin-d-g -kelley-what-did-cedric-robinson-mean-racial-capitalism.

Kobayashi, Audrey. "The Dialectic of Race and the Discipline of Geography." *Annals of the Association of American Geographers* 104, no. 6 (2014): 1101–15.

Lewis, Diane. "Anthropology and Colonialism." *Current Anthropology* 14, no. 5 (1973): 581–602.

Lewis, Jovan Scott. "Releasing a Tradition: Diasporic Epistemology and the Decolonized Curriculum." *Cambridge Journal of Anthropology* 36, no. 2 (2018): 21–33.

Lipsitz, George. *How Racism Takes Place*. Philadelphia: Temple University Press, 2011.

Livingstone, David N. *The Geographical Tradition: Episodes in the History of a Contested Discipline*. Oxford: Wiley-Blackwell, 1993.

Malkki, Liisa. "National Geographic: The Rooting of Peoples and the Territorialization of National Identity among Scholars and Refugees." *Cultural Anthropology* 7, no. 1 (1992): 24–44.

Massey, Doreen. *For Space*. Thousand Oaks, CA: Sage, 2005.

McKittrick, Katherine. "Commentary: Worn Out." *Southeastern Geographer* 57, no. 1 (2017): 96–100.

McKittrick, Katherine. *Demonic Grounds: Black Women and the Cartographies of Struggle*. Minneapolis: University of Minnesota Press, 2006.

McKittrick, Katherine. "Diachronic Loops/Deadweight Tonnage/Bad Made Measure." *Cultural Geographies* 23, no. 1 (2016): 3–18.

McKittrick, Katherine. "On Plantations, Prisons, and a Black Sense of Place." *Social and Cultural Geography* 12, no. 8 (2011): 947–63.

McKittrick, Katherine. "Plantation Futures." *Small Axe: A Caribbean Journal of Criticism* 17, no. 3 (42) (2013): 1–15.

McKittrick, Katherine, and Clyde Woods, eds. *Black Geographies and the Politics of Place*. Boston: South End, 2007.

Morrison, Romi. "Decoding Possibilities." Accessed December 12, 2018. https:// elegantcollisions.com/decoding-possibilities/.

Oswin, Natalie. "Planetary Urbanization: A View from Outside." *Environment and Planning D: Society and Space* 36, no. 3 (2018): 540–46.

Pulido, Laura. "Reflections on a White Discipline." *Professional Geographer* 54, no. 1 (2002): 42–49.

Reese, Ashanté. *Black Food Geographies*. Chapel Hill: University of North Carolina Press, 2019.

Robinson, Cedric J. *Black Marxism: The Making of the Black Radical Tradition*. 1983. Chapel Hill: University of North Carolina Press, 2005.

Robinson, Cedric J., and Elizabeth P. Robinson. "Preface." In *Futures of Black Radicalism*, edited by Gaye Theresa Johnson and Alex Lubin. London: Verso Books, 2017. Ebook.

Shabazz, Rashad. "How Prince Introduced Us to the 'Minneapolis Sound.'" *Zocalo Public Square*, September 7, 2017. http://www.zocalopublicsquare.org/2017/09/07/prince-introduced-us-minneapolis-sound/ideas/nexus/.

Shabazz, Rashad. *Spatializing Blackness: Architectures of Confinement and Black Masculinity in Chicago*. Urbana: University of Illinois Press, 2015.

Shange, Savannah. *Progressive Dystopia: Abolition, Antiblackness, and Schooling in San Francisco*. Durham, NC: Duke University Press, 2019.

Simone, AbdouMaliq. *City Life from Jakarta to Dakar: Movements at the Crossroads*. New York: Routledge, 2010.

Trouillot, Michel-Rolph. "Anthropology and the Savage Slot: The Poetics and Politics of Otherness." In *Recapturing Anthropology: Working in the Present*, edited by Richard G. Fox, 17–44. Santa Fe, NM: School of American Research Press, 1991.

Vasudevan, Pavithra. "Performance and Proximity: Revisiting Environmental Justice in Warren County, North Carolina." *Performance Research* 17, no. 4 (2012): 18–26.

Vergès, Françoise. "Racial Capitalocene." In *Futures of Black Radicalism*, edited by Gaye Theresa Johnson and Alex Lubin. London: Verso Books, 2017. Ebook.

Wilson, Bobby M. *America's Johannesburg: Industrialization and Racial Transformation in Birmingham*. Lanham, MD: Rowman and Littlefield, 2000.

Woods, Clyde. *Development Arrested: The Blues and Plantation Power in the Mississippi Delta*. London: Verso Books, 2017.

Woods, Clyde. "Life after Death." *Professional Geographer* 54, no. 1 (2002): 62–66.

Wright, Michelle M. *Physics of Blackness: Beyond the Middle Passage Epistemology*. Minneapolis: University of Minnesota Press, 2015.

Wright, Michelle M. "Postwar Blackness and the World of Europe." Österreichisches Zeitschrift *für Geschichtswissenschaften* 17 (2006): 113–22.

PART I

Praxis

1

Call Us Alive Someplace

Du Boisian Methods and Living Black Geographies

DANIELLE PURIFOY

The story goes like this. In 1899, W. E. B. Du Bois was on his way to the office of the *Atlanta Constitution* to write an editorial he hoped might calm a public bent on lynching a Black man in central Georgia for the alleged murder of his white employer and rape of the employer's wife. Following the example of journalist Ida B. Wells-Barnett in Memphis, Du Bois wanted to use his voice as a scholar and leader in Atlanta to condemn lynchings as racial terror, anathema as he saw it to the promise of the US legal system. But somewhere along his journey through downtown Atlanta, someone informed Du Bois that Sam Hose had been "barbecued" the previous day and his knuckles put on display at the general store, blocks from where Du Bois stood. Stunned, he reversed course, walking back to his post at Atlanta University. He wrote later that Hose's lynching was a turning point in his life's work, as he realized two things: "One could not be a calm, cool, and detached scientist while Negroes were lynched, murdered and starved; and secondly, there was no such definite demand for scientific work of the sort that I was doing."[1]

There was another, less cited, reason why he probably needed to break with disengaged science. In the same year, one month and one day after Hose's lynching, Du Bois's only son, Burghardt, died of diphtheria, by then a highly treatable disease, having been refused treatment by white physicians. As Du Bois later wrote: "We could not lay him in the ground there in Georgia, for the earth there is strangely red; so we bore him away to the northward, with his flowers and his little folded hands. In vain, in vain!—for where, O God! beneath thy broad blue sky shall my dark baby rest in peace,—where Reverence dwells, and Goodness, and a Freedom that is free?"[2]

The sequential devastation of preventable Black deaths that neither pedigree nor relative wealth nor geography could change marked a moment for Du Bois in which his life course changed and he was transformed into a prominent public figure in the twentieth-century movements for Black lives. Within a decade of these dual tragedies, Du Bois had cofounded the Niagara Movement, the National Association for the Advancement of Colored People (NAACP), and the *Crisis Magazine*. But just prior to those events, he took on another, curious journey deeper south.

In the summer of 1906, Du Bois traveled to Lowndes County, Alabama, to conduct a comprehensive study of Black labor and economic life in the Cotton Belt region for the US Department of Labor. Around the same time, he was commissioned to write a social novel, which he completed four years later, based in the same region. The latter work, *The Quest of the Silver Fleece*, is the only surviving text from those two endeavors. *Silver Fleece* is a work grounded in Du Bois's rigorous scientific empiricism, from which he builds a speculative fantasy of a free Black place embedded within a plantation, where land is no longer treated as property, and cotton symbolizes liberation.

Silver Fleece offers an epistemological framework that engages social science, history, and fiction to create other Black worlds, an earlier form of both speculative fiction and Black studies.[3] Forever altered by the racial terror that created the space around him, Du Bois erased the lines between positivist inquiry and creative speculation, building what *could be* from what *is*. This strategy not only set a precedent for his subsequent work as a communist and a Pan-Africanist scholar but also created a template for Black studies and the future of knowledge production that has not yet been fully realized.

This chapter traces the echoes of Du Bois's scientific reckoning and intervention through *Silver Fleece* and through a collaborative study I conducted on social and environmental conditions in Lowndes County with Torkwase Dyson, a Black abstract painter and conceptual artist. The year 2016 was steeped in Black deaths at the hands of US police and deputized white civilians, and uprisings across the Black diaspora to affirm that Black lives matter. These persistent and gratuitous killings demanded far more of my consciousness than the academy and my discipline wanted me to give. By that summer, as Torkwase and I were traveling south through Atlanta, where Du Bois lived and taught, and into Lowndes County, where he conducted what he considered his best study, I recognized that I could not, especially at that moment, spend my time in this historic Black place, one of my own ancestral homeplaces, asking questions that would lead inevitably to an unnuanced inventory of Black death and deprivation.[4] I did not know what protocol I would follow, but I knew the one I had been taught was inadequate.

What followed was a long series of conversations, narrative histories in which the Black residents and community leaders talked about their commitments to building their dreams in the Black Belt, despite other possibilities that might await them in white cities and towns mere miles away. More than a century after the publication of Du Bois's *Silver Fleece*, in landscapes that still resembled what he described in 1906, Black people in Lowndes County were reproducing parts of Du Bois's speculative fantasy, particularly in their relations to land, labor, and conceptualizations of place.

Though these respective works, Du Bois's *Silver Fleece* and our *In Conditions of Fresh Water*, were produced 105 years apart, both were created in the afterlife of slavery, in conditions described by Christina Sharpe as "the weather"—the pervasive ubiquity of anti-Blackness manifested in patterns as predictable and recurrent as the climate that orchestrate inexorably toward Black suffering and death. In the efforts to make seemingly impossible Black lives possible in the weather, Sharpe asks, "What must we *know* in order to move through these environments in which the push is always toward Black death?"[5]

I make the case that Du Bois's counterdisciplinary approach to *Silver Fleece*, which he referred to as "an economic study," is an important example of the epistemology Sharpe queries in the twenty-first century for Black people to move through the weather, and that Clyde Woods identifies in the late twentieth century as critical to Black life in the Mississippi Delta. Taking for granted the weather and its impacts, the Du Boisian method in

Silver Fleece uses the characters in the novel to advance speculative knowledges that develop a place centered around what Katherine McKittrick calls "Black livingness" amid a cotton economy where the US North and South covenant to continue building global capital through Black death dealing.[6]

Both in his writing of *Silver Fleece* and in the arc of the novel itself, Du Bois abandons detached science to advance a way of knowing that is aimed at preserving Black lives and livingness, rather than at monitoring the weather. In so doing, Du Bois created an opening across generations for my work with Torkwase to consider the infrastructures of Black livingness that we found in the same Alabama county, under similar weather conditions, still living, as he imagined.

I argue for a Du Boisian methodology in pursuing Black geographies—attention to the political, the economic, and the poetic in the service of rejecting social death as the primary means of characterizing Black life and place-making. The reason for this is more than just about beauty or truth—it is about creating an alternative to measuring Black life against white life, rather than Black life on its own terms.

It is not hyperbole to suggest that 1899 marked a profound shift in Du Bois's life. The year brought into clearer focus the difficult to reconcile tension between his work as a Harvard-trained empirical social scientist and his lived experiences as a Black man born out of slavery whose northern Black middle-class upbringing and academic pedigree did not shield him from white supremacy. The lynching of Sam Hose and the preventable death of his firstborn child, Burghardt Du Bois, represent a cracking of Du Bois's relationship to a nation that he knew was morally corrupt, but that he believed he could influence reform through his knowledge production.

In the face of those realizations, Du Bois had to decide how he would proceed to live and to work toward understanding Black life and pursuing Black liberation, however he might interpret the latter. Thus, experiencing the weather, he pursued other modes of knowledge that could build toward Black livingness, or at least something beyond Black death. Living with (as opposed to under) the weather required a break with positivist science and perhaps even epistemic traditions rooted in advocacy to contend with Black death as integral, not antithetical, to the racial capitalist project of the United States.[7] Du Bois's exclamations in the aftermath of his son's preventable death and his seeking to bury Burghardt far away from the "strangely red" soil of the South gesture toward geography being integral to the other knowledges he sought. *Where* can dark babies rest? *Where* do goodness and reverence and freedom dwell?

Du Bois's epistemic shift also required a connection to something beyond the "real"; it mandated a deep engagement with the realm of the imagination. Knowledge production "in the wake," in this case, encompasses the speculative—an integration of "what is" and "what could be" despite it. While we cannot know for certain all the forces influencing Du Bois's choice to write his first novel during this period of his life, we do know that *Silver Fleece* represents a substantial pivot away from a body of work that was already eclectic.[8] An essayist and arguably the founder of modern sociology, Du Bois had published at least one piece of fiction prior to 1911 in the *Fisk Herald*, the student-run newspaper of Fisk University, the historically Black institution where Du Bois earned his baccalaureate degree in 1888.[9] He was also an early data scientist, producing handmade graphics and charts that influence current data visualization aesthetics.[10] Yet *Silver Fleece* started a trajectory away from empirical social science and toward a life of political and intellectual organizing that spanned nearly fifty years.

The nexus between this new era in Du Bois's life and his embrace of the possibility of free Black life in the US South is of particular significance for considering the weight of the epistemic shift. Under most positivist epistemic traditions, the US South represents the "shadow" side of the nation, the region that the nation purportedly seeks to escape, but that keeps it from achieving the equity that it says is its commitment. The studies of US politics and social relations conducted by Alexis de Tocqueville in 1831 and by Gunnar Myrdal over a century later in 1937 demonstrate for the former an idea of the South as a lazy, morally backward place that would never progress to the status of the North and in which Black people could never live on equal terms with white people and, for the latter, the idea that the South as a region would eventually live up to the country's democratic ideals as whites got better educated about the harms of white supremacy.[11] Both highly influential, the Tocqueville and Myrdal studies seem to ignore the economic and social dependence of the North on the South, construing the systems of slavery-based plantation agriculture and subsequent industries centered around debt peonage as independent from the vast wealth and power manifested in the North and across the colonizing nations of the Western Hemisphere. Separating these systems from US wealth effectively separates Blackness from that wealth as well. Blackness then becomes bounded with the South, the abjection that makes the country poorer. One cannot properly grapple with the weather without a shift in geographic perspective about the South.

Jarvis McInnis argues that *Silver Fleece* marks a shift in Du Bois's engagement with and perspective on the South; whereas Du Bois the social scientist regarded the South as "a political and socioeconomic wasteland for Black Americans," Du Bois the novelist wrote the South as a site where another, more vital Black life could be imagined and created.[12] The shape and contours of that life would necessarily need to look different from white idealized visions of vital lives. That Black paradise in *Silver Fleece* is a swamp community within a plantation requires a change and geographic orientation not only with regard to the South, but also with regard to the meaning and possibility embedded within the precarities of the swamp and violences of the plantation. *Silver Fleece* inverts all these macro- and microgeographies to make impossible Black lives possible.

In *Silver Fleece*, Du Bois refuses to deny how integral chattel slavery, the plantation, and the South are to how Blackness is constituted. Rather than answering the question of what kind of place Black freedom divorced from slavery would produce, Du Bois uses *Silver Fleece* to imagine what kind of place would be created by Black lives that were *insistent* in slavery's wake, committed to building an existence that exceeded the confines of white ideological and spatial enclosures.[13] That imagining necessarily confronts, rather than circumvents, the meaning of spaces like the South, the plantation, the swamp—all degraded geographies—for Black people, and rather than deny their weight or simply reconcile them, Du Bois integrates them into living Black geographies.

Silver Fleece subverts the plantation romance genre by utilizing the lives of the two main Black characters, Blessed Alwyn and Zora Cresswell, to demonstrate the irredeemable and persistent brutality of the plantation in the aftermath of slavery, the fallacy of the North as a geography independent of plantation power and anti-Blackness, and the lie of capitalism as an economic system predicated on freedom and equality. And rather than end with that subversion of plantation logic, Du Bois offers a vision of Black place that shifts Black relationship to both land and labor, creating lives not predicated on violence and extraction.

Blessed arrives in Tooms County (a fictional version of Lowndes County) from his native Atlanta to attend a school for Black people run by a white woman from the North, Sarah Smith. Zora is a descendant of people enslaved on the Cresswell plantation where the school is located; she and Blessed meet as teenagers grappling with the meaning of freedom and the value of the formal, white-structured education that is said to be the pathway to that freedom. Blessed views the school as an opportunity to know what white people know, the "things that give them power and wealth and make them rule."[14] Zora sees the school as a waste of her time, insisting that she "knows more than [white peoples]" and that the "things" that white peoples know are "heavy, dead things." "We black peoples is got the *spirit*. We'se lighter and cunninger; we fly right through them; we go and come again just as we wants to."[15]

While Zora's indifference to "formal" education and her investment in building a Black community engaged primarily in cotton cultivation appears to echo the familiar debate about the role of education in Black freedom between Du Bois and his contemporary Booker T. Washington, Zora is much less interested than Washington in participation in the larger capitalist economy. Indeed, a critical juxtaposition can be made between Zora's vision of economics and that of John Taylor, the white, New York–based brother of one of Zora's and Blessing's schoolteachers, Mary Taylor. Demonstrating the fundamental reliance of northern industrialists on southern labor and land resources, John encourages his sister to teach in the cotton region so that he can get better connected to the Cresswell family for the purpose of buying land to control large shares of the cotton market. Cornering this global market for exponential wealth gains is the essence of plantation power—it requires exclusive private property ownership and domination of land and labor. The place created by such practices persists only through extractive, nonregenerative ecological and social consequences.

Zora's own vision of Black freedom is predicated on shifting the relationship to land and labor away from the plantation logics that have ruled over her family members' lives for generations. Zora possesses not just the knowledges necessary to survive the plantation but also a range of counterlogics required to maintain a life and place apart from white rule—including mistrust of white education systems, lack of interest in individualism, and attentiveness to the function of ecosystems beyond commodities. Du Bois brings in through Zora what might be considered an early version of Clyde Woods's blues epistemology; a way of knowing and of creating place predicated on the insistent lives of Black people in the face of structured death.[16] Though Blessed's reliance on the formal education of the Negro school is encouraged as a means of personal and collective Black uplift, it nonetheless directs him ultimately toward being a higher-stakes participant in the same kind of capitalist economy reproduced by Taylor, bolstering his class status without changing fundamentally the social structure of the society. He lands far north of Tooms County, in Washington, DC, a city where his education grooms him to separate himself from land and the physical labor of agriculture, to forget how his increasingly elite Black experience is reliant on extractive relations with the southern states. But even that form of geographic forgetfulness is tempered by the weather of anti-Blackness.

Having experienced this paradox firsthand, Du Bois uses *Silver Fleece* as a kind of narrative experiment, speculating an alternative form of existence apart from, but not wholly separable from, the plantation. In the end, having attained formal educations and forays up North—the world in the novel most resembling Du Bois's own Black elite existence—life there becomes untenable for both Blessed and Zora. They eventually abandon the false promises of Black elitism to return to Tooms County, where first Zora, then Blessed, become committed to resisting insurgent white supremacy by organizing themselves and their Tooms County community into a Black place predicated on abundance and cooperation—a Black commons—where they could collectively refuse the social, economic, and political confines of whiteness.[17]

They establish a maroon-like community in the same swamp where Zora was born and where her ancestors were enslaved, and where present generations were still functionally in bondage from economies centered around sharecropping and convict leasing. Through a cooperative economy based on cotton—another subversion of plantation power in which community members grow and sell cotton to meet their collective needs rather than for individual profit—Zora and Blessed commit to Black livingness while embedded within the literal plantation. They do this despite its history and ultimately despite the mob violence and massacre that befall their community toward the end of the book, after which they rebuild and continue, ever insistent even in close proximity to death.

In writing *Silver Fleece*, Du Bois did what is forbidden to scientists—he refused to pretend that his life, and indeed his proximity to death, was not tethered to the forces that he studied. Imagining insistent Black lives on the plantation meant he need not surrender to or be complicit in the death-making structures identified by his own scholarship. His life could be insistent, too.

While there is little evidence to directly connect the novel to his future work, the events of Du Bois's life at the time of *Silver Fleece*, combined with his articulated shift away from traditional academia and the themes of the novel, signal an expansion of his political consciousness and appetite for social change. Further, the medium of what Walidah Imarisha calls "visionary" or "speculative" fiction is part of the practice of "creating and envisioning another world."[18] Du Bois used this form in *Silver Fleece* to imagine a future for Black liberation and cooperative living in a region pronounced dead by many of his contemporaries—himself included. Such uses of the fantastic to revive and revise the possibilities of the Cotton Belt arguably laid the groundwork for his future mobilizations of art, journalism, essays, and activism toward the global liberation of Black people through Pan-Africanism and socialism.

The stretch of Highway 80 running through Lowndes County is disorienting, a wide screensaver landscape outside the capital city of Montgomery. The fields are sown with cotton and corn and soybeans, cut into straight rows with industrial precision, mathematically distributed to the fence lines. There are fields at rest, red clay laid bare beneath the sun. And then there are the trees: miles of pines stretched along rolling hills, deep green masses thrust against skies that appear to bow low to the earth.

It is difficult to argue against trees in a place this hot—the temperature stayed well above ninety degrees when Torkwase and I were there in mid-August 2016. The humid air hovered as thick as the clouds. We hauled Torkwase's mobile solar-powered artist studio—Studio South Zero (ssz)—549 miles from North Carolina with a diesel pickup truck. The solar panels powered two desk fans inside ssz, which mostly moved the heat from corner to corner. We were grateful for any shade, any breeze that might pass through those dense stands often planted where Black homeplaces used to be. Those absentee-owned tree plantations.

Torkwase and I traveled to Lowndes County to better understand how the economic and political structures of one of the Blackest geographies in the United States systematically denied Black people access to what the twenty-first century considers the most basic resources for human dignity—clean water and sanitation. Our project, *In Conditions of Fresh Water*, was intended to do the interdisciplinary work of bringing together the structural analysis of social science with the poetic imaginary of visual abstraction to explore the nuances and possibilities of Black places living under regimes of ecological and social harm.[19] Torkwase focused on learning how Black people in Lowndes County and the larger Black Belt contended with the "political abstraction" of anti-Black spatial enclosures and

FIGURE 1.1. US Route 80 in Lowndes County, Alabama, 2015.

denials—such as refusal of water and sewer infrastructure—and countered with their own approaches to spatial justice.[20]

More than fifty years after the passage of the Voting Rights Act of 1965—preceded by the Voting Rights March through this exact stretch of highway from Selma to Montgomery—and decades after the first Black elected officials were installed in the Black Belt, descendants of enslaved Black people on these lands could not rely on any governing body to provide reliably clean water and sanitation services.[21] In some places, the infrastructure available for treating sewage was little different from what Du Bois likely encountered in 1906. The timber industry, which boomed here after Reconstruction, eventually took King Cotton off its throne and dominated the economy—approximately 70 percent of Alabama's land is controlled by the timber industry, largely private absentee planters who have a powerful hold over the state's present and future.[22] In Lowndes County, as with most of the Black Belt, because most of the land is owned by people who do not live there, the absentee planters have both the tax incentives and the political power to block public infrastructure development in the region, including wastewater sanitation systems.[23] Indeed, some people suspect the timber industry influenced the criminalization of failed private sanitation systems. In the first decade of the twenty-first century, several Black residents in the Black Belt were arrested for endangering public health due to failed or nonexistent septic tanks.[24] Such penalties made properties owned by accused Black families more vulnerable to state-sanctioned seizure, making them available for expansion of timberlands, and the foreclosure of the development plans of the communities left behind.

The Black Belt ecologies that eventually birthed King Cotton and pine plantations and nourished the Creek, Chockaw, Chickasaw, and Cherokee peoples before are so thoroughly cultivated for the weather that every element of this bucolic place has a second face. We were here in this Black rural place in 2016, during one of the largest political mobilizations of Black people in defense of Black lives, as people were being daily slaughtered in public by state and deputized actors, with no real accountability.[25] We were surrounded by loud Black death in the cities and suburbs, but here, it sounded different.

Nearly everyone I spoke with on my first visit to "Bloody" Lowndes County recalled a relative or friend who had disappeared or was found dead in the 1960s and 1970s as the Black freedom movements came through the Black Belt. The Lowndes Interpretive Center in the town of White Hall—where the Student Nonviolent Coordinating Committee (SNCC) fought to elect the first Black Panther Party representatives years before the eponymous party appeared in Oakland, California—had a range of memorials to the innumerable Black people who died violently for insisting on living.[26] Everyone knew the descendants of the white people responsible for those disappearances were now sitting in public office, picking up where they left off. More recently, in 2019, the Lowndes County sheriff, a Black man named "Big" John Williams, was murdered by the white son of a deputy sheriff from a neighboring county after trying to disperse a largely white crowd of young people at a gas station.[27] Black people in Lowndes County, which is over 70 percent Black, fought the local white power structure for decades for the privilege of having a Black sheriff, to have at the very least something other than another armed white face claiming to represent safety.[28]

Death sounds different here because this place had already been presumed dead, cast off as the old backward South where every Black person who valued their own life and the possibility of progress had already left. To be Black and to be in the Alabama Black Belt, or most any rural area in the twenty-first century, means encountering the weather out of sight and largely out of national consciousness. The city, even if not in the North, is still considered the future. We *know* the city is the future, just like our predecessors knew the North and West were the future, because we need to believe there is somewhere where the weather is better or has progressed.

Du Bois called "second sight" a gift, an epistemology that offered Black people in the United States (and beyond) clarity about the structure of the society and our place in it.[29] His own second sight arguably enabled his recognition that detached science could free neither him nor the Black people he was studying. Second sight enables the critique of the weather, but there is an important and not inevitable step between that critique and attending to the Black livingness Du Bois imagines in *Silver Fleece*. To see oneself "through the revelation of another world" sometimes means to be engaged in a persistent measurement of oneself from the vantage point of that world.[30] Science often relies on calculations of Black suffering, a detailed inventory of Black death with the objective of prompting progress.[31] But inasmuch as the logics of progress rely endlessly on an ever-changing and indifferent white referent, the practice of defensively measuring Black death can never account for Black life. The gift of second sight, then, must not delimit the imagination, seeing oneself and other Black people—and the places where Black people are—past the long gaze of whiteness.

I knew that the Black Belt was not dead, but I did not quite understand what it meant for it to live. I did not know how to consider places outside of frameworks of progress, growth, and development. But I did know that I would not ask questions that sought the region's death. So, for those few hot weeks in Lowndes County, parked by the Piggly Wiggly Express and the bingo hall, surrounded by loblolly pines and empty storefronts, I asked questions about living.

People trickled in, curious. Some people stopping at the Piggly Wiggly Express saw us hanging around ssz and asked if we were starting a food truck. When we said no, they looked puzzled. What were we doing *here*? They had been asked so many times about the sanitation problem. The weather is the weather. They did not want to talk about it. Instead, they talked about what they were making of their own lives, their own memories, their own dreams of their futures in that place.[32]

Some people came to talk with us because there was scarcely anywhere in the region where someone could get $25 for one hour of their time. A woman in her midthirties named Beatrice said $10 per hour, or $9.50 starting, would be good there, even "eight dollars all right you can get by a little bit." She and her husband, Keon, had five children and lived in the city of Montgomery for a while, just a forty-five-minute drive from Lowndes

FIGURE 1.2. Piggly Wiggly Express in White Hall, Alabama, 2016.

County. The jobs paid better in the city, and both she and Keon could only find odd jobs around White Hall, sometimes installing septic systems or other plumbing. But Beatrice said she made this arrangement work because she liked living in the country better: "You can feel free. You can sit on your porch, and you speak to your neighbor … you play your music, fire up your grill, you ain't got to worry about the police coming through saying turn your radio down, you can't sit here, drink your beer, you know, things like that. To me it feel kinda, it's a little private."

"Feeling free," even when not explicitly stated, was a central theme in my conversations and interviews. Making that feeling possible outside of traditional forms of political power and capital required the kind of improvisation practiced by Zora—living at the margins of the dominant political economy but never seeing yourself as marginal. When Torkwase and I first arrived in White Hall, we met up with John Jackson, the town's former mayor and a member of the SNCC, who was ousted from office by state officials while pursuing long-awaited development for the town. He drove us around in an old police car, pointing out the various sites where the community was trying to develop and how the infrastructure challenges hindered their progress.

The Piggly Wiggly Express, a grocery store that Jackson owned along with the other empty storefronts in the town's strip mall, was demonstrative of both the promise of development and their hindrances. Other than John Jackson's own car and two seemingly abandoned police vehicles parked at White Hall's city hall, we did not encounter any signs of police during our entire visit, something seemingly impossible in any Black place within any major or minor city in the United States, including Montgomery, mere miles away. To feel free here, as Beatrice expressed, also encompasses safety but not, as it seemed, the kind ruled by force. Indeed, this phenomenon of community safety without policing is also identified in Celeste Winston's scholarship on historic Black communities in Maryland, as a model for organizing around abolition of the prison-industrial complex.[33]

Beatrice and Keon, like most other people I interviewed, lived on land that had been in their family for several generations. The homeplace typically had three to five homes or trailers, with a central family home where the elders lived. Du Bois visited Lowndes County within a generation after many land parcels on plantations had been sold to Black families, many of whom bought the land from the same planters who had enslaved them or their ancestors. Decades after the publication of *Silver Fleece*, after his politics grew increasingly socialist, Du Bois delivered a speech to the closing session of the 1946 Southern Youth Legislature in Columbia, South Carolina. To his young audience, he stressed the importance of "taking up land" as a Black freedom strategy, as a means of creating safety and protecting its future by taking it out of the hands of "thugs and lynchers, the mobs and profiteers, the monopolists and gamblers who today choke its soul and steal its resources."[34]

Though we do not today witness Du Bois's imaginings of interracial class solidarity and democracy, Black people's relationship to land in Lowndes County—and in many other Black rural places across the United States—exceeds his own mandate. Although Black land is subject to a legal regime of private, exclusive, and dominated property, Black land as a practice is neither merely property nor capital. From the homeplace to the co-op, Black land is a site-based strategy of refuge, political resistance, love, and longevity.[35]

Catherine Coleman Flowers, a Lowndes County native, educator, writer, and award-winning environmental justice activist who first taught me about Lowndes County's ongoing battles against plantation power, told me about the history of Black family land in Lowndes County and explained why she was taught it was important: "Our families taught us to purchase land, or to keep land, or to always keep the family property, because that's the place where the family could always go. So, no matter what, you always make sure you keep some land that holds the family together.... And those places too, were where the seeds of resistance were planted."

We visited some of these family lands, tucked-away openings amid the hovering pines. Grandmothers were on porches or in the garden or busy somewhere in the house. Grandchildren were running and riding bikes and yelling from house to house. Sometimes there was food growing on a plot out back that could feed whoever needed it, and sometimes not. But there was always some sign of longevity—something weathered and long unused, like an old well or an abandoned trailer. Something that said, we've been here, we've seen it all, and we're still here, like the historic marker across the street from Ruby Rudolph's homeplace. That land belonged to her mother, Rosie Steele, who during the Voting Rights March set up an evening camp for the marchers, including the Reverend Martin Luther King Jr.

We did not have an opportunity to visit the juke joint where James Brown and Bessie Smith used to come play on their chitlin circuit tours, later sleeping at someone's house, but Lyndon and Ben, cousins and brickmasons who build churches and other major buildings together across the country, told us about how it's still a good place to have a beer, to unwind, to meet your future spouse, as one of them did. There are homes far out along back roads where the best card players show up for late night tournaments. There is the Holy Ground—the sandy shore of the Alabama River everyone calls a beach and gathers there for family reunions and cookouts and hot swimming days—where one battle in the Creek War was fought. Some people complained about the county's lack of infrastructure, but they were more likely to tell me why they were still here in spite of those challenges. There were few places they knew of where they could live in peace and safety, where they could count on community to take care of them if they needed it. They had no plans to leave.

Our maps could never contain all the livingness. As I traced the spatial and familial and infrastructural networks through these conversations, mapping them onto other Black places I know from life, from literature, from poetry, from scholarship, Torkwase spoke back to the Lowndes County residents and to me through architectural paintings and mixed-media representations of these fugitive Black spatialities, aimed at the "abilities of Black bodies to expressively inhabit and negotiate the coercive construction of space in real time."[36] Her paintings and installations, which were displayed in a six-month exhibition at Duke University's Center for Documentary Studies, were named for the moments in these conversations when people described the spaces they inhabited and articulated how they used their public and private spaces to anchor and build their lives. These artistic abstractions collectively exemplify what Torkwase calls "Black compositional thought"—a Black practice of shifting space, energy, and scale to create alternative possibilities for Black liberation, much like what Zora, Blessed, and their community practiced in Tooms County 105 years earlier.

And suddenly it was time for us to return to our own places in the city.

We made one last visit, to a place called Epes, for the annual meeting of the Federation of Southern Cooperatives. The grounds of the rural training facility had been constructed in a hidden clearing through narrow and hilly terrain in a town of fewer than two hundred people, originally to protect the organizing efforts of rural Black farmers who saw little difference in their lives in the post–civil rights period. They sought cooperative rural economies, run by Black farmers for Black farmers—a way around the plantation. For more than fifty years, and across at least twelve states, they built their own vision of Black living, straight out of Du Bois's imaginary in *Silver Fleece*. On the day we were there, a group of women members of the Federation of Southern Cooperatives met with Francia Márquez, an Afro-Colombian human rights and environmental justice organizer and

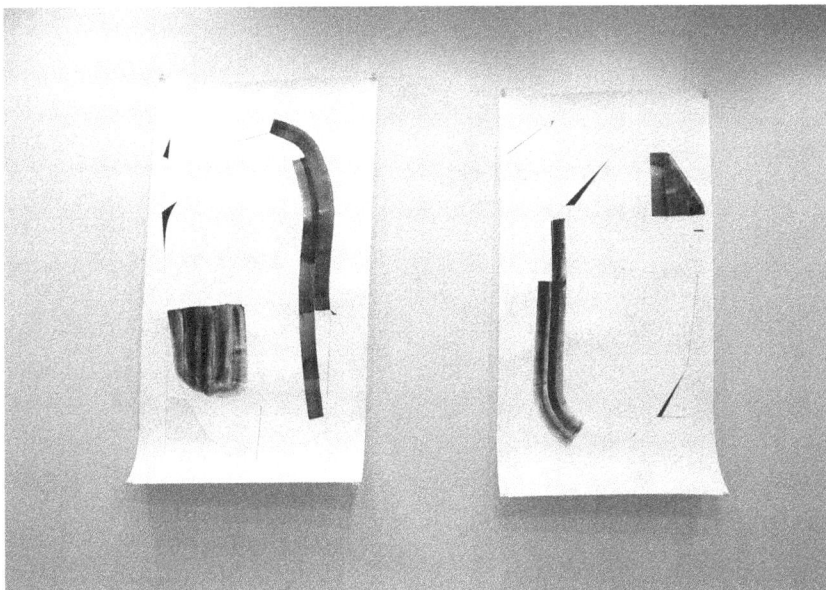

FIGURE 1.3. Torkwase Dyson, *Our Own Good Time Place #1* (*right*) and *Our Own Good Time Place #2* (*left*), 2017. Gouache and ink on paper. Photo by Tamika Galanis.

future vice president of Colombia.[37] Their goal was to build an international network of Black women land protectors that would descend on Colombia's Cauca region in opposition to the pillage and erasure of ancestral lands for gold, which was poisoning waterways essential for Afro-Colombian survival. Over a century after his departure from this region, Du Bois's vision of Pan-African solidarity struggles, on which he worked until his death in Ghana in 1963, were being realized right in front of us.

Even as Du Boisian sociology is a thriving and necessary enterprise and is rewriting the history of a discipline deeply implicated in anti-Blackness, I want to reflect with a few notes on "Du Boisian methodology," which I argue is applicable for scholars of any discipline (or no discipline) who are interested in Black or other subaltern groups and the places they inhabit.[38] Du Bois's approach in *Silver Fleece* has important relevance to ongoing conversations about Black epistemic traditions and problematics of science, and the role of the imaginary in knowledge production.[39]

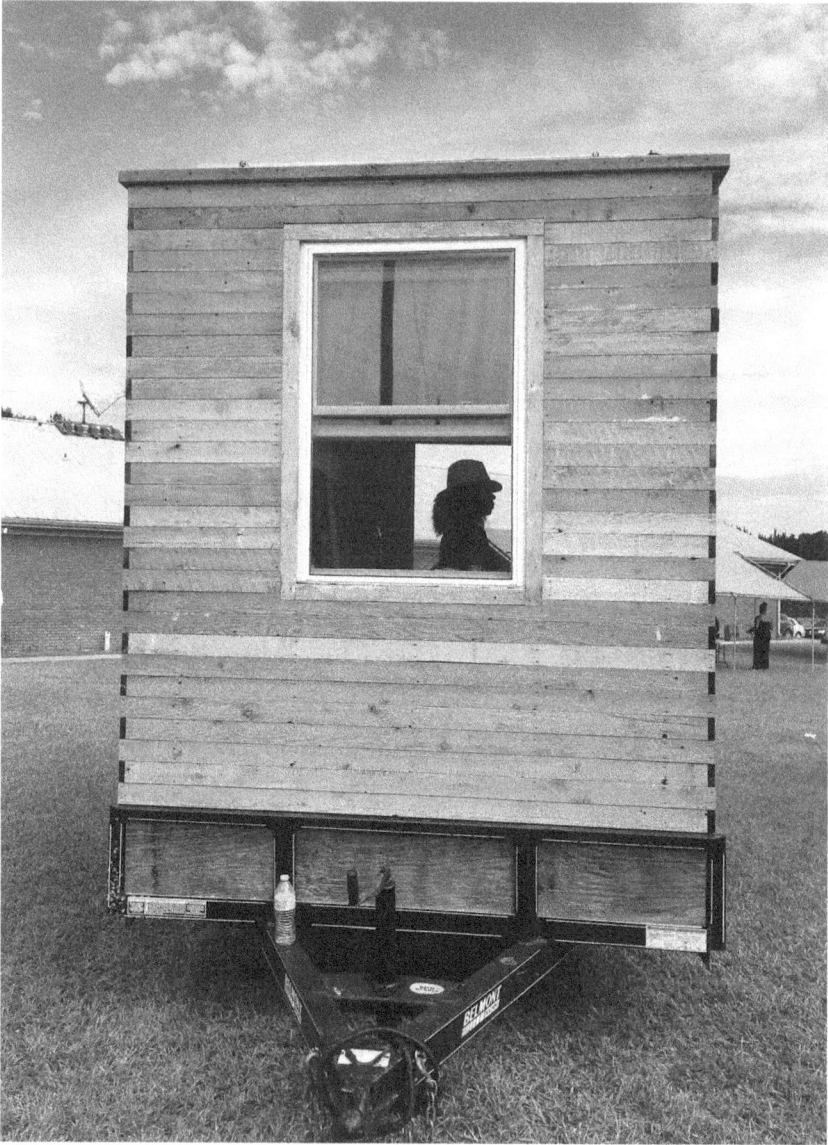

FIGURE 1.4. Torkwase Dyson in Studio South Zero, Epes, Alabama, 2016.

Du Bois's methods onward from "Negro Labor in Lowndes County" and *Silver Fleece* seemed absorbed with the question of "where" Black people could be free when the weather of anti-Blackness was everywhere. At least some part of the answer to that question came from addressing Sharpe's question—"What must we *know* in order to move through these environments in which the push is always toward Black death?"[40]

The knowledge about Blackness produced by positivist social science is, almost by its nature, knowledge about Black suffering and death, because whiteness is the unacknowledged social referent against which Black life is measured. When whiteness is the litmus test for what it means to live and even thrive, then the everyday practice of Black living within white supremacy, not to mention the possibilities of other modes of life beyond the present geographic order, are rendered as irrelevant knowledge.[41] Breaking that cycle of death and death epistemology requires both imagining that some other way of life must exist, even when the weather does not change. Though we gather from Du Bois's letters at the time that at least part of his aim in writing a novel was to broaden his audience beyond scholars and to reach a Black public, his decision to write *Silver Fleece* reflects not only a refusal of a singular discipline as a scholar but also a recognition that there is a *necessary relationship* between epistemic practices that have been normatively separated.[42] The math of Black existence under plantation regimes, for instance, offers one way of seeing that requires science fiction or speculation to open the trap of perpetual white referential calculus, to see something beyond lack or burden in Blackness. Part of the disciplining involved is the practice of disallowing colonial epistemologies and standards to define every possibility. Just as the novel (or an art exhibit) can also be an "economic study," the plantation can have a different kind of future.[43]

In Conditions of Fresh Water took up this Du Boisian method by redirecting the center of the research from the weather, manifested through systematic denial of basic infrastructure in Lowndes County, Alabama, to the kind of places that Black people had created within and around those imposed constraints. Where positivist social science would have concluded with numbers of underserved, development disparities of Black places vis-à-vis white places and, at best, a summary of the political resistance to these disparities, the questions I asked about Black residents' memories, histories, and attachments to Lowndes County produced entirely different interpretations and understandings of the place, all of which had very little to do with whiteness generally, and the infrastructure disparities more generally. The specific emphasis that Black Lowndes County residents placed on the kind of safe and connected lives they created for themselves in that place did not diminish the importance of infrastructure problems, but it rejected a conflation of the "disparities" they suffered with the lives they were living.

Beyond considerations of measurement, Du Boisian methods also require a level of improvisation and vulnerability disfavored by positivist inquiry. The precision prized by positivism is also quite narrow—so much so that the knowledge it produces is often narrow and unnuanced. While it is not useless, the primacy of such inquiry does lead to the kind of conclusions and conflations refused by Black residents of Lowndes County. McKittrick insists that an approach to knowledge production beyond positivism, as practiced in Black studies—of which Du Bois is certainly an early practitioner—is precise, but I interpret precision in this sense to mean the nuances of Black lives and geographies that cannot be measured. What, then, does it mean for a trained scientist to study something that cannot be measured? Du Boisian methods, which are Black studies methods, require an openness to a range of approaches to knowing beyond the limits of any one form of training, such as speculation and fiction, as well as the possibility of the unknowable. This means a commitment to the vulnerability of not knowing, of conceding expertise, while maintaining curiosity about various possibilities of what could be in the spirit of finding ways toward Black freedom(s).

Notes

The chapter title, with gratitude to Danez Smith, is from their poem "Summer, Somewhere."

1   Du Bois, *Dusk of Dawn*, 67.
2   Du Bois, *Souls of Black Folk*, 160.
3   See, e.g., McKittrick, *Dear Science*; brown and Imarisha, *Octavia's Brood*.
4   McKittrick, "Diachronic Loops."
5   Sharpe, *In the Wake*, 106 (my emphasis).
6   McKittrick, *Dear Science*.
7   See, e.g., Woods, *Development Arrested*; Robinson, *Black Marxism*.
8   In the introduction to *The Quest of the Silver Fleece*, Herbert Aptheker indicates Du Bois was partly influenced to attempt *Silver Fleece* by the tide of social novels by his contemporaries, such as Paul Laurence Dunbar.
9   On Du Bois as the founder of modern sociology, see Morris, *Scholar Denied*.

10 Battle-Baptiste and Rusert, *W. E. B. DuBois's Data Portraits*.

11 Tocqueville, *Democracy in America*; Myrdal, *American Dilemma*.

12 McInnis, "'Behold the Land,'" 71.

13 Hawthorne, "Black Matters Are Spatial Matters," 7.

14 Du Bois, *Quest of the Silver Fleece*, 29.

15 Du Bois, *Quest of the Silver Fleece*, 29.

16. Woods, *Development Arrested*, 25.

17 Roane, "Plotting the Black Commons," 241–44.

18 brown and Imarisha, *Octavia's Brood*, 3.

19 Dyson and Purifoy, "In Conditions of Fresh Water."

20 On political abstraction, see Dyson, "Black Interiority."

21 Winkler and Flowers, "America's Dirty Secret," 184–85.

22 Bailey, Gopaul, Thomson, and Gunnoe, "Taking Goldschmidt to the Woods," 51.

23 Bailey and Majumdar, "Absentee Forest and Farm Land Ownership," 146.

24 Winkler and Flowers, "America's Dirty Secret," 191–92.

25 See Khan-Cullors and bandele, *When They Call You a Terrorist*.

26 Jeffries, *Bloody Lowndes*, 143–79.

27 Robinson, "Lowndes County Sheriff Killed."

28 Jeffries, *Bloody Lowndes*, 241.

29 Du Bois, *Souls of Black Folk*, 3.

30 Du Bois, *Souls of Black Folk*, 3.

31 McKittrick, "Mathematics Black Life," 18.

32 Excerpts of some of these conversations are available at https://www.danielle purifoy.com/media.

33 Winston, "'How to Lose the Hounds'"; Winston, "Maroon Geographies."

34 Du Bois, "Behold the Land."

35 See, e.g., Roane, "Plotting the Black Commons"; McInnis, "'Behold the Land.'"

36 Dyson, "Black Interiority."

37 In June 2022, Francia Márquez was elected the first Black vice president of Colombia. See Turkewitz, "Francia Márquez."

38 On Du Boisian sociology as a thriving and necessary enterprise, see Morris, *Scholar Denied*.

39 See, e.g., Woods, "Life after Death"; Woods, *Development Arrested*; McKittrick, *Dear Science*.

40 Sharpe, *In the Wake*, 106 (my emphasis).

41 See Quashie, *Black Aliveness*.

42 See Aptheker, introduction, *Quest of the Silver Fleece*; Collins, *Black Feminist Thought*; McKittrick, "Diachronic Loops."

43 McKittrick, "Plantation Futures."

Bailey, Conner, Abhimanyu Gopaul, Ryan Thomson, and Andrew Gunnoe. "Taking Goldschmidt to the Woods: Timberland Ownership and Quality of Life in Alabama." *Rural Sociology* 86, no. 1 (2021): 50–80.

Bailey, Conner, and Mahua Majumdar. "Absentee Forest and Farm Land Ownership in Alabama: Capturing Benefits from Natural Capital Controlled by Nonresidents." In *Rural Wealth Creation*, edited by John L. Pender, Bruce A. Weber, Thomas G. Johnson, and J. Matthew Fannin, 152–68. Abingdon, UK: Routledge, 2014.

Battle-Baptiste, Whitney, and Britt Rusert, eds. *W. E. B. Du Bois's Data Portraits: Visualizing Black America*. New York: Princeton Architectural Press, 2018.

brown, adrienne maree, and Walidah Imarisha, eds. *Octavia's Brood: Science Fiction Stories from Social Justice Movements*. Chico, CA: AK Press, 2015.

Collins, Patricia Hill. *Black Feminist Thought: Knowledge, Consciousness, and the Politics of Empowerment*. New York: Routledge, 2000.

Du Bois, W. E. B. "Behold the Land." 1946. http://credo.library.umass.edu/view/full/mums312-b198-i047.

Du Bois, W. E. B. *Dusk of Dawn: An Essay toward an Autobiography of a Race Concept*. 1940. New Brunswick, NJ: Transaction, 2011.

Du Bois, W. E. B. *The Quest of the Silver Fleece*. 1911. Repr. ed. Mineola, NY: Dover, 2008.

Du Bois, W. E. B. *The Souls of Black Folk*. 1903. New Haven, CT: Yale University Press, 2015.

Dyson, Torkwase. "Black Interiority: Notes on Architecture, Infrastructure, Environmental Justice, and Abstract Drawing." *Pelican Bomb*, January 9, 2017. http://pelicanbomb.com/art-review/2017/black-interiority-notes-on-architecture-infrastructure-environmental-justice-and-abstract-drawing.

Dyson, Torkwase, and Danielle Purifoy. "In Conditions of Fresh Water." 2016. https://www.daniellepurifoy.com/in-conditions-of-fresh-water-1.

Hawthorne, Camilla. "Black Matters Are Spatial Matters: Black Geographies for the Twenty-First Century." *Geography Compass* 13, no. 11 (2019): 1–13.

Jeffries, Hasan Kwame. *Bloody Lowndes: Civil Rights and Black Power in Alabama's Black Belt*. New York: NYU Press, 2010.

Khan-Cullors, Patrisse, and asha bandele. *When They Call You a Terrorist: A Black Lives Matter Memoir*. New York: St. Martin's Griffin, 2018.

McInnis, Jarvis C. "'Behold the Land': W. E. B. Du Bois, Cotton Futures, and the Afterlife of the Plantation in the US South." *Global South* 10, no. 2 (2016): 70–98.

McKittrick, Katherine. *Dear Science and Other Stories*. Durham, NC: Duke University Press, 2021.

McKittrick, Katherine. "Diachronic Loops/Deadweight Tonnage/Bad Made Measure." *Cultural Geographies* 23, no. 1 (2016): 3–18. https://doi.org/10.1177/1474474015612716.

McKittrick, Katherine. "Mathematics Black Life." *Black Scholar* 44, no. 2 (2014): 16–28. https://www.tandfonline.com/doi/abs/10.1080/00064246.2014.11413684.

McKittrick, Katherine. "Plantation Futures." *Small Axe: A Caribbean Journal of Criticism* 17, no. 3 (42) (2013): 1–15.

Morris, Aldon. *The Scholar Denied: W. E. B. Du Bois and the Birth of Modern Sociology*. Berkeley: University of California Press, 2015.

Myrdal, Gunnar. *An American Dilemma: The Negro Problem and Modern Democracy*. 2 vols. New York: Harper and Brothers, 1944.

Quashie, Kevin. *Black Aliveness, or A Poetics of Being*. Durham, NC: Duke University Press, 2021.

Roane, J. T. 2018. "Plotting the Black Commons." *Souls* 20, no. 3 (2018): 239–66.

Robinson, Carol. "Lowndes County Sheriff Killed, Suspect Surrenders." *AL.com*, November 24, 2019. https://www.al.com/news/montgomery/2019/11/lowndes -county-sheriff-big-john-williams-shot-and-killed-in-the-line-of-duty.html.

Robinson, Cedric J. *Black Marxism: The Making of the Black Radical Tradition*. 3rd ed. Chapel Hill: University of North Carolina Press, 2020.

Sharpe, Christina. *In the Wake: On Blackness and Being*. Durham, NC: Duke University Press, 2016.

Smith, Danez. *Don't Call Us Dead: Poems*. Minneapolis: Graywolf Press, 2017.

Tocqueville, Alexis de. *Democracy in America*. Vol. 1. New York: Colonial Press, 1899.

Turkewitz, Julie. "Francia Márquez—a Former Housekeeper and Activist—Is Colombia's First Black Vice President." *New York Times*, June 19, 2022. https:// www.nytimes.com/2022/06/19/world/americas/francia-marquez-vice-president -colombia.html.

Winkler, Inga T., and Catherine Coleman Flowers. "America's Dirty Secret: The Human Right to Sanitation in Alabama's Black Belt." *Columbia Human Rights Law Review* 49 (2017): 181–228.

Winston, Celeste. "'How to Lose the Hounds': Tracing the Relevance of Marronage for Contemporary Anti-police Struggles." PhD diss., City University of New York, 2019.

Winston, Celeste. "Maroon Geographies." *Annals of the American Association of Geographers* 111, no. 7 (2021): 2185–99. https://doi.org/10.1080/24694452.2021.1894087.

Woods, Clyde. *Development Arrested: The Blues and Plantation Power in the Mississippi Delta*. London: Verso, 1998.

Woods, Clyde. "Life after Death." *Professional Geographer* 54, no. 1 (2002): 62–66. https://doi.org/10.1111/0033-0124.00315.

2

Shaking the Basemap

JUDITH MADERA

Black geographies are openings into multiple worlds. They are not limited to the bounds of any singular representational system. Instead, they cut across far-reaching practices and spaces. This chapter looks at early narratives from the long epoch of abolition. It considers different kinds of situated knowledges and geographic practices developed in the writings of Black abolitionists. Abolitionist print genealogies traffic in a range of forms: spiritual texts, poetics, exploratory accounts, fugitive narratives, newspaper imprints, fiction, editorials, letters, and local histories. Their formal fluidity reflects the variable conditions of their production and reception.[1] Yet, Black geography was never a practice limited to patterned confinement or teleologies of resistance. From the earliest records we see that author-activists insisted on the primacy of first-person experience. They suggested modal possibility for vibrant Black life. And they recognized that the ways places were shared mattered.

The author-activists I discuss envisioned new place-making strategies as an expressive politics of connection. In this chapter, I will look at three arenas of advocacy revealed by the Black archive: the development of critical literacies—especially expressed in Black women's civics; strategies against commodification inside colonial-capitalist systems; and the political geographies amplified in early literature. I begin in the Black narrative archive because it signals the shapes of radical geographic risk and venture.

Archives beyond Archives

There is an impossibility to beginning with the subject of the archive since to trace Black geographies through print records, we must first deal with histories riddled by silences. We also contend with the freight of racist hierarchies that obscured Africana women's voices and the knowledges of those made disposable through colonialism and late-plantation capitalism. Not surprisingly, dominant historiographies reflect institutionalized vanishing points. They are largely codified to suppress the very place experiences that were already discarded in master inventories. C. Riley Snorton reminds us to "consider that an archive serves as 'proof' not only of the questions we bring to it but also of a set of political procedures and institutional forces that make it available to us."[2] It is a valuable point. For generations of enslaved and indentured peoples who were doubly expendable as bodies and as historical subjects, the archive registers absences. Often all that can be deduced is the echo of presence. Marisa Fuentes reflects: "One must persist for years in this 'mortuary' of records to bring otherwise invisible lives to historical representation in a way that challenges the reproduction of invisibility and commodification."[3] Black feminist aesthetics reject a telos of closure. Instead, its practices produce new mappings and different frames for belonging.

I will not expend space here discussing the imperialist roots of geography as a discipline or the forms of proslavery US expansion supported by cartography firms and map copyright consolidators.[4] These points have already been well established. Suffice it to say that unsettling the timelines and genres of categorization—the broader project of radical geographic praxis—is not reducible to programmatic formulation. It requires approaches that interrogate representational practices. It also takes a willingness to disrupt historical storage units (commonly called *traditions*) by bringing people's place-based experiences to account.

To this end, Black feminist cultural historians have advanced a range of curatorial praxes. Saidiya Hartman calls for a critical, fabulatory methodology to "make visible the production of disposable lives."[5] Jacqueline Goldsby advocates a relational methodology, something constituted by the archival encounter itself, and correspondences invoked by the plastic arts.[6] Other approaches focalize narrative differentiation, or what Nicole Aljoe describes as a testimonial "disembedding" from colonial contexts.[7] Feminist heuristics attend to the back-end work of archival record-making and thick assemblage. They extend public history into communities. Much of this work has to be done in the absence of licensed cartographic records or existing print indexes.

Early Black political geographies were likewise born of the need to reinvent both places and practices. Black women had to first write the ramp to new imaginations of history through activism. Decades prior to the American Civil War, women were doing the activist, place-making work of convening the Colored Conventions movement. The strategies of the movement grew to encompass major civil rights campaigns.[8] Women's organizing, including minute keeping and dispatch writing, were integral to nineteenth-century place-making. By bringing attention to the discursive and community-making practices of those who were largely omitted from sociohistorical records, we can better account for the lived connections that made Black political geographies.

Going back further, women's voices were noticeably absent from the Laws of the African Society (1802), one of the earliest mutual aid stateside societies that flourished in the early 1790s. But it was the womanist curatorship of Howard University librarian Dorothy Porter that daylighted these abolitionist tributaries. She brought the meeting documents and letters of redress into conversation with each other—and staged their debates for a twentieth-century reading public.[9] In a parallel way, authors like Alice Dunbar-Nelson and Zora Neale Hurston who explored Black regional life during dynamic eras of change had to devise new literary modes to depict extranational community histories. Their literature reflects vastly different experiences of national subzones and interspaces than are found in the genres and periodicities to which their writing is typically assigned. By complicating what constitutes authorship and locating place-making practices beyond an imposed historicity, we get closer to the progressions of abolitionist geography.

For these reasons, I look at the Black geographic archive not as an artifact set but as a network. The archive can be a place and an event at the same time. It can be a multiscaled church like the African Methodist Episcopal ecclesiological spaces archived by the Afrofuturist avatar, editor, and historian Pauline Hopkins in *Contending Forces* (1900).[10] In Hopkins's novel, the church becomes a syncretic, open archive. It is at once an abolitionist platform, a financial support structure, a deliberative political sphere, a hospital, a kitchen, and an educational forum. The Black archive takes manifold forms. It can be a house like Arturo Schomburg's home in Bedford-Stuyvesant, which spilled out into the now famous holdings of Harlem as contour trails of a life's work. Schomburg's project was to make a reparative record of a cultural and linguistic Black tradition of Africana cultural production in the Americas. His geographic reach encompassed West Indian archipelagoes, continental Africa, and the hemispheric Americas. Schomburg pursued a vast tradition that we no longer think of as singular.

Even surpassing Schomburg's extensive collections are archaeologies of human-environment relations that constitute Black tension ecologies—often at the edges of plantation precincts. These sites are palimpsests; they collate radical Black geographies as transitive movements. They include caves, cockpits, and the mobile Black undergrounds, where refugees defied dominant territorializations. Moreover, if we think about sites as actors in their own right, then the archive can be something as intractable as a peat swamp that decomposed its human histories in acid and ooze. Only trace material artifacts remain in the Great Dismal Swamp that nineteenth-century authors Solomon Northup and Moses Grandy described as a trial space that redirected linearity. But the swamp remains an integrative biome that invoked abolitionist cultural imaginaries. It stands as an archive of Black resistance. In transformative ways, the Black archive resists containment. It is ongoing and connects to the stories it yields.

Feminist Print and Praxis before Du Bois

Geographies are material and discursive. So are archives. Both are shaped through currencies, memories, and people's stories. Print was an important vehicle for extending spatial networks. From Briton Hammon's 1760 account to Phillis Wheatley's elegiac poetics (1770), Ignatius Sancho's letters (1782), and beyond, a common threadline is the high premium enslaved peoples placed on obtaining literacy and writing their stories. Frederick Douglass described reading as "the pathway from slavery to freedom."[11] And the poet Juan Francisco Manzano, enslaved in Cuba, stated in his 1840 autobiography, "In vain was I forbidden to write."[12]

Early nineteenth-century contemporaries Nancy Gardner Prince, Maria W. Miller Stewart, and Harriet Wilson used their writing to project foundations for Black women's political representation in the young Republic. They immediately insisted on improved access to schools for Black girls and called for greater opportunities for higher education. Prince would go so far as to travel from her home base of Boston, Massachusetts, through slave installations in the Gulf of Mexico to reach Kingston, Jamaica, in an effort to help establish a free school for Jamaican girls in 1840. It was a trip she repeated despite threats of violence and imprisonment. Through expressly situated narratives, including ethnographies, domestic memoirs, and community treatises, Black women authors called for a civics that they first needed to build.

Some seventy years before W. E. B. Du Bois's 1903 popularization of an elite, male representational politics ("the Negro Race, like all races, is going to be saved by its exceptional men"), Maria Stewart rejected the premise and directly proffered alternatives.[13] In a dual indictment of the American Colonization Society and a US nation divided by its own legal system, Stewart in 1833 argued: "It is of no use for us to wait any longer for a generation of well-educated men to arise."[14] She was clear that the marginalization of Black women as intellectual and political leaders would hinder long-arc abolition. At great personal risk, she took on the mantel of a spiritual and political leader—an activist. In her "Farewell Address to Her Friends in the City of Boston," Stewart invited women from all corners of social life to the revolution, telling them to bring their "voice in moral, religious, and political subjects" in a reclamation of a Black participatory demos.[15] This was considered very controversial in the early nineteenth century—certainly for its reach into the male-only sphere of politics. But hers was an injunction to seek out unsanctioned forms in the project of Black civic organization.

Late nineteenth-century authors and journalists like Frances E. W. Harper, Pauline Hopkins, Victoria Earle Matthews, and Ida B. Wells-Barnett took up Stewart's call. They amplified local knowledges and connected communities of color through print abolitionism.[16] Harper, Hopkins, and Matthews were literary-based activists. In their poetry and fiction they envisioned a range of community praxis sites for women. Rarely was a praxis site something fixed in shape. Instead, it was a network. Networks could be speculative or already vested. But by featuring practice geographies (those showing myriad ways of enacting space) and characters drawn into place-making by a range of affinities, Black women authors developed a self-reflexive literary spatial aesthetics. They recast known worlds and looked to new collectivities for shared abolitionist purposes. Their writing transformed possibility into materiality and movement.

All of these authors put women's access to safe housing and employment at the center of their published writings. Pauline Hopkins's novel *Contending Forces* is a case study of a Boston-based women's political sphere at the turn of the century. The text illustrates the ways Black women mediate multiple interpublic spaces and institutions. Their current event discussion groups, civic clubs, and workspaces are all venues where Black political futures get deliberated—with clarity and humor. The characters mobilized by Hopkins take on difficult present-day issues as well, including gender-based violence and homelessness. Yet, the author shows that women's voices are marginalized by the nationally organized Colored League, a precursor to the National Association for the Advancement of Colored People (NAACP). Much of the political discussion is centered on representative race men, Booker T. Washington and W. E. B. Du Bois, the latter depicted as a native son of Massachusetts.

In Hopkins's novel, both Du Bois and Washington fail to adequately account for Black women's political agency. The author observed the ways women's antilynching coordination and civil rights activism had been obscured in men's leadership fora and sociological publications. Washington, it is worth noting, was a professional rival of Hopkins who wrested editorship of her *Colored American Magazine* from her in 1905 with a leveraged buyout.[17] Intent on decentering Hopkins's plainly racial focus with more conciliatory rhetoric, he changed what was a magazine about Black education, race relations, community organization, and current affairs into a vocational education bulletin. The *Colored American*'s readership and circulation plummeted.

While Hopkins's devotion to both Black literary culture and urban sociological study brought her into closer alignment with Du Bois, she took issue with the models of progress he ventured. She did not see how he adequately accounted for women's voices or women's mobility as features of place-making. She was likely disappointed by his repeated failure to credit women in his social activism and writing, including women like Anna Julia Cooper and Ida B. Wells-Barnett, whose work he used without attribution. In her series "Famous Women of the Negro Race" (1902), Hopkins archly declared: "We know that it is not 'popular' for a woman to speak or write in plain terms against political brutalities, that a woman should confine her efforts to woman's work in the home and church." But casting aside this prescription, she argued, "The colored woman must have an intimate knowledge of every question that agitates the councils of the world; she must understand the solution of problems that involve the alteration of the boundaries of countries, and which make and unmake governments."[18]

Discursive geographies, then, were not just representations of material space. They did not simply represent space. Rather, they unmasked the terms by which places were produced and were concourses for new ways of visioning connectivity. Narratives extended material spaces. Harper and Hopkins used fiction to model alliances between Black people inhabiting very different worlds, from Ethiopia to the wider Caribbean and New England—not through a logic of generalization but by situated approaches attendant to cultural translation and circulation. Hopkins, like Harper, Matthews, and Wells-Barnett, took an interest in supporting Black women's intranational mobility through urban planning and settlement housing. All of these author-activists fundraised for Black women migrants. Hopkins and Wells-Barnett were also political reporters and editors. Both became small-newspaper owners, directing readers' attention to Black educational disparities. Through their editorials and print contributions they placed Black women's rights at the core of civil rights. Abolitionist geographies grew up in reading societies, church organizations, cottage industries, women's leadership groups, social clubs, and political debate fora. Author-activists transformed what was taken to be nonpolitical and private into embodied political speech. These women were forerunners for an intersectional discursive feminism. Their work was grounded concretely by efforts to develop critical literacies.[19]

Archipelagic Networks from the Eighteenth Century

If we take a more expansive view of Black literary history as practice-based and community-informed discourses, then the eighteenth-century roots of Black geography, *geo* (world) *graphia* (writing), become clearer. For the Ghana-born Quobna Ottobah Cugoano, who toiled in the 1770s-era plantation economy of Grenada before arriving in England, the abolitionist petition was a form of spatial redress that both historicized and expanded Black place-based experiences. Cugoano maintained that colonialism defrauded the protections of citizenship and the possibility of national identity for

African-descended peoples. Like Briton Hammon, who sailed between Massachusetts, coastal Florida, Cuba, and London in the middle decades of the eighteenth century, he gave weight to trajectories of movement that could not be confined to any national geography or spatial teleology. Traversing nearly all of England, Cugoano petitioned King George III directly to demand an end to "the infernal traffic of slavery" and insisted on publishing under his African name—not his assigned English name of John Stewart.[20]

Cugoano's activism brought him into affiliation with Black abolitionists like Ignatius Sancho and Olaudah Equiano, both of whom had cultivated relationships with London publishers and bookbinders. Though their narratives are very different, they all reveal systems of racial capital hidden by official maps. Taken together, their accounts counter what liberal humanism made the material of history or what Frantz Fanon termed simply "History," or *l'Histoire*, "a historicoracial schema, by which the other, the white man, who had woven me out of a thousand details, anecdotes, stories" could lay claim.[21] Nor were Cugoano's or Equiano's narratives dependent on white paratexts or trajectories of nation-based (British rise of the novel) emplotment. Instead, early abolitionist narratives foregrounded the potential of Black spatial topology, the work of rescaling figuration in Caribbean worlds politically and linguistically atomized by colonialism.

A little-examined feature of Olaudah Equiano's *Interesting Narrative* (1789) is how the text makes a political space out of mutable Antillean geographies—and puts the flesh of place at the core. Claiming to "have visited no less than fifteen" islands, Equiano compiled archipelagoes as sites of witness, drawing his readers into a dystopic panorama of the Caribbean.[22] Archipelagoes translate into stepping stones in a system of captures that he nonetheless eludes and refigures through writing. Glossing whole Caribbean worlds in short paragraphs, the narrative sutures different island shapes to colonial violence: Montserrat was about roofless living and returning to wetness "with open pores."[23] The whole term of a field slave's life on this fertile volcano, Equiano claims, is eleven years. St. Kitts, the first Caribbean island to be colonized by the British, is a locus of wasted flesh—brands and broken bones.[24] Martinico (Martinique) puts on a more pleasant face: St. Pierre was "more like a European city than any I had seen in the West Indies."[25] But behind its impressive harbor and *grande rues*, he reported, were sugarcane fields where mulatto overseers spawned their own field labor. No dissociative aesthetics characterize these place stories, but rather the enmeshed sites of body and environment. The compendium of

Caribbean geographies aggregates embodied, material realities into a place archive.

Equiano's spatial index of Caribbean life extended the reach and application of an early Black political geography by accounting for lives not accounted for. He situated enslaved people in physical environments they could not leave, save by death. And he showed the hand of colonialism in all of it. Islands are projected as connective nodes that expended Black Atlantic life as the calculated churn of an already-strained commodity system. The arteries of this traffic were colonialism and slavery. Mesologically (scaled to environment and government) the islands Equiano staged together demanded new abolitionist mobilizations—a new geostrategy. It is fitting that a text about linked island worlds would bring readers into overlapping communities of struggle.[26] *The Interesting Narrative* was published in eight British editions in the author's lifetime, and in one US edition, ultimately making it one of the most widely read Black narratives in England. Equiano's testimony was instrumental in turn-of-the-century parliamentary deliberations about the international slave trade.

To wit, the author was at the forefront of efforts to publicize the *Zong* massacre of 1781 in Jamaican coastal waters. He delivered news of the event to Granville Sharp and to London abolitionists, who were, in turn, responsible for the first newspaper printing of the incident—nearly two years after the 1781 mass killings were debated as a cargo jettison or "general average." In fact, the homicides reached British courts as a property underwriting case. The administrative classification itself reveals the economic and legal system Equiano was up against. But by 1788, he had petitioned the House of Commons to stop the transport of Africans on slave ships. Though he would not live to see the passage of the Slave Trade Act of 1807, his narrative testimony at a critical juncture during British slavery debates disrupted transnational logistics and its British legal armature in significant ways. It all branched from a personal narrative about the perilous life of a Black sailor.

Basemap and Countercartography

One major way Black Atlantic authors exposed infrastructures of racism was by interrogating the colonial basemap, or the notion of a stable referent that supported white supremacist alignment systems.[27] The basemap that Cugoano repeatedly called in his *Narrative* "the fashionable way of traffic" was a human extraction system at the nexus of critical Black geographies.[28]

As he more pointedly stated in his emancipation proclamation, *Thoughts and Sentiments on the Evil and Wicked Traffic of the Slavery and Commerce of the Human Species* (1787), the basemap was a geopolitical map of European trade outlets, logistics, and supply chains—inclusive of West Indian colonies and coastal access points to Africa. It was a nautical scheme of expropriation, facilitated by "an act of parliament, Anno 1697" and the Royal African Company, which built "forts and factories on the western coast of Africa," from "the North part of Guinea … Gambia, Sierra Leone, and Sherbro; and on the South part of Guinea," to Ghana, and beyond.[29]

The very construct of a basemap, a selected arrangement of geographic data that constitutes a map's setting, depends on the notion of a stable referent. That is, the basemap accords value to a projected framework for spatial epistemology. It presents itself as an official (orthorectified) alignment system and as an accessible generic context. But it is nonetheless contingent and reflective of the leverages of power. Denis Wood describes the modern map's statist affirmation as an extension of colonial cartography: "From their inception it had been essential that states appear as facts of nature, as real enduring things, things like mountains; and at all costs to obscure their recent origins in violence."[30] For the wider work of Black geographic praxis, the basemap is an index of who gets to control scale, borders, and vectors—and whose interests imposed standardizations serve.

Unlike a latitudinal point zero on the equator to indicate altitude or horizon, longitude measures time. And textual longitude placed the Royal Observatory, Greenwich, London, at the center of nautical history. Britain bestowed chronology, attached to the value of the colonial encounter. Much like the prime meridian (a product of eighteenth-century colonial cartography and not fully adopted until 1850), the basemap is a context that is presumably shared and foundational. Yet, mapping and representation produced political territory, a point not lost on the eighteenth-century abolitionist Ignatius Sancho. Commemorated as the first Black British voter, Sancho got a primary education inside the grid lines of institutional geography, being enslaved as a child in Greenwich—until escaping for better prospects. In a 1778 letter, he contrasted the freedom of England's residents to the disadvantage of its territories: "I say it is with reluctance that I must observe your country's conduct has been uniformly wicked in the East West Indies—and even on the coast of Guinea."[31]

The nineteenth-century Trinidadian antislavery journalist and novelist Michel Maxwell Philip asserted that the basemap was supposed to be invisible in official histories. It was blended into the organizational aesthetics of authorized maps. His novel *Emmanuel Appadocca; or, Blighted Life* (1854), a revenge story set aboard the *Black Schooner* in the circum-Caribbean, goes to some lengths to illustrate the ways the modern map is a mediated product. Using the same language of "fashionable movement" and extortion as Cugoano, Philip stated: "A fashion springs up at a certain time to have others to labour for our benefit…the map of the world is opened."[32] He described colonialism as the "axis" on which "the civilized world turns."[33] But by exploiting conventions of Victorian buccaneer fiction, dark Romanticism, and the British colonial cartographic alignment system, the author imagined counterspaces of exchange for Black piracy. Revealing vulnerabilities in policed cargo sites and Atlantic fueling stations, Philip projected economic opportunities for Africana peoples of the Caribbean. His novel explored possible forms of redress and trade predation in reclamation of colonial plunder in what was then the colonized British and Danish West Indies, and the French Antilles.

What geographers can gain from literary texts and narrative-based cognitive maps is both conceptual and creative in nature. Philip saw things differently from others around him. He could, not surprisingly, anticipate a Southern Caribbean economic future, freighted by backwater debt and extractive malfeasance. Yet, he could also envisage an insurrectionary movement between island nations at the crossroads of the North Atlantic and South America. The Black Orinoco delta is transformed by the author into a site of joint revolt between Caribbeans and the Venezuelan *llaneros*, whom he called the "new world children of the Savannahs," and the Bedouins of South America.[34] (Philip read the military potential of the *llaneros* soundly insofar as they proved to be the mixed-race infantry decisive in Simón Bolívar's defeat of the Spanish.) The spaces of Black enterprise he expanded in his literature connected an oil-rich Gulf of Paria and major river plains of the largest coastline in the Caribbean—that of Venezuela. The countermap took the form of an adventure story and a song of destruction in different acts. *Emmanuel Appadocca* plots ways to make late-plantation speculative valuations insolvent. The protagonist's aim is to destabilize dominant territorial and logistical enforcements. Through waterways and island straits, Philip brought channels for Black piracy into the foreground.

Philip's literature intensified an anticolonial countercartography. His novel was built on dis-orienting a British-centered commercial basemap that held together island chains and naval bases as military-market sites. To achieve this in episodic form, he told a multi-arc story of colonialism from its archipelagoes, from the voices of those living on the islands. Such a countercartography made legible something that was not supposed to be advertised: exploitable logistics and imperial sea routes for shipping traffic. It also brought obscured agencies into consideration.

Countercartographies contest statist claims to space by rewriting the rules and enforcements that underlie territory. The challenge can simply be in the presentation of a different point of view. By shifting the viewpoint or frame of reference for a map, alternative configurations become more prominent. This element of perspective shifting connects to another feature of countercartographies: they expand the stories that maps can tell. They are modes of acting, writing, and re-creating place that destabilize exclusionary representations. By realigning spatial claims and representations, countercartographies denormalize official maps. They flip the script.

Anticolonial Ecologies

Black discursive geographies did not adhere to standard forms—or those that supported colonial extraction. And why would they? Ashton Warner's *Negro Slavery Described by a Negro* (1831), dictated to Susanna Strickland, extended the textual politics of Black narrative as a focused, economic-based counter to the sugar plantation. Contrasting the volcanic, rocky topographies of St. Vincent and the Grenadines with British colonial land practices in service of a value-depressed monocrop, the narrative evokes a picture of drastic ecological misalignments. Strickland (who later ventured into homesteading and agriculture) would not let such a distorted model of export economics out of sight. On an archipelago ill-suited for imperial sugar, slavery-based production operated heedless of prevailing weather patterns and the division of Southern Caribbean wet and dry seasons. St. Vincent's drought-impacted climate and rocky geology did not support the livestock production system demanded by plantation owners: "The grass grows in tufts, often scattered over a great space of ground, and, when the season is dry, it is very scarce and withered, so that the slaves collect it slowly and with difficulty."[35] Everything about the model of input and supply is economically inefficient.

As early (and lesser-known) critiques of environmental hubris, Caribbean narratives like Warner's situate the violence of slave-driven land management systems inside a broader system of extractivism, a violence against whole-form ecologies. Extractivism meant the joint exploitation of human labor and land—for diminishing returns. As Warner shares, slave drivers demanded futile work like gathering dry sticks in the high noon sun from an already-famished captive labor. Using the language of contamination and illness ("When we were hard pressed, and had much sugar to pot, the manager would often send to the sick-house for the people who were sick, or lame with sores, to help us"), Warner shows slavery's commodities as vitiating bodies and biomes alike.[36] His counternarrative to the Caribbean plantation life cycle is a situated critique; he shows how a model of accumulation devalues and expends the same natural resources it relies on.

Warner's text signals the fused plantation estate and a market liberalism (administered by the British Colonial Office) that would come to absorb attenuated systems of African slavery. His narrative situates Black geographic praxis as a countermovement to colonial production at home on the Windward Islands, named (as were the Leeward Islands due north) for how they facilitated European trade. Presenting Black freedom as work stoppage, his account extends the purchase of refusal by radical acts of island crossing. As a fugitive, Warner traveled by boat from the Grenadines to Grenada, Martinique, Trinidad, St. Kitts, and ultimately St. Catherine's docks in London, where in 1830 he sued his former owner and estate for defrauding him of freedom. He further suggests the potential for efficiency (more calculable information and less human redundancy) as a commercial value that could devoid the straining slave system of its exigency. More than anything, his narrative shares a counterecology with readers. It stresses the unsustainability of cultivation standards inside dominant spatializations. And it does this by foregrounding actual usage. As Warner's narrative illustrates, Black geography could be shared operational knowledges targeted to market disruption.

The joint impacts of racialization and environment were most starkly expressed in the first published narrative by an enslaved woman, *The History of Mary Prince: A West Indian Slave Related by Herself* (1831). Prince's political and ecological narrative reaches readers as a compound of voices that pull in different directions. It is a text manipulated according to protocols of witness statements by her abolitionist editor, Thomas Pringle, and primed by the amanuensis she shared with Ashton Warner, Susanna Strickland.[37] To be sure, how Mary Prince's "otherness" reached British readers was a mixed geopolitical curation. Yet, rather than try to pare away mediating voices or to authenticate the presence of Mary Prince, I take the text to be part of a discursive complex. Prince's *History* shows how open signification and material indexes of presence evolved together in the Black archive. That is to say, as much as archival histories are sites of contest, so too are individual texts.

In Prince's narrative, body and discourse are mutually constitutive. Her embodied geography was a volatile eastern Caribbean environment of earthquakes, sinkholes, and floods (encompassing experiences in Bermuda, Antigua, and Grand Turk Island). She described how in salt ponds, which produced salt for markets in North America, she stood for seventeen straight hours in water up to her knees—given Indian corn for lunch and dinner, and exposed to direct sun overhead. Things only got worse when she was sent to Antigua. Cold pond laundry work left her crippled with both rheumatism and Saint Anthony's fire. Her body was coterminous with environmental exposure. The environment was chronic pain and deep exhaustion. It was the outside coming in.[38] She reached her nadir alone in an outhouse of vermin, where only the kindness of a neighbor in the next yard who brought her food and boiled bark saved her life. Like so many of the women accorded only a first name, if named at all, in the extant archive, she was driven to the very edge—the death zone of colonial world systems. (Marronage was not a prominent trait for Black fugitivity on the small, flat islands without fresh water and canopy cover—places like Anguilla, Bermuda, Antigua, and Barbados.) As Prince tells it, the closest physical escape was death, "for life was very weak in me, and I wished more than ever to die."[39]

Mary Prince was not a stand-in for other women, or the Marys, Marías, and Mollys repeated in Caribbean inventories and ledgers, whose movements and performances do not cancel back to any metonym. Nor does the recognition of Mary Prince's embodiment resolve any contradictions in the fusion of modernity, plantocracy, and enslaved labor that enabled the discipline of geography of which we speak, something requisite for colonial-capitalist expansion. Rather, in her testimony, the body emerges as both spatially contingent and irreducible to a commodified discursive site. Prince's *History* reveals how textual geographies can be spaces for expressions that cannot be synthesized by reference to preexisting categories or customs.

Put another way, Mary Prince was not supposed to have a voice in British Parliament or be represented in West Indian history. She was gendered, raced, and defined as property. And though denied epistemic credibility as a universal (disembodied) subject, she opened an archipelago to a metropole with the publication of *The History of Mary Prince.* It is a text that makes feeling, soma, and the capacities that come from being a feeling person the very basis of conduct—not the Enlightenment touchstone of reason and not an English legal system that denied her rights of personhood. Instead, from the very zones of humanist fracture, she defined a biopolitics of colonial ecosystems. Prince conjured what Nelson Maldonado-Torres, following

Sylvia Wynter, calls a turn to life that "generates epistemologies and politics which affirm the idea that 'another world is possible.'"[40] It also brings to bear Katherine McKittrick's heuristic for a Black geographic analytic that "does something new to the Black body—dislodging it as the only source of Black knowledge (and therefore liberation), while also honoring it as the location through which Black anti-colonial praxis emerges."[41] Her published narrative became a countercartography in its own right. It expanded the forms politics could take by an appeal to the sensory registers of lived experience. Prince defied dominant territorializations. She was pivotal in producing awareness of a supposedly benign Bermudan slavery, and she narrated acts of resistance inside the master's house(s), culminating in her unsanctioned marriage. Her story of exposing racist infrastructures brings us to that of Nancy Gardner Prince—no relation, but a kin in abolition.

Abolitionist Place-Making

A radical reversal of colonial cartographies and coordinate systems animated Nancy Gardner Prince's contribution to modal Black geography. Born "free" on the North Atlantic waterfront in Newburyport, Massachusetts, in 1799, Price knew about precarity and place-as-contestation. She also knew firsthand about the currents and undertows that made Black Atlantic venture an obviously dangerous undertaking. Yet as an abolitionist, women's rights activist, progressive educator, and author, she survived poverty and abuse as a child domestic to publish an ethnography of the Caribbean: *The West Indies: Being a Description of the Islands, Progress of Christianity, Education, and Liberty among the Colored Population Generally* (1841). It was informed by her efforts to start a labor school for destitute girls in Jamaica and was written for a Black northeastern audience who knew practically nothing about Jamaican lives. Her *Narrative of the Life and Travels* (1850) was an extraordinary telling of her life's intertwined journeys across the Atlantic, including a vivid account of nine and a half years in St. Petersburg, Russia, where her husband, Nero Prince, served as a sentry for the Russian czar. Her writing bears startling witness to the epochal flood of 1824, the Decembrist Revolt of 1826, and the cholera epidemic of 1831.

But by her admission, she faced some of the most exacting struggles in her life trying to reach the newly emancipated Jamaica in 1840. Deliberately steered off course by a captain seeking a cargo upcharge, she uncovered the ways that packet ships and commercial routes in coastal Louisiana were policed to ensure slaveholder territorial installations. She writes that in a New Orleans terminal, "every inducement was made to persuade me to go ashore, or set my feet on the wharf."[42] However, Prince recognized that geographies could be slippery legal constructs. She warned her northeastern Black audiences to be attentive to the reaches of jurisdiction, the relationship between law and land. This was particularly critical in unfamiliar spaces. Abolitionists knew that laws reflected power and not justice. She writes: "A law had just been passed that every free colored person coming there, should be put in custody on their going ashore."[43] Instead, she strategically occupies the boat. Her refusal to leave it enrages her fellow travelers, but they cannot trick her into coming ashore. Prince confronts proslavery interests both with spoken rebukes (her antagonists start to suspect she is protected by Russia) and with the more permanent imprint of the pen. And she published the first and last names and places of residences of her racist tormentors in her *Narrative*. Prince's countercartography of free Black travel reveals just how much slavery's agents and enablers preferred invisibility. So it is critical that she assigns them names and addresses for circulation, which she does. In fact, she makes proslavery logistics and enforcements readable to wider audiences. This is again the work of countercartography: denormalizing statist enforcements and presenting Black-accessible codes and tools to claim space.

In Jamaica, Prince stressed the gap between political emancipation and limited outlets for recovery. Lives fell into this gap. Her repertoire of resistance targeted the commercialization of the postemancipation plantation—its production and trade—at the root. She stretched her thin financial resources (she was by this point a widow) to self-publish her discoveries, and to warn US Blacks about British indenture schemes on silk farms, aka the House of Corrections in St. Anne's Parish. Prince's narrative quickly dispels any Romantic versions of diasporan interspace. Coastal waters in the Gulf of Mexico are subzones for statist policy; they are networked into the same liquid republic that perpetuated generations of bondage. But Prince ultimately finds a modal resource in the Trelawny Town Maroons of Jamaica. Deported to both Nova Scotia and Sierra Leone, they manage to get back home. Prince makes a point of meeting with the Maroons and speaking with them. She honors their Jamaican return as paradigms of Black statist refusal and a calculated geos of overcoming forced displacement.

What is especially memorable about the spatial trajectories recorded by Nancy Gardner Prince is that far from depicting the Caribbean corridors of the Middle Passage Atlantic as an abyss of representation, she channeled them as experiences in laying claim to direction. Her counter to the basemap was navigational literacy and applied cartographic learning. A descendant of generations of Black seafarers, Prince knew that the ocean could not be controlled, but she was clear about seeding her own radical praxis against a field of doubt. She writes: "After leaving Jamaica, the vessel was tacked to a south-west course. I asked the Captain what this meant. He said he must take the current as there was no wind. Without any ceremony, I told him it was not the case, and told the passengers that he had deceived us."[44]

A hallmark of Nancy Gardner Prince's work is its insistence on first-person mapping. She had to rely on her own readings and measurements. In fact, she demanded a reorientation of knowledge so that Black experiences were accounted for. In scenes of transit, all of her resources are tested. While to her readers she described islands, straits, Mercator curves, and longitudinal and latitudinal coordinates, she had to deal with other points of location, too. Prince knew that Black geography meant traveling under the signs of gender and race. These were costs registered as a body in the world.[45] Her narrative of travel and discovery shows that the body is inextricable from geography. During her final voyage from Jamaica, she was extorted by American agents and lost everything material, including all her luggage. Exposed to the cold-facing Atlantic wind on the upper deck, because a Captain Comstock of New York would not allow her cabin passage, she lost the free use of her limbs. She returned home sick, wet, and unfed. But she got home alive. Her journey was not in vain. She came to change the lives of children. And she recorded configurations for experiences that were neither normalized nor condoned.

Literary study is especially pliable for examining geography because it tracks confrontations about place in relation to human projection and imagination. Discourse and place-making, as I have discussed, can be mutually constitutive. When we approach places as compositions that reflect territorial strategy and user design, then mechanisms for social control become more apparent. Black geographic praxis has long been invested in locating the seams and slippages of statist power. But it is not confined to resistance paradigms. Instead, it is practically concerned with mobility and social organization. It contends with repair and with alternative forms that justice can take. This is why stories shared across fractured sites are so integral to spatial praxis. Black geographies are conjured in soundscapes, in poetics, and in the forms of elegy that sew together vastly different experiences. They are in the evocation of the ocean at night, and in echoes heard by

Nancy Gardner Prince and those who passed before her. They are in the traces of undocumented voices that can be discerned as diaspora. Black archival records reveal networked worlds at the edges of official histories.

Notes

1. In the 1850s, the decade that launched the rise of the Black novel and the first generation of African American novelists, including William Wells Brown, Frank J. Webb, Harriet Wilson, and Martin Delany, no incorporated or nationalized commercial market could be tapped—as was the case for the rise of the Anglo novel in the eighteenth century. Black authors had to target multiple publics within the slaveholding United States and colonial Britain. Even the best-known nineteenth-century authors, including Frederick Douglass and Harriet Jacobs, had to enlist a white witness or amanuensis to vouch for authorial authority. See Madera, *Black Atlas*, 8–10.
2. In Bychowski et al., "'Trans*historicities,'" 674.
3. Fuentes, *Dispossessed Lives*, 147.
4. See Madera, *Black Atlas*, 118–21.
5. Hartman, "Venus in Two Acts," 11.
6. See Goldsby, "Keynote: Parting the Waters."
7. Aljoe, *Creole Testimonies*; see also Aljoe et al., "Obeah and the Early Caribbean Digital Archive."
8. See Foreman, "Colored Conventions Project."
9. See Porter, *Early Negro Writing*; see also Nunes, "Cataloging Black Knowledge."
10. See Hopkins, *Contending Forces*.
11. Douglass, *Narrative of the Life of Frederick Douglass*, 275.
12. Madden and Manzano, *History of the Early Life of the Negro Poet*, 79.
13. Du Bois, "Talented Tenth," 31.
14. Richardson, *Maria W. Stewart*, 62.
15. Richardson, *Maria W. Stewart*, 68.
16. See Cooper, *Voice from the South*; Hopkins, *Contending Forces*; Wells-Barnett, *Southern Horrors*; Knight, *Pauline Hopkins and the American Dream*; Quigley, *Just Another Southern Town*.
17. "Announcement," 1–2.
18. Hopkins, "Famous Women of the Negro Race. IV."
19. Madera, "Early Black Worldmaking," 484.
20. Cugoano, *Thoughts and Sentiments*, 179–80.
21. Fanon, *Black Skin, White Masks*, 111.

22 Equiano, *Interesting Narrative*, 226.

23 Equiano, *Interesting Narrative*, 222.

24 Equiano, *Interesting Narrative*, 224.

25 Equiano, *Interesting Narrative*, 250.

26 See Lowe, *Intimacies of Four Continents*. Lowe reminds us that "the antislavery agenda became a powerful pretext for the expansion of Britain's colonial interventions in Africa, accompanied by the shift to 'legitimate' trades with African merchants" (68–69).

27 Madera, "Early Black Worldmaking," 487.

28 Cugoano, *Narrative*, 120, 125.

29 Cugoano, *Thoughts and Sentiments*, 166–67.

30 Wood, *Rethinking the Power of Maps*, 33.

31 Sancho, *Letters of the Late Ignatius Sancho*, 2:4.

32 Philip, *Emmanuel Appadocca*, 113.

33 Philip, *Emmanuel Appadocca*, 217.

34 Philip, *Emmanuel Appadocca*, 171.

35 Warner, *Negro Slavery Described by a Negro*, 35.

36 Warner, *Negro Slavery Described by a Negro*, 39.

37 Thomas Pringle, secretary of the British Anti-Slavery Society, was a poet who romanticized settler colonialism among the San, Khoi, and Xhosa in South Africa's Cape frontier. See Shum, "Thomas Pringle's 'The Emigrant's Cabin,'" 35–58.

38 For racialized political hierarchies that take their reference points in human flesh, see Weheliye, *Habeas Viscus*.

39 Prince, *History of Mary Prince*, 8.

40 Maldonado-Torres, "Enrique Dussel's Liberation Thought," 18; see also Wynter, "Unsettling the Coloniality of Being/Power/Truth/Freedom," 257–337.

41 McKittrick, "Commentary," 99.

42 Prince, *Narrative*, 75. Prince is notified that if she had gone ashore, "they intended to beat you. John and Lucy Davenport of Salem laid down the first ten dollars towards a hundred for that person who should get you there" (81).

43 Prince, *Narrative*, 81.

44 Prince, *Narrative*, 74.

45 Prince, *Narrative*, 65.

Bibliography

Aljoe, Nicole N. *Creole Testimonies: Slave Narratives from the British West Indies, 1709–1838*. New York: Palgrave, 2012.

Aljoe, Nicole N., Elizabeth Maddock Dillon, Benjamin J. Doyle, and Elizabeth Hopwood. "Obeah and the Early Caribbean Digital Archive." *Atlantic Studies* 12, no. 2 (2015): 258–66. doi:10.1080/14788810.2015.1025217.

"Announcement." *Colored American Magazine* 1, no. 1 (May 1900): 1–2.

Bychowski, M. W., Howard Chiang, Jack Halberstam, Jacob Lau, Kathleen P. Long, Marcia Ochoa, C. Riley Snorton, Leah DeVun, and Zeb Tortorici. "'Trans*historicities': A Roundtable Discussion." *Transgender Studies Quarterly* 5, no. 4 (2018): 658–85.

Cooper, Anna J. *A Voice from the South: By a Black Woman of the South.* Chapel Hill: University of North Carolina Press, 2017.

Cugoano, Quobna Ottobah. *Narrative of the Enslavement of Ottobah Cugoano, a Native of Africa; Published by Himself, in the Year 1787.* London: Hatchard and J. and A. Arch, 1825. https://docsouth.unc.edu/neh/cugoano/cugoano.html.

Cugoano, Quobna Ottobah. *Thoughts and Sentiments on the Evil and Wicked Traffic of the Slavery and Commerce of the Human Species.* London, 1787. Reprinted in *Unchained Voices: An Anthology of Black Authors in the English-Speaking World of the Eighteenth Century*, edited by Vincent Caretta, 145–84. Lexington: University Press of Kentucky, 2004.

Delany, Martin R. *Blake; or, The Huts of America: A Tale of the Mississippi Valley, the Southern United States, and Cuba.* 1859–62. Reprinted as *Blake; or, The Huts of America.* Edited by Floyd J. Miller. Boston: Beacon Press, 1970.

Delany, Martin R. *The Condition, Elevation, Emigration and Destiny of the Colored People of the United States.* 1852. New York: Arno, 1968.

Delany, Martin R. *Official Report of the Niger Valley Exploring Party.* 1861. In *Martin R. Delany: A Documentary Reader*, edited by Robert S. Levine, 336–57. Chapel Hill: University of North Carolina Press, 2003.

Douglass, Frederick. *Narrative of the Life of Frederick Douglass, an American Slave.* In *The Classic Slave Narratives*, edited by Henry Louis Gates Jr., 243–331. New York: Penguin, 1987.

Du Bois, W. E. B. "The Talented Tenth." In *The Negro Problem: A Series of Articles by Representative Negroes of To-day*, 31–76. New York: AMS Press, 1903.

Equiano, Olaudah. *The Interesting Narrative of the Life of Olaudah Equiano, or Gustavus Vassa, the African. Written by Himself.* Ninth edition enlarged. London, 1794. Reprinted in *Unchained Voices: An Anthology of Black Authors in the English-Speaking World of the Eighteenth Century*, edited by Vincent Caretta, 185–318. Lexington: University Press of Kentucky, 2004.

Fanon, Frantz. *Black Skin, White Masks.* Translated by Charles Lam Markmann. New York: Grove Press, 1967.

Foreman, P. Gabrielle. "The Colored Conventions Project and the Changing Same." *Common-place.org* 16, no. 1 (Fall 2015): n.p.

Fuentes, Marisa. *Dispossessed Lives: Enslaved Women, Violence, and the Archive.* Philadelphia: University of Pennsylvania Press, 2016.

Goldsby, Jacqueline. "Keynote: Parting the Waters: CLIR's Pathways in the Archive." In *Innovation, Collaboration, and Models: Proceedings of the CLIR Cataloging Hidden Special Collections and Archives Symposium.* March 2015. https://www.clir.org/wp-ontent/uploads/sites/6/goldsby.pdf.

Grandy, Moses. *Narrative of the Life of Moses Grandy; Late a Slave in the United States of America*. London: Gilpin, 1843.

Hartman, Saidiya. "Venus in Two Acts." *Small Axe: A Caribbean Journal of Criticism* 12, no. 2 (2008): 1–14.

Hopkins, Pauline. *Contending Forces: A Romance Illustrative of Negro Life North and South*. 1900. New York: Oxford University Press, 1988.

Hopkins, Pauline. "Famous Women of the Negro Race. IV: Some Literary Workers." *Colored American Magazine* 4, no. 4 (March 1902): 277–80.

Knight, Alisha R. *Pauline Hopkins and the American Dream: An African American Writer's (Re)Visionary Gospel of Success*. Knoxville: University of Tennessee Press, 2012.

Lowe, Lisa. *The Intimacies of Four Continents*. Durham, NC: Duke University Press, 2015.

Madden, Richard Robert, and Juan Francisco Manzano. *The History of the Early Life of the Negro Poet, Written by Himself; to Which Are Prefixed Two Pieces Descriptive of Cuban Slavery and the Slave-Traffic*. London: Thomas Ward, 1840.

Madera, Judith. *Black Atlas: Geography and Flow in Nineteenth-Century African American Literature*. Durham, NC: Duke University Press, 2015.

Madera, Judith. "Early Black Worldmaking: Body, Compass, and Text." *American Literary History* 33, no. 3 (2021): 481–97. muse.jhu.edu/article/836720.

Maldonado-Torres, Nelson. "Enrique Dussel's Liberation Thought in the Decolonial Turn." *Transmodernity* 1, no. 1 (2011): 1–30.

McKittrick, Katherine. "Commentary: Worn Out." *Southeastern Geographer* 57, no. 1 (Spring 2017): 96–100.

Nunes, Zita Cristina. "Cataloging Black Knowledge: How Dorothy Porter Assembled and Organized a Premier Africana Research Collection." *Perspectives on History*, November 20, 2018. https://www.historians.org/publications-and -directories/perspectives-on-history/december-2018/cataloging-Black -knowledge-how-dorothy-porter-assembled-and-organized-a-premier -africana-research-collection.

Philip, Maxwell. *Emmanuel Appadocca; or, Blighted Life. A Tale of the Boucaneers*. Edited by Selwyn Cudjoe. Amherst: University of Massachusetts Press, 1997.

Porter, Dorothy, ed. *Early Negro Writing 1760–1837*. Boston: Beacon Press, 1971.

Prince, Mary. *The History of Mary Prince, a West Indian Slave. Related by Herself*. London: F. Westley and A. H. Davis, 1831. Reprint, The Digital Schomburg, New York Public Library, 1997. File number 1997wwm97262.sgm. http://digilib .nypl.org/dynaweb/digs/wwm97262/.

Prince, Nancy. *A Narrative of the Life and Travels of Mrs. Nancy Prince*. 2nd ed. Boston: Nancy Prince, S.P., 1853.

Prince, Nancy. *The West Indies: Being a Description of the Islands, Progress of Christianity, Education, and Liberty among the Colored Population Generally*. Boston: Dow and Jackson, 1841.

Quigley, Joan. *Just Another Southern Town: Mary Church Terrell and the Struggle for Racial Justice in the Nation's Capital*. New York: Oxford University Press, 2016.

Richardson, Marilyn, ed. *Maria W. Stewart, America's First Black Woman Political Writer: Essays and Speeches*. Bloomington: Indiana University Press, 1987.

Robinson, Cedric J. *Black Marxism: The Making of the Black Radical Tradition*. London: Zed Books, 1983.

Sancho, Ignatius. *Letters of the Late Ignatius Sancho, An African. In Two Volumes. To Which Are Prefixed, Memoirs of His Life*. Vol. 2. London: J. Nichols, 1782.

Shum, Matthew. "Thomas Pringle's 'The Emigrant's Cabin' and the Invention of Settler Colonialism." *English in Africa* 38, no. 3 (2011): 35–58. http://www.jstor .org.go.libproxy.wakehealth.edu/stable/23268989.

Smith, Venture. *A Narrative of the Life and Adventures of Venture, a Native of Africa: But Resident above Sixty Years in the United States of America. Related by Himself*. New London, CT: C. Holt at The Bee-office, 1798. http://docsouth .unc.edu/neh/venture/venture.html.

Soja, Edward W. *Postmodern Geographies: The Reassertion of Space in Critical Social Theory*. New York: Verso, 1989.

Warner, Ashton. *Negro Slavery Described by a Negro: Being the Narrative of Ashton Warner, a Native of St. Vincent's. With an Appendix Containing the Testimony of Four Christian Ministers, Recently Returned from the Colonies, on the System of Slavery as It Now Exists*. Edited by Susanna Strickland. London: Samuel Maunder, 1831.

Weheliye, Alexander G. *Habeas Viscus: Racializing Assemblages, Biopolitics, and Black Feminist Theories of the Human*. Durham, NC: Duke University Press, 2014.

Wells-Barnett, Ida B. *Southern Horrors: Lynch Law in All Its Phases*. New York: New York Age Print, 1892.

Wood, Denis. *Rethinking the Power of Maps*. New York: Guilford Press, 2010.

Wynter, Sylvia. "Unsettling the Coloniality of Being/Power/Truth/Freedom: Towards the Human, after Man, Its Overrepresentation—an Argument." *CR: The New Centennial Review* 3, no. 3 (2003): 257–337.

3

"My Bad Attitude toward the Pastoral"

Race, Place, and Allusion in the Poetry of C. S. Giscombe

CHIYUMA ELLIOTT

Early in my life I learned some things about geography—by which I mean here where places such as cities and countries are and where border-lines are drawn—from unlikely sources: stamp collecting, an obsession with railway schedules, and popular songs and rhymes. Years later I'm still interested by the ways places appear in song and how the language of songs—and poetry—documents place.
—C. S. GISCOMBE, "Haf Owre, Haf Owre to Bonny Aberdour"

C. S. Giscombe's book-length poem called *Here* documents twentieth-century urban life in the American North. His often elliptical, highly lyric verse explores the ways the urban North is shaped by the rural, the South, and by race and racism. In Giscombe's poem, urban and rural geography blur together; this blurred geography offers an account of why someone might have a "bad attitude toward the pastoral"—that is, a bad attitude toward idealized or romanticized versions of country life.[1] With its focus on "the ways in which racial violences ... shape, but do not wholly define, black worlds," Giscombe's 1994 poem anticipates some of the key aspects of a "black sense of place" articulated by Katherine McKittrick (2011). *Here*'s extended exploration of the role that race plays in shaping people's relationships to both urban and rural spaces and places also offers an alternative to "the broad-brushed ascription of anti-Black racism onto the entire [South] region" lamented by Adam Bledsoe, Latoya Eaves, and Brian Williams in their 2017 introduction to a special issue on "Black Geographies in and of the United States South."[2] Giscombe's poetic speaker perceives southern-inflected racism existing potentially all over the map; but his ascription of its reach is careful, inquisitive, and accretive, and it marshals swift juxtapositions between different types of material, emotional, and historical evidence. It is a fundamentally interrogative poetic project because the speaker wonders throughout if, when, and where he and other African Americans are safe.

Here offers an extended exploration of the role that race plays in shaping people's relationships to both urban and rural spaces and places. The hybridity of locations is the primary way the long poem investigates the relationship of geographic scale and identity. In "The Space That Race Makes," David Delaney points out that "forms of nativist racism may articulate 'the local,' 'the regional,' 'the national,' and 'the international' in complex and shifting ways."[3] Giscombe's poem explores shifts in—and blurring across—the latter three categories. It reads as a kind of thought experiment wherein the extent to which safety exists is also the extent to which abstract, undifferentiated space exists as a meaningful Black geographic category. Yi-Fu Tuan points out that "the ideas 'space' and 'place' require each other for definition," the movement allowed by the latter juxtaposed by the pause in movement required for locational transformation.[4]

The limits on Black space reflect back on Black place in Giscombe's work; both are meaningfully shaped by social relations, and both reflect the consensus knowledge about hierarchies, laws, and conventions of what Henri Lefebvre terms "social space."[5] McKittrick's arguments about a Black sense of place and Lefebvre's about social space hinge on the legibility of their socially stratified geographic arrangements. In contrast, what Giscombe posits is a gradual process by which an African American individual develops an awareness of that social consensus; rather than legibility (carceral or otherwise), what *Here* describes is the unevenness, uncertainty, and ambiguity within collective locational constructions and individual human responses to them.

If Black space cannot exist as a stable material category in *Here*, it certainly can and does exist as a conceptual category. Tuan notes that spatial experience "can be direct and intimate, or it can be indirect and conceptual, mediated by symbols."[6] The racial constraints on direct and intimate spatial exploration and consideration mean that indirect and conceptual exploration become more important. In the latter types of human experience, as in poetry, symbols loom large. Poetry is well suited for such indirect, abstract, and conceptual geographic exploration, and Giscombe leverages the genre's investigative aptitudes throughout this book. Indeed, his poetic treatment of material processes emphasizes the ways in which Blackness itself is historically and geographically situated.

I begin my close reading by tracing Giscombe's poetic influences and subtle references to twentieth-century racial conflict in order to explain how *Here* racializes its places, spaces, and regional landscapes. I use symbolism and quoted song lyrics to argue that the poem makes some of the same key claims as geographers who work on shifting regional boundaries and identity. Specifically, I contend that Giscombe documents the presence of "Dixie Islands," much like Shrinidhi Ambinakudige. But Giscombe's poetic presentation of the geographic phenomenon allows him to do something additional: to spell out the emotional stakes of living in such a shifting world full of latent potential danger, blurry racialized boundaries, and moments of quiet reprieve. Because Giscombe's 1994 book also offers an example of how the language of songs—and poetry—documents place, analysis of this intricate poem involves reading techniques and strategies that may be useful for scholars working in fields in which poems and poetry are often invoked but rarely evaluated in a systematic way.

Giscombe's long poem was inspired by a 1923 book called *Cane* by Jean Toomer. Giscombe wrote the following in 2009 to explain Toomer's influence:

> Of course I remember "discovering" Jean Toomer's *Cane* when I was a sophomore at university and what a powerful moment that was for me; I read it the same year I went to Goose Lake—the music festival was a mixed experience…but nothing good or bad about it was particularly unnerving. Toomer's complex blackness married to issues of migration and sex and to his book's own unwieldiness as a book, on the other hand, unnerved me a great deal. My book *Here*, begun 15 years after I read *Cane* for the first time, is a belated response—an homage, really—to it.[7]

Giscombe's long poem presents an intriguing paradox: there is no absolutely clear-cut, direct reference to *Cane* in the book. But Toomer's 1923 work is still (somehow, almost mysteriously) omnipresent in Giscombe's long response poem through hints, echoes, elaborations, and digressions, and also through shared themes, strategies, and geographies. *Here* makes the most sense when one approaches it not expecting to find a single "smoking gun" or instance or reference that suddenly explains everything. Instead, what we find is an agglomeration of evidence from across the book, which points us repeatedly to the same things. As Giscombe wrote in a different poem, "Location's what you come to; it's the low point, it usually repeats."[8] We are looking for a metaphor over here, and a place-name over there, and a word that keeps showing up in odd and conspicuous ways. Our job as readers is to make sense of those book-length patterns and repetitions because they help us (slowly) identify and make sense of the poem's big claims.

There is a big claim underlying this approach: great works of literature teach us how to read them. I think these works present us with a world and, step by step, show us how to make sense of that world so we can answer important questions such as the following: How is the world that the book projects distinctive? How is it different from another book (e.g., from a sociological setting of the same problem or issue)? What ideas or beliefs do you have to embrace for the world of the book to seem plausible? What anchors the world? What divides it up? And how do (or might) we use the book for evidence? Giscombe's book is about race, place, belonging, and many other things. It is initially mysterious. But, step by step, the poem teaches us how to figure it out.

Here is sixty-two pages long and is divided into three sections of unequal length. Parts of it are set in Ohio, where Giscombe himself grew up. A list of poem subsection titles from the first part of the book points to the dramatic ways the poem moves around physically and temporally:

> (February 1978)
> (1978, remembering 1962)
> (1962)
> (1978, etc.)
> (the recent past)
> (the future)
> (the long view)
> (all time)
> (1978 itself)
> (the very recent past)
> (3 ideas about the future)

(1962 at the edge of town)
(the 1970s—UltraSuede)
(the distant past-B.W.I.)
(the 1-2-3)

The title and subtitles in *Here* make me think of the arrows on maps that say, "YOU ARE HERE" (maps typically designed for visitors who are walking through unfamiliar large buildings, in malls, across college campuses, or in airports). If this book were a map, it would need to have many such arrows. Or perhaps just one, provided that arrow could keep changing direction and location. "Here" could be any number of places in the book *Here* because the poem's speaker travels around dramatically in space and time. At one point in the poem, he is a child visiting his extended family in Birmingham, Alabama. Then, on the next page, he is a middle-aged adult in Ohio, thinking back to his childhood. Two pages later, he is a young adult, remembering those same childhood memories a little differently. And then, a page later, the speaker is in "the future." And so on, and so on.[9]

Even before the expansive patterns of spatial and temporal movement become legible to readers, we form some strong impressions. By the second page of this poem, our impression is of the uncomfortable "melodious southern wild" the speaker so vividly remembers from his childhood. We also notice how the location's latent menace is intertwined with his abstract reflections, as in the subsection "(1978, remembering 1962)":

> Essentially description, night
> comes down to connect,
>
> becomes endless talk
>
> becomes principle served by "shape":
>
> the melodious southern wild comes into the cities:
>
> my sister & I inside but watching 2 German shepherds
> out in the slope of my grandmother's back yard
> —2 o'clock, 3 o'clock in the morning, they
> having knocked over the cans which woke us—
>
> eating garbage & watching us watch them
>
> as though they were heat
> seeped right in off the godhead,

or the lyrical element in a string
of repetitions,

or the patter itself.

                      "I don't like," she sd, "looking down
on big dogs at night—"

                              it being the 1-2-3, all
facts unbroken whatever
happens,

            all stories non sequiturs,

all chance made present[10]

This poem segment is made up of two long sentences, the second of which is incomplete. The first sentence's series of subordinated clauses demands careful attention if we want to understand the various things night is and does. The sister voices the discomfort of the scene; the abbreviated orthography of the word *sd* (instead of the standard English *said*) also might make us readers a little uncomfortable because it signals the fact that this poem is making its own rules. Our literary and linguistic analysis runs in tandem with our tracking of the literal scene taking place in the speaker's memory: he is eleven years old, it is the middle of the night, and he is standing with his kid sister, looking through a window at big, unfamiliar dogs that are eating the garbage outside. And the dogs are looking back at them. No adults are awake or close enough to help should the dogs decide to target the children rather than the garbage cans.

The particular type of dogs the children are watching (and being watched by) further amplifies the tension in this scene. German shepherds are the breed most used by American police. Because, in the 1960s, there were so many notorious incidents in which police dogs attacked unarmed African American protesters, two of the most famous statues commemorating the civil rights movement feature life-size images of German shepherds attacking peaceful demonstrators.[11] Such statues use synecdochic logic: they present a single part of activist experience that is meant to stand in for the whole terrifying and vicious institutional response to civil rights reformers.

Imagine that you are twenty-seven years old, thinking back on this particular childhood memory. Why might this event stand out to you? The speaker says it was as if the dogs were "the lyrical element in a string / of repetitions," and later claims that all stories are non sequiturs, meaning conclusions or statements that do not follow logically from the previous arguments or statements. Despite the speaker's assertion, I want to suggest that, in a deeper sense, the stories in this poem *do* follow a logical order, but it is an emotional logic that reflects what it feels like to be a Black person growing up and living in a virulently racist country. In this context, sometimes things seem confusing because American racism often is confusing. And sometimes the world is unsettling, like having big, unfamiliar dogs making a mess and a ruckus in your yard at night.

The supposedly fixed positions of North and South blur into each other in Giscombe's book, as do distinctions between urban and rural and between past, present, and future. Even sleeping and waking lose their discrete edges and become contiguous and overlapping territory. For the poem's speaker, the myriad distinctive places in *Here* are also a palimpsest in which racialized identity is forged, and through which one must struggle in order to understand one's being. One of my favorite moments of urban-rural blurring happens in the long center section of Giscombe's book, in a subsection simply titled "(in)":

> —some few blocks in from the 3rd St bridge
> the big Kroger's chain store
> & its big parking lot dug into the hillside all
> around it rt below Dunbar House on Summit, words
> & pictures for idyll's source (an unbroken
> line to *near* here (or its implied continuation this *way* to
> recur near here,
>   the corporate heart of Negro Dayton in the 50s
> & 60s, the store's big porticos facing open
> onto the lot:
>   market-days—Friday late,
> Saturday—men & women sold greens
> & fish to other Negroes & a few white people as well out
> of the trunks of their cars parked there &
> there & there among those of customers
> some little distance in
> some little distance creeping back in from over land *like* this,
> these out-
> lying areas,
> from alongside water[12]

So many of *Here*'s northern and southern places are hybrids or palimpsests. The parking lot of a Kroger's grocery store near the Third Street Bridge, right below the Dunbar House on Summit, is one of "these out- / lying areas" like the war zone in the dream and is also "dug into the hillside." The parking lot is the heart of "Negro Dayton" in the 1950s and 1960s because it hosts an unofficial farmers market on Fridays and Saturdays, where "men & women sold greens / & fish to other Negroes & a few white people as well out / of the trunks of their cars parked there & / there & there among those of customers."[13] The fact that there is neither white sanction nor any officially designated space for this event does not stop these sometimes interracial transactions from happening in the interstices of official commerce, literally between the cars of shoppers. Giscombe's descriptions make us readers aware that, at certain times, the places (market and lot) overlap, and human paths cross in unexpected ways. The speaker in *Here* continually wonders and worries about the nature of the place he is currently at because of geography's inherent hybridity, its penchant for change and encroachment. What I think we readers are meant to notice here is that the rural sometimes springs up in the heart of the city, albeit fleetingly. The rural is a sweet potato sold from the trunk of a car in a grocery store parking lot on West Third Street in Dayton, Ohio; sold perhaps by Black people like the folks who lived and grew big gardens on the fringes of Birmingham, Alabama (the clients who often paid the speaker's physician grandfather for his services with hams and "baskets of greens & fruit").[14]

The book *Here* constantly jumps around in time and space, and it does so, I would argue, because it is trying to make sure we readers do not miss its other big point about geography: that it is racially inflected. One of the first things we learn about geography in the book is that it is racially demarcated. The speaker uses racialized place terminology, such as "Negro Dayton." The poem's speaker also reminds us twice fairly early on that he remembers racial segregation, and he uses that unambiguous and racially loaded name "Jim Crow" for it.[15] In the poem, legally enforced racial segregation (though theoretically ended when the speaker was a child) still affects where people live, and what different places mean to them. In the poem's South, many Black neighborhoods are located on the peripheries of cities (on the edges of cities, where urban space and industrial space and countryside merge), as in the following quote:

> Hard luck on the long way in from the airport
> in through the New to the first Negro edge
> of Birmingham:

the nomenclature can't keep up w/the sub-industrial, no lyric
intensity
to the network of low roads, no image
for the hidden facts ahead, for the economy of push
& take in place forever.[16]

Southern neighborhoods are even racially marked in the speaker's
dreams, as in the section called "(the recent past)":

> when the train stopped across a road I
> climbed up
> into the spare ribs of a gondola, how those boys arrived—I knew
> too—
> in Scottsboro,
> but when we started again
> it was a single car trolley through the suburbs *up*
> *on the mountain* sd my father, where
> the white folks w/money still live
> in Birmingham
>
> (not of course a real mountain but boulevards
> over high ground,
> big houses bespeaking the harmony of all parts[17]

Because the speaker is discussing segregated space, maybe we readers are
supposed to hear an echo of the term *big house* when the speaker says "big
houses" (a colloquialism that can mean the owner's mansion on a slave plantation or can designate a prison). Maybe we are also supposed to think of
the famous Scottsboro Boys, nine African American teenagers who were
accused of raping two white women on a train in Alabama in 1931.[18]

In Giscombe's poem, there are clear racial divisions in the South. The
northern neighborhoods are also similarly racially divided. Late in the
poem, the speaker defines the word *edge* in five different ways, one of which
is the following:

> —on the bridges across into downtown from Negro Dayton
> (& outlying areas on 3rd, 5th, Washington, & Stewart[19]

Six pages later, the speaker describes this neighborhood near the Third
Street Bridge in a way that makes it clear it is also a personally meaningful place: "my side" and "my side of the river," the speaker says.[20] In this

poem, the edges of African American neighborhoods are easy to identify (in Dayton and Cincinnati, and all the places in between). And those discrete edges are also shifting edges. On page 33, the speaker describes the changes in this way:

> By the 50s & 60s we'd been well-ensconced for years
> all along the road from Cincinnati Gateway
> to the South, had pushed in down Germantown hill
>
> in fact as far as the Miami to the east, Wolf Creek
> to the north,
>
> Dunbar's house on Summit overlooked Wolf Creek,
> grandly misnamed Riverview Av across the bridge

In describing the places Black people live, the poem's landmarks include bridges, streets, bodies of water, and a house that belonged to the most famous African American poet of the nineteenth century: Paul Laurence Dunbar.

Back in 2012, Giscombe wrote, "I'm still interested by the ways places appear in song and how the language of songs—and poetry—documents place." If I were a demographer, or a historian interested in, say, the Great Migration or urban demographics in northern cities, I might build my own picture of this Dayton, Ohio, neighborhood by looking up census data from 1950 to 1970, to figure out the exact racial makeup of each dwelling over time (to determine whether I could "see" racial edges on a neighborhood map). I might try to figure out if the real-life borders and timelines I could reconstruct matched what the poem's speaker describes and remembers. I might try to find oral histories about Negro Dayton, or interview people myself, to see if they identify the same landmarks and boundaries and changes. If I were a geographer, I might use all those place-names to tell a story about the city's inhabitants over time: Germantown Hill, the Miami River, Wolf Creek, Summit Avenue, Riverview Avenue.

Because I am a poet and a literary critic, I wonder about those things but am focusing on something else that this confluence of poetic data about race, location, borders, and names is signaling to me: how the people in the poem decide where they do and do not belong. Boundaries and belonging tell me about location and identity in the poem; one thing they emphasize is that locations are hybrids of other locations. The last poem segment in the twenty-six-page first section of *Here* presents regional hybridity and also asserts that it is something that is literally embodied inside people.

On page 25, the speaker says: "—I remember / my sister's birth in Ohio / but thought for years our mother had borne me / down in Birmingham."[21] His long confusion about birthplaces matters because one of the poem's big revelations is that to be Black and from Ohio also means to be fundamentally southern ("part of that same map" is how the speaker articulates it). The speaker's retrospective reflection on his Dayton, Ohio, childhood describes all the children there (himself included) as "different from one another / except for the south, the unbroken border / at all centers." Later on, he says even more about his place of birth:

> I was born here 50 miles across
> the Ohio, my parents came
>
> like everyone
>
> from the south ('tho not the land)[22]

Here, "the Ohio" means the Ohio River, where it demarcates the boundary between Ohio and Kentucky (formerly the boundary between slave state and free state); "the land" means the rural space "out past the gates / to the city" where there might be horses standing around waiting. Everyone came from the South, the speaker in the poem asserts. The North and the South blur together very quickly in this book: in the exterior world, in life experience, and also inside the very bodies of the people in the poem. To be from one place implies deep connections with the other place. That deep interconnectedness is true for North and South, and it is true also for urban and rural.

Claudia Rankine's book *Citizen* (2014) is about racist microaggressions; it makes a number of claims about microtraumas: they are frequent; they have a cumulative effect on the people who experience them; part of what makes them damaging is the myriad ways other people deny their import or significance; and the host of small traumas sets the context for the occasional big, dramatic, overt acts of racial animus, where someone clearly is trying to hurt another person. I think Giscombe's book *Here* tells a related story. Giscombe's poetic speaker constantly is trying to figure out what kind of place he is in. Beneath the question, "What kind of place is this?" is another really serious question: "Am I safe?" Am I going to be targeted like the Scottsboro Boys? Or blown up by vigilante Ku Klux Klan members, like the four little girls at choir practice at the Sixteenth Street Baptist Church in September 1963 (children who were the same age as Giscombe's speaker, and who that speaker possibly meets in 1962 at his grandfather's church funeral on page 11). Often, the speaker is not sure about either thing: what kind of place he is in, or whether he is safe there. But usually he does not declare that problem outright. Unlike in Rankine's book, where racism is the overt subject, in Giscombe's poem *Here*, there are accretions and echoes, but readers do not get easy narrative clarity about race and racism. We have to piece together the book's different incidents and images and inferences to make sense of what happens, and what it means.

A category of story that I call "nothing happened" helps clarify how race works in Giscombe's book:

> 4.
> Out abroad of an evening in 1960-something, way
> across Wolf Creek w/a white boy my age
> the 2 of us—waiting for buses—reclined
> on some lawn, at
> some intersection:
>
>   nothing happened
> my bus came first
> it was a warm clear night among the dark houses
> this far up in
> (myself this present in
>
> the set-up, the sequence
> of description, not its demand[23]

What does it mean to be "present" in a description, but not present in or to what that description demands? Let me pose what I think is a related question: Why would a person tell a story in which nothing happens? One possibility is to emphasize how dull things are in their world. Another possibility: because the fact that nothing bad happened in that particular time and place is a *really big deal*. This poem section is set at night in "1960-something" (meaning during the height of the American civil rights movement), near the edge of a Black neighborhood ("way / across Wolf Creek"). And there are a white boy and a Black boy, both waiting for buses. No one dies, or gets attacked, or goes to jail. It is 1960s America, and they can loaf in the same place for a while without incident. The moral of this quiet little story: depending on where you are from, sometimes it is a big deal if white people and Black people cross each other's paths and nothing happens. It is worth making the uneventful encounter into a section of a poem.

The closest thing to a smoking gun in Giscombe's poem *Here* is the word *Dixie*, which connects the act of looking to a racially freighted song. The word *Dixie* appears twice in the opening section of the poem, first on page 16 (after the speaker tells us that he is old enough to remember the Jim Crow era):

> ensconced in Dixie I am piss elegance,
> nameless dread, I am the route of escape
> & approach both,
> the absence of meaning,[24]

In the second instance, in the subsection titled "(very recent past)," the word *Dixie* appears in a series of questions. After asking about how "dams & turpentine forests / back / red dirt roads became the godhead," the speaker wonders:

> (If metaphor by nature kicks in before the fantasy's revealed
> was it ever true
> what they say about Dixie?)[25]

The term *Dixie* has become a widely understood synonym for the American South, but many additional things (both true and false) are also said about it frequently, especially in Ohio, particularly about the famous antebellum song of that name and the racial politics it evokes. As historians Howard Sacks and Judith Rose Sacks note:

> To most contemporary listeners, "Dixie" conjures images of the ante-bellum South because of its historical association with the Confederacy. When Southern states seceded from the Union in 1861, they adopted "Dixie" as their national anthem.... New lyrics were composed celebrating the Confederacy, whose soldiers marched into battle to the strains of "Dixie" played on fife and drum. Today, the song is no less a source of pride to some Southerners.... But to other Southerners, "Dixie" is a hateful reminder of generations of segregation, an auditory code cheering racial oppression.[26]

Dixie is a deeply contested term in America, and has been for more than a hundred years; starting in the 1960s, Black students protested the song's inclusion at campus events in the South (where it was regularly played, along with the national anthem, and a school's alma mater).[27] Especially during the antilynching campaigns of the 1920s and 1930s, Black poets, including Langston Hughes, evoked and revised the song's lyrics in poems to criticize white supremacy.

It is not just the term *Dixie* that is important in Giscombe's poem but also the way the song lyrics themselves echo and repeat, sometimes overtly, sometimes ambiguously (and maybe more ominously because the links are suggested sonically but not absolutely clear). Giscombe's poem quotes a variant of the 1859 "Dixie's Land" refrain, which has itself been varied and echoed in most (if not all) subsequent versions of the song:

> I wish I was in de land ob cotton,
> 'Cimmon seed an sandy bottom,
> Look away—look 'way, way Dixie Land.
> In Dixie land whar I was born in,
> Early on one frosty mornin;
> Look away—look 'way, away Dixie Land.[28]

This same refrain is focal in the Confederate anthem version of "Dixie," which juxtaposes the words "look away" with a deep yearning and affection for the enduring historical memory of the southern "land of cotton."

The speaker quotes "Dixie" song lyrics explicitly at the end of the segment titled "(1978, etc)":

> it was the apparent lack of meaning to our place
> that left nowhere else to look but back,
> but around,
>
> it was principle burning off over time,
>
> it was the refrain Look away, look away[29]

The song's refrain directs us to look away. But look a little closer, and "Dixie" also becomes a way into another porous border at the center of American identity, a porous racial border. While authorship of the song is ascribed traditionally to the white minstrel performer Dan Emmett, African Americans in rural Knox County, Ohio, have long credited "Dixie" to a different local author: an African American family of musicians named the Snowdens. As Sacks and Sacks note, "'Dixie' conjures images of the South and was first performed in the North, but the song's origins rest in the association of African Americans and European Americans in the western frontier. There, people of diverse backgrounds met and created communities and a common culture very different from the Old South and the growing urban population centers."[30] So "Dixie" the song is paradoxical because it represents the Old South of the Confederacy but also tells a hidden story about Ohio, and America's western frontier. In other words, for those in the know, it tells a complex story of cross-cultural and cross-racial contact and influence.

The boxcars that show up over and over in Giscombe's poem repeat the Southern Railway's slogan: "Look Ahead, Look South." What the speaker notices is the way the train company slogan is a vague sonic echo of the song "Dixie" ("look away, look away"). In the poem, the trains may be mobile signifiers that carry Dixie all over the continent.[31] For the speaker, the train slogan's sonic similarity to the refrain to "Dixie" connotes and evokes a long reckoning with Black racial selfhood that is tied inextricably to questions of southern place, even in faraway Syracuse, New York. As the speaker reflects,

> The attitude worries the line through the service belt around
> Syracuse
> like anyplace:
>
> what the line of boxcars says, where
> & how it says to look meant
>
> Look at yourself, I saw[32]

The "Dixie" lyrics provide a way to reflect on the legibility of white supremacy in and on the land, and its effects on the people shaped by its racial codes and geographic boundaries.

Starting in 1976, the geographer J. Reed and colleagues set out to answer two questions: "Where is the South?" and "Where is Dixie?" This was part of what was meant to be an "unobtrusive measure" of regional identification. Reed demonstrated that "the South" and "Dixie" were two separate and distinctive regions by mapping the two terms based on entries in metropolitan telephone directories (compiled by looking at business names and place-names). He argued that the term *Dixie* evokes the Old South of plantation agriculture, whereas *South* connotes the New South of commerce and industry. Reed concluded that while southern identity was strong and more geographically expansive than Dixie, Dixie was more about group identity than it was about location. When Reed and his colleagues repeated the survey in 1998 (four years after Giscombe's book was published), they found that the border of "the South" had shifted slightly south and east, but "Dixie" shrank dramatically.[33] When Shrinidhi Ambinakudige used a similar method to study those same vernacular regional boundaries in 2009, he identified what he referred to as "Dixie islands" in the northern and western United States, as well as surprising identity islands in Utah and Ohio. Ambinakudige concluded that, in important ways, Dixie identity was both eroding and unpredictably dispersed.[34] According to geographers, and according to Giscombe's poem, Dixie, though islandized, is moving, and it is literally all over the map. Dixie might be located anywhere.[35]

The implications of this are deadly serious. In Jean Toomer's book *Cane*, which inspired Giscombe, the northern urban protagonist Ralph Kabnis becomes frightened that he is going to be lynched while temporarily living and teaching in rural Georgia. But Kabnis is sure he will be safe if he can get out of the Georgia countryside, and back to the urban North. In Giscombe's response poem, by contrast, there is no clear place of safety. If you are a Black person growing up in America, you learn (slowly) that racial menace potentially is everywhere. And you might develop a bad attitude toward the pastoral because you might fear being the victim of a lynch mob along a red country road a piece. The recurring signs and sounds of racial menace make you look away repeatedly, and they also make you look closely at yourself.

Giscombe could have declared, in so many words, that times and places blur together. He did not do so in this book, and I think that choice matters because, in real life, we are not born knowing our country's history, or our society's rules, or the places we are and are not safe. We have to learn those things over time, and the learning process is uneven, and frequently confusing, and sometimes also scary. Here is my theory about *Here*: the poem tells its stories about race and racism in such a piecemeal and confusing way because part of the point is for us readers to know what that kind of confusion feels like, that is, constantly puzzled (and sometimes threatened) by the connections of race and geography. As the speaker says in a segment called "(the future)":

> Looking at my bad attitude toward the pastoral
>
> & only seeing myself on one of those red dirt roads
> I'd seen from the air, caught unlucky
>
> w/ night more palpable every minute, that
> for future[36]

One way we readers can register the confusion engendered by racism is by imaginatively traveling along with the poem's speaker as he tries to figure out where the boundaries are between North and South; urban and rural; past, present, and future; and self and pastoral (those idealized country landscapes that so little resemble the tangle of the real world).

Speaking of real-world tangles, I want to conclude by proposing several ways that Giscombe's book *Here* helps us think about the current disciplinary intersections of poetry and geography. In the introduction to the anthology *Geopoetics in Practice* (2020), coeditor Eric Magrane offers thoughts on the state of the field, and a basic taxonomy of the genres of geopoetic work:

> A growing number of geographers incorporate creative/artistic practices into their geographic work, and a growing number of artists and writers seem to be entering the field of geography.... In the article "Situating Geopoetics" (Magrane 2015), I begin to outline different "modes" of geopoetics: as creative geography, in which poetry itself is produced as geography and geography is practiced as poetry/poetics; as literary geography, in which geographers interpret poetic texts; and as geophilosophy, in which the "earth-making" of geopoetics is theorized in forms that are not necessarily recognizable as "poetry."[37]

Here participates in at least the first two categories; it is a creative geographic work and also an extended literary critical response to *Cane* (an early work of the Harlem Renaissance and also the first recognized African American modernist book).[38] Indeed, one of Giscombe's larger claims is accomplished through *Here*'s hybridity itself: the assertion that geography and literary history are co-constituted.

Arguably, taking Giscombe's claim seriously means paying closer attention across the disciplines of geography and poetry. His crossing of genres is useful because, by helping us notice and think about poetry's capacity to accomplish both poetic and literary critical work, it helps us consider also the various ways poetry can do geographic work. Later on in the same introduction, after a discussion of the different literatures and citation practices privileged by poets and geographers, *Geopoetics in Practice* coeditor Craig Santos Perez lists some of the different ways that poems do geography: "I appreciate the aesthetic diversity of geopoetic methodologies: narrative poems that story certain places, lyric poems that express emotions about certain landscapes, modernist poems about fragmentation of space, postmodern poems that deconstruct geographical concepts, documentary poems that include archival sources about places, visual poems that embody geographic features, map poems that reimagine cartography, and so much more."[39] Proposing literary style or mode itself as a methodology gestures toward the bundle of methods used routinely by poets and literary critics, some of which (like the close reading I employ in this chapter) can be quite fruitful for geographers who want to ascertain the geographic claims of poems. Indeed, many geographic claims are downright indecipherable without careful attention to the elements from which poems are made. I think it is inadequate to conceive of geopoetics merely as geographers using creativity to explore space, place, and environment. Geographers who are serious about using poetic sources or employing poetic modes of writing would do well to look outside their primary discipline for best practices for studying literary objects and expression.

Finally, I want to point to the activist potential of geopoetic work because I think that is part of Giscombe's point in telling these particular stories about human experiences of fear: the uncertain and perpetual toggle between anxiety and alarm that makes *Here*'s social commentary on American racism so poignant and pointed.[40] Magrane, Santos Perez, Linda Russo, and Sarah de Leeuw imagine geopoetics as an activist endeavor: "Perhaps the ultimate goal of geopoetics as a route-finding practice, then, is to acquire perspective, gain empathy, and try to make something that does not fuck things up further but instead reimagines and resets earthly relationships in the hope of creating more informed and more equitable dynamics."[41] This is what the field-shaping work of McKittrick and literary critic Judith Madera points us to also: an awareness that geography is political, including when its contours seem most natural and neutral or most made (in the pages of a book).[42] The nonlinear route finding of *Here*'s unnamed speaker points us toward that same conclusion, motivated as it is by the complicated ways racism manifests in places, spaces, and landscapes.

Notes

1 Giscombe's poem is obviously about location and repetition, but some clarifications about vocabulary are important up front if the disciplines of poetry and geography are to be mutually intelligible. What I mean by *geography* is the study of human encounters with, and understanding of, our environments; I am designating how we understand our relationships to where we live, or where we find ourselves. What I mean by *space* is an abstract geography; it is a location that

does not have social connections for a person (in this case, the poem's speaker). When I use *place*, I mean a location that is personally significant; it is a location created in some meaningful sense by legible human experiences. Following Denis Cosgrove (*Social Formation and Symbolic Landscape*), Dolores Hayden (*Power of Place*), and Richard Schein (*Landscape and Race in the United States*), by *landscape*, I mean to evoke both literal and imaginative vistas and territories that reflect shifting human desires and power relations.

2 Bledsoe, Eaves, and Williams, "Introduction," 7.

3 Delaney, "The Space That Race Makes," 8.

4 Tuan, *Space and Place*, 5. In *Landscapes of Fear*, Tuan later blurred the distinction between categories by describing all human constructions, mental and material, as landscapes of fear—including those constructions that denote and define places and spaces.

5 In *State, Space, World*, Lefebvre writes, "All space is social: it involves assigning more or less appropriated places to social relations ... social space has thus always been a social product" (186–87).

6 Tuan, *Space and Place*, 6.

7 Giscombe, "Natural Abilities and Natural Writing," in *Border Towns*, 35.

8 Giscombe, "Downstate," in *Prairie Style*, 3.

9 Giscombe's locational and temporal multitudes resonate with McKittrick's centering of sets of locations—disparate and sometimes geographically and temporally far-flung—with shared histories of normalized racial violence and similarly racialized patterns of power relations. McKittrick, "On Plantations, Prisons, and a Black Sense of Place," 950.

10 Giscombe, *Here*, 10.

11 Ronald S. McDowell's bronze sculpture *The Foot Soldier* (1995) stands in Kelly Ingram Park in Alabama, part of the National Park Service's four-block Birmingham Civil Rights National Monument. James Drake's *Police Attack Dog* (1991) lines both sides of the sidewalk, requiring people to pass between life-size lunging and snarling metal dogs in order to continue on the park's Freedom Walk path.

12 Giscombe, *Here*, 48–49.

13 Giscombe, *Here*, 49.

14 Giscombe, *Here*, 22.

15 Giscombe, *Here*, 15, 23.

16 Giscombe, *Here*, 18.

17 Giscombe, *Here*, 13.

18 The Scottsboro Boys were threatened by a lynch mob and required the protection of the Alabama National Guard. Their case ultimately went to the US Supreme Court, which set an important legal precedent when it ruled that having all-white juries was unfair to African American defendants. Most of the Scottsboro Boys served prison time, though decades later all of them were either

pardoned or had their convictions overturned because of what came to be acknowledged as gross, racially motivated miscarriages of justice.

19 Giscombe, *Here*, 42.

20 Giscombe, *Here*, 48.

21 Giscombe, *Here*, 25.

22 Giscombe, *Here*, 31.

23 Giscombe, *Here*, 35.

24 Giscombe, *Here*, 16.

25 Giscombe, *Here*, 19.

26 Sacks and Sacks, *Way Up North in Dixie*, 3–4.

27 "Since the 1960s Black students at Southern state universities have protested the song's performance at football games and have in some cases been successful in eliminating it from the halftime repertoire, which traditionally has included 'Dixie' along with the alma mater and the national anthem. As recently as 1989, *Jet* magazine noted the protest of the song by three Black state senators from Georgia, Arthur Langford, Horace Tate, and Gary Parker; they left the Georgia chamber when the song was sung by Miss Georgia Sweet Potato Queen—incidentally the niece of a white Georgia senator, Walter Ray." Sacks and Sacks, *Way Up North in Dixie*, 4.

28 Sacks and Sacks, *Way Up North in Dixie*, vi.

29 Giscombe, *Here*, 12.

30 Sacks and Sacks, *Way Up North in Dixie*, 8.

31 Derek Alderman and Daniel Good perhaps come closest to addressing mobile sites in their 1997 study of southern identity on the web, but their focus on proposing an ideologically based southern cybergeography de-emphasizes liminality and flux, even when focused on time-delimited web events such as cyberpreparation for the 1996 Olympics. As they note, "One moment's 'snapshot' of the Web is unlikely to differ from another if we are primarily interested in ideologies 'between the lines' of Web pages." Alderman and Good, "Exploring the Virtual South," 28.

32 Giscombe, *Here*, 21.

33 Reed, Kohls, and Hanchette, "Dissolution of Dixie," 221–33.

34 Ambinakudige commented, "The actual reason for a strong Dixie identity in Ohio is unknown. It may be related to the fact that Ohio is the birthplace of Dan Emmett, writer of the famous song 'Dixie.'" Ambinakudige, "Revisiting 'the South' and 'Dixie,'" 245–47, 249.

35 While I was revising this chapter, a group of residents of San Rafael, California (just north of me, in Marin County), asked me to review some historical documents about their school district's history. The Dixie School District in San Rafael was named in 1863, in the middle of the Civil War; it was a controversial name back then, and it is still controversial, especially for people who know its local history. The activists in San Rafael wanted me to assess whether

their claims about the name's history were accurate. It turned out they were correct; the name clearly was meant to evoke and support the Confederacy. While reviewing those primary sources about 1860s California, I found myself asking: If you are an African American child, walking down a street in San Rafael, California, and you see a sign that says "Dixie School," are you safe there? What kind of place are you in? I did not check, but this little corner of Marin County may be one of the Dixie islands that cultural geographers have identified recently.

36 Giscombe, *Here*, 14.

37 Magrane et al., *Geopoetics in Practice*, 2.

38 Possibly also a third if one considers the extended prose, verse, and prose poetic exploration of the concept of "value" across his books, particularly *Here* and *Prairie Style*. Giscombe's prose poem "Negro Mountain" is included in the *Geopoetics in Practice* anthology. Looking at this recent work in progress focused on race, racialization, and place-names helps us differentiate *Here's* distinctive form and its uses of geographic materials.

39 Magrane et al., *Geopoetics in Practice*, 9.

40 Yi-Fu Tuan writes, "What is fear? It is a complex feeling of which two strains, alarm and anxiety, are clearly distinguishable. Alarm is triggered by an obtrusive event in the environment. . . . Anxiety, on the other hand, is a diffuse sense of dread that presupposes an ability to anticipate. . . . Anxiety is a presentiment of danger when nothing in the immediate surroundings can be pinpointed as dangerous. The need for decisive action is checked by the lack of any specific, circumventable threat." Tuan, *Landscapes of Fear*, 5.

41 Magrane et al., *Geopoetics in Practice*, 1.

42 Madera, *Black Atlas*.

Bibliography

Alderman, Derek H., and Daniel B. Good. "Exploring the Virtual South: The Idea of a Distinctive Region on the Web." *Southeastern Geographer* 37, no. 1 (1997): 20–45.

Ambinakudige, Shrinidhi. "Revisiting 'the South' and 'Dixie': Delineating Vernacular Regions Using GIS." *Southeastern Geographer* 49, no. 3 (2009): 240–50.

Bledsoe, Adam, Latoya E. Eaves, and Brian Williams. "Introduction: Black Geographies in and of the United States South." *Southeastern Geographer* 57, no. 1 (Spring 2017): 6–11.

Cosgrove, Denis. *Social Formation and Symbolic Landscape*. 1984. Madison: University of Wisconsin Press, 1998.

Delaney, David. "The Space That Race Makes." *Professional Geographer* 54, no. 1 (2002): 6–14.

Giscombe, C. S. *Border Towns*. Victoria, TX: Dalkey Archive Press, 2016.

Giscombe, C. S. *Here*. Victoria, TX: Dalkey Archive Press, 1994.

Giscombe, C. S. *Prairie Style*. Victoria, TX: Dalkey Archive Press, 2008.

Hayden, Dolores. *The Power of Place: Urban Landscapes as Public History*. Cambridge, MA: MIT Press, 1995.

Lefebvre, Henri. *State, Space, World: Selected Essays*. Minneapolis: University of Minnesota Press, 2009.

Madera, Judith. *Black Atlas: Geography and Flow in Nineteenth-Century African American Literature*. Durham, NC: Duke University Press, 2015.

Magrane, Eric, Linda Russo, Sarah de Leeuw, and Craig Santos Perez, eds. *Geopoetics in Practice*. New York: Routledge, 2019.

McKittrick, Katherine. "On Plantations, Prisons, and a Black Sense of Place." *Social and Cultural Geography* 12, no. 8 (2011): 947–63.

Rankine, Claudia. *Citizen: An American Lyric*. Minneapolis: Graywolf Press, 2014.

Reed, John Shelton, James Kohls, and Carol Hanchette. "The Dissolution of Dixie and the Changing Shape of the South." *Social Forces* 69, no. 1 (1990): 221–33.

Sacks, Howard L., and Judith Rose Sacks. *Way Up North in Dixie*. Washington, DC: Smithsonian Institution Press, 1993.

Schein, Richard, ed. *Landscape and Race in the United States*. New York: Routledge, 2006.

Tuan, Yi-Fu. *Landscapes of Fear*. 1979. Minneapolis: University of Minnesota Press, 2013.

Tuan, Yi-Fu. *Space and Place: The Perspective of Experience*. Minneapolis: University of Minnesota Press, 1977.

PART II

Resistances

4

Blackness Out of Place and In Between in the Sahara

AMPSON HAGAN

Stopped by the Police and Asked for *Pièce d'Identité*

Earlier in the week, Malcolm and Morris attempted to go see the driver who held their luggage to request that they be allowed to go into their bags to change their clothes, as they had been wearing the same few clothing items for weeks. Their plan was to secretly retrieve some of the cash they had stored away in their bags; I hoped they would be able to sneak off with enough of their hidden money to pay off their debt without the driver noticing. I also thought it would be a miracle if they were to find their bags untouched, and that no one had gone through them. I thought that surely the men holding the bags hostage wanted to inspect them to make sure the bags actually contained some valuable items. Malcolm and Morris were two young Liberian men and were unauthorized migrants in

Niger whom I met a month prior to this encounter. In Algeria in search of money, Morris worked for a few years doing various menial jobs, while Malcolm was unable to secure employment during the few months he was there. They entered Niger from the north after having escaped imprisonment by smugglers in Algeria, only to have their driver confiscate their luggage after they arrived in Niamey for failure to pay for the travel. Their identities as African and Black, as well as their shared ontological condition as out of place and subject to police harassment by African (Nigerien) authorities, highlight the complexities of Black geographies within Africa. That Europe has poured hundreds of millions of euros into strengthening Niger's migration controls has added to the complexities of geographies that Black African migrants chart in Niger. As they avoid police deportation and humanitarian or intergovernmental organizations' efforts to help them by way of repatriation, Malcolm, Morris, and other Black African migrants carve out a space in between police and aid. That space, along with related experiences of Black migrant illegality and policing in Niger, constitutes the geographies of what I call the in-between.

One day, Malcolm asked me if we could meet that night, and I agreed. After a long taxi ride, I reached *l'échangeur* (the interchange, a highway overpass that bisects Mali Bero Road and lies near the national stadium, the International Organization for Migration (IOM) migrant camp for men, and the Sonef bus station) where Malcolm and Morris told me to meet them. I arrived near *l'échangeur* at around midnight and saw Malcolm and Morris a few meters up the road. We exchanged greetings while walking, and they decided it would be safest to step under the overpass to talk. In hushed tones, Malcolm and Morris said they wanted to show me something. In the dark of night, few people were around, and the three of us, out in the open, talking secretly, looked suspicious. We scurried underneath the overpass, against a concrete barrier that hid us from view from the adjacent Mali Bero Road. Morris kneeled down to pantomime for me a demonstration of the length of the box where they kept their money. They had used their clothes to quickly grab what few bills they could, and that is what they wanted to show me. We were positioned behind a stone column supporting the ramp above to conceal the transfer and inspection of the money—their money—they had smuggled out of the warehouse, escaping the watchful eyes of the warehouse workers. Morris, wearing a crisp new black T-shirt, reached into his pocket and handed me some folded bills. Euros. I hoped there would be many euros in my hands, but I held only fifty. I went to my calculator to confirm what I already knew: this was only a little more than

25,000 Francs de Communauté financière d'Afrique (FCFA), nothing compared with what they still owed their driver (who had taken them across the desert to Niamey, after they were arrested in Algeria and deported to Niger, and was now holding their precious luggage as collateral until they pay), which was more than 1,000 euros (approximately 645,000 FCFA). I told them that 50 euros is "little money" that does not come close to solving their problems, including being able to find housing, pay for food, and pay for ID cards so they could legally work in order to pay off their debt.

They asked me about exchanging the fifty euros for FCFA, and I told them I would ask a man who exchanges money at a good rate. I quickly folded the bills and slid them into my back left pocket. As we talked, two trucks filled with gendarmes/police bearing automatic rifles pulled over to the side of the overpass, across the road, upon having seen the three of us. One man quickly hopped off the truck bench, followed by another, and they came over to us, both sporting their rifles and wearing red berets and desert camouflage uniforms. I don't quite know their military branch but have seen these divisions or platoons of military/police before. One officer delivered a preamble in which he said to us, "We are protecting the city and the people," to preface the police questioning that soon followed. Were we not people, too? Did he not think we deserved protecting? With his colleague behind him, calmly clutching his rifle, the officer asked for our ID cards, *les pièces d'identité*.

At this point, our out-of-placeness met the juridical crosshairs of the state, which has targeted Black outsiders like us since the European Union (EU) started flooding Niger with moneys contingent on stepping up its antimigration policing and border controls for the past few years. But how did the police know to stop us? I saw the trucks coming up the ramp of the expressway, but they stopped so abruptly, it led me to believe they just happened across us, perhaps realizing that the three of Malcolm, Morris, and I seemed peculiar as we entered their field of vision. But why did they stop? What was it about the three of us standing and talking that led them to believe we required investigation? How did we register as out of place and/or foreign? Our Blackness did not protect us from being perceived as outsiders in a predominantly Black country such as Niger. Geographer Julien Brachet notes that trans-Saharan migrants passing through Agadez, Niger, on the way toward Algeria and Libya arrive in Agadez via regular means of transport (e.g., buses and taxis), and at times the foreign origin of migrants may be more obvious. He goes on to say that travelers who appear to be migrants are often treated differently from other passengers by the police or by their drivers at their entry into Niger or during their transit through Niamey, including receiving hostile and violent treatment by the police.[1] Not "looking like" Nigeriens and possibly fitting the description of "migrants" (e.g., wearing clothing that may mark us as foreign Black Africans), we were subjected to what Simone Browne calls "racializing surveillance."[2]

Somehow, our being Black but "different" (the police did not mistake us for Nigeriens, so they assumed we were unauthorized Black migrants from elsewhere) fit neatly into the globalized notions of "illegal migrants" as criminal agents. This scene demonstrates how race and specifically Blackness are not constituted only through epidermalization (e.g., when Frantz Fanon records a white child exclaiming to his mother, upon seeing Fanon, "Look! A Negro!").[3] They also are understood through bodily movements, sartorial choices, hairstyles, or perceived physical differences that mark someone as an "outsider" or perhaps differently Black.[4] Writing about Blackness in Ghana, anthropologist Jemima Pierre explained that Ghanaian identity formation must be understood within broader processes of racialization, and that local meanings of Black Ghanaian selfhood have always been constructed through a complex set of imbricated histories that are set within transnational understandings of race and Blackness.[5] Relatedly, local or vernacular meanings of African Blackness and selfhood are shaped through the interactions between Black people's agency and a European-dominated Atlantic political-economic complex.[6] The fact of racialized subjectivity in Niger, and within West Africa more broadly, emerges from a vernacular interpretation of Blackness, which is articulated through perceived Africanness or assumed belonging to an Indigenous ethnic group, having been born and raised on the continent, and the ability to speak African language(s). Anthropologist Charles Price noted in his ethnography of racialization and Black identity formation among Jamaican Rastafari that the moral economy of Blackness orients us toward racialized "ways of life that include ideas about social welfare, tradition, community, and identity."[7] All these elements of Black African racial identity are perceived, and thus are processes of perception and cultural/community surveillance. This Blackness out of place and the surveillance of it circumscribe geographic possibilities for Black migrants, and push migrants to the in-between, the space between humanitarian aid and repatriation, and police arrest and deportation.

Reflecting on how David Theo Goldberg's conceptualization of power and self-disciplining through surveillance reckons with the policing of Black peoples, Browne considers racializing surveillance to signal the moments when the deployment of surveillance reifies borders and bodies along racial lines, often preceding the discriminatory treatment of those who are negatively racialized by such surveillance.[8] However, in the case of Malcolm, Morris, and me, we were stopped precisely because we looked suspicious under *l'échangeur*, and the fact that the gendarmes asked only for our ID cards and nothing else suggests that our Blackness was deemed to be that of another place. The gendarme's utterance, "We are protecting the city and the people," revealed his institutionalized object of protecting people, but from whom and from what?

My intuition convinced me that this sort of migrant profiling was the case here, but it was actually months later that I received confirmation from others—outside of my own understanding and experiences of racial profiling and migrant policing—that this was in fact a scene of profiling that relied on phenotypic *difference* from Nigeriens—namely, that we looked foreign, in dress and countenance. This was a practice in telling Nigeriens (who are almost all Black) from non-Nigerien Black peoples. At a two-day police workshop in July 2019 hosted by the United Nations High Council for Refugees (UNHCR), a UNHCR representative and scholars from the Université Abdou Moumouni were training Nigerien police officers on how to properly identify what UNHCR refers to as stateless persons and migrants within the country, so as to properly assess both their chance for asylum and their legal presence in Niger. On the first day of the workshop, an older police officer complained that one of the common methods for ascertaining one's Nigerien citizenship and/or country of origin—by family surname—is no longer as useful as it once was, as the "traditional" Nigerien family names are being replaced by Nigerian and Maghrebi names; he lamented that it was becoming more difficult for him and his colleagues to determine who is Nigerien and who is not. In response, the presenter mentioned that another method of ascertaining Nigerien citizenship, in which police officers *identifier le pigment* (identify the pigment) of the person in question, still works as a citizenship-determining tactic. I think this process of identification is not necessarily about pigment; rather, it is a metaphor for phenotypic traits such as recognizable facial markings associated with specific ethnic groups and vernacular processes of facial-based ethnic recognition.[9] When I witnessed this exchange in the migration workshop, my head started spinning. Stunned, my mind jolted me back to the gendarme situation with Malcolm and Morris, and I thought about how the police probably profiled us based on our skin tones and facial features, which differ from those commonly found among Nigeriens. We were speaking softly as the gendarmes loudly drove by us, so I doubt they could hear us speaking English. However, upon having seen us standing under the overpass, and me with my long locs, they reversed their truck and got out to meet us. While this scene undermines the notion of ethnolinguistics being the reason for why we were policed, or why police stopped Malcolm and Morris at other times during their stay in Niger as they simply walked along the streets, dress, posture, and bodily comportment mark us as different from most others in Niamey. Along with the specter of unauthorized migration, the police and gendarmerie were primed to be hypervigilant about suspicious characters, foreign-looking ones like us.

The investigation and questioning of our belonging via our identification documents meant that the people the gendarme swore to protect did not include Malcolm, Morris, and me. The people, absent from the scenario, performed a psychic labor in this drama by serving as the referent value of *good* against which we were measured and deemed *not good* and an ontological threat to the good, which is the people. This was a test, or perhaps a pop quiz, on whether we could prove coverage under the auspices of state-sanctioned documentation legitimating our presence in Niger, protection under the humanitarian regime of the nearby IOM migrant camp (sanctioned by the Nigerien state and endorsed by the EU and the United Nations, representing a range of international political and racial interests), or neither. The first two options articulate different versions of belonging to a juridical-spatial place. Our racialization by the prevailing racial schema in Niger marked the three of us as foreign, with me marked differently than Malcolm and Morris. This process of affixing our out-of-place Blackness with illegality also circumscribed our possible geographies; my ID card allowed me to travel somewhat freely, but Malcolm and Morris's lack of ID, coupled with their Liberian nationality, marked them as "illegal" migrants and, within Niger, as threats to Nigerien national sovereignty.

Racialization of Migrants and the Policing Migration in Africa

The migrant is a sociohistorical category of concern, constructed as a problem of state policy, national unity, and racial consciousness and is racialized via persistent racist discourses and hierarchies forming a "racial system" with global reach.[10] This globalized racial system constructs (im)migrants as abject subjects of the European nation-state, via the "savage slot."[11] The savage slot, the "Janus-faced projection" of the West and utopia, is the category of the savage or primitive that is the alter ego the West constructed for itself, and against which the West, with its notions of civilization and being, frames itself.[12] In this vein, deservingness seeks to separate migrants, who are already less deserving than refugees, into hierarchies of vulnerability and deservingness of care within the savage slot. Although the racial and racist schema in which migrants are racialized as the others of Europe was perfected in Europe, the racialization of migration and migrants works particularly well in "sub-Saharan" or Black Africa, even while the migrants themselves are Black.[13] Colonialism was deeply concerned with the regulation of African movement and human mobility as a challenge to the stability of colonial rule, and the West and postcolonial states alike continue to racialize Black mobility as a threat to the nation-state and the rule of law.[14] Since the colonization of Africa and the related system of chattel slavery, Black migration has long been constructed as ontologically wayward and as a transgressive act against the overdetermined racial geographies that assign particular racialized peoples with certain places and nation-states, viewing the state as a racial (and "cultural") container.

Within Africa, Black movement has been restricted and policed by colonial powers in the recent past and by African governments themselves in the present. In West Africa, Niger is policing and arresting Black African migrants on behalf of Europe. At the behest of the EU, the Nigerien police arrest, detain, and deport unauthorized African migrants throughout the country, while select humanitarian organizations work to "manage" migration by facilitating repatriation of African migrants. Such comprehensive and heavily financed police and military activity represents the Nigerien state's interests, along with those of the EU, in keeping Black Africans from reaching Europe and ultimately disrupting the global racial order.[15] After World War II, the centuries-old global racial order, solidified during the era of colonialism and transatlantic slavery, adapted to the egalitarian and antiracist demands of the late twentieth century, to reflect a "color-blind" and "nonracialist" version of racial inequality and white supremacy.[16] The Europe-backed policing of Black migrants by Black African governments obscures the white supremacist foundations of this antimigration apparatus, precisely because of this re-formed racism that persists in Africa, where the idea of race is often considered an anomaly, attached only to the unique history of apartheid South Africa.[17] Religion is also a category used as grounds on which governments harass and expel migrants. Some Christian-dominated countries with Muslim immigrants from West Africa have reframed Islam as alien to the local cultures and stigmatized those Muslims by linking them with Islamist armed groups and terrorism.[18] However, the European backing of increased border policing in Niger and along the southern border of Europe specifically to prevent Africans from entering Europe has invigorated the border control efforts of West African countries like Niger, despite the fact that circular migration of Africans within the region has been commonplace for hundreds of years. This EU strengthening of Nigerien border policing, mapped onto local notions of sovereignty, masks the racial dynamics of a globalized anti-Blackness with a distinctly vernacular presentation of African ethnolinguistic or religious difference, as well as an antipolitical border control.

Such policing of Black Africans by a majority Black nation-state occurs throughout the Republic of Niger. The Nigerien state and international humanitarian organizations are targeting Black African migrants. Many migrants in Niger evade both the authorities and the humanitarian groups, existing outside of them but between them as those entities seek to converge on migrants from "both sides." The marriage of humanitarian organizations concerned with providing assistance to migrants and police/military forces of the state enacting surveillance, arrest, and deportation of migrants produces several forms of limited and restricted movement for Black migrants like Malcolm and Morris. Humanitarian and nongovernmental actors like IOM coerce or at least facilitate unauthorized migrants to pursue voluntary repatriation as a form of economic aid, and such organizations work alongside the police and the state, upholding the latter's mandate to control the flow of migrants into and out of Niger. Similarly, the Nigerien police and military execute various migrant-seeking tactics, including ID checks at checkpoints within the territory (not just at border crossings) and migrant profiling. Such tactics result in arrest, deportation, and even exploitation of migrants by police, which casts these police and related humanitarian efforts into relief as actively antimovement and anti-migrant relations.[19] Moreover, these forms of humanitarian policing link together state and international actors in a system of xenophobic, carceral, and anti-Black oppression of Black African migrants. These forms of limited and blocked movement result in alternate geographies rooted in *dispossibility* and a practice of shadow mapping among Black migrants, where Black peoples counter their surveillance by the state with their own sousveillance of the state, tracing a shadow or complementary (but hidden from plain sight) set of geographic mapping. One of the particular spaces that is created via state-blocked and humanitarian-resistant movement is the space of the in-between. It is here where many unauthorized Black migrants live, engaging in sousveillance of the chasing state-humanitarian apparatus and enacting a Black countergeography. This countergeography or alternative geography is created both in relation to and in between the state and the humanitarian apparatus, and it is a refuge from the otherwise out-of-placeness migrants experience in the broader geography of the policed nation-state territory.

Fortress Europe and IOM in Africa

For many West Africans hoping to reach Europe, traveling to Western Sahara (and Morocco) via Mauritania and Senegal was the easier route, as the Canary Islands lie in the Atlantic Ocean less than one hundred kilometers off the southernmost coast of Morocco. From the late 1990s to 2020, thousands of people from West and Central Africa engaged in unauthorized migration to Europe via North Africa in search of economic opportunities not found in their home countries.[20] The Canary Islands constitute an autonomous community of Spain. Migrants traveled to southern Morocco and northern Western Sahara in the hopes of taking clandestine boat travel to the Canary Islands, which represent the most distant outpost of "fortress Europe."[21] The IOM, in conjunction with Spanish maritime patrols, launched humanitarian "interception" campaigns and policed the waters, looking for suspicious vessels that could be harboring undocumented migrants. These efforts were influenced by European interests in securing the borders in order to protect European society and ensure its potential prosperity remains unfettered with the responsibility of supporting unwanted noncitizens.

After the Canary Islands route was closed off, many Africans hoping to reach North Africa from elsewhere in the continent attempted to cross the Sahara, traveling through Niger. Since the 1990s, the EU has been slowly extending Europe's border with Africa southward through the act of border externalization. By pressuring North African countries to tighten their border controls, stop irregular migration into and out of their member states, and commit to bilateral antimigration agreements in exchange for aid, border externalization effectively shifted the borders of Europe into Africa.[22] Under the direction of the EU and the United Nations (IOM is a UN agency), IOM polices the Sahara as a humanitarian organization providing care and assistance to migrants, while simultaneously shaping international efforts to govern and surveil the Sahara and the migrants attempting to cross it. Niger gained relevance for European countries and policymakers as a transit country following the so-called migrant crisis of 2015 that linked Niger and Europe via African migrants crossing from North Africa to European shores.[23] As a result, Europe has increased its cooperation with Niger to shore up Nigerien borders and antimigration efforts via binational and regional partnerships.[24] Actors performing migration policy governance in Niger, such as IOM and UNHCR, have seen their roles as implementing partners with the EU increased since enactment of the 2015 Niger law that criminalized smuggling and smuggling-related activities.[25]

The journey for most trans-Saharan migrants hoping to reach Europe begins far from the sea, occurring in long stages of transit migration through towns along the way.[26] On their way, migrants often settle temporarily in towns located along migration routes to work and save enough money for the next phases of their journeys.[27] With many migrants choosing to remain in such towns, positioning themselves to continue their journeys, the police and IOM have come to signify the two entities operating to arrest and repatriate (deport) migrants, respectively. Despite Europe's efforts and projects to block African migration and intercept migrants, many migrants are still traveling northward through Niger, where they live in the *in-between*.

Subverting the Geographies of Institutionalized Identification (Cards)

I nervously fumbled for my Maryland driver's license in my right front pocket—the only form of identification I had on my person at the moment—and handed it to the policeman. I figured it was official enough and that he surely cannot expect folks to walk around with passports. He turned it over in his hands, clearly interested in the strange-looking card with raised font and multiple holograms.[28] "It's in English," I explained to the officer in French, with an ambivalently useless and powerful metonym, why this card was so strange and how it simultaneously legitimated my presence in Niger via my American foreignness. The ID card denotes belonging to a particular place and, in my case, represented evidence of my belonging to a foreign, English-speaking country, definitely one outside of Niger. The letters *USA* are written in small script in the upper-left corner of the card, but perhaps that was unnecessary to determine my origin; the many holograms and the raised lettering of the card might have screamed "American security" to the officer, and he could have made a connection between my

Blackness and the United States. This diasporic location of my Blackness may have prompted him to say to me, "You must be their sponsor!" referring to me as the financial sponsor of Malcolm and Morris. By exclaiming that I was their sponsor, he assumed that I was supporting them financially by giving them money. My having an ID card from the United States satisfactorily excused me from police anti-Black migrant aggression, but Malcolm and Morris could not escape our presumed illegal presence in Niger, which was based on how we looked relative to the other Black people in Niger. Looking different, even looking *differently* Black, positioned all three of us as illegal outsiders in the eyes of the authorities, and certain forms of Blackness in Africa remain associated with illegality and out-of-placeness. However, my otherness was different from the shared otherness of Malcolm and Morris, and mine provided cover for theirs.

However, Malcolm and Morris were unable to produce any documentation, a tangible artifact of the normative liberal state's designs to atomize life to a printed series of names and dates on a card. Malcolm explained to the gendarme that he and Morris do not have any identification and that they are migrants staying at IOM (he pointed in the direction of the nearby IOM transit center as he said this, all in English). He said, "We are *les migrants*," mixing English with French. The gendarme snidely retorted (in French), "You two don't have IDs, but he does," referring to me. My heart rate quickened, and I felt my temperature rise as the gendarmes initially walked over, even as soon as their trucks stopped nearby. As he looked at my *pièce d'identité* and talked to the two of us who had none, I could feel the other officers—about fifteen of them in total—staring at us, at me, from across the road. Then the interrogating officer asked Malcolm if I was his and Morris's *patron* ("boss," or, in this case, a person to whom others owe favors in return for assistance). Malcolm said no and quickly added that I was simply his friend. The police officer was satisfied with that, handed me my ID, said, "C'est bon," and walked off with the other officer. After the soldiers left, we all decided it was time to go home. It was very late, and Malcolm and Morris needed to get back to the SONEF guard's house before he gets home from work and finds that they are not there. The guard thought they were home sleeping and not out late, according to Malcolm and Morris. Here, the officers represent the incomplete process of postindependence deracialization in newly independent African states. Jemima Pierre argues that "the appropriation by Africans of certain administrative positions did not fully mean the erosion of the accumulated privilege of Whiteness in the former colonies."[29] On the contrary, the racial character of colonial rule institutionalized whiteness and European rule within economic and social relations, and the antimigrant and anti-Black gendarmes are the fundamental embodiment of this European rule that forcibly acts, in a simulacrum of colonial control, on Black Africans. I inferred that the gendarmes believed it would be (or is) disrespectful to be outside in the city at an hour when their host assumed they were home, especially since something could have happened to Malcolm and Morris out at night without any identification documents; all of this could have easily annoyed the host and potentially jeopardized their stay in the home. Again, we see here how the gendarmes' aggression toward Black migrants sutures the gendarmes' sovereign power to the vulnerability and powerlessness of Black peoples within the territory, a power that emanates from European colonial rule and shapes the ways the state racializes (and thus polices) Black peoples.

We escaped that night. More specifically, Malcolm and Morris escaped the unspoken threat of deportation. My read on this moment is that my identification card worked in such a way that it helped override Malcolm's and Morris's lack of identification.[30] However, I am unsure if this was what in fact saved me (and us). If not for the Maryland ID, I could have appealed to the gendarmes in English and stated that I was American and should have received some dispensation from Nigerien laws. However, from my personal experiences in the region, police and gendarmes have often doubted and rejected my claims to American nationality and said that I "looked Nigerian" or declared that I must have been from an Anglophone African country. Thus, my linguistic background may not have helped me at all without the accompanying ID. However, based on the fact that the gendarme accepted this Anglophone card without having pressed me for my passport and/or visa, I assume that he decided that I was "legit" as in, an acceptable Black foreigner, unlike Malcolm and Morris. This racializing surveillance technology of identification, or "seeing things" via informants, works across multiple geographies in order to historically and socially locate individuals within a social frame of security and risk that determines people's potential of risk to the greater population and the state.[31]

I thought back on that gendarme's preamble. His charge to "protect the people" in Niger required that he recognize any possible threats to "the people," and migrants have been classically categorized as an existential threat to the nation-state. Similarly, Didier Bigo's notion of the Banopticon articulates how the state abandons those whom it racializes as potential risks, via the practice of profiling individuals into risk categories and then projecting these categories "by generalization upon the potential behavior of each individual pertaining to the risk category."[32] Browne extends this idea further, noting how the Banopticon labels certain groups and individuals as potentially dangerous. She explains that the labeling itself is dangerous, as it determines the risk of entire nations and their citizens as well as those outside the bounds of citizenship, where "anxieties and the anticipation of risk stemming from those deemed 'dangerous minorities' then shape security measures at borders, on city streets, and [in] other spaces that come to be associated with risk, or with being at risk of becoming risky."[33] In the case of Black migrants in Niger, however, the idea of a dangerous minority is replaced by the continued (re)production of the migrant figure as a harbinger of crime and illegality. While Nigerien authorities do attack African migrants, the Nigerien police and gendarmerie occasionally harass and attack citizens to assert their authority.[34] However, Europe does not frame nonmigrant African citizens as a geographic threat to its territorial sovereignty and racial self-identity in the way that Europe frames African migrants as threats. Europe turned its psychological fears of Black African migrants into material support of policing and police violence in Africa. Extending Browne's point here, it is the anxieties and the resulting constellations of antimigrant technologies and tactics that emerged from the reproduction of the migrant figure that reify the idea of the Black migrant as a potential threat to Niger and, by extension, a threat to Europe.

While my ID definitely saved me from potential trouble, being able to point to IOM across the road definitely helped out Malcolm and Morris. They were geographically close to a plausible location where their existence as different-looking Black people (but not different in a way that avoids suspicion that they might be Black African migrants) can be located. In fact, Malcolm and Morris deliberately recognize their in-between status, and their actual inhabitance of the geographies of the in-between, when they invoke IOM as a metonym and explanation for who they are and where they belong. The attempt to locate themselves spatially and institutionally with IOM and specifically the nearby IOM migrant camp shows how Black migrants here in Niger often use widely known ideas of police and humanitarian behaviors toward migrants against one another to escape their grasp, to survive outside of each. It also shows how migrants are positioned between the state and the nongovernmental organizations (NGOs) such as

IOM. Malcolm and Morris are trying to maintain an existence in Niger that is outside of and in between those two entities, the only way they can try and make enough money to pay off the ransom for their luggage. We escaped the state in a way, but risk of arrest and the threat of deportation for Malcolm and Morris remained as potent as ever.

Humanitarianism as the Flip Side of Police Action

On a humid May night in Niamey, I met the IOM communications officer in the parking lot of a bus depot. She told me that she was facilitating a sensitization program called Cinema Caravan, in which IOM hosts sensitization events around town and throughout the country to educate people—Black African migrants and pre-migrants—about the dangers of migration to dissuade people from migrating. As people trickled into the large lot inside the depot walls, attracted by the familiar Naija beats awakening the otherwise sleepy, dull Monday night, Linda turned to me and asked, "What do you want to know about IOM?" Perhaps having seen my nonchalant response about being interested in IOM programming as vague, Linda enthusiastically launched into an advertisement for IOM touting all the goals, objectives, and programs of the organization. According to her and the organization's standard operating procedure, IOM works only with pre-migrants, migrants, and internally displaced persons. She added that IOM provides numerous services for these groups, including crisis kits, food, temporary shelter in transit centers, job training, and voluntary repatriation to migrants' countries of origin.

Linda went on to state that the sensitization work in Niamey and Agadez was important preventive work that is critical to addressing the migrant situation in the country because it seeks to dissuade (read: prevent) potential migrants from engaging in international migration at all. With all this IOM information and IOM/development-speak, I could not help but find this illusory. While IOM does in fact do a lot of humanitarian and crisis work, its migration programming is hardly migration-preventative. It spends considerable energy and resources to convince Black Africans that they will face violence, poverty, and racism in North Africa and in Europe and that they should stay home even though they face economic precarity and have few opportunities there. Since 2015, Africa has experienced a surge in migration policy efforts backed by the EU and implemented by IOM.

Such policies include bilateral agreements to provide technical assistance, develop aid and arms to limit irregular or unauthorized migration, and secure borders.[35] Even though EU bilateral agreements deploy language of cooperation and mutual benefit for both countries, they aim to block Africans' movements to Europe.[36] As the migration policy implementing agency, IOM's goal is to manage migration and secure European borders through deportations and increased cooperation with antimigration police efforts. Thus, IOM's work involves keeping Black Africans within Africa and out of Europe.

The IOM transit centers throughout the Saharan region are "open," meaning that accommodation for migrants is "voluntary" and that migrants can leave at any time. However, in order to be accommodated at an IOM transit center, migrants must agree to voluntary repatriation to their countries of origin.[37] It is increasingly difficult for migrants in Niger to find temporary housing, as their presence is evermore criminalized.[38] Arrest could lead to deportation, representing an interruption of migrants' dreams of elsewhere—a failed migration.[39] With safe housing and access to food and water for unauthorized migrants in Niger available only through NGOs but contingent on repatriation, migrant health in Niger exhibits a form of paternalism that contributes to policies of containment. Unlike sovereign states that exhibit compassion for refugees in exceptional moments amid the common and socially acceptable repression of those refugees, IOM performs compassion and repression both as a rights-based organization (compassion) and as a facsimile of states' and local communities' antimigrant demands for containment and repatriation (repression).[40]

Some migrants in Niger criticize this double mission of IOM and ultimately the care it provides. I have asked Malcolm and Morris as well as other migrants living on the outskirts of Niamey why they do not like IOM, choosing instead to live outside of IOM care, risking arrest as undocumented persons. Malcolm once responded that "IOM wants to deport you" and that "they don't care about you." Even during our many meetings with each other in town to strategize and brainstorm about what Malcolm and Morris "can do now," I asked them if they went to IOM for any help at all, but their response was the same. Malcolm said, "No, I don't go there," and Morris concurred. They both eschew the aid of IOM and the restrictions on Black movement that very aid demands. They know that IOM means repatriation, something that Malcolm and Morris, like many other undocumented migrants biding their time in Niger, want to avoid.

Sousveillance from the In-Between

That Malcolm and Morris used the premise of being migrants with IOM to evade police scrutiny indicates this space of the in-between. In itself a cruel irony, I wondered how it is also a demonstration of a politics of elsewhere, of a space that cannot be apprehended or colonized. They were surveilled, as we were on this night, but were easily able to subvert notions of where they were by relying on authorities' expectations of where they belong. The work of Simone Browne on Black vulnerability, policing, and Black activities of sousveillance—a counterwatching by Black peoples contesting the subjecthood they face via surveillance by an oppressive sovereign power—resonates here. Conditions and vulnerabilities that Black African migrants endure and inhabit represent generative sites of being through which practices of surveillance and sousveillance are articulated and contested.[41] This focus on the surveillance of Black migrants in Niger reflects Europe's surveillance of Black migrants in Europe. As a result, cross-border security networks have emerged, linking the regime of surveillance in Europe with migration management in African nations known to be hubs for migrants moving northward to the Mediterranean. These cross-border surveillance networks are essential elements of transnational governance and rely heavily on governance through the intertwining of crime control and immigration control, what Katja Aas calls "crimmigration."[42] Acts of crimmigration and opposing migrant sousveillance played out in the streets of Niamey and in the desert-swept corners of Agadez, like a game of cat and mouse, between the (non)state apparatus wanting to consume out-of-place Black peoples and those people invisibilizing themselves to evade capture.[43] Turning back to the police stop where the officer said, "We are protecting the people," the suggestion was that Malcolm, Morris, and I represented ontological threats to "the people" (Nigerien citizens), from whom we were excluded as soon as the officers saw us. Migrancy appears to be the same as criminality, thus necessitating policing.[44] On our many walks together through town, we would often spot groups of police officers and gendarmes a few meters ahead of us, with groups of young to middle-aged men languidly sitting in the cabins and beds of the police pickup trucks under the shade of verdant neem trees. On one occasion, we walked by, keeping our gaze focused on the path ahead of us, but once we were out of earshot, Malcolm dryly chuckled. He shook his head as he sardonically said, "These police! They want to embarrass you!" On another occasion, we spotted a group of gendarmes secluded under the shade of another tree, near the national hospital at the center of town. They appeared to be hiding from view as much as they were hiding from the beating sun. Again, this prompted a smirk and more head shaking from Malcolm and Morris.

In September 2019, a few months after the gendarme episode, Malcolm was missing. I called Malcolm and Morris multiple times over the course of twenty-four hours and did not hear back from them. Even though they share a phone, one of them usually finds phone credit to call me or borrows someone else's phone to get in touch with me, so I thought the long silence unusual. The next day I went to Talladjé, the community where they live, to look for them. I finally found Morris, who told me that Malcolm was being deported. Scared for both of them, I decided to go with Morris to the police stations (all of them, because we did not know where Malcolm was being held) early in the morning to try to reach him before he was to be bused back to Liberia sometime the following evening. However, the following afternoon, Malcolm returned alone. He informed us that plain-clothes police officers, working undercover to catch unauthorized and undocumented migrants, had caught him and some other men in one of the large markets. He said that these tactics of hunting Black migrants are the same methods of capture that the Algerian authorities use in their racist arrest and expulsion of Black Africans.

Since the year 2000, Algeria has expelled Black African migrants in raids such as the type that Malcolm described, and Niger's antimigrant actions reflect the manner in which its Algerian neighbors treat the same Black migrants. In a further extension of racial logics of bordering and the disregard for the lives of Black peoples, Algeria has allegedly abandoned more than thirteen thousand black African migrants in the Sahara Desert since 2017, including children and pregnant women.[45] Malcolm and Morris know all too well how their presence and spatiality have serious consequences for their safety. Sousveillance by unauthorized migrants living in between the state and the humanitarian NGO is crucial to their survival. Without the ability to constantly perceive, from the vantage point of the elsewhere space of the in-between, the police and the NGO humanitarian actors may capture them. Malcolm and Morris performed an act of sousveillance that positioned them as responsible parties and demonstrated their right to be there (despite not having documentation) vis-à-vis their proximity to the transit center and associated claim of being migrants. They also simultaneously deployed the political claim of their in-betweenness to both escape and remain.

The in-between is not solely a space produced by insecurity and migrant vulnerability to police violence and social stigmatization; rather, it is itself a condition, a result of refusing both care and carcerality, the two dominant biopolitical logics the state uses to control persons. The scene under the overpass demonstrates how Malcolm, Morris, and other migrants embody the in-between, through the violences they suffer but also through the spaces they inhabit. By inhabiting the in-between and invoking it through the register of migrancy on the precipice of repatriation (e.g., saying they are with IOM, when being "with IOM" usually means repatriation), they made use of their space that is both outside of and between the various structures attempting to consume them, playing those entities off one another to re-main exterior to them. Being a migrant significantly places individuals in ambiguous and often hostile relationships to the state.[46] As is the case for many migrants in Niger, the category of migrant positions them against humanitarian aid as well.

Accompanying the sousveillance of the police throughout Niamey, Malcolm and Morris also performed a countermapping against the geog-raphies of which they are excluded via the state-humanitarian apparatus. They took (and made) shortcuts from their faraway migrant community on the outskirts of Niamey into town in order to avoid police scrutiny. They lived in the small, modest community of Talladjé, on the road to the Hamani Diori Airport, about three miles from the center of town. Even if the Liberian community members were not always in solidarity with each other, Malcolm and Morris have told me several times that they were all suspicious of outsiders in Talladjé, which was their site of refuge. It was also their space where they have, with a sense of comfort in protection, existed in the in-between away from the threat of the police. As Morris once told me regarding the police, "They don't come here." They also demonstrated acute awareness of much of Niamey and the enclaves and routes of other unauthorized migrants living throughout Niamey and especially within the community of Talladjé, geographic knowledge that the authorities did not possess. Sousveillance against crimmigration tactics unlocked other possibilities for migrants in Talladjé, including a possible life in Niger and one outside of, but alongside, the state. Considering the in-between as a space of ontological interiority, that new interiority embodies a spatial transformation, and bell hooks explained that the "transformed interior space is expansive."[47] Similarly, Carole Boyce Davies refers to this poten-tial inherent in a new home space, a new interiority, as "a new site for the imaginative."[48] Such counter-mapping of alternate geographies that Black migrants inhabit within the in-between of trans-Saharan migration reflects a new knowledge system "produced outside the realms of normalcy" that is forged in the critical space/place of the in-between.[49]

Mapping and Studying Geographies of the In-Between

In terms of Black movement across space and time, what happens to Black peoples and Blackness at the borders of transitions between spaces, between sociojuridical imaginaries, such as the nation-state and the humanitarian state? What happens at the inflection point? What happens during the long journey between A and B? Douglas Allen, Mary Lawhon, and Joseph Pierce explain the difference between place and relational place-making, noting that "while place-bundles include material components and are formed in relation to material conditions and experiences, relational place is a fundamentally conceptual product, continually produced, altered, and maintained through socio-political processes."[50] I argue that those socio-political processes include citizenship, mythmaking, and scapegoating of migrants from elsewhere in Africa, as well as notions of political belonging and deservingness. Put another way, the formation of the post-colonial Nigerien nation-state reinforced notions of who belongs through pressure from other countries to control migration and through this process established who is inappropriate or out of place within its borders. Conversely, migrants like Malcolm and Morris engage in what Deborah Martin describes as a collective place-making that affirms their social and political goals while expressing or enacting a geographic vision.[51]

Malcolm and Morris inhabit a geographic space of the in-between, where they negotiate the rules and inclusion/exclusion norms of the nation-state, as well as the repatriation-oriented humanitarian and NGO apparatus. In her analysis of M. Nourbese Philip's essay "Dis Place—the Space Between," Katherine McKittrick notes that while the feminine Black body is seemingly kept in place by the "space between her legs," this space between "constructs contextual and subjective outsides."[52] Thus, the space between or the in-between produces outsides and forms the subjective contours of those outsides through its own being. The in-between forms what McKittrick calls a "paradoxical space" inscribing paradoxical geographies that mark the tensions in geography.[53] They do not, however, foreclose geographic strategies for surviving that domination and critiquing it.[54] An in-between space offers geographic possibilities for living within oppressive regimes as well as making space and moving through them. Black peoples like Malcolm and Morris are considered "out of place" by the hegemonic logics of the geography of Man, where Man is an overdetermined category of existence and assumed universality, and Blacks occupy the spaces of Otherness. McKittrick sees Blacks as being in place, but the geographies of Man and his sense of place are naturalized as normal and thus overlook "the under-represented conceptions of being *in place*" that emerge from Black people's "differential encounters with geography."[55]

While the relatively minor encounter between Malcolm, Morris, and the police appears typical of many encounters young African men may have with police across the continent, I highlight this scene as a demonstration of tensions in geography because it is not so much like "typical" migrant-police encounters in West Africa. Again, the EU funding and support of Nigerien antimigration efforts in the territory animate this rather trivial scene with the racist demographic anxieties and political exigencies of European societies. Thus, these scenes between Black Africans (all migrants and Others) and (Black) police forces are not solely African affairs, ones that would tend to fall on ethnic or political grounds rather than racial ones, with Black Africans being of the same "race." Rather, white European imperatives infect and transform these encounters between African migrants and African police to reflect white political and geographic desires, and ultimately do so while masking themselves as African sovereign and geographic imaginaries.

I am concerned about the in-between and how Black people can be driven to it when their desires for life lie outside of the predetermined destinies prescribed by the global world order. This is a demonstration of the need for the sustained, empirical, and philosophical study of life outside of the Western-inflected normative sociojuridical and even humanitarian conceptions of life, especially in the locales of the non-West. The in-between for many Black migrants in West Africa represents a refuge from forces conspiring to polarize their geographic positioning. By polarization, I am referring to the programmatic and juridical actions by the state and the humanitarian regime to pull migrants into one or the other, to capture and sequestrate migrants within one of the two opposing poles of the global antimigrant apparatus. That these actions include racializing surveillance by the Nigerien state and accompanying antimovement measures, such as voluntary repatriation in exchange for care in a migrant camp, demonstrates the dire situation migrants face when they both evade the police and eschew the humanitarian.

Through the concept of and concern for the in-between, I want to advance an analytical focus on Blackness interned in the middle of all its movements and critical study of how that space functions as a place that is bounded and defined by the subjectivities of being both outside of home and outside of a future, unrealized home, as well as outside of the normalizing structures within the global postcolonial, neoliberal environment. People residing within that intermediate space experience acute effects on the *condition* of Blackness vis-à-vis their movement (dis)possibilities. This intermediate zone does not necessarily define Black life, but it shapes it and influences it, as much as it may protect it and the dreams of reaching elsewhere, to which Black migrants may cling. Echoing Katherine McKittrick, Black lives are "necessarily geographic," as Black Africans embody spatiality on several registers.[56] African Blackness shares important connections and histories with diasporic Black peoples, and Black identity is constituted through transnational histories and within transnational understandings of race and Blackness. The categorization of "migrant," of course, renders the lives of Black African migrants as extrinsically geographic, as the word *migrant* describes a sort of movement across sovereign space. What I want to highlight and what the in-between gestures to is that the restriction of movement of Black peoples also has geographic manifestations. Black movement is geographic, and the unmovement that Black migrants like Malcolm and Morris experience in Niger results in geographic dispossibilities, charting alternative sets of spatial realities that concede the nation-state and citizenship-based normative modalities of life in favor of existing outside of those destructive normative modes.

Conceptualizing Black Geographies in Black Africa

What is at stake in this project, and what does it have to do with Black Geographies? Blackness is ontologically and diametrically opposed to the nation-state, no matter "where" the nation-state is or how Black are the people who constitute it. The misrecognition or illegibility of Blackness as human and, similarly, the illegibility of "migrants" as belonging to a place subjects Black migrants to the purgatory of existence that is *lower than* that of white peoples (e.g., in Europe) or Nigeriens in Niger; their gender and sexual identities as illegitimate denizens of the national territory form part of the perception that they are biologically deviant, diseased, and immoral persons. Their sexuality and gender are immediately and always pathological in relation to the white heteronormative nation-state, and a countergeographic praxis of mapping speaks to this queered racio-sexual imaginary and representation of the illegal Black migrant. I spoke with several migrants who told me that they navigate between these forms of carcerality and attempt to make space within the interstices of these forms of oppression. Malcolm and Morris, as well as others, live in Niamey without papers and, therefore, without the security citizenship endows to all citizened persons. As a result, they effectively live in the terra nullius of life, a subjecthood that is both in direct opposition to and still subject to the state. The in-between spaces are outside the contours of the state but are still subject to the state, producing a contingency of subjectivity, migrant safety, and even migrant autonomy. All is precarious and unsettled. In this in-between, there is no rest, and unlike the lack of rest that citizens experience from trying to remain in place in the fast-moving neoliberal hamster wheel of high economic needs with little economic opportunity or security, these Black migrants do not have the appurtenances of citizenship (e.g., access to the welfare state, access to jobs) on which to rely.

A Black geographic praxis that attends to the political and the poetic is an analytical (and ethnographic) focus on Blackness *in between* and the in-betweenness that Blackness can create and occupy. What does this mean? According to McKittrick, "Space and place give Black lives meaning."[57] Here, I contend that movement does as well. Approaching studies of lived Black geographic kinesis from the *middle* of movement through space, as well as examining the in-between as both a space and a place, may tell us a lot about how Blackness and Black peoples engage with movement between various political and sociojuridical structures. Black movement and inhabitance of the in-between represent a *politics* of living alternative geographies, charting different futures, and ultimately doing otherwise.

Notes

1   Brachet, "Constructions of Territoriality in the Sahara," 240.

2   Browne, *Dark Matters*, 16.

3   Fanon, *Black Skin, White Masks*, 89.

4   Wright, *Physics of Blackness*, 2.

5   Pierre, *Predicament of Blackness*, 157.

6   Matory, "Afro-Atlantic Culture," 36–44.

7   Price, *Becoming Rasta*, 27.

8   Goldberg, *Threat of Race*, 67.

9   Ake, "What Is the Problem of Ethnicity in Africa?," 1. See also Ojo, "Beyond Diversity"; Coetzee et al., "Facial-Based Ethnic Recognition," 464–66.

10 Silverstein, "Immigrant Racialization and the New Savage Slot," 364; Winant, *New Politics of Race*, 94–107.

11 Trouillot, "Anthropology and the Savage Slot," 17–45.

12 Trouillot, *Global Transformations*, 18.

13 Throughout this chapter, I use the term *Black Africa* rather than *sub-Saharan Africa*, which emerged in the 1950s as a replacement for the racially charged term *Black Africa*. However, today, owing to the West's overall reluctance to address race and anti-Black racism, while Western studies of the continent simultaneously attempt to efface the racial characteristics of Africans, *Black Africa* is a more direct term that forces all to reckon with the actual peoples of Africa as raced beings. *Sub-Saharan* divides Africa via Euro-American (white) notions of race and reifies North Africa as a space of proximal whiteness, while separating the rest of Africa as Black without acknowledging such. Similarly, I use the term *Black Africans* instead of merely *Africans* to avoid the slippage that occurs when *African* is equated with *Black*. This slippage elides the various groups of Africans that do not necessarily fall into the racial category of Black and, more important, refuse that categorization. For example, in Niger, there is a sizable Arab population as well as a large Tuareg (Berber) population, of which some within the ethnoculture are coded as "white" Tuaregs while others are phenotypically and racially considered Black. Thus, to highlight this distinction and simultaneously refuse the racial assumption that African means Black, I use *Black African* when precisely talking about Blacks to the exclusion of Arabs and certain Tuareg peoples. While many of these peoples are indigenous to the continent, many of them are not Black and therefore are not exposed to the same vulnerabilities and demanding stereotypes as are Black African migrants in Niger.

14 Silverstein, "Immigrant Racialization and the New Savage Slot," 364; Browne, *Dark Matters*, 38.

15 Winant, "Modern World Racial System in Transition," 100.

16 Winant, "Modern World Racial System in Transition," 101.

17 Pierre and Niaufre, "L'Afrique et la question de la blackness," 85.

18 Gaibazzi, "West African Strangers," 475.

19 Various interlocutors mentioned that the police would often ask for inconsistent fine amounts from migrants they had arrested, and that those amounts were negotiated between police and migrants, calling into question the legality and legitimacy of the fines.

20 Adepoju, "Migration in West Africa."

21 Andersson, *Illegality, Inc.*, 7.

22 Brachet, "Policing the Desert," 10.

23 Frowd, "Developmental Borderwork," 1662–63.

24 Jegen, *Political Economy of Migration Governance in Niger*, 8–22.

25 Loi n° 2015–36 du 26 mai 2015, https://sherloc.unodc.org/cld/uploads/res
    /document/ner/2015/loi_relative_au_trafic_illicite_de_migrants_html/Loi
    _N2015-36_relative_au_trafic_illicite_de_migrants.pdf.

26 Collyer, "In-Between Places," 669.

27 Brachet, "Constructions of Territoriality in the Sahara," 242.

28 Maryland adopted the RealID card system in 2016; the RealID federal law was
    passed in 2005 in response to the terrorist attacks of September 11, 2001; Mar-
    bella, "Is Your Driver's License Up to Speed?"

29 Pierre, *Predicament of Blackness*, 40.

30 Perhaps the card's Englishness, denoting specific geographies of foreignness that
    are outside of West Africa, may have elevated me beyond the possible categori-
    zation of "migrant" myself. The name USA is written in small letters perpendic-
    ular to the much larger name MARYLAND at the top of the card.

31 Göpfert, "Surveillance in Niger," 51.

32 Bigo, "Security and Immigration," 81.

33 Browne, *Dark Matters*, 38.

34 Beek and Göpfert, "Police Violence in West Africa," 477.

35 Conteh-Morgan, "Danger of Supplementing Aid to Africa with Weapons."

36 Landau, Kihato, and Postel, *Future of Mobility and Migration*.

37 International Organization for Migration, "German Chancellor Visits IOM
    Transit Centre in Niger."

38 Dean, "Migration after Rebellion in Niger."

39 Chua, *In Pursuit of the Good Life*, 154.

40 Fassin, "Compassion and Repression," 375.

41 Browne, *Dark Matters*, 21.

42 Aas, "'Crimmigrant' Bodies and Bona Fide Travelers," 332. See also Stumpf,
    Crimmigration Crisis, 367.

43 Browne, *Dark Matters*, 21.

44 Aas, "'Crimmigrant' Bodies and Bona Fide Travelers," 332. To see how the
    notions of "illegality" and frequent criminalization of migrants contribute to
    their vulnerability to state violence, see also Willen, "Migration, 'Illegality,' and
    Health."

45 "Algeria Accused of Abandoning More Than 13,000 Migrants."

46 Castañeda et al., "Immigration as a Social Determinant of Health," 378. See also
    Fleischman et al., "Migration as a Social Determinant of Health for Irregular
    Migrants," 90.

47 hooks, "Zora Neale Hurston," 22.

48 Boyce Davies, *Black Women, Writing and Identity*, 149.

49 McKittrick, "Plantation Futures," 11.

50 Allen, Lawhon, and Pierce, "Placing Race," 1001–19.

51 Martin, "'Place-Framing' as Place-Making," 730–33.

52 McKittrick, *Demonic Grounds*, 49.

53 McKittrick, *Demonic Grounds*, 43.

54 McKittrick, *Demonic Grounds*, 44.

55 McKittrick, *Demonic Grounds*, 132–33.

56 McKittrick, *Demonic Grounds*, xiii.

57 McKittrick, *Demonic Grounds*, xiii.

Bibliography

Aas, Katja Franko. "'Crimmigrant' Bodies and Bona Fide Travelers: Surveillance, Citizenship and Global Governance." *Theoretical Criminology* 15, no. 3 (2011): 331–46.

Adepoju, Aderanti. "Migration in West Africa." *Development* 46, no. 3 (2003): 37–41.

Ake, Claude. "What Is the Problem of Ethnicity in Africa?" *Transformation* 22 (1993): 1–14.

"Algeria Accused of Abandoning More Than 13,000 Migrants in Sahara Desert without Food or Water." *Independent*, June 25, 2018. https://www.independent .co.uk/news/world/africa/algeria-migrants-sahara-desert-denies-women -children-without-food-drink-a8415681.html.

Allen, Douglas, Mary Lawhon, and Joseph Pierce. "Placing Race: On the Resonance of Place with Black Geographies." *Progress in Human Geography* 43, no. 6 (2019): 1001–19.

Andersson, Ruben. *Illegality, Inc.: Clandestine Migration and the Business of Bordering Europe*. Oakland: University of California Press, 2014.

Beek, Jan, and Mirco Göpfert. "Police Violence in West Africa: Perpetrators' and Ethnographers' Dilemmas." *Ethnography* 14, no. 4 (2013): 477–500.

Bigo, Didier. "Security and Immigration: "Toward a Critique of the Governmental- ity of Unease." *Alternatives: Global, Local, Political* 27 (2002): 63–92.

Boyce Davies, Carole. *Black Women, Writing and Identity: Migrations of the Subject*. 1994. New York: Routledge, 2002.

Brachet, Julien. "Constructions of Territoriality in the Sahara: The Transformation of Spaces of Transit." *Vienna Journal of African Studies* 8 (2005): 236–53.

Brachet, Julien. "Policing the Desert: The IOM in Libya beyond War and Peace." *Antipode* 48, no. 2 (2015): 1–21.

Browne, Simone. *Dark Matters: On the Surveillance of Blackness*. Durham, NC: Duke University Press, 2015.

Castañeda, Heide, Seth M. Holmes, Daniel S. Madrigal, Maria-Elena D. Young, Naomi Beyeler, and James Quesada. "Immigration as a Social Determinant of Health." *Annual Review of Public Health* 36 (2015): 375–92.

Chua, Jocelyn L. *In Pursuit of the Good Life: Aspiration and Suicide in Globalizing South India*. Berkeley: University of California Press, 2014.

Coetzee, Vinet, Jaco M. Greeff, Louise Barrett, and S. Peter Henzi. "Facial-Based Ethnic Recognition: Insights from Two Closely Related but Ethnically Distinct Groups." *South African Journal of Science* 105, nos. 11–12 (2009): 464–66.

Collyer, Michael. "In-Between Places: Trans-Saharan Transit Migrants in Morocco and the Fragmented Journey to Europe." *Antipode* 39, no. 4 (2007): 668–90.

Conteh-Morgan, Earl. "The Danger of Supplementing Aid to Africa with Weapons." *IPI Global Observatory*, August 15, 2017. https://theglobalobservatory.org/2017/08/aid-weapons-merkel-ecowas-g-20/.

Dean, Laura. "Migration after Rebellion in Niger." *International Reporting Project*, June 6, 2017. https://internationalreportingproject.org/stories/view/in-agadez.

Fanon, Frantz. *Black Skin, White Masks*. London: Paladin, 1970.

Fassin, Didier. "Compassion and Repression: The Moral Economy of Immigration Policies in France." *Cultural Anthropology* 20 (2005): 362–87.

Fleischman, Yonina, Sarah Willen, Nadav Davidovitch, and Zohar Mor. "Migration as a Social Determinant of Health for Irregular Migrants: Israel as Case Study." *Social Science and Medicine* 147 (2015): 89–97.

Frowd, Philippe M. "Developmental Borderwork and the International Organization for Migration." *Journal of Ethnic and Migration Studies* 44, no. 10 (2018): 1656–72.

Gaibazzi, Paolo. "West African Strangers and the Politics of Inhumanity in Angola." *American Ethnologist* 45, no. 4 (2018): 470–81.

Goldberg, David T. *The Threat of Race: Reflections on Racial Neoliberalism*. Malden, MA: Wiley-Blackwell, 2009.

Göpfert, Mirco. "Surveillance in Niger: Gendarmes and the Problem of 'Seeing Things.'" *African Studies Review* 59, no. 2 (2016): 39–57.

hooks, bell. "Zora Neale Hurston: A Subversive Reading." *Matatu: Journal for African Culture and Writing* 3, no. 6 (1989): 22.

International Organization for Migration. "German Chancellor Visits IOM Transit Centre in Niger." October 11, 2016. https://www.iom.int/news/german-chancellor-visits-iom-transit-centre-niger.

International Organization for Migration. "IOM Transit Centers in Niger." January 26, 2017. https://www.iom.int/video/iom-transit-centers-niger.

Jegen, Leonie. *The Political Economy of Migration Governance in Niger*. Freiburg, Germany: Arnold Bergstraesser Institute, 2019.

Landau, Loren B., Caroline Wanjiku Kihato, and Hannah Postel. *The Future of Mobility and Migration within and from Sub-Saharan Africa*. Princeton, NJ: Liechtenstein Institute on Self-Determination, 2019.

Marbella, Jean. "Is Your Driver's License Up to Speed? Real ID Requirements Cause Confusion in Maryland." *Baltimore Sun*, May 11, 2019. https://www.baltimoresun.com/maryland/bs-md-real-id-problems-20190510-story.html.

Martin, Deborah G. "'Place-Framing' as Place-Making: Constituting a Neighborhood for Organizing and Activism." *Annals of the Association of American Geographers* 93, no. 3 (2003): 730–50.

Matory, J. Lorand. "Afro-Atlantic Culture: On the Live Dialogue between Africa and the Americas." In *Africana: The Encyclopedia of the African and African American Experience*, edited by Kwame Anthony Appiah and Henry Louis Gates Jr., 36–44. New York: Basic Civitas Books, 1999.

McKittrick, Katherine. *Demonic Grounds: Black Women and the Cartographies of Struggle*. Minneapolis: University of Minnesota Press, 2006.

McKittrick, Katherine. "Plantation Futures." *Small Axe* 17 (2013): 1–15.

Ojo, Olatunji. "Beyond Diversity: Women, Scarification, and Yoruba Identity." *History in Africa* 35 (2008): 347–74.

Pierre, Jemima. *The Predicament of Blackness: Postcolonial Ghana and the Politics of Race*. Chicago: University of Chicago Press, 2013.

Pierre, Jemima, and Camille Niaufre. "L'Afrique et la question de la blackness: Exemples du Ghana." *Politique africaine* 4 (2014): 83–103.

Price, Charles. *Becoming Rasta: Origins of Rastafari Identity in Jamaica*. New York: NYU Press, 2009.

Silverstein, Paul A. "Immigrant Racialization and the New Savage Slot: Race, Migration, and Immigration in the New Europe." *Annual Review of Anthropology* 34 (2005): 363–84.

Stumpf, Juliet. "The Crimmigration Crisis: Immigrants, Crime and Sovereign Power." *American University Law Review* 56, no. 2 (2006): 367–419.

Trouillot, Michel-Rolph. "Anthropology and the Savage Slot: The Poetics and Politics of Otherness." In *Recapturing Anthropology: Working in the Present*, edited by Richard G. Fox, 17–45. Santa Fe, NM: School of American Research, 1991.

Trouillot, Michel-Rolph. *Global Transformations: Anthropology and the Modern World*. New York: Palgrave Macmillan, 2003.

Willen, Sarah S. "Migration, 'Illegality,' and Health: Mapping Embodied Vulnerability and Debating Health-Related Deservingness." *Social Science and Medicine* 74, no. 6 (2011): 805–11.

Winant, Howard. "The Modern World Racial System in Transition." In *Rethinking Anti-racisms: From Theory to Practice*, edited by Floya Anthias and Cathie Lloyd, 100–110. New York: Routledge, 2002.

Winant, Howard. *The New Politics of Race: Globalism, Difference, Justice*. Minneapolis: University of Minnesota Press, 2004.

Wright, Michelle M. *Physics of Blackness: Beyond the Middle Passage Epistemology*. Minneapolis: University of Minnesota Press, 2015.

5

Words Re(en)visioned

Black and Indigenous Languages for Autonomy

DIANA NEGRÍN

Inhuac tlahtolli ye miqui,	*When a language dies,*
cemihcac motzacuah	*then, a window, a door closes*
nohuian altepepan	*For all peoples of the world.*
in tlanexillotl, in quixohuayan.	*A glance*
In ye tlamahuizolo	*in a different way*
occetica	*at everything that exists*
in mochi mani ihuan yoli in tlalticpac.	*and is life on earth.*

—MIGUEL LEÓN-PORTILLA, "Cuando muere una lengua," 1998

Now it is the intellectuals of Man who "own the Word," while, like pre-Renaissance lay intellectuals, it is the "native" intellectuals who now have only the use of Man's Word, who therefore can only "echo."

—SYLVIA WYNTER, "Unsettling the Coloniality of Being/Power/Truth/Freedom," 2003

We speak of linguistic revitalization, but who will speak those languages when they are killing us, the speakers? If us, the speakers, are being dispossessed of all that we name?

—SELENE GALINDO, O'dam speech given at State Congress of Durango, 2019

But Chicano Spanish is a border tongue which developed naturally. Change, *evolución, enriquecimiento de palabras nuevas por invención o adopción* have created variants of Chicano Spanish, *un nuevo lenguaje. Un lenguaje que corresponde a un modo de vivir.* Chicano Spanish is not incorrect, it is a living language.

—GLORIA ANZALDÚA, "How to Tame a Wild Tongue," 1987

During the last three hundred years, the African American working class has daily constructed their vision of a non-oppressive society through a variety of cultural practices, institution-building activities, and social movements. By doing so, they have created an intellectual and social space in which they could discuss, plan, and organize this new world. The blues are the cries of a new society being born.

—CLYDE WOODS, *Development Arrested: The Blues and Plantation Power in the Mississippi Delta*, 2017

[The Rastafarians] learned to speak a new language. And they spoke it with a vengeance. They learned to speak and sing. And in so doing, they did not assume that their only cultural resources lay in the past.

—STUART HALL, "On Postmodernism and Articulation," 1986

In January 2019, the United Nations General Assembly declared the International Year of Indigenous Languages based on recommendations made by the institution's Permanent Forum on Indigenous Issues. This declaration—which has now been catapulted into a decade of promotion of Indigenous languages—was a response to the disappearance of nearly 40 percent of the world's estimated sixty-seven hundred languages. The declaration affirms that "the complex knowledges and cultures [Indigenous languages] foster are increasingly being recognized as strategic resources for good governance, peace building, reconciliation, and sustainable development."[1] This announcement rippled through some halls of power concerned with expanding the rights of Indigenous peoples and, as 2019 unfolded, multiple cultural and academic activities in Latin America took place to bring attention to the threatened survival of Indigenous languages in the colonized hemisphere.

On October 3, 2019, Selene Galindo, an O'dam cultural anthropologist and filmmaker from the locality of Mezquitán in the northwestern Mexican state of Durango, stood before legislators and gave a brief speech in her native language as part of the state government's own recognition of the UN's themed call. With her dyed blue hair and traditional O'dam dress, Galindo elegantly critiqued the abstraction of official linguistic celebrations: "I would have liked to have spoken about the language itself, the pretty things about it." Life is at the center of language, and revitalization is meaningless if the lives of the speakers are considered superfluous within the context of the economic, political, and cultural violence that is omnipresent in so many of the communities that hold what are increasingly labeled endangered languages. Further, Galindo noted how language exists in relation to territory: "Our languages are tied to a territory that we can no longer access, to a house to which we can no longer return, to all that is and once was there and that we can no longer name, that hurts to name." She could have followed the more traditional protocol of using this platform to recite verses in O'dam and to speak of the "pretty things." But instead she signaled the complicity of state actors with the violence of the drug economy and its associated international war on drugs that has threatened, killed, and displaced ancestral O'dam communities: "Or do we speak of a linguistic revitalization in which we need to begin to create new words for the AK-47s and the bazookas and the grenades?" How could the world speak of linguistic revitalization and at the same time not confront the conditions of violence and dispossession the speakers of these languages endure, negotiate, and resist?

Following Katherine McKittrick and Clyde Woods's call for the creation of a "global community of scholars," and considering Sylvia Wynter's insistence on a Black and Indigenous "third perspective," this chapter threads together some conceptual possibilities that exist in the convergence of critical Black and Indigenous scholarship as these draw on decolonizing alternatives to centuries of violence waged upon Black and Indigenous geographies.[2] Placing these critical voices together provides an opportunity for dialogue, one that weaves together distinct traditions of decolonial thought and practice that can provide what Wynter calls an "autonomy of cognition."[3] Here, I center the role of language and forms of orality as sources of knowledge that contain key elements for decolonial and autonomous praxis. I do this by holding a dialogue between Black geographic scholarship linked to a "third perspective" and Indigenous linguistic concepts that manifest both a poetics and a construction of livelihoods that uphold the Zapatista phrase that "another world is possible."

I concur with Tiffany Lethabo King's emphasis that Black and Indigenous peoples and epistemologies must not be brought together solely through "their separate and respective emergences."[4] I write attentive to the reality that Black peoples are also Indigenous peoples native to various geographies, and I thus invite scholars to more readily engage the interconnections between Black and Indigenous scholarship. By curating the present dialogue, I push against academic and real-world borders that continue to limit the "unexpected openings" that emerge when "different voices are brought into relationship" and, in this convergence, interrupt hegemonic and colonial structures of space and belonging, and create "new worlds antithetical to the exploitative aims of the agents of capitalism."[5] Beyond creating an interruption to Man's "overrepresented" voice, my focus on language is an attempt to write beyond the ongoing presence of violence by paying attention to the ways in which forms of orality are a "terrain through which different geographic stories can be and are told."[6] Through a dialogue that threads together Black geographic thought and Indigenous linguistic concepts, I seek to shine a light on examples of cognitive autonomy and cultural and political possibility. By no means is this an exhaustive study of critical geography and its relationship to language and orality; rather, it is an initial effort and invitation to contribute to spatial thinking by drawing on the liberatory thought and praxis of Black and Indigenous epistemic traditions. The present text is thus a working dialogue that reflects on the ways that language—in its spoken, written, or sung forms—advances "a different way of knowing and imagining the world."[7] In doing so, it presents autonomous articulations of space, movement, and "life politics."[8]

Epistemic Redescriptions

Raúl Zibechi remarks that the forms of colonialism that communities of the broadly diverse Global South experience today are expressed through the extractive industry and megaprojects, the neo–plantation economy, and the imposition of the power of the state through the use of police and military forces.[9] Selene Galindo's O'dam community sits at the crossroads of these forces, yet, in the diaspora, she holds to her language so that she can remember the "pretty things" and resist disappearance through activating a political struggle that is inseparable from the commitment to preserve other ways of knowing and inhabiting the world. Language is not only a form of expression but is a "constitutive element of culture" and a "weapon of political struggle" within the context of settler colonialism and the global diasporas that have formed through ongoing structures of dispossession.[10] Language, in its various spoken, sung, and written forms, is intrinsically tied to knowledge. If, as Sylvia Wynter cautions, our language is limited to "the Man's Word," then we run the danger of only murmuring "echoes" of "Man" as "the Western bourgeois conception of the human" that, through the workings of the long colonial project, has managed to "overrepresent itself as if it were the human itself."[11]

The polyvalent project of decolonization, then, inescapably implies a preservation, recovery, and creation of words and languages that provide autonomy and dignity for the lives of those peoples who have survived hundreds of years of linguistic, cultural, political, and economic violence. With this omnipresent violence as a backdrop, Fred Moten suggests Black musical and performative traditions as illustrative of the "power to speak and break speech" by the commodified Black subject whose act of speech carries the capacity of "revaluation and reconstruction of value."[12] Beyond a breaking of speech, language permits the articulation of subjectivities that create a counterposition and a place beyond the reach of hegemonic society. Stuart Hall makes this clear when referring to the articulation of the Rastafarian tradition in Jamaica: "They learned to speak a new language. And they spoke it with a vengeance. They learned to speak and sing. And in so doing, they did not assume that their only cultural resources lay in the past."[13] Decolonization can thus speak through the polyvalent openings found in language and oral expression and its capacity to provide what Édouard Glissant identifies as opacity and what the Congreso Nacional Indígena and the Zapatistas express through the lexicon of autonomy—thus gathering rooted and routed traditions to create languages and spaces for liberation in the present and future.

In light of deep colonial wounds, Gloria Anzaldúa expresses how the experience of shame toward her mother tongue and its systemic silencing taught her that language is intricately tied to one's sense of self: "I am my language" and "I will have my voice."[14] Within settler colonial society, to claim or reclaim language is a profoundly political act at both an intimate and a collective scale. Linda Tuhiwai Smith emphasizes that to decolonize is to "center our concerns and world views" in order to create theory and praxis that responds to the purposes of colonized and formally colonized peoples.[15] The "decolonizing methodologies" that Tuhiwai Smith discusses are innately tied to narrative forms that exist beyond the confines of coloniality and demonstrate the resilience of orality despite the material impositions and spatial displacements of the colonial political economy. Sharing parallels with Moten's description of Black music as a "sounded critique of the theory of value," Clyde Woods's blues epistemology becomes a powerful "ethnoregional" response and critique to the still hegemonic "plantation bloc," utilizing words, sounds, and movements that present a "theory of social and economic development and change."[16] The blues epistemology crystallizes an alternate narrative of a lived geography, an autonomous selfhood, and collective politics that exists within Black and Indigenous oral traditions, both prior to conquest, during colonialism, and in the transformation away from coloniality.

Wynter notes that "we cannot 'unsettle' a 'coloniality of power' without a redescription of the human outside the terms of our present descriptive statement of the human"—one in which Europe, the West, and capitalism have all been "overrepresented."[17] In a similar vein, Glissant asserts the need to "return to the sources of our cultures and the mobility of their relational content" as a means of confronting the chaos of ongoing conditions of coloniality.[18] In this chapter, I suggest that this redescription can find answers in linguistic traditions and their contemporary critical redeployment that name conditions of oppression and liberation while dignifying the experiences of those who confront dispossession through everyday forms of state and social power. The contention is that a redescription of our being requires a decolonial focus whose end point is not to create a new hegemonic narrative, but to work for multiple articulations in which "emancipatory knowledges" are found in the "worldviews" and in the "experiences of life/resistance" of Indigenous, Black, and mestizo peoples.[19] Boaventura de Sousa Santos states that the Global South—understood as a broad, decentered geography that is a metaphor for suffering and survivance—must uplift its "ecologies of knowledge" as part of a political project based on an ontological and epistemological transition: a decolonization.[20] Orality and language can thus be understood as a form of epistemic redescription that stretches ideas of space, identity, and belonging by way of pushing against the grain of the colonial imaginary. Ultimately, the opacity that exists within linguistic and oral praxis provides space for autonomy while becoming an emergent cultural and political project at once.

Oral Tradition and Resilience

In addition to informing their daily lives and the life of the United States as a nation, their vision of social, economic, and cultural affirmation and justice is the mother of several global languages and philosophical systems commonly known as the blues, jazz, rock and roll, and soul.

—CLYDE WOODS, *Development Arrested*, 2017

In his discussion of "epistemologies of the south," Boaventura de Sousa Santos points to the limited capacity that northern intellectual thought has for meeting the political, economic, and social crises that societies are confronting across the globe. Specifically, he criticizes the breadth of "strong questions" that are nonetheless accompanied by a proliferation of "weak answers."[21] Noting this weakness, Santos urges use of a theoretical praxis that is rooted in popular, situated yet rhizomatic, decolonial epistemologies, languages, and political alternatives. He refers to a South that is "a metaphor of unjust and systematic suffering caused by capitalism, colonialism and patriarchy."[22] But this South is not mere victim; instead, it is an active resister to these various forms of oppression. This South is not a delineated geographic area but a concept that critically relates the conditions of life and death of communities from across the globe, not by collapsing them into homogeneous subalterns but by recognizing their vast heterogeneity and continued existence under threats and practices of dispossession. Much as when we utilize the term *Indigenous*, it is important to acknowledge that there is no uniform experience of what it means to inhabit the South. Nonetheless, unifying categories like Indigenous can become strategic by being "politicized as a powerful signifier of oppositional identity."[23] Speaking and practicing epistemologies of the South, blues epistemologies, or Indigenous epistemologies articulates the idea that liberation is enunciable, possible, and unifying.

In her discussion of the "overrepresentation" of Western Man, Sylvia Wynter motions that all our contemporary struggles—from global warming to poverty—are "differing facets of the central ethnoclass Man vs. Human struggle."[24] For Wynter, this struggle identifies the need for oppressed people to restore "full cognitive autonomy and behavioral autonomy" that was distorted or lost as the secularizing forces of the Enlightenment and the birth of the biological sciences edified a language that would be globalized through imperialism and made common sense through settler colonialism.[25] In her contemplation of the "origin of the Americas," Wynter pauses on the effects of the "juridico-theological order" imposed on the so-called New World, which placed the celestial and terrestrial worlds in opposition to one another, thereby creating a universalized "subjective understanding" of the world that was to be transparently transferred to different places of the globe.[26] The imposition of both Christian and Western juridical worldviews on life on Earth presents a particular problem as it relates to language. As we will see in the ensuing pages, the Wixarika language is fundamentally nonsecular and multilayered by being anchored to a cosmogony that unites the celestial and terrestrial realms. For in Wixarika tradition, materiality (most appreciated in agricultural labor) is intricately tied to spiritual practice and to a collective relationship with the ancestors who themselves are anchored to territory. As with other Indigenous peoples, for Wixaritari (plural), the ability to speak one's native tongue translates into the ability to participate in ceremonies and endure arduous pilgrimages that irreplaceably inform the collective community's broader political and economic sustenance.

The languages that have evaded disappearance and re-created themselves across space and time through permanence and hybridization offer an example of a "third perspective" that Wynter positions as a "new synchronizing cultural matrix of the now-emerging world civilization of the Caribbean and the Americas."[27] This leads us to Black and Indigenous geographies and geographic thought as modes of critical expression that are able to reach across the very real overlapping physical, human, and disciplinary borders that we live with today, becoming models through which a "new society" is born.[28] Undoubtedly, the Western Hemisphere uniquely exemplifies the creation of new societies, many of which have sprung forth with the intention of liberation and autonomous life, such as the notable cases of the Zapatista and Maroon communities.[29] This envisioning of another world and a way of inhabiting it occurs in autonomous communities that present an exit from the confines propelled by the incipient colonial capitalism of earlier centuries or the neoliberal nation-state. Alternately, Gloria Anzaldúa shows us how a nurturing of one's cognitive autonomy is related to the reclaiming of words that can liberate the colonized. Most famously, Anzaldúa theorized *nepantla,* a Náhuatl word that roughly translates to "in between," as a "threshold" space that can enable personal empowerment and provoke "new forms of community and new types of social action."[30] Much like King's use of the shoal, *nepantla* connotes physical and psychic spaces that exist in relation to one another and that are always in emergence. For King, the shoal is "a place and time of liminality where one becomes an ecotone, a space of transition between distinct ecological systems and states. A place to come to terms with a changing terrain that demands that you both walk and swim to shore—and whatever the shore may bring."[31] In this way, the *nepantla* and the shoal are geographic spaces that can invoke in-betweenness and a state of ongoing formation that, despite not having any guarantees, permit the possibility for the birth and continuity of "other worlds."

This envisioning of "other worlds" also shows up in the public realm, in state capitals where words of protest rage after yet another violation, whether the construction of contested development projects or in response to continuing police brutality across all Black communities of the hemisphere. Bodies converge, and the spoken word—ancient and new—becomes a strategy for reframing, survivance, and collective decolonization.[32] Following Woods's articulation of blues epistemologies, it is possible to understand how forms of oral expression contain the wisdom on which new social relations are constructed, even under conditions of severe oppression.[33] For instance, Tuhiwai Smith points to the ways in which song and the practice of naming are intricately tied to Maori identity and territorial belonging: the land is sung into existence, while mountains and ancestors become geographic, political, and genealogical identifiers.[34] Similar to Selene Galindo's warning to the congress members, Indigenous identities and languages exist in relation to place; dispossession thus presents a painful challenge when one must remember how to name those elements of life that are no longer tangible.

In light of this dispossession, the blues demonstrates the power of transcendence in the spoken and sung word, as well as its ability to pull from distinct roots in order to create new traditions linked to geographies that hold opportunity and foreclosure at once. As such, Woods takes note of the oral tradition's centrality in shaping our social, political, and economic envisioning. Music is thus a key element of orality that traveled, faced silencing, yet still sprung forward dynamically: "In various parts of Africa, griots, musical families, and orchestras serve as historians, genealogies, counselors, reporters, diplomats, and social, cultural, and economic innovators. It was not a great leap from the stringed instruments of Africa to the diddly bo, the violin, the banjo, and, later, the guitar in the Americas. Despite intense efforts at suppression, the African musical sensibility and scale were preserved."[35] What Woods brings to the surface so poignantly in *Development Arrested* are the ways in which the blues provided an outlet for expression and autonomy for Black people in the Mississippi Delta and their subsequent northward diaspora. Returning to Santos, the knowledge systems of the West only partially provide the language that can offer the necessary description of suffering or the pathways for change that communities of the South require. Conversely, languages, like the blues, offer both a description and a vision. Wynter references a talk given by Aimé Césaire in 1946 in which he makes a complementary argument by stating his belief that the sciences offered humanity very little knowledge from where to meet the real challenges of the day. Instead, he proposed an elaboration of a "new science" and a new "study of the Word" that offered distinct narratives, codes, and forms of consciousness.[36] In effect, the revitalization of ancient languages and the embrace of emergent oral traditions provide an exceptional path toward the epistemologies that may offer the strong answers that hegemonic language continues to limit. By understanding autonomy as a counterpoint to hegemony, in the following pages I offer a few examples of how Indigenous linguistic concepts and Black geographic thought provide personal and collective forms of autonomous life and, borrowing from Wynter, autonomous cognition.

Autonomy/Movement

I'm possessed of my own spirit / This is the music of the African muse / I just want to be of use to my ancestors.
—ABBEY LINCOLN quoted in Moten, *In the Break*, 2003

Wixarika (singular) religious and socioeconomic organization is intimately related to territorial practices that span various states of northwestern and central Mexico and that continue to direct their political struggles today.[37] Since time immemorial, Wixaritari (plural) have practiced yearly pilgrimages to distinct sacred places related to particular ancestors who are linked to the reproduction of *tukari*, which signifies collective life, vital energy, and spiritual strength. Ancestors continuously manifest themselves in the daily materialities of life through cycles of planting, growth, and harvest and through their connection to specific sacred territories. Each one of these dispersed sacred places, when held in relation, harbors a renewal of ancestral practices and, thus, a reproduction of land-based traditions. Renewing these practices requires personal and collective sacrifice due to the arduous journeys and a series of mandates that are asked along the way, such as fasting, ritual hunting, and service to the community. The interconnectivity between agricultural and ritual practices appears in Wixarika linguistic distinctions between the everyday spoken form and its complex religious counterpart that requires time to learn as well as active participation in religious life. Words thus can be defined along a spectrum—from more literal meanings to textured concepts. For instance, the word *yeiyari* is used to describe walking from one point to another, but it holds deeper conceptual ideas as well. *Yeiyari* "derives from the verb *yeiyá*, to go, walk, traverse, and from the word *'iyari*, the heart that takes form and reflects all sorts of memories by tracing the path marked by the footsteps of Our Collective Ancestors."[38]

Here I want to direct attention to the relationship between cultural, linguistic, and territorial autonomy by emphasizing how the practice of language works reciprocally with the reproduction of land-based cultural, economic, and political life. Although Wixarika communities maintained substantial autonomy during the colonial period due to the combination of steep terrain and a series of rebellions, from the mid-nineteenth century onward, the rise of the Mexican nation-state has perpetuated a series of direct challenges to conceptions and practices linked to Wixarika territory and movement. As private property gained traction, the Repúblicas de Indios of the colonial period were dismantled through a series of land transfers that benefited the new liberal elites whose power grew in a similar form as the "plantation bloc" that Woods analyzes in the Mississippi Delta. Nineteenth-century Mexico was marked by a massive territorial expropriation from Indigenous communities, coupled with continuous rebellion and resistance from these same communities.[39] While Wixaritari were able to maintain legal title to a good portion of their highland communities, the vast territorial network they traversed beyond these spaces was radically reconfigured and continues to be altered to the present date. This is experienced through ongoing conflicts related to land use and series of economic interventions (mining, tourism, agro-industry, and drug trafficking) that affect not only the preservation of ancestral sacred places but also the Wixaritari's own abilities to carry out their pilgrimages across what are now increasingly parceled sections of private property. As with other Indigenous communities of Mexico, the expansion of capitalism and its more recent neoliberal manifestations has decreased the ability of many families to live sustainably in their homelands, making migration to near and far plantations and cities an increasingly important source of survival.

Emigration has caused significant preoccupation over the ability to preserve languages and reproduce ancestral religious practices, which are often place-based. As noted by Selene Galindo, the act of naming objects in one's mother tongue is limited if one cannot maintain a connection with those objects, places, and practices that allow language to be alive. At the same time, both the political and the economic elites and broader mestizo and white society view urban Indigenous peoples as culturally anomalous—albeit economically essential—to city spaces and life. This places Indigenous migrants in a geographic bind caused by an ever-existing hegemonic colonial mentality that limits their political, social, and economic life to the periphery. Indigenous migrants find themselves existing within a *nepantla* state of in-betweenness and liminality—where belonging, dignity, and agency are confronted with a racialized and spatialized common sense that fixes identities to place and status. Increasingly, this is compounded by outright xenophobic attitudes that reject all forms of human migration and reterritorialization.[40]

In contrast, the Wixarika word *makuyeika* offers a counterpoint that provides an exit from spatial confines of citizenship and being. *Makuyeika* is most commonly defined as "he or she who walks in many places." The word speaks to the long tradition of Wixarika movement across territory and the requisite of the pilgrimage for *tukari*—vital energy and life—to be maintained. Francisco Talavera notes in his work on the seasonal migration to the coast of Nayarit that the concept of *makuyeika* dignifies the experience of Wixaritari working under the exploitative conditions of the coastal plantations, by allowing them to see themselves existing beyond the space of just the tobacco fields.[41] While Wixaritari have visited the coast as part of their ancestral pilgrimage to bring offerings to Tatéi Haramara, Our Mother Ocean, and later return to the highlands with salt and other goods, Talavera argues that *makuyeika* provides meaning to the current seasonal movements that now satisfy both economic and cultural purposes.

The word *makuyeika* also embraces the experiences of Wixaritari living outside of their communal territories by allowing them to assert their belonging in more than one place. So while popular discourse and public policy continue to fix Indigenous bodies to specific nonurban and nonmodern spaces, *makuyeika* releases Wixaritari from these confines in a similar vein as the *nepantla* offers a dignified word to affirm Xicanx life on the borderlands. *Makuyeika* permits many young Wixarika urban residents to see themselves as belonging to multiple spheres of public and private life, rural and urban, Western and Wixarika. As a concept, it signals permission of movement within the context of a hegemonic order that seeks a more transparent and fixed geography attached to identity.[42]

Juan Castillo Cocom describes the Maya T'aan (Yucatec Mayan) word *iknal*, which holds strong parallels with *makuyeika*, as "the potential to omnipresence: the state of being present in all places at all times."[43] Like their Wixarika counterparts, the various Indigenous communities grouped under the category of Maya hold a long history of interpellating and resisting coloniality. Castillo Cocom problematizes the ways in which the identities of Mayan peoples have been reduced by academic disciplines, political parties, and the tourist gaze: "Or perhaps I was unsettled by the arbitrariness by which academics split time into recognizable points of reference, as to where exactly forms of Maya Yucatec identity took place—such as the Spanish Conquest and its subsequent imposition of the race concept, the Caste War of the nineteenth century, and the emergence of ethnic politics in the twentieth century."[44] He thus argues for an exit from the ethnogenesis that created the idea of "the Maya" and argues for a (re)integration of the word *iknal* that stands as "an extension of social agency, of *perspective, presence, action,* and *attitude.*"[45] Within the universalizing vision brought by the colonial West, acting out one's *iknal* is a personal "escape from status, from how one fits into social structures": a form of "ethnoexodus."[46] This complements Wynter's insistence that the descriptive-statements-turned-truth made by the Western colonial tradition conditioned modes of being human: "These truths had therefore both commanded obedience and necessitated the individual and collective behaviors by means of which each such order and its mode of being human were brought into existence, produced, and stably reproduced."[47] Castillo Cocom notes that the ethnogenesis of "the Maya" became the index of truth through which popular discourse and political relations would be mediated with the diverse Mayan communities of the Yucatan Peninsula. This concern with the creation of a distinct yet abstracted ethnic identity is shared by Wynter, whose discussion of the "overrepresentation of Man" hinges on the way the *longue durée* of colonialism sought to collapse "all such knowledges of the physical cosmos, all such astronomies, all such geographies" into "ethno-astronomies, ethno-geographies."[48] These knowledge systems thus become a mere echo, a peripheral perspective to the "overrepresented Man."

For this reason, Castillo Cocom emphasizes the limits of utilizing the language of "the Man" as it does not fully attest to the realities of a more heterogeneous Mayan collectivity, one that is also increasingly diasporic. And it is partially due to the diaspora that Castillo Cocom theorizes *iknal* as an important alternative for describing the multiple spaces in which his people live, as its meaning affords a person the ability to be present, physically or not: "With a focus on *presence* . . . one's *iknal* is the embodied *context* and *product* of social relations. Thus, *iknal* has to do with where a person is physically and habitually present but is not caught in the power game of status."[49] Much as in King's discussion of the shoal, *iknal* allows identity to be in movement and to inhabit more than one space. By departing from a distinct epistemological framework, it does not reduce or spatialize ethnic and racialized belonging in the way that Western discourse and practice have attempted to do with their own classificatory systems.

Édouard Glissant argues that "when identity is determined by a root, the emigrant is condemned . . . to being split and flattened," whereas a relational understanding of identity allows for a rhizomatic sense of the self, particularly given the human diasporas that have formed as a product of colonial and capitalist dispossession.[50] While coloniality has continued to fix peoples to specific root identities and geographies, *makuyeika* and *iknal* are two words and concepts that acknowledge fluidity, simultaneity, and a form of emplacement that is linked not to one fixed coordinate, but to many. Perhaps more than ever, these two words reflect the contemporary reality of Indigenous peoples who participate in the cultural, economic, and political life of ancestral and diasporic communities. The sense of openness toward movement and relationality found in these terms provides what Castillo Cocom describes as an exit from the status imposed by colonial and nation-state categories. Fundamentally, by calling on a distinct linguistic tradition, these words offer autonomy from the categorical dictates of where and how identity resides and identifies—itself a potential activator for a different type of "life politics."[51]

Autonomy/Life Politics

One of autonomy's central meanings conveys the capacity for self-determination and rule. Colonialism and different forms of capitalist accumulation have rested on an opposite premise, where containment and elimination of autonomy have been central to its operation. This is most notable in the ways in which Black and Indigenous communities across the Western Hemisphere have continuously struggled for individual and territorial autonomy in the face of powerful political and economic blocs. In the American South this is characterized by the plantation's own omnipresence in society: "The plantation classificatory grid has at its center the planter as the heroic master of a national ethnic, class, gender, and environmental hierarchy."[52] Beyond particular historical and geographic differences, peasant communities throughout Latin America and the Caribbean confronted similar plantation blocs that were reconstituted at different historical moments via new political and economic forms. Clyde Woods's own Gramscian reframing of historical relations in the Mississippi Delta affirms the constant presence of the "blues bloc" as a "working class African American worldview" deeply embedded in geography: "The ontology, or worldview, embedded in these communities has provided a sense of collective self and a tectonic footing from which to oppose and dismantle the American intellectual, cultural, and socioeconomic traditions constructed from the raw material of African American exploitation and denigration."[53] As Woods argues with his theorization of a blues epistemology, the reconstitution of a personal and collective self is greatly expanded through the summoning of a language that can describe, activate, and liberate.

In Chiapas, languages of oppression and resistance have been at the heart of its past five hundred years of history. Like the Mississippi Delta described in Woods's work, the plantation and extractive economy of Chiapas has found multiple ways to maintain its hegemony through time and across federal and regional political regimes. It is no coincidence that the Zapatista rebellion of 1994 was birthed in this southern state's highland communities, themselves survivors of extreme colonial and capitalist violence. Poetics and language have been a central element of Zapatismo, made visible in its globally circulated communiqués or in the everyday exchanges of its base communities.

It is the practice of the everyday language of politics that Mariana Mora takes up in her discussion of *kuxlejal* politics as a "life existence" or "life force" reminiscent of the Wixarika word *tukari*. To hold a fuller understanding of this word as an expression of autonomy, Mora emphasizes the need to understand the pursuit of Zapatista autonomy as part of an intergenerational experience of being racialized, gendered, and spatialized by regional plantations and political institutions.[54] *Kuxlejal* posits a redescription of the ongoing neoliberal present through autonomous and decolonized Zapatista epistemics and practice that activate a collective and autonomous "life politics," exercised through the lens of everyday culture, economics, and politics:

> Autonomy as the foundation of life politics thus is expressed in gathering fallen branches for firewood, in harvesting corn in the fields, in praying for abundant water, . . . in taking care of the children and the

elderly, in sharing memories of past events so as to produce knowledge affecting changes in the present. It is the sum of activities in such arenas that allowed for the dignified reproduction of life, not only as a physical presence but as a series of cultural processes that allow for the perpetuation of *kuxlejal* in its collective form and as a collective force.[55]

In its most essential manifestation, this autonomy becomes articulated through dialogue and practice, by the literal act of walking. Mora engages *kuxlejal* as a form of life politics that holds a spectrum of more precise meanings within the Tzeltal language, yet as a concept it can help articulate a broader project of decolonization by providing a radical alternative to the "dehumanizing conditions of racialized colonial states of being."[56] Resistance is part of an extended way of life, and it lives in the distinct forms of making and practicing politics through an "everyday claimed power to be" that stands in direct contrast to the "overrepresented Man." Again, Mora's discussion of Zapatista autonomy complements Woods's description of the blues epistemology as an essential, life-affirming oppositional response to the "totalizing practices of the plantation's institutions."[57] Much as the word *kuxlejal* is put into practice by Zapatista communities, Black life in the Mississippi Delta has been articulated through embedding political acts into the everyday practices of working on the land, spirituality, orality, and musicality that provide a more dignified reproduction of life. In this case, autonomy is achieved by politics becoming seamlessly embedded in everyday life, and the reproduction of this life politics is a fundamental act of resistance within the hegemonic order of coloniality.

Nepantla, makuyeika, iknal, and *kuxlejal* are examples of words that, by providing a distinct description of the self in the world, can help move those who encounter and enunciate them toward a more "fully realized autonomy of feelings, thoughts, and behaviors."[58] This brief discussion of these words is meant to point toward some of the broader possibilities for radical change through the centering of various decolonial epistemic variations (Indigenous, southern, blues) and their old and new linguistic expressions. Further, *nepantla, makuyeika, iknal*, and *kuxlejal* all incorporate a sense of praxis in space, whether in the Zapatista communities of Chiapas through the everyday acts of autonomous politics or in the affirmation of an autonomous personal identity that embodies its rhizomatic histories and geographies. In her speech at the Durango congress, Selene Galindo told a story of how language is vital for our relations with territory, and she stressed that the threatened disappearance of O'dam is of grave significance: "What we speak, names what we live and how we live." In 1998, renowned Mexican scholar Miguel León-Portilla translated the anonymously written Náhuatl poem *When a Language Dies*, drawing on a lifelong study of Mesoamerican humanities and a deep understanding of the global significance of Indigenous languages in their various forms and depths: "Quinihcuac motzacua nohuian altepepan in tlanexillotl, in quixohuayan / When a language dies, then, a window, a door closes for all peoples of the world." To speak of the transformative or radical capacity of language is thus partly to speak of the "pretty things" (the land, the sacred, the poetic), but it also serves as a potent form of opposition by providing a window and door into personal and collective spaces for autonomy.

Notes

1   United Nations, "2019 International Year of Indigenous Languages," January 12, 2019, https://www.un.org/development/desa/dspd/2019/01/2019-international -year-of-indigenous-languages/.

2   McKittrick and Woods, *Black Geographies and the Politics of Place*; Wynter, "1492: A New World View." By speaking of Black and Indigenous epistemic traditions, language, and orality, I am attentive to the problematic geographic dualism that is created when the word *Indigenous* inherently suggests geographic permanence and nonmovement, while *Blackness* is understood as meaning non-Indigenous and thus foreign, migrant, or displaced. In "Strategic Anti-essentialism," Nandita Sharma works against such a dualism precisely because the geographies of subjectivity are part of the colonial project. Relatedly, in her book *Black Shoals*, Tiffany Lethabo King's theorization of the "shoal" seeks to complicate the association of Blackness with water's spatial liminality and indigeneity solely with territorial rootedness, turning our attention to the shoal as an alternate space that cannot be fixed in place.

3   Wynter, "Unsettling the Coloniality of Being."

4   King, *Black Shoals*, 28.

5   King, *Black Shoals*, 30; Wright, "Morphology of Marronage," 1135.

6   Wynter, "Unsettling the Coloniality of Being"; McKittrick, *Demonic Grounds*, x.

7   McKittrick, *Demonic Grounds*, xxvi.

8   Mora, *Kuxlejal Politics*.

9   Zibechi, "Movimientos antisistémicos y descolonialidad," 105.

10 Fernández and Sepúlveda, "Pueblos indígenas, saberes y descolonización," 4.

11 Wynter, "Unsettling the Coloniality of Being," 260.

12 Moten, *In the Break*, 14–17.

13 Hall, "On Postmodernism and Articulation," 54.

14 Anzaldúa, "How to Tame a Wild Tongue," 30–40.

15 Tuhiwai Smith, *Decolonizing Methodologies*, 41.

16 Woods, *Development Arrested*, 17–20.

17 Wynter, "Unsettling the Coloniality of Being."

18 Glissant, *Poetics of Relation*, 126.

19 Zibechi, "Movimientos antisistémicos y descolonialidad," 113.

20 Santos, "Construyendo la contrahegemonía," 30.

21 Santos, "Introducción," 14.

22 Santos, "Construyendo la contrahegemonía," 30.

23 Tuhiwai Smith, *Decolonizing Methodologies*, 6. In recent years, some constitutional recognitions have been won in Latin American countries that recognize Afro-descendant populations as Indigenous peoples. Under the presidency of Andrés Manuel López Obrador, who was elected in 2018, Mexico is undergoing a major reform to grant Indigenous and Afro-descendants new rights to political, economic, cultural, and territorial autonomy.

24 Wynter, "Unsettling the Coloniality of Being," 261.

25 Wynter, "Unsettling the Coloniality of Being," 260.

26 Wynter, "1492: A New World View," 26.

27 Wynter, "1492: A New World View," 9.

28 Woods, *Development Arrested*, 290.

29 Santos, "Construyendo la contrahegemonía"; Wright, "Morphology of Marronage."

30 Keating, "From Borderlands and New Mestizas," 6.

31 King, *Black Shoals*, 9.

32 Tuhiwai Smith, *Decolonizing Methodologies*.

33 Woods, *Development Arrested*, 4.

34 Tuhiwai Smith, *Decolonizing Methodologies*, 129.

35 Woods, *Development Arrested*, 34.

36 Wynter, "Unsettling the Coloniality of Being," 328.

37 Liffman, *Huichol Territory and the Mexican Nation*.

38 Personal communication, Juan Negrín, July 18, 2007.

39 Reina Aoyama, "Introduction," 11.

40 Negrín, *Racial Alterity, Wixarika Youth Activism*.

41 Talavera Durón, "Las venas del tabaco."

42 Glissant, *Poetics of Relation.*

43 Castillo Cocom, "Ethnoexodus."

44 Castillo Cocom, "Ethnoexodus," 47.

45 Castillo Cocom, "Ethnoexodus," 50.

46 Castillo Cocom, "Ethnoexodus," 50.

47 Wynter, "Unsettling the Coloniality of Being," 271.

48 Wynter, "Unsettling the Coloniality of Being," 271.

49 Castillo Cocom, "Ethnoexodus," 64.

50 Glissant, *Poetics of Relation*, 143–44.

51 Mora, *Kuxlejal Politics.*

52 Woods, *Development Arrested*, 29.

53 Woods, *Development Arrested*, 29.

54 Mora, *Kuxlejal Politics*, 17.

55 Mora, *Kuxlejal Politics*, 19.

56 Mora, *Kuxlejal Politics*, 233.

57 Mora, *Kuxlejal Politics*, 55.

58 Wynter, "Unsettling the Coloniality of Being," 331.

Bibliography

Anzaldúa, Gloria. "How to Tame a Wild Tongue." In *Borderlands/La Frontera: The New Mestiza*, 33–45. Iowa City: Aunt Lute Books, 1987.

Beyyette, Bethany J., and Lisa J. LeCount, eds. *The Only True People: Linking Maya Identities Past and Present.* Boulder: University Press of Colorado, 2017.

Castillo Cocom, Juan, Timoteo Rodriguez, and McCale Ashenbrener. "Ethnoexodus: Escaping Mayaland." In *The Only True People: Linking Maya Identities Past and Present*, edited by Bethany J. Beyyette and Lisa J. LeCount, 47–71. Boulder: University Press of Colorado, 2017.

Escobar Ohmstede, Antonio, ed. *Indio, nación y comunidad en el México del siglo XIX.* Mexico City: Centro de Estudios Mexicanos y Centroamericanos, 1993.

Fernández, Blanca, and Bastien Sepúlveda. "Pueblos indígenas, saberes y descolonización: Procesos interculturales en América Latina." *Polis: Revista Latinoamericana*, no. 38 (2014): 1–7.

Glissant, Édouard. *Poetics of Relation.* Ann Arbor: University of Michigan Press, 1997.

Grossberg, Lawrence. "On Postmodernism and Articulation: An Interview with Stuart Hall." *Journal of Communication Inquiry* 10, no. 2 (1986): 45–60.

Hyatt, Vera Lawrence, and Rex Nettleford, eds. *Race, Discourse, and the Origin of the Americas: A New World View.* Washington, DC: Smithsonian Institution Press, 1996.

Keating, Ana Louise. "From Borderlands and New Mestizas to Nepantlas and Nepantleras: Anzaldúan Theories of Social Change." *Human Architecture: Journal of the Sociology of Self-Knowledge*, no. 4, special issue (2006): 5–16.

King, Tiffany Lethabo. *The Black Shoals: Offshore Formations of Black and Native Studies*. Durham, NC: Duke University Press, 2019.

León-Portilla, Miguel. "Cuando muere una lengua / Ihcuac tlahtolli ye miqui." *Revista de la Universidad de México*, no. 569 (April–May 1998): 24–25.

Liffman, Paul. *Huichol Territory and the Mexican Nation: Indigenous Ritual, Land Conflict, and Sovereignty Claims*. Tucson: University of Arizona Press, 2011.

Mañé, Bet, and Alvise Vianello, eds. *Formas-Otras: Saber, nombras, narrar, hacer*. Barcelona: CIDOB Edicions, 2011.

McKittrick, Katherine. *Demonic Grounds: Black Women and the Cartographies of Struggle*. Minneapolis: University of Minnesota Press, 2006.

McKittrick, Katherine, ed. *Sylvia Wynter on Being Human as Praxis*. Durham, NC: Duke University Press, 2015.

McKittrick, Katherine, and Clyde Woods. *Black Geographies and the Politics of Place*. Boston: South End, 2007.

Mora, Mariana. *Kuxlejal Politics: Indigenous Autonomy, Race, and Decolonizing Research in Zapatista Communities*. Austin: University of Texas Press, 2017.

Moten, Fred. *In the Break: The Aesthetics of the Black Radical Tradition*. Minneapolis: University of Minnesota Press, 2003.

Negrín, Diana. 2019. *Racial Alterity, Wixarika Youth Activism, and the Right to the Mexican City*. Tucson: University of Arizona Press, 2019.

Reina Aoyama, Leticia. "Introducción." In *Indio, nación y comunidad en el México del siglo XIX*, edited by Antonio Escobar Ohmstede, 11–17. Mexico City: Centro de Estudios Mexicanos y Centroamericanos, 1993.

Sandoval, Rafael, ed. *Pensar desde la Resistencia anticapitalista y la autonomía*. Mexico City: CIESAS, 2015.

Santos, Boaventura de Sousa. "Construyendo la contrahegemonía: Traducción, interculturalidad entre los movimientos sociales." In *Pensar desde la Resistencia anticapitalista y la autonomía*, edited by Rafael Sandoval, 27–44. Mexico City: CIESAS, 2015.

Santos, Boaventura de Sousa. "Introducción: Las epistemologías del sur." In *Formas-Otras: Saber, nombras, narrar, hacer*, edited by Bet Mañé and Alvise Vianello, 9–22. Barcelona: CIDOB Edicions, 2011.

Sharma, Nandita. "Strategic Anti-essentialism: Decolonizing Decolonization." In *Sylvia Wynter on Being Human as Praxis*, edited by Katherine McKittrick, 164–82. Durham, NC: Duke University Press, 2015.

Talavera Durón, Luis Francisco. "Las venas del tabaco: La migración de los wixaritari en la costa de Nayarit." Bachelor's thesis, Escuela Nacional de Antropología e Historia, Mexico City, 2013.

Tuhiwai Smith, Linda. *Decolonizing Methodologies: Research and Indigenous Peoples*. London: Zed Books, 2012.

Woods, Clyde. *Development Arrested: The Blues and Plantation Power in the Mississippi Delta*. 1998. London: Verso, 2017.

Wright, Willie Jamaal. "The Morphology of Marronage." *Annals of the American Association of Geographers* 110, no. 4 (2020): 1134–49.

Wynter, Sylvia. "1492: A New World View." In *Race, Discourse, and the Origin of the Americas: A New World View*, edited by Vera Lawrence Hyatt and Rex Nettleford, 5–57. Washington, DC: Smithsonian Institution Press, 1996.

Wynter, Sylvia. "Unsettling the Coloniality of Being/Power/Truth/Freedom: Towards the Human, after Man, Its Overrepresentation—an Argument." *CR: The New Centennial Review* 3, no. 3 (2003): 257–337.

Zibechi, Raúl. 2015. "Movimientos antisistémicos y descolonialidad." In *Pensar desde la Resistencia anticapitalista y la autonomía*, edited by Rafael Sandoval, 105–20. Mexico City: CIESAS, 2015.

6

Blackness in the (Post)Colonial African City

JORDANNA MATLON

It is exceptional that a black accepts the need to carry out his effort beyond the simple task in order to increase his gains. For that to happen, he must have been profoundly Europeanized, he must have adopted our motivations and accepted our own necessities. In a word, he has retained nothing African except the color.
—1953 FRENCH OFFICE DES ÉTUDES PSYCHOTECHNIQUES, in Frederick Cooper, *Decolonization and African Society*, 1996

Because black urban residents have had to maneuver their residency across incessantly shifting lines of inclusion and exclusion, overregulation and autonomy, their experiences provide an incisive platform for coming to grips with the combination of possibility and precariousness that seems to be at the forefront of urban life.
—ABDOUMALIQ SIMONE, *City Life from Jakarta to Dakar*, 2010

What Is This "Black" in the Black Geographic?

That an identity could become a color was bound in the violently extractive impulses of the merchant, plantation, and industrial capitalists of the transatlantic slave economy. The appropriation of African bodies demanded a total negation of the multitude of stories, experiences, intellects, and capacities for pain or for joy, power, and beauty that would have otherwise made them intelligible to those who gained from their commodification. It was a mandate, Cedric Robinson writes, that the "'Negro,' that is the color black," have "no civilization, no cultures, no religions, no history, no place, and finally no humanity that might command consideration." To reify racial difference was, in short, to collapse capital and labor in the Blackness that embodied both.[1]

This hollowing out of African humanity to produce a vessel for European profit tells the origin story of Blackness as racial identity, as cultural politics, and as political possibility. It is an origin story of capture and displacement. It is negation and objectification, achieved by and in the interest of an uprooting, the production of capital through an extraction of labor at once geographic and metaphysical. It is Blackness born from a denial of home, intended to exist as *matter out of place*. And it is that experience of homemaking, that *re*-membering after dismemberment, that process of locating, that constituted the diaspora as a theoretically rich position from which to interrogate the modern subject and a Black Atlantic spatial imaginary.[2]

Yet the multilayered and multisited "fact of Blackness produced by Western imperialism" extends well beyond a geography of transatlantic displacement, full stop.[3] As Walter Rodney so thoroughly established, Europe's underdevelopment of Africa was a palimpsest; slavery was itself the precondition for continental conquest.[4] Africa as signifier, residual, employed fundamentally as a means to an end—"roots and routes to engage the question of unity and identity of transnational Black communities"— rather than equal part to a "hybridity that constitutes the modern Black experience" is, Jemima Pierre observes, a "move away from theorizing the continent as a living and modern place."[5]

Situating the multiple spatialities and referentialities of Blackness elaborates the manifold operations of power and resistance that structure Black identities in the contemporary world. In some spaces anti-Blackness might hover over Black life as ever-present, interpersonal acts of racial violence—the police stop, or the home foreclosed. In other spaces its antagonisms are most frequently insidious and "silent" violences.[6] They compel historical acuity to connect the political economy of empire to famines or debt regimes, informal economies, or the wage as it was simultaneously raced and gendered. Contending with and seeking to escape territorialized negations have in turn produced situated intersectionalities—patriarchy, class privilege, regime affiliation, dual citizenship—to mediate harms, evidence of the fabric of white supremacy interwoven in Black-majority spaces. Or, a distant Blackness evokes reterritorialization-as-freedom: a movement "back to Africa," a clandestine migratory journey, a "mediascape."[7] These transcontinental spatialities and cross-continental referentialities attend to how "Black African and diaspora populations [are] continually and mutually engaged in dialogues and practices that race back and forth across the Atlantic."[8]

In this chapter, I elaborate the African Black Geographic, where affirmations and contestations of a Blackness born of negation but not erasure vie among disrupted yet unbroken ancestral lineages and homemaking claims. In particular, I interrogate the African colonial and postcolonial city. This vantage point centers the ideological and experiential intersectionalities that differentially enable or deny Black people's access to the rights, privileges, and "expectations of modernity."[9] At the same time, it offers the burgeoning tradition of Black Geographies a rich parallel conversation regarding the "possibility and precariousness" of Black life.[10] I begin from the vestiges of French empire, whose *mission civilisatrice*, or civilizing mission, deeply conflated the terms of race and culture to articulate the *right to the city*.[11] I examine two iconic sites where the *mission civilisatrice* powerfully structured norms and aspirations: the colonial municipalities of the Four Communes in Senegal whose residents attained exceptional citizenship privileges in the French empire, and the postcolonial regional hegemon of Abidjan, Côte d'Ivoire, in which urban-national belonging was tightly linked to salaried work and the forms of domesticity and sociality it enabled. I then engage AbdouMaliq Simone's theorization of "black urbanism," which disrupts imperial denouncements of Blackness in the city to posit alternative, always and already livelihood strategies, mobilities, and meaning-making practices to offer a vital contribution to the Black Geographic spatial imaginary.

La Mission Civilisatrice

In the Code Noir that regulated colonial slavery from 1685 onward, France made explicit the link between racial debasement and bodily exploitation: to be Black was to be a slave and vice versa. The French term for the slave trade was *la traite des noirs* (the trade of Blacks) or, more derogatorily, *la traite des nègres*.[12] Abolition in 1848 would entail not autonomy but another form of capture. An alibi for imperial expansion, abolitionist societies proposed "free" colonial labor on the Continent as a more efficient method of resource extraction while saving Africans from the specters of the native despot and the Arab slave trader.[13] As such it was also an act of historical revision, a disavowal of ongoing racial logics in metropole and colonies.[14] Thus, while France constructed a nation-building narrative of "liberty, equality, fraternity" that implied unity and human dignity for all those subjected to its authority, it simultaneously pursued a colonial project that further demarcated and entrenched the presumptive citizen within the boundaries of whiteness.

Adapting racialized knowing as the iconography of capitalism, empire visualized Africans across diverse territories according to the roles it intended for them. While in the metropole and the Caribbean colonies there was no imperative to incorporate Blackness beyond enslavement's object-rendering status, on the Continent, Africans were to be colonial *subjects* as well as commodity *objects*: consumers for the expansion of metropolitan markets as well as compulsory laborers on stolen land. Moreover, the small ratio of Europeans to Africans compelled dependence on African interlocutors, promoting an elite stratum of citizens-in-the-making.[15] Those Africans who adopted French language and culture, and by profession or trade lubricated colonial and capital circuits, were denoted *évolué*—literally, "evolved." Forged out of material necessity and cultivated by the ideology of the *mission civilisatrice*, the *évolué* African signified proximity to whiteness and offered an assimilatory project as benevolent cover to racial capitalist expropriation. *Évolué* acculturation bore the promise of civilization via the new modes of production and consumer lifestyles of the colonial economy.

Thinking with Stuart Hall, a "non-reductive approach to ... the interrelationship between class and race" is attentive to the "culturally specific quality of class formations in any historically specific society."[16] Slavery and colonialism are the historically specific modes through which the world capitalist system incorporated Black bodies and shaped the culturally specific quality of class formations in economies built on their foundations. On the African continent, the production of an elite stratum was instrumental to consolidating colonial rule and promoted a kind of racial passing among those Africans who adopted the ways of the colonizer. Opportunities for improved livelihoods if not basic recognition of one's humanity immersed in the colonial schema, African subjects swept into the white man's world faced the imperative, Frantz Fanon wrote, to "turn white or disappear."[17] And it was this constituency, the African bourgeoisie who rose against the colonial regime while nevertheless embracing the registers and privileges of whiteness, that Fanon warned would advance the accumulation of metropolitan capital upon independence.[18] Situated at the nexus of race and culture, *évolués* embodied colonial *hegemony*; not only for whom but also in the modes by which they worked, and in their sartorial expressions, forms of sociality, expressed tastes and proclivities, *évolué* livelihoods and lifestyles signaled entrenchment within the racial capitalist superstructure, the foundations for consent.[19] Hegemony, Hall observed, subjects "the victims of racism to the mystifications of the very racist ideologies which imprison and define them."[20] Affirming the material and ideological tenets of racial capitalist expansion, *évolués* upheld an imperial economic order constructed of white dominance and Black subordination, the politics of representation a crucial component of capitalist exploitation.

The Hybrid City

Originating from the struggles of South African activists and intellectuals, theories of racial capitalism first named and operationalized the political economy of apartheid. Cedric Robinson later employed the term to encompass the world capitalist system. "While the South Africans particularize," Peter James Hudson observes, "Robinson universalizes."[21] Yet this historiography would be less provincializing if considered in the context of Mahmood Mamdani's important observation that apartheid was unique to South Africa only in name.[22] As it produced a new political economy, the colonial civilizing mission was also an act of place-making, a *here, not there* apartheid geography where *here* was to constitute entitlement and privilege, and *there*, ever an exterior of humanity rendered disposable. Across colonial Africa, the European settler city carved out a territory and jurisdiction apart, its mode of inhabitation and permissible mobility demarcating citizen from subject.[23] To travel freely, to earn a living, to access services, to build a home—the right to the city as the right of the citizen making claims on the body politic, *the right to life itself*, this was at once spatialized and racialized. The polarity of racial exclusion and exception, the latter empire's collaborators and assimilationist triumphs, were constitutive of gradated colonial citizenship classifications and rights.

These logics formed dramatic relief in France's first sub-Saharan African territories, the Four Communes of Senegal composed of Saint-Louis, Gorée, Rufisque, and Dakar. Initiated with the settlement of Saint-Louis in 1659 and colonized in 1817, the Four Communes emerged as privileged municipalities in the *mission civilisatrice*.[24] Upon the formation of the imperial administrative body of French West Africa, or Afrique Occidentale Française (AOF) in 1895, the capital was designated Saint-Louis, moving to Dakar in 1902. A city of French administrators and African elites, Dakar became known in the late colonial period as the "Paris of Africa."

Those living in and around the Four Communes were grouped according to consequential and at points overlapping social, professional, religious, biological, and territorial distinctions that included *habitant* (established resident, rights-bearing), *originaire* (native of Four Communes, rights-bearing), *indigène* (native outside of Four Communes, rights-excluded), *sujet* (subject, rights-excluded), *signare* (African women in relationships with Europeans), *gourmet* (African Catholics), *métis* (of European and African ancestry), and *évolué* (French-educated, working in the interest of foreign capital).[25] Citizenship rights in the Four Communes would be periodically revoked and reinstated until citizenship to all *originaires* and their descendants was affirmed by the 1916 Blaise Diagne laws, after which nearly two decades of more relaxed citizenship regulations followed.[26] The region's strong anchor in Islam long nurtured a cosmopolitan identity: worldly, literate, and highly educated; yet pointedly oriented away from the *mission civilisatrice*, a recurring point of contestation was Islamic tenets that undermined French civil law.[27] Polygamous marriages and extended family units in particular generated a major flash point for the European modernist project that established the nuclear family not only as a fundamental civilizing force but also as the means by which to organize productive labor and inheritable property, thereby guaranteeing the expansion of capitalism.[28]

This African exceptionalism was objectionable to and yet functional for empire. The meeting of diverse ethnic groups and Islamic factions in the colonial municipalities facilitated extensive networks for communication and commerce. Autonomous expression of native traditions and networks, albeit adapted, thus also served European capital accumulation. The Four Communes' rights-bearing status was accorded in no small part to the metropole's heavy dependency on local elites for imperial expansion and colonial settlement. As "agent[s] of cross-colonization," interlocutors "transcended the discursive boundaries of 'Europe' and 'Africa.'"[29] Ties forged with the metropole were, in other words, concentrated around regime interests. Colonial policy was here "the products of two apparently contradictory enterprises: on the one hand, a colonial project founded on the logic of French assimilation . . . and on the other, a long historical accumulation of many commercial transactions."[30]

Like the Four Communes municipalities, innumerable manifestations and compromises resulted from the cultural hybridity that proliferated within colonial cities. Continuous political struggle belied the tension between hegemony and hybridity, and the means by which either could be employed for the imperial pursuit of profit. This tension would play out in the colonial project via strategies of assimilation versus association, direct versus indirect rule. Whatever degree of cultural autonomy that African *évolués* maintained in the private sphere at least, most significant to the metropolitan connection was the assertion of status through working and consuming in the money economy. This new economy was in turn fundamental to the socialization and spatialization of a "new urban elite."[31] Their "social, cultural, political, and economic practices . . . were expressed in an urban space, incorporated in a French imperial economy that determine[d] its ebb and flow, with its conflict of interests."[32] And the city, locus of the civilizing mission and a space apart, maintained the territorial bifurcation of rights: an urban elite citizenry whom the French came to generalize as *évolué* and, as cause and consequence, rights contingent if not altogether denied for those whose claims to the city the colonial authority refused to recognize. The confinement of citizen rights to administrative borders in the exemplary case of the Four Communes of Senegal explicitly located those rights in urban space.[33]

In short, *évolué* identity was from the start premised on regime embeddedness and the advance of capitalism. Thus formed the boundaries Africans were to navigate or traverse to ensure life and livelihood in the colonial order, and structured inhabitation of the colonial city. These boundaries, with the capitalist economy and urbanity the indices of proximity to the metropole and metropolitan/white privilege, persisted in the postcolony to divide elites from masses, center from periphery, and formal from informal.

The Salary City

In the decade prior to African independence, the confluence of Third World solidarity, postwar racial reckoning, and workers' movements pushed for imperial powers to realize the social and economic dimensions of their civilizational promises. At the nexus of both, wages intended to Europeanize African workers by incorporating them into the incentives and rationality of the capitalist economy. Subsequent labor struggles would involve not only ridding colonial arrangements of compulsion, which continued to manifest in nominally "free" labor on plantations, in the extractive industries, or for public works, but also agitating for pay and benefits—especially with regard to family allowances—equivalent to those of metropolitan workers among civil servants who constituted the great majority of salaried employees in the colonial economy.[34]

It was through attaining the right kind of work—salaried, contractual, pensioned—that the African *man* (empire envisioned *évolué* women not as workers but as wives) would gain the right to the colonial city and thereby be *affirmatively* incorporated into racial capitalist modernity. In the vision of the civilizing mission, this right promised to encompass ever more workers and their nuclear families, tasked with producing future generations of worker-citizens. Just as the city was the socioterritorial nexus of the colonial experiment, the salary, dually a mechanism of capitalist expansion and consent, became the predominant colonial instrument of social engineering in the African city. It was a means of connecting metropole to colony as well as a construct separating production from reproduction along the same gendered bifurcations established in industrializing Europe. As it did, it linked a masculinized remunerated work to a feminized domestic realm, ensuring that this particular mode of *production* (wage labor) would privilege social reproduction—*provision*, neatly packaged together in the breadwinning ideal. In a victory of hegemony, as the money economy carved out a new existence in the city, the salary became a prerequisite to marriage, itself the signifier of modern African manhood.[35] The modern and urban as intertwined, racializing constructions, lent a particular resonance to the articulation of both Black and masculine identities on the Continent.[36]

Limited access to the salary, access that was facilitated by and large by regime entrenchment, was a primary means of circumscribing the *évolué* elite. As they conformed to the colonial work ethos and family arrangements that ensured their reproduction, *évolués* properly inhabited the colonial city and embodied the hegemonic racial order. Those engaged in economic activities not easily captured by the colonial regulatory machine, including market women's commerce, were subject to nonrecognition if not derision and degradation.[37] The salary and the breadwinning ideal man it engendered were, in short, dual expressions of empire and patriarchy. They provided evidence of the gendered *and* racialized dimensions of capitalism taking root in African cities, both to satisfy material needs and to restrict social expression in accordance to a normative European standard.

What resulted was a racialized and gendered register of inclusion in and exclusion from urban life with the salary its organizing principle. Thus comprised the social architecture of racial capitalism in the African city, mapping the limits of permissible and navigable space for African men (as workers) and women (as wives), as well as a gateway for those who successfully embodied its civilizing narrative. It divided citizen from subject but also promised the possibility of crossing over through participation in the colonial economy, itself a primary means and measure of acculturation.

Upon independence, what had constituted the colonial wage economy transitioned into the formal economy, entrenching an elite-formal/mass-informal divide in which life-sustaining, dignifying, and normatively masculine work remained in the purview of the few. Its underlying racialism came to manifest as party, class, or ethnic privilege. Still, such work maintained deep ideological and often direct material orientations to the racial capitalist world political economy.

The Paris of Africa

Abidjan, Côte d'Ivoire's economic, cultural, and administrative center, was a city in which the *mission civilisatrice* and its politics of representation powerfully articulated in the colonial and postcolonial social imaginary. From the start, French colonial rule partitioned land and organized labor in Côte d'Ivoire according to its principles of efficient colonial extraction and, coupled in the colonial imaginary, the population's perceived ethnic dispositions.[38] Within this material and ideological construction, French colonists acted as civilizational gatekeepers while designating Ivoirian civil servants as *évolué* in-betweens and men migrating from the Ivoirian north and neighboring countries, working in *petits métiers* ("little jobs," a diminutive), backward savages. Abidjan was situated as a "stepping stone" between Africa and the West with sociogeographic hierarchies so firmly entrenched that by independence in 1960, to fully embody an Abidjanais identity entailed embracing the alterity of the French.[39]

In colonial Abidjan, the urban bourgeoisie worked in the highest echelons of the administration and in trade, although the latter were few in number and frequently foreign or of mixed European and African parentage. Although the number and proportion of Ivoirians in elite administrative positions increased steadily as independence approached, the majority were employed as midlevel bureaucrats with limited authority vis-à-vis the French. The French administration and private companies met demands for skilled and manual labor in Abidjan's port and industrial zones by recruiting Africans from other colonies, and subordinated the urban proletariat and contingent classes into forced labor.[40] Amid a significant foreign population that remained in the nation's workforce after independence, Ivoirians secured their place in the public sector.[41]

The distinction between coerced and voluntary labor disappeared upon the abolition of forced labor in 1946, but the salary and correlated imaginaries of dignified work endured as criteria for status and mobility. Even as the number of salaried workers more than doubled in the final decade of colonization, the social demarcation between salaried manual laborers and those employed in office jobs was rigid and persistent.[42] The latter were admirably designated as those who *connaissent papier* (know paper)—in other words, the educated *évolué* who had mastered the French language.[43] Informal labor, while a constant in the colonial urban economy, never figured into official plans or assessments. At best, the colonial state perceived these populations as temporary excess in an otherwise modernizing city.

Because salaried laborers were initially either European settlers or their African administrators, urban wage labor emerged as a category of colonial exclusion. This classificatory schema persisted in the postcolony and produced an Abidjanais colloquialism for the esteemed category of wage labor: *travail des Blancs* (white people's work) or, alternatively, *travail de ville* (city work).[44] A *travailleur* (worker) inferred a salary, and could moreover be distinguished from the phrase *se débrouiller* (to get by, make do, fend for oneself, hustle), describing both informal work and unemployment.[45] As a "linguistic peculiarity," the *travailleur/se débrouiller* distinction "refers to a double anxiety," at once economic and social, the salary pitting the state and the European modern, "seats of power and wealth," against the informal, traditional, peasant, and African.[46]

Originating in France's nineteenth-century empire-building forays, the concept *se débrouiller* described "forms of everyday resistance and survival strategies" in the face of "power imbalances, unequal access to resources, or an overbearing state."[47] As the term migrated to the informal economies of poststructural adjustment in Francophone Africa, its presumed ingenuities contended with how to approximate the male breadwinner role, most often by drawing on personal "networks of interdependence, solidarity, and social cohesion."[48] *Le travailleur*, on the other hand, composed a comfortable totality: he who was gainfully employed could be supposed to have "an anchor into modernity in addition to a stable income and the possibility of turning to the state for support in times of need." *Travailleurs* constituted "a distinct social category: salaried employment is conferred as an emblem of social status."[49]

Neocolonial relations with the former metropole during first president Félix Houphouët-Boigny's reign from 1960 until his death in 1993 underwrote a French-backed peace and prosperity in Côte d'Ivoire, with the narrative being *le miracle ivoirien* (the Ivoirian miracle).[50] The colonial sociogeographic hierarchies of labor and profit persisted in the citizenship classifications of the postcolonial urban social imaginary, designating some working bodies as more or less civilized than others.[51] At the top of the hierarchy, Houphouët-Boigny staffed his administration with French personnel, increasing the French presence in Abidjan fivefold in the new nation's first decade.[52] At the bottom, West African migrant labor constituted a quarter of Abidjan's workforce, predominantly in low-status, informal trades.[53] For Ivoirians straddling an aspired French sociality and a denigrated migrant underclass, the civil service, the formal economy's main employer, provided the ultimate modern employment and central path to middle-class, *évolué* status.[54] In this way the salary became a vehicle of regime loyalty as the "state granted means of livelihood to all it had put under obligation."[55]

By the 1970s, Abidjan had gained notoriety as a hub of French population and culture and was designated the "Paris of Africa." Entrenched assimilationist doctrine delivered the ideological cover of integration between city and metropole, *évolué* elite and French citizenry.[56] It produced a modernist vision of state and economy that coalesced in Abidjan, registering terms of national belonging that conflated *citadin* (urban resident) and *citoyen* (citizen).[57]

Black Urbanism

The Four Communes of Senegal and Abidjan exemplified the race-culture nexus of the French West African *mission civilisatrice* so essential to constructing a hegemonic urban labor regime. *Évolué* aspiration and the salary were ideological and material devices purposed for a racial capitalist order that would endure well after empire's end. Through them, the right to the city was articulated as a negation of African livelihood strategies, social networks, family structures, and mobilities. Expressed in its totality, this racializing difference was productive of an otherness—Blackness—to be either acculturated away or cast out from the city, constructed as the locus of African modernity. It was a negated otherness produced from Africa's forceful integration into transatlantic capital circuits; as empire refined its modus operandi from brute coercion to elite consent, it reinforced its civilizing mission as a *here, not there* geography of inclusion and exclusion now dually expressed at the continental and municipal scale.

Blackness thus emerges as a heuristic device to think through the racialization of Africanity as well as other ways of enduring or experiencing space and sociality unseen or unrecognized in the colonial city. The cultural, economic, and territorial mappings of Blackness, read in the postcolonial vernacular as the informal, the marginal, or the peripheral, are constitutive of the Black Geographic in the African city. They induce, for the three-quarters and upward of African urbanites in the new century surviving in the informal economy, a different sort of "social death": invisibility if not predation by the state, and precarious incorporation into the networks and modalities that otherwise ensure livelihood and provision.[58] Together, they devastate the capacity for production and social reproduction, thereby devastating African men who confront the pressures of the breadwinner norm.[59]

Deprovincializing the African city in theorizations of Blackness, AbdouMaliq Simone calls *Black urbanism* a way of navigating urban life that "draws lines between different places and different ways of doing things."[60] Emerging from a generalized discussion of "peripheral urbanism"—peripheral to the urban plan, the global policy report, the formal economy, the colonial settler city—Black urbanism evokes inhabitations of the city through difference as both a category of reference and a strategy for action.[61] It is simultaneously subjectivity and a mode of survival. "Blackness as a device," Simone explains, "embodies a conceptual solidarity," and just as it has stood in for exclusion "from certain norms and rights to the city," it also "implies the existence of undocumented worlds of limited visibility thought to haunt the city's modernity or posit radically different ways of being in the city."[62] In these ways Blackness epitomizes the fluidity and potentiality of *cityness* itself, whereby "in the same place and time, another set of conditions, another way of doing things, and another reality have always already been possible."[63] Against the most exploitative and improbable of circumstances, Blackness embodies making do despite, transforming uncertainty into a mechanism to reconceive and reconstitute, a mode of seeing without being seen. Moreover, in its "incessantly flexible, mobile, and provisional intersections," and when the planner, administrator, or petty bureaucrat would otherwise see it regulated or erased, the Black body itself acts as an indeterminate "infrastructure" par excellence.[64]

Becoming Black of the World

Abidjan of the twenty-first century was a far cry from *le miracle ivoirien* of the 1960s and 1970s. When debt conditionalities gutted African states' coffers in the 1980s, Houphouët-Boigny and successive administrations were increasingly unable to assure *évolué* mobility via civil service employment, eclipsed instead by the postcolonial boogeymen: the unplanned, the peripheral, the informal. From 1980 to 2005, the number of civil servants had increased by about half, compared with a population that had nearly tripled.[65] By 1993, Côte d'Ivoire "succeeded in breaking the world record for indebtedness: 240% of its annual production."[66] Over the next decade, France and global finance institutions imposed increasingly harsh structural adjustment measures, stripping the Ivoirian government of its substantial public sector and much of its sovereignty.[67] Whereas the proportion of Ivoirians living below the poverty line of $1.90 per day in 1985 was 6.81 percent, by 2008 this figure had soared to 29.02 percent.[68]

Structural adjustment shone a hard light on the deficits of the colonial pact in its latest iteration, as developmental promise and Abidjanais dream. Bill Freund explains: "In the good times, education, access to the civil service, the move to town, and ultimately Abidjan was the golden road to success, to becoming a real *patron* [boss] to one's friends, family, and ethnic group ... [but] now the road was virtually cut off."[69] Upon the demise of the salary and the disillusionment of the *évolué* path, Abidjanais amplified "itineraries of accumulation" that, as novel survival strategies and forms of sociality, rejected the entwined economies and colonial norms that structured privilege in the postcolony.[70] Symbolizing the flexibility, mobility, and provisionality of Black urbanism, that making do *despite*, the *débrouilleur* emerged as a novel hero of *la crise* (the crisis).[71] The hustler in designer threads, earnings obscured, buying rounds for the table; the musician or athlete living it up with his one-in-a million livelihood and billionaire lifestyle, the ultimate freedom of the new economy, free to make and to spend and to fail. Alongside this new hero was a villain first nurtured in the ethnic and labor hierarchies of the colonial regime: the figure of the foreigner, as *ivoirité*, or "authentic" Ivoirianness, became the rallying cry

FIGURE 6.1. MC Black wearing Black Power jersey. MC Black, a market vendor, hip-hop artist, and my research assistant in Abidjan, poses in his Black Power jersey. What Stuart Hall (1993, 109) says of Black diasporic cultures is so also of residents of the African urban periphery, a *we* encompassing the continental and diasporic Black Atlantic forged in the singular: *We* "have used the body—as if it were, and it often was, the only cultural capital we had. We have worked on ourselves as the canvases of representation." Author's photo, 2008.

for an exclusionary nationalism that would pit southerners against northerners and migrants in a decade-long civil war (2002–11), even as (and in fact because) both vied for a place on the periphery, for a hustle, for a piece of a shrinking pie. Just as *évolué* identity surfaced a racial-colonial legacy, faithful national adherence to a racialized, civilizational ideal reproduced its postcolonial other.

Work, however exploitative, is a "unique configuration of social wealth and social relations."[72] This configuration bestows value on the bodies whose labor renders them agential subjects in capitalist circuits; the body, racialized and gendered, maps onto the value of the labor it performs. Concurrent with the rise of industrial society in the metropole, the stigma of nonwork and its legalized dictum of vagabondage produced a "proto-racialization" that perpetuates across time and space to exclude both the lumpen and the racial other from the status of "relational beings," a "capital relation [bound] to the social" out of which respect and self-worth are so fundamentally derived.[73] A racial logic thus naturalizing work, the meritorious working subject, and the banished, race acts as "the final arbiter of waste and wastage."[74] "Race," in other words, "is an instrumentality that makes it possible both to name the surplus and to commit it to waste."[75] This racialized capital relation simultaneously presupposed a male subject, consigning men throughout the Black Atlantic to the interstices of masculine entitlement and racialized disposability. The enduring contradiction of Black masculinity lays bare its *long* history of crisis in racial capitalism.[76]

The *mission civilisatrice* was to evolve the African man into the salaried worker so that he might take his place among a community of men. This compromise between capital and labor was a social contract, a patriarchal dividend, that incentivized compliance even among racially marginalized men. Posited for much of the twentieth century as a normative reality, this compromise was in fact an aspirational model afforded only to the dominant group within a given social order. For Black men, failure came at the double cost of racial and gender denigration: the emasculating colonial subject designation of *grand enfant* (big child). As the late capitalist regime of nonwork spills over boundaries previously fixed by race and gender, it disrupts the patriarchal and white supremacist compromise of which the breadwinner was to evidence the advance of civilization. It is feminized work *and* the "*becoming Black of the world*."[77] Thus it is proof at once of the malaise of late capitalism and the incomplete conquest of capital, portending a civilization in decline or as yet unrealized. The expansion of precarious economies indicates the underlying fragility of the gender and racial privileges on which capitalism is built.

Blackness, incorporated into the world capitalist system from slave to forced laborer to interlocutor in colonial civilizing missions, encapsulates wide-ranging expressions of the race-gender-labor tripartite. In Abidjan as elsewhere, the right to the city manifested as the state-society contract, a contract underpinning participation in the formal economy. As the urban labor regime encompassed the double realm of the modern and the nation, it asserted hegemony over competing imaginaries, such as the cosmopolitan orientation to Islam in the Four Communes of Senegal and a peripheral yet globetrotting Black urbanism—even while these iterations persist as powerful alternative "worlding[s] of African cities."[78] In other words, the conditions under which the right to the African city is realized speak to the contradictions in modern projects of citizen-making and their implicit colonial legacies. They indicate how, as projects of subject formation, cultural and socioeconomic inclusion have always been deeply racialized, evoking specters of whiteness even in the everyday absence of white bodies. The colonial city demonstrated the sovereign's strategic "capacity to define who matters and who does not, who is *disposable* and who is not."[79] But it also demonstrates how those who "had to play by the rules governing urban life [despite not having] recourse to these same rules as a way of guaranteeing that they had the same chances in the city" engage "practices and technologies that bring an increasing heterogeneity of calculations, livelihoods, and organizational logics into a relationship with each other."[80] It is a "constitutive paradox" that renders the African city a rich site for thinking through the multisited complexities of hegemonic projects in histories of Black place-making.[81]

Prior modes of production—and productive potential—foment the conditions for the next, and the gender and racial ideologies of patriarchal privilege and proximity to whiteness that produced the salaried subject have been instrumental for generating consent in racial capitalist economies of surplus labor, be they the informal economies of debt-ravaged African cities or the postindustrial underground economies of cities in Europe and North America. Preempting the proliferation of surplus bodies across boundaries of race and gender, in the glamorized mediascape of hustler capitalism men of the Black Atlantic are simultaneously marginalized and venerated for engaging in alternative forms of economic participation. As embodiments of economic survival outside the social contract, their extralives—lives and livelihoods in excess, pushed from and pushing out the formal boundaries of the capitalist world system, infrastructures of Black urbanism—model afterlives of surplus to propose an alternative future, whether utopic or dystopic, for all. As *possibility*, Black urbanism rejects those palimpsests of racialized dispossession, denigration, and devastation to make claims on the city. Yet the global structures of racial capitalism firmly in place, deathly *precarious* remain the means to nourish or embellish the Black body.

Notes

1   Robinson, *Black Marxism*, 81.
2   Gilroy, *Black Atlantic*.
3   Pierre, *Predicament of Blackness*, 214.
4   Rodney, *How Europe Underdeveloped Africa*.
5   Pierre, *Predicament of Blackness*, 212, 214, 213.
6   Cf. Watts, *Silent Violence*.
7   Appadurai, "Disjuncture and Difference in the Global Cultural Economy"; Matlon, "Il Est Garçon."
8   Pierre, *Predicament of Blackness*, 214.
9   Ferguson, *Expectations of Modernity*.
10   Simone, *City Life from Jakarta to Dakar*, 281.
11   Lefebvre, *Writings on Cities*.
12   Cohen, *French Encounter with Africans*.
13   Cohen, *French Encounter with Africans*; Conklin, *Mission to Civilize*; Cooper, "Conditions Analogous to Slavery."
14   Cooper, *Citizenship between Empire and Nation*; Fleming, *Resurrecting Slavery*.
15   Cohen, *French Encounter with Africans*, ch. 4.
16   Hall, "Gramsci's Relevance for the Study of Race and Ethnicity," 42.
17   Fanon, *Black Skin, White Masks*, 100.
18   Fanon, *Wretched of the Earth*.
19   Gramsci, *Selections from the Prison Notebooks*.
20   Hall, "Gramsci's Relevance for the Study of Race and Ethnicity," 27.
21   Hudson, "Racial Capitalism and the Dark Proletariat."
22   Mamdani, *Citizen and Subject*.
23   Mamdani, *Citizen and Subject*.
24   Diouf, "French Colonial Policy of Assimilation."
25   Conklin, *Mission to Civilize*; Diouf, "French Colonial Policy of Assimilation"; Genova, *Colonial Ambivalence*.
26   Cooper, *Citizenship between Empire and Nation*; Genova, *Colonial Ambivalence*; Semley, "'Evolution Revolution.'"
27   Diouf, "French Colonial Policy of Assimilation."
28   Cooper, *Decolonization and African Society*; Diouf, "French Colonial Policy of Assimilation"; Ferguson, *Expectations of Modernity*.
29   Genova, *Colonial Ambivalence*, 22.
30   Diouf, "French Colonial Policy of Assimilation," 677–78.
31   Genova, *Colonial Ambivalence*, 22.
32   Diouf, "French Colonial Policy of Assimilation," 675.
33   Genova, *Colonial Ambivalence*.

34 Cooper, *Decolonization and African Society*; Cooper, "Conditions Analogous to Slavery." The same contestations that Muslim inhabitants of the Four Communes of Senegal confronted regarding citizenship rights arose here, with the French positing that African family types, namely size and structure, rendered a producer-provider wage unviable.

35 Lindsay and Miescher, "Introduction."

36 In rural areas, on the other hand, colonial whiteness as a reference category for masculinity was neither as constant nor as hegemonic.

37 Cooper, *Decolonization and African Society*.

38 Banégas, "Côte d'Ivoire"; Chauveau and Dozon, "Ethnies et état en Côte d'Ivoire."

39 Newell, "Enregistering Modernity, Bluffing Criminality," 179; see also Touré, *La civilisation quotidienne en Côte d'Ivoire*.

40 Coquery-Vidrovitch, *L'Afrique occidentale au temps des Français*; Loucou, *La Côte d'Ivoire colonial*.

41 Cohen, "Urban Policy and Development Strategy."

42 Loucou, *La Côte d'Ivoire colonial*.

43 Bazin and Gnabéli, "Le travail salarié," 699.

44 Bazin and Gnabéli, "Le travail salarié."

45 Bazin and Gnabéli, "Le travail salarié"; Murphy, "Brief History of *Le Système D*."

46 Bazin and Gnabéli, "Le travail salarié," 698–99.

47 Murphy, "Brief History of *Le Système D*," 353.

48 Murphy, "Brief History of *Le Système D*," 367–68.

49 Bazin and Gnabéli, "Le travail salarié," 699.

50 Bouquet, *Géopolitique de la Côte d'Ivoire*; Koulibaly, *Les servitudes du pacte colonial*.

51 Le Pape, *L'énergie sociale à Abidjan*; Newell, *Modernity Bluff*.

52 Crook, "Patrimonialism, Administrative Effectiveness and Economic Development in Côte d'Ivoire."

53 Sandbrook and Barker, *Politics of Africa's Economic Stagnation*; Zartman and Delgado, *Political Economy of Ivory Coast*.

54 Dozon, "L'étranger et l'allochtone en Côte d'Ivoire"; République de Côte d'Ivoire, *La Côte d'Ivoire en chiffres*; Woods, "State Action and Class Interests in the Ivory Coast."

55 Mbembe, *On the Postcolony*, 45.

56 Loucou, *La Côte d'Ivoire colonial*.

57 Newell, *Modernity Bluff*, 9.

58 On social death, see Patterson, *Slavery and Social Death*.

59 See Matlon, "Racial Capitalism and the Crisis of Black Masculinity."

60 Simone, *City Life from Jakarta to Dakar*, 307–8.

61 Simone, *City Life from Jakarta to Dakar*. Black urbanism joins theorizations of the plot/provision grounds and maroon communities to critically posit other possible worlds through the lived experiences of Black modernity.

62 Simone, *City Life from Jakarta to Dakar*, 285.

63 Simone, *City Life from Jakarta to Dakar*, 8.

64 Simone, "People as Infrastructure," 407.

65 République de Côte d'Ivoire, *La Côte d'Ivoire en chiffres*.

66 Verschave, *La Françafrique*, 132.

67 Bouquet, *Géopolitique de la Côte d'Ivoire*.

68 World Bank, "Poverty Headcount Ratio at $1.90 a Day."

69 Freund, *African City*, 182–83.

70 Banégas and Warnier, "Nouvelles figures de la réussite et du pouvoir," 6.

71 Kohlhagen "Frime, escroquerie et cosmopolitisme"; Newell, *Modernity Bluff*.

72 Yates, "Human-as-Waste," 1688.

73 Melamed, "Racial Capitalism," 81.

74 McIntyre and Nast, "Bio(necro)polis," 1472.

75 Mbembe, *Critique of Black Reason*, 34–35.

76 Matlon, *A Man among Other Men*.

77 Mbembe, *Critique of Black Reason*, 6 (emphasis in original).

78 Simone, "On the Worlding of African Cities."

79 Mbembe, "Necropolitics," 27.

80 Simone, *City Life from Jakarta to Dakar*, 281, 280.

81 Simone, *City Life from Jakarta to Dakar*, 282.

Bibliography

Appadurai, Arjun. "Disjuncture and Difference in the Global Cultural Economy." *Public Culture* 2, no. 2 (1990): 1–24.

Banégas, Richard. "Côte d'Ivoire: Les jeunes 'se lèvent en hommes.' Anticolonialisme et ultranationalisme chez les Jeunes patriotes d'Abidjan." *Les Études du Centre de recherches internationales (CERI)* 137 (2007): 1–52.

Banégas, Richard, and Jean-Pierre Warnier. "Nouvelles figures de la réussite et du pouvoir." *Politique africaine* 82 (2001): 5–21.

Bazin, Laurent, and Roch Yao Gnabéli. "Le travail salarié, un modèle en décomposition?" In *Le modèle ivoirien en questions: Crises, ajustements, recompositions, hommes et sociétés*, edited by B. Contamin and H. Memel-Fotë, 689–705. Paris: Karthala et Orstom, 1997.

Bouquet, Christian. *Géopolitique de la Côte d'Ivoire: Le désespoir de Kourouma*. Paris: Armand Colin, 2005.

Chauveau, Jean-Pierre, and Jean-Pierre Dozon. "Ethnies et état en Côte d'Ivoire." *Revue française de science politique* 38, no. 5 (1988): 732–47.

Cohen, Michael. "Urban Policy and Development Strategy." In *The Political Economy of Ivory Coast*, edited by I. William Zartman and Christopher L. Delgado, 57–75. New York: Praeger, 1984.

Cohen, William B. *The French Encounter with Africans: White Response to Blacks, 1530–1880*. 1980. Bloomington: Indiana University Press, 2003.

Conklin, Alice L. *A Mission to Civilize: The Republican Idea of Empire in France and West Africa, 1895–1930*. Palo Alto, CA: Stanford University Press, 1997.

Cooper, Frederick. *Citizenship between Empire and Nation: Remaking France and French Africa, 1945–1960*. Princeton, NJ: Princeton University Press, 2015.

Cooper, Frederick. "Conditions Analogous to Slavery: Imperialism and Free Labor Ideology in Africa." In *Beyond Slavery: Explorations of Race, Labor, and Citizenship in Postemancipation Societies*, edited by Frederick Cooper, Thomas C. Holt, and Rebecca J. Scott, 107–49. Chapel Hill: University of North Carolina Press, 2000.

Cooper, Frederick. *Decolonization and African Society: The Labor Question in French and British Africa*. New York: Cambridge University Press, 1996.

Coquery-Vidrovitch, Catherine. *L'Afrique occidentale au temps des Français, colonisateurs et colonisés (c. 1860–1960)*. Paris: Éditions la Découverte, 1992.

Crook, Richard C. "Patrimonialism, Administrative Effectiveness and Economic Development in Côte d'Ivoire." *African Affairs* 88, no. 351 (1989): 205–28.

Diouf, Mamadou. "The French Colonial Policy of Assimilation and the Civility of the Originaires of the Four Communes (Senegal): A Nineteenth Century Globalization Project." *Development and Change* 29 (1998): 671–96.

Dozon, Jean-Pierre. "L'étranger et l'allochtone en Côte d'Ivoire." In *Le modèle ivoirien en questions: Crises, ajustements, recompositions, hommes et sociétés*, edited by Bernard Contamin and Harris Memel-Fotê, 779–98. Paris: Karthala et Orstom, 1997.

Fanon, Frantz. *Black Skin, White Masks*. Translated by Charles L. Markmann. 1952. New York: Grove Press, 1967.

Fanon, Frantz. *The Wretched of the Earth*. Translated by Constance Farrington. 1961. New York: Grove Press, 1963.

Ferguson, James. *Expectations of Modernity: Myths and Meanings of Urban Life on the Zambian Copperbelt*. Berkeley: University of California Press, 1999.

Fleming, Crystal Marie. *Resurrecting Slavery: Racial Legacies and White Supremacy in France*. Philadelphia: Temple University Press, 2017.

Freund, Bill. *The African City: A History*. Cambridge: Cambridge University Press, 2007.

Genova, James Eskridge. *Colonial Ambivalence, Cultural Authenticity, and the Limitations of Mimicry in French-Ruled West Africa, 1914–1956*. Washington, DC: Peter Lang, 2004.

Gilroy, Paul. *The Black Atlantic: Modernity and Double Consciousness*. Cambridge, MA: Harvard University Press, 1993.

Gramsci, Antonio. *Selections from the Prison Notebooks*. Translated by Quintin Hoare and Geoffrey Nowell Smith. New York: International Publishers, 1971.

Hall, Stuart. "Gramsci's Relevance for the Study of Race and Ethnicity." *Journal of Communication Inquiry* 10, no. 2 (1986): 5–27.

Hall, Stuart. "What Is This 'Black' in Black Popular Culture?" *Social Justice* 20, nos. 1–2 (1993): 104–14.

Hudson, Peter James. "Racial Capitalism and the Dark Proletariat." Forum Response. To Remake the World: Slavery, Racial Capitalism, and Justice. *Boston Review*, February 20, 2018. http://bostonreview.net/forum/remake-world-slavery-racial-capitalism-and-justice/peter-james-hudson-racial-capitalism-and/.

Kohlhagen, Dominik. "Frime, escroquerie et cosmopolitisme: Le succès du 'coupé-décalé' en Afrique et ailleurs." *Politique africaine* 100, no. 4 (2005–6): 92–105.

Koulibaly, Mamadou. *Les servitudes du pacte colonial.* Abidjan: CEDA/Nouvelles Éditions Ivoiriennes, 2005.

Lefebvre, Henri. *Writings on Cities.* Translated and edited by Eleonore Kofman and Elizabeth Lebas. 1968. Malden, MA: Wiley-Blackwell, 1996.

Le Pape, Marc. *L'énergie sociale à Abidjan: Économie politique de la ville en Afrique noire, 1930–1995.* Paris: Karthala, 1997.

Lindsay, Lisa A., and Stephan F. Miescher. "Introduction: Men and Masculinities in Modern African History." In *Men and Masculinities in Modern Africa*, edited by Lisa A. Lindsay and Stephan F. Miescher, 1–29. Portsmouth, NH: Heinemann, 2003.

Loucou, Jean-Noël. *La Côte d'Ivoire coloniale, 1893–1960.* Abidjan: Éditions du Centre de recherche et d'action pour la paix (CERAP), 2012.

Mamdani, Mahmood. *Citizen and Subject: Contemporary Africa and the Legacy of Late Colonialism.* Princeton, NJ: Princeton University Press, 1996.

Matlon, Jordanna. "Il Est Garçon: Marginal Abidjanais Masculinity and the Politics of Representation." *Poetics* 39, no. 5 (2011): 380–406.

Matlon, Jordanna. *A Man among Other Men: The Crisis of Black Masculinity in Racial Capitalism.* Ithaca, NY: Cornell University Press, 2022.

Matlon, Jordanna. "Racial Capitalism and the Crisis of Black Masculinity." *American Sociological Review* 81, no. 5 (2016): 1014–38.

Mbembe, Achille. *Critique of Black Reason.* Durham, NC: Duke University Press, 2017.

Mbembe, Achille. "Necropolitics." *Public Culture* 15, no. 1 (2003): 11–40.

Mbembe, Achille. *On the Postcolony.* Berkeley: University of California Press, 2001.

McIntyre, Michael, and Heidi J. Nast. "Bio(necro)polis: Marx, Surplus Populations, and the Spatial Dialectics of Reproduction and 'Race.'" *Antipode* 43, no. 5 (2011): 1465–88.

Melamed, Jodi. "Racial Capitalism." *Critical Ethnic Studies* 1, no. 1 (2015): 76–85.

Murphy, Libby. "A Brief History of *Le Système D.*" *Contemporary French Civilization* 40, no. 3 (2015): 351–71.

Newell, Sasha. "Enregistering Modernity, Bluffing Criminality: How Nouchi Speech Reinvented (and Fractured) the Nation." *Journal of Linguistic Anthropology* 19, no. 2 (2009): 157–84.

Newell, Sasha. *The Modernity Bluff: Crime, Consumption, and Citizenship in Côte d'Ivoire*. Chicago: University of Chicago Press, 2012.

Patterson, Orlando. *Slavery and Social Death: A Comparative Study*. Cambridge, MA: Harvard University Press, 1982.

Pierre, Jemima. *The Predicament of Blackness: Postcolonial Ghana and the Politics of Race*. Chicago: University of Chicago Press, 2013.

République de Côte d'Ivoire. *La Côte d'Ivoire en chiffres*. Abidjan: Ministère de l'Économie et des Finances—Direction Générale de l'Économie, 2007.

Robinson, Cedric J. *Black Marxism: The Making of the Black Radical Tradition*. 1983. Chapel Hill: University of North Carolina Press, 2000.

Rodney, Walter. *How Europe Underdeveloped Africa*. 1972. New York: Verso, 2018.

Sandbrook, Richard, and Judith Barker. *The Politics of Africa's Economic Stagnation*. New York: Cambridge University Press, 1985.

Semley, Lorelle D. "'Evolution Revolution' and the Journey from African Colonial Subject to French Citizen." *Law and History Review* 32, no. 2 (2014): 267–307.

Simone, AbdouMaliq. *City Life from Jakarta to Dakar: Movements at the Crossroads*. New York: Routledge, 2010.

Simone, AbdouMaliq. "On the Worlding of African Cities." *African Studies Review* 44, no. 2 (2001): 15–41.

Simone, AbdouMaliq. "People as Infrastructure: Intersecting Fragments in Johannesburg." *Public Culture* 16, no. 3 (2004): 407–29.

Touré, Abdou. *La civilisation quotidienne en Côte d'Ivoire: Procès d'occidentalisation*. Paris: Karthala, 1981.

Verschave, François-Xavier. *La Françafrique: Le plus long scandale de la République*. Paris: Stock, 1998.

Watts, Michael J. *Silent Violence: Food, Famine, and Peasantry in Northern Nigeria*. 1983. Athens: University of Georgia Press, 2013.

Woods, Dwayne. "State Action and Class Interests in the Ivory Coast." *African Studies Review* 31, no. 1 (1988): 93–116.

World Bank Development Research Group. "Poverty Headcount Ratio at $1.90 a Day (2011 PPP) (% of Population). Côte d'Ivoire." Washington, DC, 2017. http://data.worldbank.org/indicator/SI.POV.DDAY?locations=CI.

Yates, Michelle. "The Human-as-Waste, the Labor Theory of Value and Disposability in Contemporary Capitalism." *Antipode* 43, no. 5 (2011): 1679–95.

Zartman, I. William, and Christopher L. Delgado. *The Political Economy of Ivory Coast*. New York: Praeger, 1984.

7

Marielle Franco and Black Spatial Imaginaries

SOLANGE MUÑOZ

On March 14, 2018, in Rio de Janeiro, Brazil, Marielle Franco, the first elected Black councilwoman from a favela (slum community), strongly supported by her constituents and celebrated as an up-and-coming political figure and activist for Black women, LGBTQ individuals, and favela inhabitants, was gunned down. At the time, she was coming home from a roundtable event titled "Young Black Women Moving Power Structures" that she had attended in her capacity as a Black woman, councilwoman, and activist. Tragically and ironically, one of the last things she said before leaving that meeting was, "We must occupy every place with our bodies."[1] Like many Black individuals in positions of power, Marielle Franco was seen as a threat to Brazil's political institutions and status quo. To many elite conservatives, her presence in politics, as well as her politics and programs, shook the white supremacist foundations on which Brazil was founded and on which the favelas continue to be imagined and reified.[2] Franco's presence and outspokenness in government challenged these narratives and flipped them on their head.

Positioning this research in the frameworks of human and Black geographies, this chapter employs the concepts of racialized spaces and imaginaries to examine the ways in which Black women occupy spaces and public positions of political power, despite persistent white supremacist violence by individuals and institutions that try to keep them out of those spaces and "in their place." This chapter asks, What is the symbolic and spatial power/significance/threat of Black women in political positions? Why is the presence of Black women in political power perceived as an aberration? What are potential spaces and the collective subjectivities they produce? When Black women employ these subjectivities within white supremacist, misogynist spaces of power, what is their might?

This research examines the significance of Black women in political positions of power and representation, with a particular focus on Councilwoman Marielle Franco's life, death, and legacy in Brazil. I explore Franco and the social and spatial significance of her intersectionality and positionality as an outspoken activist, a Black woman, a *favelada*, an LGBTQ person, and a single mother who was elected to the city council and then assassinated in Brazil. By focusing on Franco, I hope to both further introduce her to a US and English-speaking audience as a way to analyze, commemorate, and promote her life and struggle, and to acknowledge her broader social, spatial, and symbolic importance as an elected official from the margins and by and for marginalized communities.

By positioning a discussion about Franco within a Black geographies framework that examines her assassination in Brazil in the context of white nationalism, Black genocide, and spatial violence, I want to move beyond the national and local contexts in which race and racism are usually understood and analyzed. Brazil and the United States share a racial and economic history that was founded on the transatlantic slave trade.[3] Both Brazil and the United States continue to struggle with extreme levels of racial inequality, anti-Blackness, violence, and segregation.[4] At the time of writing, both countries' leaders openly represented white supremacist, conservative ideologies and used nationalist rhetoric to promote their policies and justify racial violence and exclusion. Like the rise of Donald Trump to the US presidency, in Brazil the election of Jair Bolsonaro and the assassination of Marielle Franco also "revealed to the world" that, like the United States, Brazil remains "racist, sexist, misogynist and LGBTQ phobic."[5]

Through this analysis, I argue for scholarship on race that more profoundly considers the shared geographies of Black women and their histories, struggles, and experiences across the Americas and the world. While I acknowledge contextual, historical, and geographic differences, I also believe that "serious engagement between researchers and [research] of [race] and marginality throughout the Americas" can provide a more profound understanding of the myriad ways in which white supremacy, race, and racism are manifested, imposed, lived, and resisted.[6] Similarly, a regional approach that includes all of the Americas can identify the many different geographies, alternative projects, ways of life, struggles, and solutions that are currently challenging hegemonic capitalist, racist, and misogynist institutions throughout the region.

Although this chapter rests at the intersection of white supremacy, how it is wielded, and how it is resisted, my goal is to center the story, life, and politics of Marielle Franco as one example of the many Black women who "occupy every place with [their] bodies" in order to challenge and resist white supremacist institutions. I draw on scholars such as Jaime Alves, Ta-Nehisi Coates, LaToya Eaves, George Lipsitz, Katherine McKittrick, Luciane de Oliveira Rocha, and others to unpack how Black geographic approaches can provide a framework for both analyzing and giving meaning to Black women who figuratively and literally sacrifice themselves through their person, bodies, and lives to position themselves at the center of white supremacist political institutions in order to center the work and narratives of other voices and experiences, and to produce alternative visions and projects that strive for social justice, equality, and collective and inclusive agendas.

Theoretical Framework: A Black Sense of Place

One of the objectives behind the violence of white supremacist strategies (i.e., xenophobic and misogynist narratives, imagery and ideology, physical violence, death threats, and death) is to question, undermine, and eliminate the credibility, rights, and access to spaces, positions of power, and representation of Black individuals.[7] These narrative strategies and violence employ and reproduce a "fear of a Black planet," one that is grounded in the myth that geography and power are and should be "white."[8] They are also illustrative of what Ta-Nehisi Coates has described as "racism's true breadth" or "the need to fix Black people in one corner of the universe so that white people may be secure in all the rest of it."[9] Coates's statement alludes to how the fear of a Black planet is one that is globally rationalized—even when it is managed and manifested through local and national racialized spaces and narratives used to control and contain the movement and access of Black individuals and communities.[10] This spatialized logic of race and racism impacts how Black bodies are perceived and denied access to spaces and power, and the way their presence and authority in particular spaces and positions are challenged, delegitimized, and denied.

Yet, in the same way that power and domination are spatialized, so is resistance to domination and violence, as well as the production of alternative spaces, practices, and ways of being.[11] This chapter considers the ways that resistance is spatialized, and embodied, as Black women employ their presence, their bodies, and their identities in order to resist, challenge traditional power structures, and push for social justice and change from positions of power. Resistance here is understood through the production of racialized spaces and subjectivities that are part of continuous and dynamic struggles for survival and social justice and includes the ways in which bodies and individuals (are both denied and able to) access and move within particular spaces, and how they are positioned and resist that positioning.[12] Beyond resistance, this chapter also explores how Black geographies provide alternative visions and projects for traditionally marginalized communities that can challenge, expose, and move beyond racial hierarchies, exclusionary projects and spaces, and white supremacist institutions.

The racialization of space highlights the ways in which power, race, access, and ownership are spatialized and weaponized. It provides a framework for thinking about the subjectivities of space, mobility, and power within a logic of white supremacy, settler colonialism, racial capitalism, and imperialism.[13] As spaces are racialized, so are the material and symbolic meanings, experiences, and opportunities of bodies and people that inhabit those spaces.[14] The settler colonial project is one that employs the racialization of space and territory to produce and reinforce the material underpinnings of white supremacy.[15] Like Brazil, many countries throughout the Americas and beyond are founded on settler colonial projects, understood not as historical events but as ongoing structures that "continue to shape race, gender, class, and sexual formations into the present."[16] Evelyn Nakano Glenn defines settler colonialism as a race-gender project in that it produced a "racialized and gendered national identity that normalized male whiteness."[17] In this context, white masculinity is exclusively tied to both ownership of property and political sovereignty.[18] Simply put, it creates a racial and gendered hierarchy that normalizes and reserves ownership and power for white men. Under the ongoing structural logic of settler colonialism, racial violence directed at Black and brown bodies and communities has a common goal: to keep Black and brown people and communities "in their place" and "out of place."

Like Glenn's discussion of settler colonialism, McKittrick describes how power and violence operate spatially through "multiscalar discourses of ownership."[19] Through the conceptualization of "Black matters as spatial matters," McKittrick explains that the "legacy of racial dispossession underwrites how we can come to know space and place, and that the connections between what are 'real' or valuable forms of ownership are buttressed through racial codes that mark the Black body as ungeographic."[20] Following this logic, power and whiteness are also spatially manifested in ways that intentionally and violently position Black people and bodies to be controlled, (dis)possessed, and (dis)placed with few, if any, legal protections.[21]

Lipsitz's work also adds to this discussion of race and space when he claims that spatial relations and their production of racial identities must be understood not simply as reflecting "the existence of racialized space in society, [but rather how] they come to function as part of it."[22] This discussion of racialized space and the way it produces particular racialized identities, experiences, and realities can be applied in multiple ways. On the one hand, it normalizes the racialization of space and who "belongs" in different spaces. Like the racist projects that produce them, the experiences and realities of Black communities and spaces are both fetishized and denied by white supremacist narratives that normalize both segregation and exclusion of Black bodies.[23] At the same time, this naturalization "enables advocates of expressly racist policies to disavow any racial intent" and leads to what João Costa Vargas has called "hyperconsciousness/negation of race dialectic . . . a system that is on the surface devoid of racial awareness [but that] is in reality deeply immersed in racialized understandings of the social world."[24] Black geographies expose this dialectic and, as a result, also expose another outcome of racialized space: the lives, experiences, realities, violence, resistance, and situated knowledges and the "wonderfully festive and celebratory spaces of mutuality, community and solidarity" that give form to what Lipsitz calls "the Black spatial imaginary."[25]

Black experiences in a racist society and a racist world produce racialized spaces and subjectivities of meaning, identity, place, and power.[26] Black women in particular carry this burden and the power of production, resistance, and survival that it imparts.[27] In the specific context of state violence, the favela, and Brazil, Alves discusses the organizing power of mothers whose children, mostly young, Black men, have been gunned down by the state, and the public protests and acts in which they partake in order to dislocate "masculinist constructions of racial injustice...[and to]...inform a gendered spatial praxis through which Black women re-signify the meanings of space, bodies and motherhood."[28] McKittrick provides similar imagery in her discussion of Octavia Butler's novel *Kindred*, from which she notes, "Dana, by stepping into what might be considered unknown or inaccessible spaces and places,...respatializes the potential of Black femininity and Black subjectivity in general."[29] These actions are at once resistance to white supremacy and creative productions and imaginations in their own right. As McKittrick explains: "Black women's histories, lives, and spaces must be understood as enmeshing with traditional geographic arrangements in order to identify a different way of knowing and writing the social world and to expand how the production of space is achieved across terrains of domination."[30] Lipsitz employs the concept of spatial imaginaries to also consider their generative social and political significance and the ways in which these different experiences and projects provide a more inclusive and humanistic worldview. Employing a White and Black spatial imaginary dichotomy, Lipsitz claims a Black spatial imaginary is fundamentally different from the white spatial imaginary due in part to its very foundations marked by white supremacist structures and institutions.[31] This conceptualization moves beyond the mere notion of resistance and alludes to the generative possibilities of the Black spatial imaginary. This is particularly important because, as Lipsitz argues, "Struggles for racial justice require more than mere inclusion into previously excluded places. They also necessitate creation of a counter social warrant with fundamentally different assumptions about place than the white imaginary allows."[32] I draw on Lipsitz's and other scholars' discussions of spatial imaginaries and geographies to consider the particular case of Franco's "inclusion" within what are some of the most white supremacist, conservative, and exclusive spaces and institutions in society—local and national government.

The experiences of exploitation, exclusion, containment, and confinement have required that Black individuals and communities develop collective ways of coping and surviving under white supremacist institutions and spaces.[33] Black collective strategies in which individuals and families work in community to ensure their safety and survival "offer a model of democratic citizenship to everyone [and] promote solidarities within, between and across spaces."[34] Similarly, individuals from traditionally marginalized communities who run for office are increasingly elected and join government in order to transform it through mandates that make demands and offer a very different world vision. What makes Marielle Franco particularly important in this context is not only her visibility and positionality but also that she pushed agendas that not only are progressive but also are representative of a different experience and understanding of humanity and the world.

What are the collective and political spaces and subjectivities that are created when Black women are able to center their experiences, creativity, and demands in spaces of government and power from which they have historically been excluded? As Black women enter politics and voice their demands, the potential to create other ways of life and subjectivities becomes possible. Their political actions, rhetoric, and agendas can promote an alternative and inclusive worldview, which they also embody and represent through their intersectional subjectivities.[35] These subjectivities both empower Black women (and the communities they represent) and also endanger them, because of the knowledge and experiences they bring and alternative visions and imaginaries they offer, which both challenge and expose the historical social injustices of the very institutions they now occupy.

The Favela and the *Favelada*

Born in 1978 and raised in Rio de Janeiro, in the Maré favela, Marielle Franco was elected to the city council in an exceptional feat. In a city and a country in which over 50 percent of the population identifies as Black or mixed race, Franco was the only Black woman on Rio de Janeiro's fifty-one-member city council. She received 46,500 votes, the fifth-highest count of more than a hundred candidates. As a candidate for the Socialism and Freedom Party, her platform, as well as her activism, outspoken progressiveness, and her identity as a Black, bisexual woman and a single mother born and raised in the favelas, threatened and angered many within the elite conservative political establishment.[36] At the same time, these qualities made her an inspiration for many poor, Black, and mixed-race Brazilians who had also grown up in the favelas and who had never felt represented or had envisioned someone "like them" in the political institutions of government. As Dani Monteiro, another Black politician, explained the situation, "Suddenly you are no longer invisible, in a space where we had always been invisible."[37]

Marielle Franco's identity and experience as a *favelada*, a term that refers to residents of favelas, cannot be overstated in terms of her election to city council and the platform on which she ran. Franco's life and her assassination are representative of the favela and the Black experience in Brazil, figuratively, literally, and symbolically. Franco openly defended and fought for the rights of Black women, LGBTQ individuals, *favelados*, and other traditionally marginalized groups in Brazil, and she was a fierce critic of the police presence and militarization of the favelas.[38] She earned an undergraduate degree in social sciences and a master's degree in public administration, in which she was one of two Black students in the program. Her master's thesis, which was published posthumously for a general audience as a form of protest and with the goal of educating and resisting police violence and corruption, was titled, "UPP: The Reduction of the Favela to Three Letters," which analyzes and critiques the presence and violence of the Unidade de Policia Pacificadora (UPP; Pacifying Police Unit) in the favelas.

The UPP was a security program developed in 2008 to address the country's high rates of violence ahead of the World Cup and the Olympics. The goals were aimed at increasing security in the favelas and integrating the neighborhoods and residents into the formal city.[39] Yet, despite some perceived improvements in the favelas, for many, the presence of the UPP meant exchanging violence and instability brought on by gangs for violence and corruption at the hands of the police.[40]

Many believe that Marielle Franco was killed because of her outspoken criticism of the UPP and the militarization of the favela. Although this version of events is not wrong, it simplifies Franco's significance and power as a Black woman from the favelas elected to Rio de Janeiro's city council. Instead, I suggest Franco's killing was a response to her presence as a Black woman in a position of power and her ability to challenge Brazil's hegemonic narrative of the favelas and the *favelados*, as well as to provide a very different narrative from the official one that characterized the government and the UPP as a force for order and peace inside the favelas.[41]

Franco's presence as an elected political figure and activist also challenged the simplified, hegemonic framing of the favelas and their residents as poor, Black, and dangerous criminals that is often used to justify police violence and other policies of displacement and military presence.[42] Like the urban ghettos of the United States or the Black townships of South Africa under apartheid, the favelas of Brazil have long been normalized as poor, violent, Black spaces.[43] The myth of racial democracy on which Brazil's interpretation of its racial history and configuration is based, and Brazil's impulse to deny or conflate race with class have meant that although favelas are some of the most violent places in the world, *because* of their imposed status as Black spaces they have remained largely void of racial analyses and understandings.[44] Increasingly, however, scholars have argued that state violence and militarization in the favelas are first and foremost forms of racial and spatial control and discipline that work to contain what Vargas sarcastically calls the "evils before they spill over into the wider polity."[45]

Important here is not only the racialization of favelas and their inhabitants but, rather, the ways in which these spatial and racial imaginations are used to justify what Alves calls "macabre" violence: the constant threat of destruction of individuals and their families and communities.[46] Under racist systems and white supremacist logics, the status of favelas as Black, informal spaces makes them and their inhabitants ungeographic or placeless.[47] Both Smith and Perry argue that the violence in the favelas against Black bodies from death squads and the far right, respectively, must be understood within a broader historical context as "a phenomenon imbued with multiple layers of racialized, gendered, sexualized and classed meaning, simultaneously territorialized as a continuous part of the landscape of inequality and Black suffering in Brazil."[48] Similarly, Alves's work on the necropolitics of favelas in São Paulo, Brazil, also describes the favela as a space marked by death.[49] However, he also argues that "the dialectic of life and death, violence and resistance, territorial captivity and placelessness produce ... an alternative spatiality in which a Black 'spatial praxis' and a Black subjectivity come into being."[50] Alves's argument is resonant of Clive Woods's earlier work *Life after Death*, in which Woods highlights the destruction of African American communities in the United States but argues for greater recognition of the social movements and production of Indigenous knowledge from within these spaces.[51]

Despite spatial practices of extreme violence and militarization inflicted and endorsed by the state and its institutions, *favelados* continue to survive, resist, and construct other realities, subjectivities, opportunities, and solidarities.[52] Franco's position on the city council and her public and political persona publicized this fact. In this sense, her life and death are representative of multiple other lives, deaths, and stories of the favelas, the *favelados*, Brazil's system of white supremacy and racism, and the Black experience and resistance. Franco, whose campaign motto was "Eu sou porque nós somos" (I am because we are), knew this.[53] Like her last words at the workshop for Black women, she occupied spaces with a powerful presence. She used her face and her body to communicate confidence, strength, and hope, and in many videos and photographs she fills the space with the image. In one video, she walks through the favela, smiling and confident, as the camera remains close to her face. It is as if she is walking up to the viewer, in a lighthearted but intense challenge to see her, to acknowledge her not individually but collectively. She is showing the favelas and their residents whose multiple spaces, lives, and experiences she both is and represents.[54]

While working as councilwoman, Franco presented sixteen bills, some individually and others that were cosponsored with other council members. Many dealt with the daily struggles of poor women and their families. For example, she proposed free nocturnal childcare for working and studying mothers (PL 17/2017), the training and education of at-risk adolescents (PL 515/2017), a campaign to raise public awareness of violence against women (PL 417/2017), and the increase and elaboration of data on women's health outcomes, social assistance, and human rights (PL 555/2017). She also proposed a bill that would dedicate one day a year to Tereza de Benguela, an icon of the Black resistance movement who led the Quilombo de Quariterê resistance against slavery (PL 103/2017). All these bills were voted into law in August 2018, five months after Franco's death. Other bills included a proposal to combat LGBTQ phobias, and another to protect women seeking an abortion, which is legal in certain cases in Brazil. Additionally, that same year, more than a thousand Black women ran in the October elections for Congress and state assemblies. Three of them were elected to the Rio de Janeiro state legislative assembly, including Renata da Silva Souza, who had previously been Marielle Franco's chief of staff. These bills highlight Franco's commitment to her constituents and to the favela communities' need and demands, previously rarely addressed in the halls of government.

Like Alves's use of praxis to describe Black women's ability to "reclaim their placeless location as a political resource for redefining themselves and the polis," McKittrick draws on Édouard Glissant's "poetics of landscape," explaining that it "discloses the underside, unapparent histories and stories that name the world and Black personhood."[55] These Black geographies, along with Franco's campaign motto, "I am because we are," provide a framework for understanding Franco's broader collective and political significance in the context of Rio de Janeiro, Brazil. Franco always carried her Blackness, her sexuality, and her status as a *favelada* in her public image, because, as her partner states in a documentary on Franco, Marielle "was a Black, gay woman from the favelas, and that is the most disposable body in this city."[56] In this way, Franco did not simply look to be included in government institutions; rather, she worked to transform government and Brazilian society from her position as an activist and elected official. Her presence in local government allowed her to represent and position the praxis and poetics of landscape inside government institutions, on television, and in other public and political spaces. This was her power and why she was killed.

Spatialized Resistances

In October 2018, two candidates of the conservative right-wing Social Liberal Party took a street plaque with Marielle Franco's name, which had been placed in the Floriano Peixoto Square next to city hall to memorialize the life and death of the councilwoman. Later that day at a rally for one of the candidates, the two men gleefully held up the broken plaque as one of them shouted to the crowd, "Me and Daniel, we went there and broke it, we are going to wipe out those people, no more PSOL, no more communist party."[57] The crowd cheered wildly after mention of the broken sign and later when one of the men threatened to "wipe out those people," the Socialism and Freedom Party (PSOL), and the communist party. The scene was eerily reminiscent of Donald Trump's rally in July 2019 in which his attacks on Representative Ilhan Omar provoked the crowd to begin chanting, "Send her back." Both of these political events are illustrative of Vargas's hyperconsciousness/negation of race dialectic; although the racial identities of both Marielle Franco and Ilan Omar are never uttered, the nature of the comments and the physical and verbal threats of doing away with the women and their followers are deeply and violently racist and misogynistic.

These and the many other acts of real, discursive, and symbolic racial violence are spatial, in terms of both where and how they happen and the imagined outcomes of their words and demands. They imply a white male imaginary of the nation that, in turn, is used to justify the possession, control, disappearance, and displacement (in any/all forms) of Black bodies.[58] These acts also highlight the ways in which white supremacist hegemonic discourses have normalized the placelessness of Black bodies and people, and importantly, the varying forms of extreme violence that white people commit in order to maintain their perceived privileged status.

A few days later, on October 14, which was the seven-month anniversary of Marielle Franco's death, her partner, Monica Benicio, and other supporters staged an event at the Floriano Peixoto Square once again, to return the stolen sign. This time, unlike the candidates' actions and their subsequent proclamations of violence and destruction, Benicio explained, the event was "an answer of resistance but with a lot of affection, solidarity and love, after the act of vandalism, the destruction of the sign that was a tribute."[59] One thousand copies were made of the street sign, which read: "Rua Marielle Franco (1979–2018) Vereadora, defensora dos Direitos Humanos e das minorias, covardemente assassinada no dia 14 de março de 2018" (Marielle Franco Street [1979–2018] Councilwoman, Defender of Human Rights and Minorities, cowardly assassinated on March 14, 2018). Protesters marched and held a copy of the street sign in their hands, each one representing Franco, her presence and role as councilwoman, democratically elected to represent the city and her constituents. Like the Mães de Maio, a human rights group made up of Black women from the São Paulo favelas whose children have been killed by the Military Police, or the Black Lives Matter movement in the United States, by staging a peaceful protest and street-naming event in Floriano Peixoto Square, Benicio and other Franco supporters and activists challenged the hegemonic narrative of Franco and the *favelados*. This reappropriation of public spaces that are closely aligned with state institutions is a reminder that all Brazilians should have the right to access and the right to be represented and protected by the state, and that, like Marielle Franco, they are also part of and represent state structures and institutions.

Many geographers have written about the power of street naming as a toponymic device that communicates how national and local identities are imagined and, as a result, who is included and excluded from those definitions.[60] The act of naming the street in front of city hall in Rio de Janeiro was a spatial and symbolic moment that not only commemorated Franco's position as councilwoman, as well as her life and death, but also represents a much more profound struggle for recognition, justice, and the right of Black Brazilians to "participate in the production of place, and to have their cultural identities and histories recognized and commemorated publicly."[61] Also, it is important to note the symbolic and political significance of street naming, not only in terms of recognition but also in terms of where that recognition and appropriation take place.[62] As societies become increasingly controlled and exclusionary, these acts of occupation and appropriation through protest and naming become even more urgent and significant.[63] At the same time, with the street sign representing both a celebration of Marielle Franco and a reminder that she was assassinated by state agents, the protesters made the state's "necropractices, [which are usually] confined to the favelas, visible in the city center."[64] Since her death, cities such as Paris, Lisbon, Berlin, Cologne, and Buenos Aires have now named different public spaces—streets, plazas, and subway stations—after Marielle Franco.

Conclusion

The threat that Franco and other Black women like her who run for office represent is real. Their presence, visibility, and political agenda work to challenge and undermine white supremacist institutions and ideology and to promote social justice, equality, and human rights. For many, the threat is based on the mere presence of Black women in powerful positions, perceived as an aberration to the settler colonial institutional foundations that exclusively position white males as embodying the nation, government, and power. The threat also comes in the form of creating and demanding laws, human rights, and protections for traditionally marginalized and invisibilized communities and individuals. Finally, the threat comes in the form of alternative agendas and collective possibilities, voices, projects, and solidarities that have historically been denied access to government institutions and representation, and that minority women's presence in government makes possible.

In these spaces, many Black women are now producing and representing projects that symbolize and reflect the collective experiences, lives and demands of Black people and communities. Their political agendas and demands reflect and push for greater inclusion, equality, and recognition in government in ways that are different from simply promoting progressive party ideology. Instead, their demands and agendas are deeply personal and historical. Franco's assassination and the threats of violence and death made against many Black women in positions of power are meant to stop these demands and the possibilities they pose. Yet, as we have seen with Franco, her assassination set off a firestorm, inspiring many Black women in Brazil and across the world to run for office and to fight for collective rights and recognition in her name.[65]

The proliferation of right-wing movements and their shift into the mainstream, along with the return of conservative and nationalist governments such as those in Brazil and the United States, have not contained the increasing centrality, visibility, demands, and activism of other voices and ways of life of traditionally marginalized groups and individuals. Furthermore, projects like the Movimento Negro in Brazil and the Black Lives Matter movement in the United States, as well as the social and political significance of productions and publications of both obscure and well-known artists, writers, scholars, activists, politicians, and countless others in Brazil, the United States, and around the world, are examples of the transformative creativity and visions of Black women who are increasingly visible and visibilizing others in the very spaces and institutions from which they have historically been denied and excluded. Despite her death, Marielle Franco continues to be a threat to Brazil's status quo.[66] She continues to "occupy spaces" through her memory and through the efforts of the millions of Black women who continue the struggle in her name.

Finally, this chapter employs the case study of Marielle Franco in Rio de Janeiro, Brazil, to argue for more transnational approaches that further link Black geographies and scholarship from around the world. Like Black diaspora studies that highlight the movement and common history of Black people around the world, Black geographies' ability to engage in multispatial and multiscalar analyses of Black experiences in global contexts can provide rich and complex analyses that are still untapped. Anti-Blackness and Black strategies of survival, resistance, and emergence move beyond local case studies and experiences and are representative of historical configurations of race, nation, and identity that are representative of shared histories and futures, linking Black communities in ways that have yet to be acknowledged, recognized, and understood. Simply put, transnational research that takes into account the shared histories, multiple scales, commonalities, and differences of Black people and Black communities around the world can expand both the theoretical and applied scholarship behind Black geographies in profound and innovative ways.

Notes

1 May, "Resilient Women."

2 Vargas, "When a Favela Dared to Become a Gated Condominium"; Alves, "From Necropolis to Blackpolis"; Rocha, "Outraged Mothering"; Dos Santos Carvalho Carinhaha, "Assassination in Brazil."

3 Robinson, "Coming to Terms"; Morgan, "Cultural Implications of the Atlantic Slave Trade."

4   Vargas, "The Inner City and the Favela"; Bledsoe and Wright, "Anti-Blackness of Global Capital"; Daniel, *Race and Multiraciality in Brazil and the United States.*

5   Erdos, "Mariel and Monica Documentary"; see also Perry, "Resurgent Far Right and the Black Feminist Struggle"; Smith, "Strange Fruit."

6   Auyero, "Researching the Urban Margins," 431.

7   Daniels, *White Lies.*

8   Baldwin, *I Am Not Your Negro.*

9   Coates, *We Were Eight Years in Power*, 37.

10 Collins, *Black Sexual Politics*; Vargas, "The Inner City and the Favela"; Lipsitz, *How Racism Takes Place*; Smith, "Strange Fruit"; Alderman, "Racialized and Violent Biopolitics of Mobility"; Perry, "Resurgent Far Right and the Black Feminist Struggle."

11 McKittrick, *Demonic Grounds*; McKittrick and Woods, *Black Geographies and the Politics of Place*; Alves, "From Necropolis to Blackpolis"; Eaves, "Black Geographic Possibilities."

12 McKittrick, *Demonic Grounds*; Vargas, "When a Favela Dared to Become a Gated Condominium"; Alves, "From Necropolis to Blackpolis"; Eaves, "Black Geographic Possibilities."

13 Robinson, "Coming to Terms"; McKittrick, *Demonic Grounds*; Lipsitz, *How Racism Takes Place*; Tyner, "Population Geography I"; Alderman, "Racialized and Violent Biopolitics of Mobility."

14 McKittrick and Woods, *Black Geographies and the Politics of Place.*

15 Glenn, "Settler Colonialism as Structure."

16 Glenn, "Settler Colonialism as Structure," 55; see also Bonds and Inwood, "Beyond White Privilege."

17 Glenn, "Settler Colonialism as Structure," 58.

18 Glenn, "Settler Colonialism as Structure."

19 Glenn, "Settler Colonialism as Structure"; McKittrick, *Demonic Grounds*, 36.

20 McKittrick, *Demonic Grounds*, 4.

21 Ferreira da Silva, "No-Bodies"; see also Smith, "Strange Fruit."

22 Lipsitz, *How Racism Takes Place*, 54.

23 Lipsitz, *How Racism Takes Place.*

24 Lipsitz, *How Racism Takes Place*, 35; Vargas, "Hyperconsciousness of Race and Its Negation," 446.

25 Lipsitz, *How Racism Takes Place*, 51.

26 McKittrick, *Demonic Grounds*; Rocha, "Outraged Mothering."

27 Rocha, "Outraged Mothering"; St. Jean and Feagin, *Double Burden*; Eaves, "Imperative of Struggle."

28 Alves, "Neither Humans nor Rights"; Alves, "From Necropolis to Blackpolis, 334; see also Rocha, "Outraged Mothering."

29 McKittrick, *Demonic Grounds*, 1.

30 McKittrick, *Demonic Grounds*, xiv.

31 Lipsitz, *How Racism Takes Place*.

32 Lipsitz, *How Racism Takes Place*, 54.

33 McKittrick, *Demonic Grounds*; Lipsitz, *How Racism Takes Place*; Eaves, "We Wear the Mask"; Bledsoe, "Marronage as Past and Present Geography"; Wright, "Morphology of Marronage."

34 Lipsitz, *How Racism Takes Place*, 56.

35 Hughes and Dubrow, "Intersectionality and Women's Political Empowerment Worldwide."

36 Araújo, "Marielle Franco's Death Is an Emblem of the Violence."

37 Londoño, "A Year after Her Killing."

38 Franco, "After the Take-Over."

39 Oosterbaan and van Wijk, "Pacifying and Integrating the Favelas of Rio de Janeiro."

40 Oosterbaan and van Wijk, "Pacifying and Integrating the Favelas of Rio de Janeiro."

41 Prouse, "Framing the World Cup."

42 Prouse, "Framing the World Cup"; Smith, "Strange Fruit"; Perry, "Resurgent Far Right and the Black Feminist Struggle."

43 Alves, "From Necropolis to Blackpolis."

44 Vargas, "When a Favela Dared to Become a Gated Condominium"; Alves, "From Necropolis to Blackpolis."

45 Vargas, "When a Favela Dared to Become a Gated Condominium," 51; see also Alves, "From Necropolis to Blackpolis."

46 Alves, "From Necropolis to Blackpolis."

47 McKittrick, *Demonic Grounds*; Ferreira da Silva, "No-Bodies"; Vargas, "Gendered antiblackness and the Impossible Brazilian Project"; Smith, "Strange Fruit."

48 Smith, "Strange Fruit," 180; Perry, "Resurgent Far Right and the Black Feminist Struggle."

49 Alves, "From Necropolis to Blackpolis."

50 Alves, "From Necropolis to Blackpolis," 329.

51 Woods, "Life after Death," 66.

52 Franco, "After the Take-Over."

53 Franco, "After the Take-Over."

54 Erdos, "Mariel and Monica Documentary."

55 Alves, "From Necropolis to Blackpolis," 323; McKittrick, *Demonic Grounds*, xxiii.

56 Erdos, "Mariel and Monica Documentary."

57 Erdos, "Mariel and Monica Documentary."

58 Vargas, "Gendered Antiblackness and the Impossible Brazilian Project"; Alves, "Neither Humans nor Rights"; Glenn, "Settler Colonialism as Structure."

59 Erdos, "Mariel and Monica Documentary."

60 Alderman and Inwood, "Street Naming and the Politics of Belonging."

61 Alderman and Inwood, "Street Naming and the Politics of Belonging," 212.

62 Alderman and Inwood, "Street Naming and the Politics of Belonging."

63 Rose-Redwood and Alderman, "Critical Interventions in Political Toponymy."

64 Alves, "From Necropolis to Blackpolis," 332.

65 Ramaswamy, "Marielle Franco Had to Resist."

66 Londoño, "A Year after Her Killing."

Bibliography

Aguirre, May. "Resilient Women: LGBTQ and Human Rights Activist, Marielle Franco." March 14, 2021. https://www.cadenacollective.com/blogs/cadena -collective/resilient-women-lgbtq-and-human-rights-activist-marielle -franco.

Alderman, Derek. "The Racialized and Violent Biopolitics of Mobility in the USA: An Agenda for Tourism Geographies." *Tourism Geographies* 20, no. 4 (2018): 717–20. https://doi.org/10.1080/14616688.2018.1477168.

Alderman, Derek, and Joshua Inwood. "Street Naming and the Politics of Belonging: Spatial Injustices in the Toponymic Commemoration of Martin Luther King Jr." *Social and Cultural Geography* 14, no. 2 (2013): 211–33. https://doi.org /10.1080/14649365.2012.754488.

Alves, Jaime A. "From Necropolis to Blackpolis: Necropolitical Governance and Black Spatial Praxis in São Paulo, Brazil." *Antipode* 46, no. 2 (2014): 323–39. https://doi.org/10.1111/anti.12055.

Alves, Jaime A. "Neither Humans nor Rights: Some Notes on the Double Negation of Black Life in Brazil." *Journal of Black Studies* 45, no. 2 (2014): 143–62. https:// doi.org/10.1177%2F0021934714524777.

Alves, Jaime A. "On Mules and Bodies: Black Captivities in the Brazilian Racial Democracy." *Critical Sociology* 42, no. 2 (2016): 229–48. https://doi.org/10.1177 %2F0896920514536590.

Araújo, Flávia. "Marielle Franco's Death Is an Emblem of the Violence against Brazil's Poor and Black." *New Statesman*, March 16, 2018.

Auyero, Javier. "Researching the Urban Margins: What Can the United States Learn from Latin America and Vice Versa?" *City and Community* 10, no. 4 (2011): 431–36. https://doi.org/10.1111%2Fj.1540-6040.2011.01370.x.

Baldwin, James. *I Am Not Your Negro: A Major Motion Picture Directed by Raoul Peck.* New York: Vintage, 2017.

Beaton, Mary Elizabeth, and Hannah B. Washington. "Slurs and the Indexical Field: The Pejoration and Reclaiming of Favelado 'Slum-Dweller.'" *Language Sciences* 52 (2015): 12–21. https://doi.org/10.1016/j.langsci.2014.06.021.

Bledsoe, Adam. "Marronage as Past and Present Geography in the Americas." *Southeastern Geographer* 57, no. 1 (2017): 30–50.

Bledsoe, Adam, and Willie Jamaal Wright. "The Anti-Blackness of Global Capital." *Environment and Planning D: Society and Space* 37, no. 1 (2019): 8–26. https://doi.org/10.1177%2F0263775818805102.

Bonds, Anne, and Joshua Inwood. "Beyond White Privilege: Geographies of White Supremacy and Settler Colonialism." *Progress in Human Geography* 40, no. 6 (2016): 715–33. https://doi.org/10.1177%2F0309132515613166.

Coates, Ta-Nehisi. *We Were Eight Years in Power: An American Tragedy*. New York: One World/Ballantine, 2018.

Collins, Patricia Hill. *Black Sexual Politics: African Americans, Gender, and the New Racism*. New York: Routledge, 2004. https://doi.org/10.4324/9780203309506.

Daniel, G. Reginald. *Race and Multiraciality in Brazil and the United States*. University Park: Pennsylvania State University Press, 2022. https://doi.org/10.1515/9780271028842.

Daniels, Jessie. *White Lies: Race, Class, Gender and Sexuality in White Supremacist Discourse*. New York: Routledge, 2016. https://doi.org/10.4324/9780203760420.

Dos Santos Carvalho Carinhanha, Ana Míria. "Assassination in Brazil Unmasks the Deadly Racism of a Country That Would Rather Ignore It." *The Conversation*, April 12, 2018. https://theconversation.com/assassination-in-brazil-unmasks-the-deadly-racism-of-a-country-that-would-rather-ignore-it-94389.

Eaves, LaToya E. "Black Geographic Possibilities: On a Queer Black South." *Southeastern Geographer* 57, no. 1 (2017): 80–95.

Eaves, LaToya E. "The Imperative of Struggle: Feminist and Gender Geographies in the United States." *Gender, Place and Culture* 26, nos. 7–9 (2019): 1314–21. https://doi.org/10.1080/0966369X.2018.1552564.

Eaves, LaToya E. "We Wear the Mask." *Southeastern Geographer* 56, no. 1 (2016): 22–28.

Erdos, Fabio. "Marielle and Monica Documentary." *Guardian*, December 18, 2018.

Ferreira da Silva, Denise. "No-Bodies: Law, Raciality, and the Territory of Justice." *Griffith Law Review* 18, no. 2 (2009): 213–36. https://doi.org/10.46560/meritum.v9i1.2493.

Franco, Marielle. "After the Take-Over: Mobilizing the Political Creativity of Brazil's Favelas." *New Left Review* 110 (2018): 135–40.

Glenn, Evelyn Nakano. "Settler Colonialism as Structure: A Framework for Comparative Studies of US Race and Gender Formation." *Sociology of Race and Ethnicity* 1, no. 1 (2015): 52–72. https://doi.org/10.1177%2F2332649214560440.

Hughes, Melanie M., and Joshua Kjerulf Dubrow. "Intersectionality and Women's Political Empowerment Worldwide." In *Measuring Women's Political Empowerment across the Globe*, edited by Amy C. Alexander, Catherine Bolzendahl, and Farida Jalalzai, 77–96. London: Palgrave Macmillan. 2018. https://doi.org/10.1007/978-3-319-64006-8.

Inter-American Commission on Human Rights. "African Americans, Police Use of Force, and Human Rights in the United States." March 25, 2019. https://

ijrcenter.org/2019/03/25/new-iachr-report-addresses-police-violence-against
-Black-americans/.

Lipsitz, George. *How Racism Takes Place*. Philadelphia: Temple University Press, 2018.

Londoño, Ernesto. "A Year after Her Killing, Marielle Franco Has Become a Rally-ing Cry in a Polarized Brazil." *New York Times*, March 14, 2019.

McKittrick, Katherine. *Demonic Grounds: Black Women and the Cartographies of Struggle*. Minneapolis: University of Minnesota Press, 2006.

McKittrick, Katherine, and Clyde Woods, eds. *Black Geographies and the Politics of Place*. Boston: South End, 2007.

Morgan, Philip D. "The Cultural Implications of the Atlantic Slave Trade: African Regional Origins, American Destinations and New World Developments." In *Routes to Slavery: Direction, Ethnicity and Mortality in the Transatlantic Slave Trade*, edited by David Eltis and David Richardson, 128–51. Abingdon, UK: Routledge, 2013.

Oosterbaan, Sarah, and Joris van Wijk. "Pacifying and Integrating the Favelas of Rio de Janeiro: An Evaluation of the Impact of the UPP Program on Favela Residents." *International Journal of Comparative and Applied Criminal Justice* 39, no. 3 (2015): 179–98. https://doi.org/10.1080/01924036.2014.97305.

Perry, Keisha-Khan Y. "The Resurgent Far Right and the Black Feminist Struggle for Social Democracy in Brazil." *American Anthropologist* 122, no. 1 (2020): 157–62. https://doi.org/10.1111/aman.13358.

Prouse, Carolyn. "Framing the World Cup: Competing Discourses of Favela Pacification as a Mega-event Legacy in Brazil." *Recreation and Society in Africa, Asia and Latin America* 3, no. 2 (2013): 1–17.

Ramaswamy, Chitra. "Marielle Franco Had to Resist—No Wonder She Didn't Survive." *Guardian*, March 19, 2018. ttps://www.theguardian.com/lifeandstyle/2018/mar/19/marielle-franco-brazilian-political-activist-black-gay-single-mother-fearless-fighter-murder.

Robinson, Cedric. "Coming to Terms: The Third World and the Dialectic of Imperialism." *Race and Class* 22, no. 4 (1981): 363–86. https://doi.org/10.1177%2Fo30639688102200403.

Rocha, Luciane de Oliveira. "Outraged Mothering: Black Women, Racial Violence, and the Power of Emotions in Rio de Janeiro's African Diaspora." PhD diss., University of Texas, 2014.

Rose-Redwood, Reuben, and Derek H. Alderman. "Critical Interventions in Political Toponymy." *ACME: An International E-Journal for Critical Geographies* 10, no. 1 (2011): 1–6.

Smith, Christen. A. "Strange Fruit: Brazil, Necropolitics, and the Transnational Resonance of Torture and Death." *Souls* 15, no. 3 (2015): 177–98. https://doi.org/10.1080/10999949.2013.838858.

St. Jean, Yanick, and Joe R. Feagin. *Double Burden: Black Women and Everyday Racism*. New York: Routledge, 2015. https://doi.org/10.4324/9781315705095.

Tyner, James A. "Population Geography I: Surplus Populations." *Progress in Human Geography* 37, no. 5 (2013): 701–11. https://doi.org/10.1177%2Fo309132512473924.

Vargas, João Costa. "Gendered Antiblackness and the Impossible Brazilian Project: Emerging Critical Black Brazilian Studies." *Cultural Dynamics* 24, no. 1 (2012): 3–11. https://doi.org/10.1177%2F0921374012452808.

Vargas, João Costa. "Hyperconsciousness of Race and Its Negation: The Dialectic of White Supremacy in Brazil." *Identities: Global Studies in Culture and Power* 11, no. 4 (2004): 443–70. https://doi.org/10.1080/10702890490883803.

Vargas, João Costa. "The Inner City and the Favela: Transnational Black Politics." *Race and Class* 44, no. 4 (2003): 19–40. https://doi.org/10.1177%2F03063968 030444002.

Vargas, João Costa. "When a Favela Dared to Become a Gated Condominium: The Politics of Race and Urban Space in Rio de Janeiro." *Latin American Perspectives* 33, no. 4 (2006): 49–81. https://doi.org/10.1177%2F0094582X06289892.

Woods, Clyde. "Life after Death." *Professional Geographer* 54, no. 1 (2002): 62–66. https://doi.org/10.1111/0033-0124.00315.

Wright, Willie Jamaal. "The Morphology of Marronage." *Annals of the American Association of Geographers* 110, no. 4 (2020): 1134–49. https://doi.org/10.1080 /24694452.2019.1664890.

PART III

Futurity

8

Rendering Gentrification and Erasing Race

Sustainable Development and the (Re)Visioning of Oakland, California, as a Green City

C.N.E. CORBIN

The West Oakland Specific Plan (WOSP) is a 530-page document developed by the City of Oakland Department of Planning and Building and the JRDV Urban International consulting team in collaboration with business and community stakeholders. The plan is said to be the "guiding framework for realizing the vision of a healthy, vibrant West Oakland."[1] Containing thirteen chapters and five appendixes with maps, tables, photos, and renderings that depict the current state and the future projection of West Oakland, it was approved by the Oakland Planning Commission on June 11, 2014. Soon after, images from appendix A, the design guidelines, proliferated in local newspapers, in online zines, on blogs, and on Facebook pages, with comment sections serving as a platform to both celebrate and contest the spaces it depicted.

Oakland, California, began its journey to become a sustainable city in 1996 by adopting its first climate change policy: Resolution No. 72809 C.M.S., "authorizing the City of Oakland to join the Cities for Climate Protection Campaign; and to apply to the International Council for Local Environmental Initiatives."[2] This and subsequent sustainability initiatives modeled from and in response to the 1992 Earth Summit and the Kyoto Protocol worked to align the municipality with cities around the world in fighting climate change. Since 2005, Oakland has been recognized and awarded for its "strong legacy of environmental leadership."[3] It has spent the last generation implementing an environmental agenda and (re)branding its municipality as a sustainable green city. A crucial part of creating a green city is the production of green spaces (e.g., parks, gardens, and urban agriculture) to improve the quality of life of urban residents, reduce negative environmental impacts, and address climate change.[4]

By examining the visual discourses embedded within the WOSP, this chapter shows how current urban sustainable development agendas are working in concert with historically rooted environmental narratives and practices that remove racialized populations identified as *undesirable* from the landscape. Analyzing the WOSP at the intersection of environmental thought, race theory, and visual media elucidates how municipal documents act as both propaganda and gentrification apparatus. Anti-Blackness is expressed by obscuring the racialization of displacement, and the visual discourse portrays acts of environmental racism in that the plan depicts and provides "whites...an *edge* in gaining access to [the] healthy physical environment," rendered in the WOSP through (re)visioning Oakland as a white and green sustainable city.[5]

Environmental Narratives, Race, and Parks

Environmental movement narratives often obscure the historic practices of displacement in the creation of parks and recreational green spaces. Because of this, the shared and similar historical patterns and practices get lost or relegated to the past, and thus are not vigilantly watched when promoting current green space creation, restoration, and beautification projects. Today, similar patterns of displacement along with exclusionary practices and forced removal are being perpetuated.

During the mid-nineteenth century, parks and green spaces began to be centered as a solution to urban human health problems.[6] City parks like

Frederick Law Olmsted's iconic Central Park, in New York City, became an urban recreational green space for the white immigrant working class and a backyard for white elites.[7] A massive project to support human health and recreation, it exemplified the environmental claims of providing healthier, cleaner air for residents and was proclaimed to be the "lungs of the city."[8] Yet, the creation of Central Park also destroyed Seneca Village, a thriving African American and Irish community of residents and property owners, using eminent domain to make way for the park.[9]

Displacement of undesirable racialized populations was also key in the establishment of the National Park System. The Native American populations living where what became Yellowstone and Glacier National Parks were forcibly removed through state-sanctioned violence following the Indian Removal Act of 1830.[10] Between the late 1820s and the mid-1850s, the Ahwahnechee people of the Sierra Nevada faced a series of attacks first from the "forty-niners," US citizens and gold rush miners, and then from militia campaigns carried out in the Yosemite Valley.[11] Indigenous traditional ecological land management practices like controlled burnings were questioned and perceived as land degradation and blight by whites, and this became a pretext for Native American criminalization and expulsion. The removal of Indigenous communities consolidated power and control over these green spaces among affluent white elites, who began using these lands for recreation in the late 1850s.[12]

The patterns within environmental narratives and practices can be seen in both the national park context and the urban park context in table 8.1. The philosophy of nature's supremacy over humans, which originated with John Muir and was embraced by the future modern environmental movements, is articulated within the national park context as a crucial need to preserve, conserve, and protect nature and the wilderness.[13] Within the urban context, nature as green space is positioned as a vital organ, the lungs of the city, which became the central argument for developing public parks, even if their construction had detrimental impacts on residents.[14]

Narratives of particular humans as questionable, harming the landscape, and lacking the capacity to use the land appropriately are (re)articulated in the rhetoric of producers of blight and empty wastelands. These narratives gave credence to the governmental practices of removing the so-called offending population(s) by force: the Indian Removal Act in the case of national parks, and eminent domain in the urban context. Forced removal is conducted through violence carried out by local, state, and federal governments using militias with genocidal intentions in national parks, while

TABLE 8.1. National Park and Urban Environmental Narratives

National Park Context	Urban Context
– Nature in need of protection.	– Green space as a vital organ.
– Narratives of an empty landscape, blighted areas, improper land uses, and the Indigenous population lacking the capacity to manage the land appropriately.	– Narratives of empty landscapes, blighted areas, urban wastelands, and residents lacking the capacity to maintain the area appropriately.
– State-sanctioned forced removal. Displacement through federal policy and militia violence.	– City-sanctioned forced removal. Displacement through eminent domain, evictions, and police violence.
– Appropriation of wilderness/natural lands for tourism and recreation for a different and more affluent white population.	– Appropriation of city lands for creating green space for tourism and recreation for a different and more affluent white population.

municipal violence is carried out through police brutality within the urban context. In both the national park and the urban context these green spaces are repopulated by a different demographic: more affluent, white urban dwellers. These are the patterns and processes of dispossession, displacement, and replacement embedded in and obscured by environmental narratives that continue to be reproduced within the green city.

The City Beautiful Movement, the Garden City Movement, and Oakland, California

The City Beautiful movement (1890s–1920s) and the Garden City movement (1898–1930s) placed parks and green space aesthetics as central components of urban design and city beautification, and they are the precursors to the suburbs and the green city. City Beautiful was introduced during the World's Columbian Exposition, the first world's fair held in Chicago in 1893, which was aptly nicknamed the White City for its white stucco buildings. The White City also reflected the society for which it was produced.[15] It was the product of "an elite movement that imposed a top-down ideal on lower economic and social classes and ignored racial considerations … it represented perfection in design as well as the perfection of Anglo society."[16] Moreover, City Beautiful brought forth a new focus in urban planning that promoted "an idealized urban environment of boulevards, buildings, and park grounds that was to be emulated by towns everywhere," including Oakland.[17] While the garden city was a "new type of community, neither urban nor rural, that combined the advantages of the city and the country … a public garden stood at the center, surrounded by a range of public, cultural, and social institutions."[18] Oakland was deemed an industrial garden and "a model of postwar urban/suburban imagining" that brought "the machine (industry) into harmony with the garden (single-family home)."[19] The garden city replicated similar practices that created the National Park System and Central Park, in that the post–World War II suburbanization process excluded racialized populations.[20] African Americans were prevented access to the green spaces that the City Beautiful and Garden City movements produced in Oakland, using then-legal segregation and racially restrictive covenants.[21] The discriminatory legacies of these movements are embedded in Oakland's urban landscape and reflected in its contemporary environmental policy and practices. Moreover, these historical racialized and classed ideologies continue to be (re)produced within the *green city* of today, albeit now grounded within an ecological sustainability framework that continues to rely on green space as a central element.

Gentrification in the Green City

In 1964, Ruth Glass coined the term *gentrification* to convey the neighborhood change taking place in London in which new individuals, the working-industrial laborers, were moving into the local modest dwellings and improving both the property and the surrounding areas through their own capital.[22] The individual actions carried out by this new population drove up property values, which led to displacement of lower-income residents. Today's gentrification has become a city planning tool, and not just the individual actions of a new workforce.[23] The current gentrification process depends on neoliberal urban policy, providing tax breaks and incentives to the private sector, to the benefit of developers and industry, while underfunding or eliminating public goods. Environmental improvements and amenities have become mechanisms for catalyzing neighborhood change, by greening while also increasing housing costs, driving up eviction rates, and catering to new wealthier residents, all of which are changing the class, racial, and cultural demographics of neighborhoods.

In 2009, Sarah Dooling introduced the concept of *ecological gentrification* as the "implementation of an environmental planning agenda related to public green space that leads to the displacement or exclusion of the most economically vulnerable human population—homeless people—while espousing an environmental ethic."[24] Dooling focuses on how both the city and its wealthy residents play a role in surveilling green spaces in which the sight of a homeless person in a *public* green space is a motive to call law enforcement and enact policy to prevent access by this population. This can be extended to Black and Brown park users who have also been rendered as trespassers, criminalized, and met by state violence historically and currently when in public green spaces.[25] Melissa Checker's term *environmental gentrification* contextualizes gentrification and displacement from green space as a neoliberal practice that benefits developers while environmental justice language is co-opted in the process.[26] According to Checker, "While it appears as politically neutral planning that is consensual as well as ecologically and socially sensitive, in practice, [environmental gentrification] subordinates equity to profit-minded development."[27] Finally, in 2012, Kenneth Gould and Tammy Lewis deployed the concept of *green gentrification* to describe the "urban gentrification processes that are facilitated in large part by the creation or restoration of an environmental amenity" in which a "greening event" attracts a more affluent population into the already improved neighborhood.[28] Green gentrification is the new process for dispossession and displacement, with similar historical patterns obscured in environmental narratives and practices. Today, the commodification of urban nature and the scarcity of green spaces within the urban landscape have become the driver for increasing property values and a pull factor to bring in a whiter and more affluent population while displacing predominantly Black communities and residents who are less economically secure. The gentrification processes described here are expressed in the West Oakland Specific Plan, yet the WOSP is only one of many plans that have been implemented since 2010 in the municipality's pursuit to (re) create itself as a sustainable green city.

History of an African American Presence in West Oakland

West Oakland has a rich African American history, with most residents having familial ties to the Second Great Migration that took place between 1940 and 1970. African Americans migrated from the South to the West, with the intention to escape Jim Crow conditions and, initially, to find gainful employment in the World War II defense industry.[29] During this time, West Oakland became a legally segregated section of the city. The Home Owners' Loan Corporation designated these neighborhoods as hazardous for housing investments, creating a container for African American residents and placing their limited housing options in and near industrial zones.[30] Due to freeway construction and the creation of the Bay Area Rapid Transit (BART) commuter train system, between the 1950s and 1970s, thousands of Black homes and businesses were razed. The transportation infrastructure divided the neighborhoods and exposed residents to freeway-based emissions.[31]

In the late 1960s and early 1970s, Oakland became the epicenter of the Black Power movement and home to the Black Panther Party for Self-Defense, which emerged from and was a response to the economic neglect and disinvestment experienced by many inner cities of the 1970s. White flight dramatically changed the demographics from a majority white middle-class city to a majority Black impoverished one. The 1970s and 1980s (re)created Oakland as a chocolate city, with surrounding vanilla suburban municipalities.[32] In 1977, Oakland elected its first black mayor, Lionel J. Wilson, and in 1983 the *Oakland Tribune* became the first African American–owned metropolitan newspaper. At a time of cultural gains, the economic loss tied to white migration and capital flows to the suburbs was compounded by the collapse of the domestic manufacturing industry, making Oakland and its Black populations economically precarious well into the first decade of the 2000s. The election of Jerry Brown as mayor in 1998 ended a generation of African American mayoral leadership as Oakland also began transitioning into a green city.

West Oakland continues to grapple with its redlined legacy and its industrial past as it contends with many environmental hazards in the present. The district is also one of the most environmentally impacted areas in the city, according to CalEnviroScreen 3.0, a public data and mapping tool of environmental hazards and social vulnerability indicators created by the California Environmental Protection Agency.[33] The Pollution Burden indicator maps and data for West Oakland show high pollution burdens due

TABLE 8.2. City of Oakland and West Oakland Racial Demographics, 2010

City of Oakland	West Oakland Zip 94607
African American/Black 28%	African American/Black 38.5%
White/Caucasian 25.9%	White/Caucasian 19.9%
Latinx 25.4%	Latinx 12.6%
Asian 16%	Asian 28.8%
Other 3.9%	Other 0.2%

to the 580, 880, and 980 freeways that encircle the area, and as an industrial site, the district is riddled with soil pollution.[34] Residents "living near these sites have a greater potential to be exposed to chemicals" than people living in other areas of the city.[35] Sustainable development and the creation of a green city are crucial for low-income residents and communities of color, who tend to be the most environmentally compromised and are less likely to have access to healthy green spaces.

According to the Bay Area Census, by 2000 the relative numbers of Black residents in Oakland decreased from about 44 percent in 1990 (163,526) to about 36 percent (142,460) in 2000, an approximate 21,066 Black population loss during a time the overall population of Oakland increased by approximately 27,000 new residents.[36] Between the 2000 and 2010 censuses, Oakland lost close to 33,000 of its African American residents.[37] Yet, Oakland still has a very diverse population when looking at demographics on a citywide scale. When focusing on West Oakland's 94607 zip code, African Americans still represent the largest segment of the population (table 8.2).[38]

The West Oakland Specific Plan

The images in appendix A of the WOSP consist of site photos and renderings of the proposed development. The existing site images show an empty and/ or blighted landscape, while the proposed development renderings show more trees and green spaces, depicting a significant greening event. A new Oakland is (re)created in which wealthier and whiter populations are rendered into this new green future while replacing the existing Black population, thus appropriating this historically African American neighborhood.

Appendix A, the design guidelines, consists of thirteen images, including the Opportunity Area map. This section focuses on five sets of pictures in appendix A, five photos of the existing opportunity sites, and five renderings of the proposed development depicting a greener future Oakland. A set of images is not included in the following analysis, but the pattern remains consistent with the images discussed. The Opportunity Area map contains four locations; Opportunity Area 1—Mandela/West Grand; Opportunity Area 2—Seventh Street; Opportunity Area 3—Third Street; and Opportunity Area 4—San Pablo Avenue. These opportunity areas represent the potential sites for development and have shared characteristics based on "factors that have impeded development, [that are] economically feasible, [with] similar land-use policies and regulations, street configurations and infrastructure systems that support future development."[39]

In what follows, the existing Opportunity Area sites are placed in comparison with each of the renderings of the proposed development. The juxtaposition of these images tells a story through visual depictions of the state of these sites and the municipality's desired outcome for West Oakland. The photos that show the existing sites express historically rooted environmental narratives and practices that remove the current population by portraying an empty, unpeopled landscape while also depicting a blighted urban landscape and wasteland. The African American population is diminished from its actual residential tract population numbers and has virtually disappeared from the site photos as well as the future renderings, which show a diverse population. The Opportunity Area map (map 8.1) is divided into eleven census tracts, labeled A through K, and corresponds to table 8.3, which identifies each tract and shows the total population and race by percentages within each of these tracts, based on the 2010 US census.[40] African Americans are the largest population in all the tracts except one area, identified as I, in which the Asian population is 51 percent (map 8.1 and table 8.3).

The Racialization of Gentrification in the WOSP

W. E. B. Du Bois's *double consciousness*, Claire Jean Kim's *colorblind talk*, and Kenneth Gould and Tammy Lewis's *green gentrification* are useful concepts that underpin this section and show how the WOSP is rendering gentrification and erasing race. The relationship between the audience and the images they are exposed to is not passive. Through interpellation, images

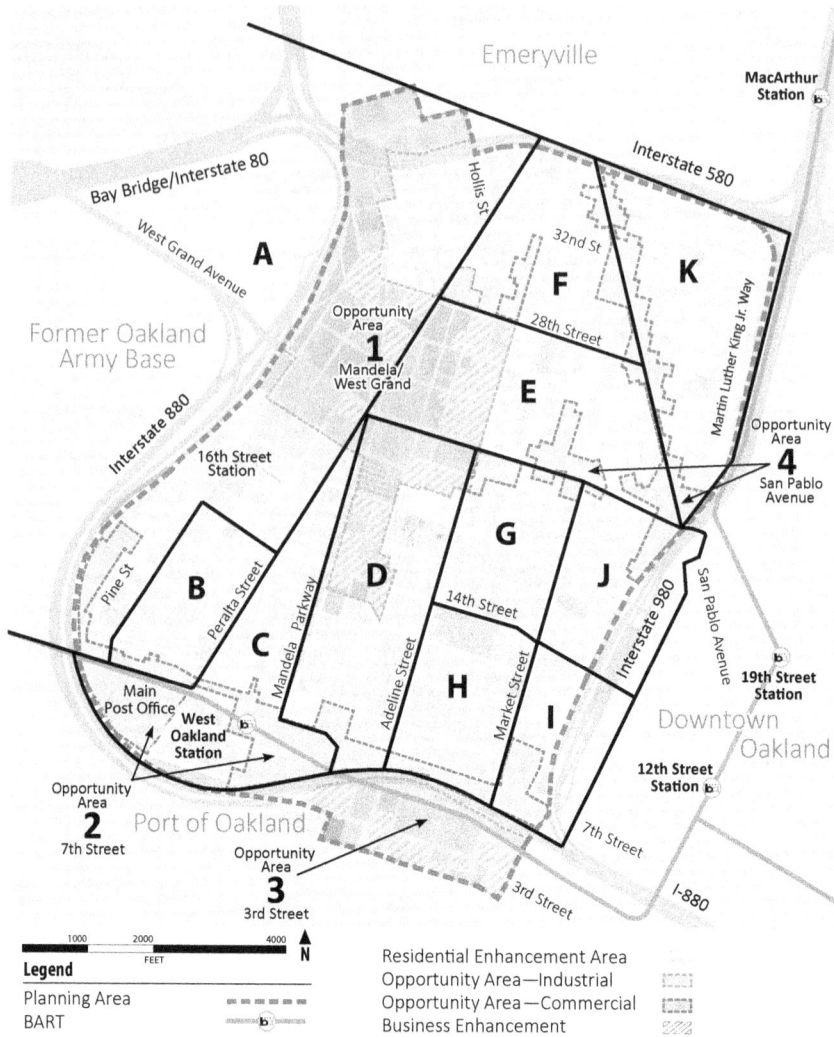

MAP 8.1. West Oakland Opportunity Areas. The tract labels correspond to total population and race percentages in table 8.3.

and renderings act on spectators, calling them "forth as subjects [and] setting conditions under which they can assume their identity."[41] For Black Oaklanders, as observers of these images, they must mentally negotiate with a type of municipal-induced double consciousness in which they are positioned as a problem, the producers of blight, and the creators of urban wastelands while also seeing through the gaze of the municipal government, which looks at them "in amused contempt and pity," by propagandizing

TABLE 8.3. West Oakland Opportunity Area Tract Data 2010 by Population Totals and Racial Demographic Percentages

Area	Popu-lation Total	Black %	White %	Latinx %	Asian %	Other %	Native Ameri-can %
A	2,667	33	26	26	10	5	—
B	1,703	57	15	19	3	5	—
C	2,385	36	16	30	12	5	—
D	2,193	62	7	9	17	5	—
E	2,163	47	16	21	12	4	1
F	2,630	53	20	15	8	4	—
G	2,351	58	13	9	14	6	1
H	1,784	67	8	5	17	4	—
I	1,151	30	11	6	51	3	—
J	1,569	56	13	16	10	5	—
K	4,314	48	13	21	10	5	1

their removal.[42] The images are not just showing an urban environment with people; rather, when situated within city plans and municipal documents, they aid in producing the very spaces they portray and invoke the populations they aim to attract and exclude.

Opportunity Area 1: Mandela/West Grand

All the site images in the WOSP convey what Claire Jean Kim identifies as colorblind talk by showing a diverse population to "hide the American racial order from view, protecting it from challenge ... by obscuring [it]."[43] Specifically, the WOSP misrepresents the current African American population through the lack of dark skin representation and rendering fewer Black people than recorded by census tract data and citywide demographic figures.[44] This can be interpreted as a type of racial ordering on display that is "classifying different [racial] groups with concrete distributional conse-quences" and with "certain privileges and/or exclusions" from healthy green spaces.[45] Lastly, the projected development renderings display a different and more affluent, whiter population and a greener landscape; thus, green gentrification is depicted in this municipal plan and exhibited in Oppor-tunity Area 1 (figures 8.1 and 8.2).[46] Applying the concepts discussed will show how the renderings of a future West Oakland privilege non-Blacks and call these populations forth as subjects to acknowledge their place as beneficiaries of this green future.

Opportunity Area 2: Seventh Street and Peralta

Kim's concepts of racial ordering and colorblind talk can also be seen in figures 8.3 and 8.4, which depict the existing view and proposed develop-ment at Seventh Street and Peralta.[47] While figure 8.3 shows another un-peopled landscape, figure 8.4 depicts an active intersection with a diverse population. These renderings evoke the erasure of the African American population (see figure 8.3) and construct a racial ordering through inaccu-rate representation (see figure 8.4). There are only three identifiable Black people: two women and a man who is half within the image and half outside the frame, connoting that he is not whole but severed from fully access-ing this new green space. Although the image shows racial diversity, it can also be understood that non-Black residents are moving through this space in numbers not reflective of the current demographics of West Oakland.

Opportunity Area 2: West Oakland BART Station at Seventh Street and Mandela Parkway

The images of Seventh Street and Mandela Parkway, also located in Op-portunity Area 2, are fraught with many contradictions and tensions in representing race and space (figures 8.5 and 8.6).[48] The existing view shows an urban landscape overwhelmed by gray and anemic green spaces, emp-tied of people and lacking community (figure 8.5). It is a far cry from rep-licating this neighborhood's standing racial demographics or activities and connotes an abandoned landscape. Either this is a well-timed photographic opportunity in an effort to display an emptied urban space or, in a more nefarious interpretation, the image could have been digitally manipulated to remove the population, thus intentionally erasing them from the land-scape in the plan.

The rendering of the proposed development of the West Oakland BART Station at Seventh Street and Mandela Parkway shows a building

FIGURE 8.1. Existing view at Twenty-Sixth Street from Mandela Parkway.

FIGURE 8.2. Proposed development at Twenty-Sixth Street from Mandela Parkway.

FIGURE 8.3. Existing view at Seventh Street and Peralta.

FIGURE 8.4. Proposed development at Seventh Street and Peralta.

FIGURE 8.5. Existing view at Seventh Street and Mandela Parkway.

FIGURE 8.6. Proposed development at Seventh Street and Mandela Parkway.

identified as the Blues Art Café (figure 8.6), which could be an attempt to "honor the culture, legacy, and history that have made West Oakland special," as articulated in appendix A.[49] Yet something very different is being conveyed. Although the image identifies the historical legacy of a Black West Oakland by centering blues, it breaks away from it by producing a visual equivalent of environmental gentrification in that this municipal document is masquerading as "ecologically and socially sensitive," yet it shows "profit-minded development."[50]

The politics of green gentrification, environmental gentrification, and historical racialized environmental narratives are more clearly revealed. An enlarged image of the proposed development of Seventh Street and Mandela Parkway shows a group of Black men playing musical instruments to a small all-white crowd (figure 8.7). The image of the band aligns with the style of music historically associated with West Oakland and the Second Great Migration of African Americans from the South. As much as this depicts a Black musical heritage through street performance, it also places these men as informal laborers, selling their music for dollars and cents to be collected in an instrument case lying on the ground. They serve as entertainment for the predominantly white residents, but they most likely cannot afford to live there themselves. In the bottom left corner, a Black woman with a Black child is also depicted, but they are walking away, heading out of the frame and out of the area (figure 8.8).

This rendering positions African Americans at the bottom of the social hierarchy and conveys that they no longer belong in this neighborhood or in West Oakland, while white populations are being called, hailed, and pulled into these same spaces. These images reflect the desired population the municipal government seeks and directly render this population into being. Caught in the spectacle of what appears to be a racially diverse future of West Oakland, the current population is lost to the promise of a better, greener, whiter, and wealthier tomorrow depicting green gentrification.

Opportunity Area 3: Third Street and Linden Street

The existing image of Third Street and Linden Street (figure 8.9) does not show the racial characteristics of this space.[51] However, it still holds to the previous patterns of emptied landscapes and a lack of healthy vegetation. The proposed developments for Third and Linden (figure 8.10) show new tree-lined streets.[52]

FIGURE 8.7. Enlarged image of street performers from proposed development at Seventh Street and Mandela Parkway.

FIGURE 8.8. Enlarged image of Black woman and child from proposed development at Seventh Street and Mandela Parkway.

FIGURE 8.9. Existing view of Third Street and Linden Street.

FIGURE 8.10. Proposed development at Third Street and Linden Street.

FIGURE 8.11. Existing view at San Pablo near West Grand Avenue.

FIGURE 8.12. Proposed development at San Pablo near West Grand Avenue.

Opportunity Area 4: San Pablo Avenue Near West Grand

This same pattern of depicting a lack of nature and population is also seen within the existing image for Opportunity Area 4 at San Pablo Avenue near West Grand, with the proposed rendering showing a greening event (figures 8.11 and 8.12).[53] The new buildings illustrated in the renderings for Opportunity Areas 3 and 4 are most likely condos and luxury apartments, housing that most current residents would be unable to afford. Moreover, the existing low-income housing is nowhere to be found. Again, the plan conveys which residents are welcomed into Oakland's sustainable green city and which are not.

Conclusion

The photos and renderings from the West Oakland Specific Plan's appendix A design guidelines demonstrate a different racialization of space than the current population in the predominantly African American district. The plan replicates and perpetuates historically rooted environmental narratives, practices, and patterns of dispossession, displacement, and replacement previously enacted in the creation of Central Park and the National Park System, and expressed in the green space aesthetics and racial exclusions of the City Beautiful movement and the Garden City movement. Moreover, these practices and movements align with the contemporary processes of green gentrification, ecological gentrification, and environmental gentrification. The erasure of the African American community from these proposed healthy green neighborhoods and the positioning of non-Black residents as the beneficiaries of these improvements elucidate the environmental racism embedded within this municipal project. In so doing, the West Oakland Specific Plan rebrands the municipality as a white and green sustainable city.

Notes

1   City of Oakland, "West Oakland Specific Plan Introduction," 1-1.

2   City of Oakland, "Oakland City Council Resolution No. 72809 C.M.S."

3   City of Oakland, "Recent Oakland Sustainability Awards."

4   Lehmann, "Green Urbanism," 1–10.

5   Bullard, "Anatomy of Environmental Racism," 17.

6   Greenberg et al., "Linking City Planning and Public Health," 235–39.

7   Spirn, "Constructing Nature," 91–113.

8   Thompson, "Linking Landscape and Health," 187–95.

9   Fordero, "Unearthing Traces of African-American Village Displaced by Central Park."

10   Taylor, "Race, Class, Gender, and American Environmentalism," 1–51.

11   Spence, "Dispossessing the Wilderness," 27–29.

12   Spence, "Dispossessing the Wilderness," 27–29.

13   DeLuca and Demo, "Imagining Nature and Erasing Class and Race," 541–60.

14   Thompson, "Linking Landscape and Health," 191.

15   Rudwick and Meier, "Black Man in the 'White City,'" 354–61.

16   Peterson, "Clarkdale, Arizona," 29.

17   Bagwell, *Oakland*, 171.

18   Parsons and Schuyler, *From Garden City to Green City*, 7.

19   Self, *American Babylon*, 25–26.

20   Finney, *Black Faces, White Spaces*, 32–50.

21   Self, *American Babylon*, 106.

22   Glass, *London*, xiii–xlii.

23   Smith, "New Globalism, New Urbanism," 427–50.

24   Dooling, "Ecological Gentrification," 630.

25   Solnit, "Death by Gentrification"; Ali, "Tamir Rice Death"; Levin, "'We're Being Pushed Out.'"

26   Checker, "Wiped Out by the 'Greenwave.'"

27   Checker, "Wiped Out by the 'Greenwave,'" 212.

28   Gould and Lewis, "Environmental Injustice of Green Gentrification," 113–46.

29   Self, *American Babylon*, 157.

30   Self, *American Babylon*, 156.

31   Self, *American Babylon*, 157.

32   Parliament, *Chocolate City*.

33   California Environmental Protection Agency, "California Office of Environmental Health Hazard Assessment."

34   California Environmental Protection Agency, "CalEnvironScreen 3.0 Pollution Burden Map."

35 California Environmental Protection Agency, "CalEnvironScreen 2.0 Pollution Burden Indicators Cleanups."

36 Bay Area Census, "City of Oakland, Alameda County."

37 Bay Area Census, "City of Oakland, Alameda County."

38 US Census Bureau, "Census.Gov," 2010.

39 City of Oakland, "West Oakland Specific Plan Introduction," 1–13.

40 California Environmental Protection Agency, "CalEnvironScreen 2.0 Census Tracts."

41 Fourie, *Media Studies*.

42 Du Bois, *Souls of Black Folk*, 3.

43 Kim, *Bitter Fruit*, 17.

44 Kim, *Bitter Fruit*, 19

45 Kim, *Bitter Fruit*, 17.

46 City of Oakland, "West Oakland Specific Plan Appendix A," A-7.

47 City of Oakland, "West Oakland Specific Plan Appendix A," A-10.

48 City of Oakland, "West Oakland Specific Plan Appendix A," A-14.

49 City of Oakland, "West Oakland Specific Plan Appendix A," A-1.

50 Checker, "Wiped Out by the 'Greenwave,'" 210–29.

51 City of Oakland, "West Oakland Specific Plan Appendix A," A-9.

52 City of Oakland, "West Oakland Specific Plan Appendix A," A-9.

53 City of Oakland, "West Oakland Specific Plan Appendix A," A-11.

Bibliography

Ali, Safia Samee. "Tamir Rice Death: Newly Released Video Shows Cop's Shifting Account." *NBC News*, April 26, 2017. https://www.nbcnews.com/news/us-news/newly-released-interview-footage-reveal-shifting-stories-officers-who-shot-n751401.

Bagwell, Beth. *Oakland: The Story of a City.* 2nd ed. Oakland, CA: Oakland Heritage Alliance, 2012.

Bay Area Census. "City of Oakland, Alameda County." Accessed November 5, 2018, http://www.bayareacensus.ca.gov/cities/Oakland70.htm.

Bullard, Robert D. "Anatomy of Environmental Racism and the Environmental Justice Movement." In *Confronting Environmental Racism: Voices from the Grassroots*, edited by Robert D. Bullard, 15–39. Boston: South End, 1993.

California Environmental Protection Agency. "CalEnvironScreen 2.0 Census Tracts." Accessed June 8, 2019. https://oehha.maps.arcgis.com/apps/MapSeries/index.html?appid=42671dba7b114509922401135ff86588&webmap=28431b9f419346d7ba38f875263iaed4.

California Environmental Protection Agency. "CalEnvironScreen 2.0 Pollution Burden Indicators Cleanups." Accessed June 8, 2019. https://oehha.maps.arcgis.com

/apps/MapSeries/index.html?appid=42671dba7b114509922401135ff86588&webmap
=28431b9f419346d7ba38f875263iaed.

California Environmental Protection Agency. "CalEnviroScreen 3.0 Pollution
Burden." Accessed June 3, 2019. https://oehha.ca.gov/calenviroscreen/report
/calenviroscreen-30.

California Environmental Protection Agency. "California Office of Environmental
Health Hazard Assessment." Accessed May 4, 2020. https://oehha.ca.gov/.

Checker, Melissa. "Wiped Out by the 'Greenwave': Environmental Gentrification
and the Paradoxical Politics of Urban Sustainability." *City and Society* 23, no. 2
(2011): 210–29.

City of Oakland. "Oakland City Council Resolution No. 72809 C.M.S." July 23, 1996.

City of Oakland. "Recent Oakland Sustainability Awards." Last modified
January 20, 2021. https://www.oaklandca.gov/resources/oaklands-sustainability
-awards.

City of Oakland. "West Oakland Specific Plan Appendix A: Design Guidelines."
Accessed June 2, 2022. https://www.oaklandca.gov/resources/read-the-final
-west-oakland-specific-plan.

City of Oakland. "West Oakland Specific Plan Introduction." Accessed June 2, 2022.
https://oaklandca.s3.us-west-1.amazonaws.com/oakca1/groups/ceda/documents
/report/oak049121.pdf.

DeLuca, Kevin, and Anne Demo. "Imagining Nature and Erasing Class and Race:
Carleton Watkins, John Muir, and the Construction of Wilderness." *Environmental History* 6, no. 4 (2001): 541–60. doi.org/10.2307/3985254.

Dooling, Sarah. "Ecological Gentrification: A Research Agenda Exploring Justice
in the City." *International Journal of Urban and Regional Research* 33, no. 3 (2009):
621–39.

Du Bois, W. E. B. *The Souls of Black Folk*. New York: Bantam Books, 1989.

Finney, Carolyn. *Black Faces, White Spaces: Reimagining the Relationship of African
Americans to the Great Outdoors*. Chapel Hill: University of North Carolina Press,
2014.

Fordero, Lisa W. "Unearthing Traces of African-American Village Displaced by
Central Park." *New York Times*, July 27, 2011.

Fourie, Pieter J., ed. *Media Studies: Media History, Media and Society*. Cape Town:
Juta and Company, 2010.

Glass, Ruth. *London: Aspects of Change*. London: MacKibbon and Kee, 1964.

Gould, Kenneth A., and Tammy L. Lewis. "The Environmental Injustice of Green
Gentrification: The Case of Brooklyn's Prospect Park." In *The World in Brooklyn: Gentrification, Immigration, and Ethnic Politics in a Global City*, edited by Judith N. DeSena and Timothy Shortell, 113–46. Lanham, MD: Lexington Books,
2012.

Greenberg, Michael, Frank Popper, Bernadette West, and Donald Krueckeberg.
"Linking City Planning and Public Health in the United States." *Journal of
Planning Literature* 8, no. 3 (1994): 235–39.

Kim, Claire Jean. *Bitter Fruit: The Politics of Black-Korean Conflict in New York City.* New Haven, CT: Yale University Press, 2000.

Lehmann, Steffen. "Green Urbanism: Formulating a Series of Holistic Principles." *S.A.P.I.EN.S. Surveys and Perspectives Integrating Environment and Society* 3, no. 2 (2010): 1–10.

Levin, Sam. "'We're Being Pushed Out': The Displacement of Black Oakland." *Guardian*, June 1, 2018. https://www.theguardian.com/us-news/2018/jun/01 /from-black-panthers-to-bbq-becky-the-displacement-of-black-oakland.

Parliament. *Chocolate City.* LP. Casablanca, 1975.

Parsons, Kermit Carlyle, and David Schuyler, eds. *From Garden City to Green City: The Legacy of Ebenezer Howard.* Baltimore, MD: Johns Hopkins University Press, 2002.

Peterson, Helen. "Clarkdale, Arizona: Built Environment, Social Order, and the City Beautiful Movement, 1913–1920." *Journal of Arizona History* 49, no. 1 (2008): 27–46.

Rudwick, Elliott M., and August Meier. "Black Man in the 'White City': Negroes and the Columbian Exposition, 1893." *Phylon* 26, no. 4 (1965): 354–61. doi.org/10.2307/273699.

Self, Robert O. *American Babylon: Race and the Struggle for Postwar Oakland.* Princeton, NJ: Princeton University Press, 2003.

Smith, Neil. "New Globalism, New Urbanism: Gentrification as Global Urban Strategy." *Antipode* 34, no. 3 (2002): 427–50. doi.org/10.1111/1467-8330.00249.

Solnit, Rebecca. "Death by Gentrification: The Killing That Shamed San Francisco." *Guardian*, April 4, 2016. https://www.theguardian.com/news/audio/2016 /apr/04/death-by-gentrification-the-killing-that-shamed-san-francisco.

Spence, Mark. "Dispossessing the Wilderness: Yosemite Indians and the National Park Ideal, 1864–1930." *Pacific Historical Review* 65, no. 1 (1996): 27–59.

Spirn, Anne Whiston. "Constructing Nature: The Legacy of Fredrick Law Olmsted." In *Uncommon Ground: Rethinking the Human Place in Nature*, edited by William Cronon, 91–113. New York: W. W. Norton, 1996.

Taylor, Dorceta E. "Race, Class, Gender, and American Environmentalism." Portland, OR: US Department of Agriculture, Forest Service, Pacific Northwest Research Station, 2002.

Thompson, Catharine Ward. "Linking Landscape and Health: The Recurring Theme." *Landscape and Urban Planning* 99, nos. 3–4 (2011): 187–95. doi.org/10 .1016/j.landurbplan.2010.10.006.

9

"Need Black Joy?"

Mapping an Afrotechtonics of Gathering in Los Angeles

MATTHEW JORDAN-MILLER KENYATTA

In the shadows of a summer night, a scattered procession of young Black socialites descends on a dimly lit, partly residential street in the postindustrial downtown area of Los Angeles. The attraction: a fledgling Black-owned business called Comfort LA catering to them by offering a "clean approach" to "Granny's" soul food. Located on the far east margins of Seventh Street, Comfort was an unsuspecting speakeasy-like tar-black building. In other words, they manifested a spatial identity out of an interstitial landscape. They collaged a Black "interdictory" space lodged somewhere between Skid Row's heart for the unhoused, the Latinx- and immigrant-dominated Fashion District, and the newly dubbed Arts District adjacent to the renowned Southern California Institute of Architecture. These gentrifying "in-beyond" spaces—as critical geographers Michael Dear and Steven Flusty once called these "internal peripheries simultaneously undergoing but resisting instrumentalization in myriad ways"—are where Black and immigrant entrepreneurial hustles often arise by necessity in the postmodern city.[1]

Barely a year earlier than that June 2017 evening, I attended the business's late-night soft launch, where I met the burly, tall, tattooed chef Jeremy McBryde. The retired actor was serving "Big Sexy" chicken platters out of the gated peephole below a blinking neon "OPEN" sign that became a to-go window while the interior seating was being renovated. McBryde's friends were mostly emerging actors in Hollywood of the Issa Rae generation who came to "Buy Black" as much as they did to fill their stomachs with food customarily not available after 11:00 p.m. in the older family-owned Black restaurants that stopped serving long before midnight. As an academic writer proposing a doctoral dissertation exploring Black culture in an age of urban displacement, I, too, was a Black creative working outside that prototypical domesticated space-time of "family hours." In between that initial encounter and my eventual candidacy in May the following year, the owners took their business to the streets. McBryde and his cofounder, Mark Walker, managed to grow their business through targeted, tactical, and tenacious street vending at "pop-up" events all over LA. In the beginning, they had repurposed their adjacent parking lot into what urban designers might call a "parklet," with benches for customers instead of room for cars. Comfort not only became an indoor restaurant but also offered ample outdoor space in the back.

That night, it was LA's turn to pop into the location for an event called the Link Up. An onyx rectangular sign above the door spelling "Come Get That Action" in red capital letters welcomed me into the already talkative and lively restaurant full of music. To my right, a middle-aged, male-presenting disc jockey stood beneath two fluorescent obelisks illuminating his sonic technology: a silver MacBook connected to a sound system humming at only a fraction of its capacity. Behind him was a collaged wall plastered with vinyl CD covers across the aural ages of Blackness—from Donna Summer to Prince and forward. But his music was not the primary purpose of this gathering. It was about becoming proximate to those patrons who, on its website, Comfort LA boasts about: "an electric mix of the downtown family, loft dwellers, pimps, hustlers, international travelers, students, artists, adventurers, bankers, entrepreneurs and entertainers holding down the spot."

A little over thirty folks who seemed to fit this bill cozied up at three pairs of mahogany wood church pew–like benches and showered the family-style tables with their smartphones, board games like Dirty Minds, and "clean soul food" from Comfort LA. With its food offerings of fried chicken wings drenched in a signature honey-based hot sauce ("That Sauce") and sprinkled with parsley accompanied by sweet cornbread and collard greens served on a compostable plate, the Link Up was a different kind of mixer. It felt more like a college game night with sports playing on the television. The flat-screen TV held a privileged axonometric view of the Black gastronomic scene, projecting the moving images onto the seated consumers. It also greeted the kitchen staff behind the register accepting new orders from the handful of prospective customers standing under the white dangling placards "Grab & Dip" and "Order & Chill" for food requests from the no-frills menu.

Two South LA natives and cultural organizers formed the Link Up in March 2017: a budding curator, Tyree Boyd-Pates, and a digital producer, Makiah Green, who eventually assumed full responsibility for the marketing service they called Black Book LA (BBLA). In fact, they were the reason I found out about Comfort LA's soft launch a year earlier. After asking the DJ to ease the music, Tyree kicked off the event that poetic full-circle night by thanking the attendees and the hosts. He reminded us of BBLA's purpose and invited everyone to come back but also pointed toward more seating available on the back patio. Rather than standing at the cocktail tables along the exposed brick wall, I elected to enjoy the patio with a handful of newly acquainted millennials—comedian Myiesha, singer Alexander, and immigration activist Tia. Under a string of outdoor lights enclosed by a canopy of trees, we sat and became friends while sipping on the restaurant's ginger-infused fresh juice version of Kool-Aid. If you happened upon the patio during a daytime Soulful Sundays event, you would encounter live music from emerging talent and wellness start-ups offering discounted samples to adult listeners.

However, in the same emailed invitation for the Link Up, BBLA was also promoting a candlelit vigil, hosted by Black Lives Matter LA cofounder Patrisse Cullors. At the Underground Museum, dozens gathered to remember Charleena Lyles of Seattle, who was slain four days earlier by Seattle police officers in her public housing. The activists also took the opportunity to continue mourning those killed by the LAPD and the sheriff's office under then district attorney Jackie Lacey's watch. Dozens of Black folks held scentless wax candles, even toddlers who were not sure what to do with them yet learning from their elders, as a curly-haired healer improvised a song above Cullors seated below her in the center of the courtyard.

Currently, geography offers few original terms to spotlight the meaningful interactions between race, place, and taste: how Blackness travels as a global cultural identity embodied, commodified, consumed, and reproduced through technology. This chapter sketches these scalar and topographic dimensions of everyday dynamic forms of cultural gatherings that constitute Blackness as *desirable* and *distinctive* urbanisms in the city, namely, through experiences marketed toward and by millennials in the metropolitan city-region of Los Angeles, California. The chapter quantifies and briefly qualifies the locations where the tastes of an undermapped spatial group—Black young people and digital natives—manifest in urbanity.

Derived from a larger transdisciplinary study of Black cultural and economic geographies in South Los Angeles, this chapter mines a three-year longitudinal dataset of over twelve hundred events, broadcast online by a four-year-old marketing start-up, Black Book LA. In mapping gathering spaces for Black folks to emplace leisure in LA, I marshal three quantitative approaches: (1) Getis-Ord hot spot analysis to highlight areas where events occur recursively, (2) demographic analysis to read the residential landscapes surrounding them, and (3) simple descriptive statistics around the costs of entry. As the opening passage illustrates, these quantitative analyses are briefly interspersed with autoethnographies, reflecting on my affective experiences as an attendee in select locations. Altogether, I feel the pulse of a valuable form of interaction to render these gathering patterns free from the realm of "elsewhere" and "no one knows."[2] I argue for three cultural heartbeats of Black geographies:

1 Black joyful space is not biogeographically determined.
2 Black joyful space can be subversive toward racialized capitalist economies.
3 Black joyful places and spaces reflect a distinctive gravitational draw.

While contributing some methods to the field-defining collective project of resurfacing Black Geographies, this chapter begins to rework concepts of the everyday to make geography more conversant with the situated knowledge of those outside the academy. This work frames Blackness as being a capacious technology *itself*: offering zones to struggle over domination, exploitation, and segregation as much as joyful sites for Black resilience and leisure.[3] Namely, I position two popular terms—*Afrotech* and *Black joy*—as traits and technologies of Black public spheres especially relevant for this digital-augmented era. Through them, I propose my own term that unites and spatializes them as *Afrotechtonics* to gesture toward a conceptual agenda that surpasses the limitations facing them individually. Black Geographies may be an intellectual home for surfacing these complexities further.

Emplacing Black Joy: The Cartographic and the Cyberspatial

While conceptualizing this prism of Black joy through technology and geography is a newer intellectual project, Black joy is an everyday reflex with a longer history at the crossroads of urban geographies, business, and information technology. Black joy is inseparable from the Black Arts Movement of the 1970s through the 1990s, which cultivated a need to express one's unique stories and desires as essential to being human and being free. With the "sociogenic principle" inspired by Sylvia Wynter and Frantz Fanon in mind, community art is the localized engine of Black joy that refuses the Westernized notion of "Man" that "over-represents itself" as humanism entirely through a parallel plane: a decolonized "counterhumanism."[45] Yet, in the cultural industries of film, television, and music (i.e., "Hollywood") anchored in Los Angeles, wherein my case takes place, that Anglocentric patriarchal worldview is still overpresent. In a sense, Black joy is a countercartography of these shadows.

Black joy is a contemporary phrase that can appear to represent an emotive state of catharsis within the microgeography of a single Black body. However, Black joy could also be understood as part of a Black "networked consciousness" or "linked fate" found in African American literature and politics that Black feminist bell hooks and philosopher Cornel West invoked at moments in the 1990s.[6] Through Gina Dent's edited volume *Black Popular Culture* (1992), West helps distinguish Black joy from an atomistic affective state of happiness: "Pleasure, under commodified conditions, tends to be inward. You take it with you, and it's a highly individuated unit.... But joy tries to cut across that. Joy tries to get at those non-market values—love, care, kindness, service, solidarity, the struggle for justice—values that provide the possibility of bringing people together."[7] Few academic works have yet to name Black joy as a metaphysical frame meriting collective use in Black study.[8] Recent groundbreaking work continues to clarify that "joy" goes beyond fleeting "happiness"; Black joy endures throughout times of struggle and simultaneously with pain.[9] Thus, Black joy is not monolithic.

In more recent years, Black joy has been politicized as a stance of "resistance" by advocacy groups like the Black Youth Project, the #BlackJoyProject, and Color of Change, which has a Black Joy Squad in various cities.[10] Despite these instantiations of public refusal, Black joy is not always an intentional rebuke. The geographic question of Black joy requires rerouting our libidinal centers away from the white gaze in space and in time toward an existence of our own making. Thus, Black joyfulness can be unbothered in its affect while cultivating physical and digital spaces that are *made* oppositional to white supremacy by the desire for freedom. Black joy is a portal to a quantum *collective* with multiple modes and symbolic sites for gathering: to relax, to release, and to reinforce the celebratory, pleasurable, free, and affirming aspects of being Black while healing and grieving and organizing around the oppressive aspects.[11] Altogether, Black joy might be understood, then, as an *oppositional* practice of Black love in the face of hegemonic cultural injustice and racist disregard for the *distinctive* desires, dreams, and delimitations found within Afrodiasporic space. Both physical and digital space must co-conspire to birth these at scale in the twenty-first century.

On Physical Space: Materializing and Spatializing Black Joy in Los Angeles

Spatial dispossession has never extinguished the emergence of Black joy in public, digitally or otherwise; it merely shapes its destination. Consider urban street corners. From W. E. B. Du Bois's study of the Philadelphia "Negro" to the 2005 music of neo-soul artist Lonnie Lynn aka Common, the corner has played a special role in urban Black life. While the popular HBO television show *The Wire* based on Baltimore depicted the corner as a site of vice (e.g., daytime drinking of liquor, heroin sales), street poets witness a virtuous struggle unfolding in and because of these same corners. While Common attests to the drug-driven economies in Chicago, he contextualizes these as emerging from existential desperation to meet material needs: "Corners leave souls opened and closed, hoping for mo' / With nowhere to go." This desire for more also motivates aspirational tactics in this small space:

The corner was our magic, our music, our politics
Fires raised as tribal dances and war cries
Broke out on different corners
Power to the people
Black power
Black is beautiful.[12]

Urban geographer Brandi Thompson Summers also takes on this tension between the intimacies of Black life hyperpresent on "The Corner" in her piercing analysis of the spatial politics of gentrification in Washington, DC, the once "chocolate city" made more vanilla through mechanisms of surveillance, ghettoization, and even discursive stigma online.[13]

The shifting loci of Black residential life keep the "Where?" of Black joy fluid, especially in Los Angeles. For much of the twentieth century, due to the Second Great Migration of African Americans from the South, urban centers hosted much of Black life. Due to rampant segregation, cities were the "chocolate" concrete cores while suburbs were the wealthy "vanilla," white-picketed outposts of American regions.[14] However, neighborhood change researchers find that places are becoming more segregated by income within racial groups regardless of spatial form, due in part to dramatic increases in income inequality since the 1970s.[15] In the top ten metropolitan areas, the Residential Income Segregation Index score has increased across nearly all of them since 1980, with Los Angeles metropolitan statistical area—the spatial unit of this analysis—being one of most economically segregated. Contrary to the dominant narrative about gentrification, most neighborhoods change slowly, and many Americans are more rooted in place than ever before.[16] It is only within the places that have seen some in- and out-migration that the residential patterns have been shifting along cultural, racial, and economic lines. As young adults have grown up and their middle-class parents have become "empty nesters," a "back-to-the-city" movement has been underway, with little signs of stopping.[17]

As critical geographers have pointed out since the 1970s, Los Angeles developed a unique morphological footprint when it came to urbanization and Blackness compared with most postindustrial cities. Many abandoned postindustrial cities of the East and Midwest were seen as formerly "gritty" but have refashioned themselves as "neo-bohemias" for the racially and economically segregated "creative class."[18] However, geographers elucidated the "privatopia" developments embraced in LA that created a litany of hostile suburban landscapes that eventually became "edge cities" unto themselves, warranting the broader terms *postmetropolis* and *postsuburbia*.[19] In restructuring itself, Los Angeles also pioneered forms of techno-surveillance and (over)policing to make transplants seeking a manufactured American dreamscape feel protected in their own "privatopia" of gated communities and single-family residentially zoned neighborhoods. Amid these factors, after 1960, the center of Black gravity in LA shifted from Central Avenue to the southwest Crenshaw district.[20]

Black LA geographies have been influenced by the "sticks" of gentrification—the push factors of unaffordability and cultural violence via increased policing.[21] But Black residential patterns have also been slightly buoyed by temporary "carrots": increased access to loans, college educations, and jobs in the suburbs. In this postmetropolis region, many Black middle-class families moved out of the inner city into underdeveloped, unfinished, initially "master planned" communities in "edge cities" like Lancaster and Fontana while still being culturally and economically overdependent on core LA. Unfortunately, despite these families' desires for "peace of mind" and "more for less" in these exurban frontiers, the Great Recession reduced those Black homeownership and wealth gains significantly.[22] While there has been an active dispersal and dispossession of Black presence in South Los Angeles in the last fifty years, Black LA as a residential assemblage is still mostly anchored by seven major neighborhoods adjacent to the north-south Crenshaw Boulevard corridor: (1) West Adams, (2) Jefferson Park, (3) Baldwin Hills/Crenshaw, (4) Leimert Park, (5) View Park-Windsor Hills, (6) Hyde Park, and (7) Inglewood.

Chocolate neighborhoods in Los Angeles have largely been predicated on housing and residential location, but Black joy amid this "chocolate city" reworlding of place defies those static boundaries and requires capacious understandings of Black mobility. While dominant narratives on Black life have centered segregation and legalized exclusion from mainstream white American institutions, a parallel vibrant history must include how these same spaces of entrapment allowed Black creatives to affordably stay, exchange ideas, and innovate in ways that became and remain mainstream today.[23] In the shadows of disinvestment, "chocolate cities" like South Los Angeles became runways and stages for Black cultural innovations that became global assets such as jazz, hip-hop cyphers, streetwear, vogue balls, and more. These same urban spaces are prime targets for a returning gentry now seeking denser housing, retail, and offices, which makes these hubs precarious today.

Black joy, like the broader idea of Blackness, is as spatially "distributed" in its discrete forms as in digital forums. However, time matters just as much as space in mapping geographies of Black joy; asking "When?" will produce a different result to the question of where. Historian Faustina DuCros offers an intergenerational history of Louisiana Creole social clubs established from the time of the Great Migration until the 1970s.[24] Cultural anthropologists and filmmakers have documented how chocolate neighborhoods in South Central, especially along Crenshaw, like Leimert Park, have incubated freedom dreams through music, especially African drumming, hip-hop cyphers, jazz, and soul.[25] Monique Azzara focuses on Black churches, which struggle with "impermanence," not always being a storefront or even a megachurch but sometimes holding services in parks and in homes.[26] Urban sociologists have pointed to LGBTQ+ dance venues and community health clubs as queer static spaces, but also to how contemporary Black queer life is ephemerally rooted in "Black nights" in majority white–run West Hollywood.[27] Black joy is a "cross-platform" institution of resilience, across digital spaces and in person.[28] Outlining the contours of that institution as a spatial imaginary requires new forms of data, science, and data scientists to find this Colored People's Space-Time along "indigenous timelines."[29]

On Cyberspace: Digitizing the Temporal Tectonics of Black Joy

Cyberspace has been a disruptive, algorithmic force on every facet of contemporary life, from the ballots to the buffet. Black Americans are one of the largest consumer groups in the economy, and that also applies to digital social media (e.g., Twitter), as they have been since the earliest periods of information technology. Due to Black dispersion to regional outskirts alongside reduced economic mobility, the meanings and mechanisms of being (dis)connected have changed. Black entrepreneurs' ability to market their products and services, for example, is mediated by technological access and algorithmic knowledge more than ever. Smartphones now steer how Black consumers decide where, when, and how they will participate in the cultural economy. These digital realities elevate the interlocutors who can streamline and curate preference-savvy advertisements to direct ever-mobile economies of attention. Put differently, the Yelps, Grubhubs, and Postmates of the world have become the new Yellow Pages for matching people with cultural places in the world.

In this chapter, tech-enabled culture is not seen as a hedonistic escape from sociopolitical life, and these cyber platforms are not neutral. Black cyberspace is also a venue to critique, speak back to dominant forces, and solidify values as a "counterpublic" sphere. One's cultural tastes in such unequal conditions are not apolitical; preferences are linked and "predisposed"by the contexts in which they arise.[30] Space is present in these tastes. Even when the product is taken away from its original context, place is in the product.[31] This taste-forming political function of space has been particularly poignant in Black musical forums, as Black geographer Clyde Woods roundly espoused in his "blues epistemology."[32] Racists also know this. That is why Yelp has been a tool for users to malign Black and Mexican restaurants in gentrifying neighborhoods in New York and Philadelphia and even act as a reliable indicator of coming gentrification in major urban centers.[33] Social life has been reconstituted by this unequal rise and domineering application of information technology.

Digital technology has shaped the possibilities for expressing Black joy since at least the late twentieth century. Interdisciplinary media scholar André Brock maps the Black roots of the internet, with BlackPlanet, established in 1999, serving as the first major Black-run social networking site. Unlike with the prior online spaces like MSBET (Microsoft + BET) and BlackVoices, Brock places this need for democratizing "discursive invention" squarely in the hands of BlackPlanet, which debuted social networking functions (e.g., votes, popularity, private messages). Teaming up with the niche website AsianAvenue's CEO in 1999, BlackPlanet cofounder Omar Wasow birthed a digital public sphere from his original New York Online site that attracted almost twenty million users by 2005.[34] Black joy became a technology itself, with everyday Black folks encoding it in ways that giants like Facebook, Instagram, and Twitter have replicated and normalized. Arguably, this power to design the digital commons has been diluted and diminished, with these mainstream websites now only allowing users to feed information into their website's design, rather than shape the form of the web 2.0 itself.

Big corporations were learning from and extracting Black preferences long before the internet, and this "attention economy" steered consumption toward (or away from) Black cultural experiences. Economic history reveals the concerted efforts that major corporations have made to secure brand loyalty from African Americans ("the Negro market")—from location siting to product placements. Hiring pioneering specialists such as Moss Kendrix and Edward J. Boyd, Pepsi created what Madison Avenue advertisers now call "niche" or "multicultural" marketing.[35] However, digital social media marketing has evolved in important ways; the cultural economy does not hinge entirely on demographic terms anymore. Tech giants like Facebook and Google have armed advertisers with a new resource—personalized consumer data—transforming marketing into a psychological battlefield over "psychographic" lifestyle. For years, it was unclear to digital marketers whether the community-driven campaigns to "Buy Black" steered consumption—that is, until the summer of 2020. Protest over systemic racism generated more pandemic-era purchases from Black-owned businesses than many had ever seen. Logistics companies like Uber Eats now had a business case for offering free curation to Black businesses, making hypervisible the taste for Black culture.

Enter Afrotech. While the term is often used to refer to an annual conference hosted by the Black millennial company Blavity since 2016, I elevate the idea of Afrotech here to mean something more than the limited context that the Black "cybergeoisie" meant. Used only once in reference to an analysis of a Black sculptor, Afrotech has not been rigorously defined.[36] Using the notion of Black public spheres, I define *Afrotech* as a neologism representing Black economic justice around information technology industries, liberation for the Black digital commons, and cultural self-determination through Afrofuturism.[37] First, the Afrotech frame invites Black communities to control their digital footprints and futures, challenging the digital apartheid of the tech industry, such as the hyperlocalization of venture capital in certain regions. Because of this, Black entrepreneurs have struggled to break into the white male–dominated industry and survive the fundraising gauntlets it takes to start a company. Further, racism and sexism in tech workplaces limit the avenues for gaining the social and human capital necessary for even a highly educated Black person (most likely a woman, given the rise of women in educational and entrepreneurial contexts) to be hired.[38] So, I invoke this word to expand its geographic use and cognitively map Black-owned companies seeking to use and shift digital space. Blavity is an example of a company doing that while also holding space for Black digital commons.

Moreover, Afrotech surpasses any machinelike understanding of "technology." Adopting a "pan-technological" stance from Black comix artist and scholar John Jennings and Beth Coleman, Afrotech draws on Blackness as an Afrofuturist technology itself that generates social delight. As Jennings once stated in an interview with *PopMatters*, "Afrofuturism . . . sees everything as a type of technology that can be hacked into, decoded, and made to function for a new agenda." Cultural scholar Clinton Fluker critically summons Beth Coleman's argument in her essay "Race as Technology" to infuse this pan-technological stance into his theorizing of Afrofuturism.[39] Like Fluker, I am critically departing from Coleman's color-blind musings on race as a "denatured object" to preserve Afrofuturism's reliance on historical specificity to perform cultural work in a racially unjust world. Afrofuturism channels Blackness as a rooted technology to hack hegemonic histories, including the racist grounds on which Black identity was forged. While racist institutions and people see Blackness as absolute abjection, Afrofuturists hack that perception with the technology of Black *joy*: the art of living through and creating pleasure and happiness alongside suffering.

Methods for Us, by Us

Considering the potentialities of Afrotech and challenging the spatialities of doing Blackness in the urban economy, what can we say about geographies of Black joy? Where does the mundane techno-hegemony leave gatherings for Black expressive culture and practices of joy? This chapter mines and maps a longitudinal dataset constructed between 2016 and 2018 by BBLA to begin locating these rhythms. Since 2016, over nineteen thousand people have become subscribers to BBLA's free-of-charge email, website, and Facebook/Instagram services. According to cofounder Makiah Green, nearly 58 percent of the BBLA subscriptions began during just the first year.[40] After being a subscriber for a year and attending some events to acclimate myself to Black culture in LA, I decided to mine the BBLA website and email announcements, which conveniently contained the location, time, and cost of each event. Initially, I created a dataset for a single year, 2017. However, in coordination with the company, the entire list was donated to this study in 2018. Thus, the data mining and data collection evoke an ethic of reflexive analysis *by* and *for* self-identified Black people.

I analyze these data with multiple ways of knowing. First, after optimizing the dataset for ArcGIS (e.g., manually standardizing addresses, field formats), I performed simple map algebra to generate summary statistics that could easily communicate frequencies of events, time of day or night, and venues. Second, I did a spatial join with the census tracts as the "target feature" and the geocoded events as the "join feature." Further, once I had the events joined (and counted) by census tract, I used an agglomerative type of spatial analysis—the optimized Getis-Ord hot spot analysis—to highlight areas where events occur repeatedly and cluster together. Hot spots are usually applied to epidemiological questions, not emotive and sociocultural topics such as "belongingness" and "joy" and "Blackness." Hot spots also are usually used to communicate a permanence rather than the occurrence of a temporality—an ephemeral sense of space and time; that is where the innovation of this approach comes in. I also draw on my own memories, reflections, and recordings (e.g., photos) to bridge that gap.

While this analysis did not systematically monitor the demographics of the attendees, an assumption was made based on the business model of the company's marketing efforts that most of the audiences were African American youth and young adults. This assumption was, again, an extrapolation bolstered in confidence partly by the fact that I was an attendee at the promoted events at least once a month. I also gathered census information—the 2016 American Community Survey (5-Year Estimates) and the 2017 Bureau of Labor Statistics Consumer Expenditure Survey—to contrast these impressions with the known residential environment nearby. The BBLA 2016–18 dataset constructed for this study has other variables such as the duration of the event, the cost of entry, promotional language, and links to event pages. However, my descriptive statistics focus on the on-site costs of entry as a proxy for economic access.

Enumerating LA's Gatherings for Black Joy

From June 2016 to December 2018, the marketed Black entertainment options were widely dispersed through the Los Angeles region. In total, more than 1,230 events occurred over this three-year period, with 92 percent of them able to be geocoded to known places and venues. Out of the 2,346 census tracts in Los Angeles County, the 245 events marketed in 2016 occurred in 98 tracts. With only 4.1 percent of tracts having an event, there is some level of nonrandom clustering here. In 2016, nearly 150 events occurred in the 40 census tracts that were considered statistically significant hot spots in the LA region, meaning they had a "Gi bin" number of 1, or were within the 90 percent confidence interval. The optimized hot spot analysis indicated that the 2016 hot spots, while statistically significant, were not the most concentrated, which is not surprising, given that this was the earliest year in which the marketing company systematically collected data. Most of the events marketed that year in these hot spots happened in venues in Downtown Los Angeles (e.g., Microsoft Theater), Central Los Angeles (e.g., UNION/Catch One Nightclub in Mid-City, Echoplex in Hollywood), and South Los Angeles (e.g., Baldwin Hills Crenshaw Mall).

However, BBLA's reach seems to have expanded and the patterns deepened. In 2017, the 378 events that successfully matched to a geocode occurred in 118 census tracts. The hot spots were far more concentrated: only 9 census tracts with 28 events. While it might seem odd that more events resulted in fewer hot spots, the degree of confidence in these hot spots increased from 90 percent to 95 percent. Once again, Downtown Los Angeles, South Los Angeles, and Hollywood-centric venues dominated this narrower set of census tracts. Finally, in 2018, the 503 events successfully matched or geocoded occurred in 130 census tracts. Over the course of the three years, the number of events marketed by BBLA grew by more than 105 percent (from 245 in 2016 to 503 in 2018), yet they occurred in only 32 more census tracts (32.6 percent). This further reinforces that Black millennial events are exhibiting a specific, recurring spatial pattern even as awareness and buzz grow. While the concentration of events deepened, the spread also dispersed to more edge places (e.g., Long Beach) and multiple cores. The degree of confidence also increased within the set of events that were determined to be held in statistically significant census tracts. Unlike 2017, these 368 events took place in 61 statistically significant hot spots—tracts that ranked in the 95 to 99 percent confidence interval. This final year showed other areas of the region above the I-10 freeway and outside of the urban core—North Hollywood, West LA, and Silver Lake.

Demographically, the events occurred in neighborhoods dominated by distinct groups. The residents are also largely millennials, with an average age of thirty-three across the study period and a median age ranging from thirty to thirty-five. However, on average, these neighborhoods were mostly non-Black: non-Hispanic white, Asian, and multiracial people (collectively 59 percent on average). Additionally, as listed in table 9.1, these areas host well-educated residents, with the majority having at least some college and the largest single group being those with an undergraduate degree.

However, these residents are not from high-income households, with a median household income of $17,562 and an average of $20,786 (not pictured in table 9.1). According to the Bureau of Labor Statistics from 2017, the average income of the Los Angeles metropolitan statistical area was $82,119. The average age of the Bureau of Labor Statistics respondents was forty-nine, much older than the populations in these tracts. That skew aside, the average household—more than 50 percent—is at least 150 percent above the poverty line, if not greater. This places relative importance on the cost of entry to make it financially inclusive.

The cost of attending events depends on many factors. It may depend on what level of and when you have information about the event to access websites or sometimes even custom apps to secure tickets. It also depends on how you plan to pay (e.g., cash at door; card via smartphone, which may incur a transaction fee). Occasionally, the costs of events also are gendered to entice women to attend and (monied) men to follow (e.g., $40 for men, $15 or $20 for women). One such party—I LOVE BEARDS—reversed that tradition and made the event free for men. Other unaccounted-for structural costs may include transportation: parking costs (which some events made clear to attendees in advance), gas to get there, a taxi or ride-share fare, cost of a TAP metro card (if the event is accessible by transit).[41]

Caveats aside, there was a wide range of events marketed at various price points, if there was an entry cost at all. Many event organizers and promoters simply wanted an audience and events have "suggested" or "donation" amounts or, more commonly, were free before certain times. As table 9.2 illustrates, the three-year average cost of entry was around $10, with a median of $1.67. With an average of 412 events promoted per year, one could attend over 52 percent of them at no cost. If these events happened every day of the year, nearly 60 percent of the year, or 211 out of 365 days, could hypothetically be filled with cultural activities if one had the information that BBLA provides its followers. Last, the median starting time for the events across all three years tended to be evening. Remarkably, for each year, the median starting time for the events was 7:00 p.m., which indicates an attempt to promote evening leisure activities, likely for working professionals who may live within these tracts.

Proposing "Afrotechtonics," or What Digitally Engaged Blackness Demands of Geographers

My findings suggest that Black cultural geographies are quantum: cosmopolitan, dispersed, complex, and often financially accessible. By using event ticketing details (place, time, fees), the marketing company's digital social media efforts, and my own experiences, I took the pulse of these gatherings for Black leisure and sought to liberate their patterns from the cognitive entrapments of "elsewhere" and "no one knows." While a fraction of the events echo what I dub a *spectacularized* Black economy—big-ticketed cultural events requiring large performative spaces (e.g., secret warehouses, centrally located stadiums)—many more gatherings were the substrate of *everyday* Black economies. These gatherings were happening in homes (e.g., House of Armour), coffee shops, restaurant allies, and more: the *interstitial* spaces of Los Angeles. The crowdsourced technologies of digital social media help memorialize and map these spaces. In interpreting my findings, I argue for three spatial understandings of Black joy that motivate

TABLE 9.1. Three-Year Social Demography of the BBLA Hot Spot Census Tracts (US Census ACS 2016 Five-Year Estimates)

Social Factor	2016 Tracts	2017 Tracts	2018 Tracts	3-Year Average	% Change
Total population	3,617	3,381	3,646	3,548	1%
Median age	35	30.2	34.2	33	−2%
% Non-Hispanic whites	12	18.4	14.8	15	21%
% Black/African American	6	4.9	6.5	6	11%
% American Indian/Alaskan Native	0	0.3	0	0	−100%
% Asian	13	21.2	12.4	15	−1%
% Native Hawaiian/ Pacific Islander	0	0.1	0	0	0%
% Other race	26	37	23.6	29	−10%
% Two races	3	4.1	3.3	3	10%
Population over 25 years old counted for education	2,500	2,032	2,302	2,278	−8%
% over 25 years old with no HS degree	7	6.4	6.3	6	−3%
% over 25 years old with HS degree	20	16	18.4	18	−7%
% over 25 years old with some college/ AA degree	21	17.6	20.4	20	−2%
% over 25 years old with bachelor's degree	20	21.5	25.4	22	27%

Social Factor	2016 Tracts	2017 Tracts	2018 Tracts	3-Year Average	% Change
% over 25 years old with graduate degree	6	6.3	6.6	6	17%
Population with annual income	3,187	2,906	2,987	3,027	−6%
Median annual income (last 12 months)	19,067	14,313	19,306	17,562	1%
Total population estimated for poverty stats	3,553	3,033	3,381	3,322	−5%
% of population living up to 100% of poverty line	27	43.7	26.7	32	−1%
% of population living 150% or more above poverty line	58	42.5	58	53	0%

TABLE 9.2. Summary Statistics on the BBLA Cost of Entry Pricing

Monetary Statistics	2016	2017	2018	3-Yr Average
Average cost	$6.78	$13.43	$10.70	$10.30
Median cost	0	$5	0	$1.67
# of free events*	185	126	323	211.33
Total events	286	424	528	412.67
% Free	65%	30%	61%	52%

*   For the purposes of this analysis, any vendor who promoted a specific donation amount (i.e., $15 suggested donation) was considered a price and not free. Other times the cost of attendance would be waived if one became a member to ensure loyalty.

new language in Black studies, geography, and information technology: what I call *Afrotechtonics*.

Black Joyful Space Is Not Biogeographically Determined

The spaces where Black millennials gathered were not predicated on dominant Black residential location patterns; the delivery of information regarding place and time seems like the biggest arbiter of accessing these Black millennial–oriented events. Despite the much-deserved attention on urban displacement, the ways in which events emerge do not conform to those same patterns of economic segregation and restructuring. Events better reflect the "post-integration" that sociologist Karyn Lacy writes about regarding Black middle-class geographies.[42] I also argue that this decades-long dispersal of Black residential locations from urban Black hot spots of cultural gathering produces the anxiety and possible alienation that motivates the very existence of companies like BBLA, which sought to reunite a fractured community by answering its own founding question, "Where are all the Black people at?" through digital space: through Afrotech.

Black place-making is more transient, indeterminate, and temporal than what may be convenient for analysts of Black space who rely on well-combed public datasets compiled about Black bodies in singular modes of being (e.g., places of slumber in Census Bureau data, places of work in Bureau of Labor Statistics data). Given the multicultural settings in which Black people move and make, one can imagine the rich terrain of potential questions place-making provokes about cultural belongingness in a cosmopolitan archipelago like Los Angeles. Our understanding of cities often takes a view of the permanent spaces—homes, businesses, schools, parks—as bastions of disbelonging. However, my work shows the temporal and interstitial elements of urban living as predicated by culture and commerce.

To the detriment of cities, Black businesses—tech-based or otherwise— are often not regarded as economic and community drivers for cities, despite their contributions to the success of all other immigrant groups' ability to amass wealth.[43] Currently, Black-run events are rarely considered as a viable form of cultural tourism—with exceptions for only the most venerated and elite Black performers.[44] Yet what legal scholar Regina Austin calls "leisure restraints" often motivates large numbers of Black consumers to regularly seek alternatives.[45] These range from structural restraints in the way public infrastructure (e.g., amusement parks, beaches) is designed to privilege non-Black populations to the microtactics of venue security enacting clothing restrictions befitting the description of working-class Black people (e.g., hoodies, jeans, tennis shoes). This creates a vacuum in the cultural economy that Black-owned businesses can fill: providing Afrotechtonic spaces where Black joy is centered and advertised effectively. In this sense, Black joy acts as a tonic to the invisibilizing effects of business as usual. As of 2020, the fact that Google Maps allows the voluntary listing of a business as Black- or woman-owned is one such indicator that Big Tech knows the public value of explicitly naming these identities for consumers and for the marketplace. Thus, like Black joy, the concept of Afrotech applies to the body politic—its micro- and macrolevel public geographies—through the vector of Black businesses and, in this case, a singular company's digital advocacy.

Black Joyful Spheres Engage Subversively with Racialized Cultural Economies

While these Black cultural events demanded time and money to host and attend, Black leisure for millennials is not strictly structured as a neoliberal pay-to-play model of cultural consumption. Amid pressures to maximize short-term profits, promoters participate in (or against) a spectrum of (non)monetization strategies. Just over half of the events in the first year, for example, had no entry fees, sometimes without requiring an RSVP. Throughout its life course between 2016 and 2020, BBLA maintained a gradient of priced and free events. While many organizers included a cost of entry, many more reluctantly suggested a donation. Given the variable pricing structure of the events yet BBLA's consistent promotion of them by a business-to-business (B2B) company, these findings beg the questions: Why would a company promote a free event? And why would a company pay another company to promote their free event? While this study did not aim to explore BBLA's pricing structure, the ambiguity still offers a partial window into the politics of Black public spheres.

One interpretation is there is a community-building intention: a socially affirmative case for doing business while Black. This mentality perhaps draws on the trait of sociality found in what George Lipsitz called the Black spatial imaginary, which operates under different oppositional logics than hegemonic white space.[46] Yet, even among socially minded cultural organizers, the reluctance to charge fees may not be an altruistic political statement but more an acknowledgment of the economic fragility of audiences and their industries. The cultural economy—regardless of race—struggles to operate with transactional payments as the mode of profit, unless the provider works at a large scale. Thus, many subsectors suffer from low profit margins, low business survival rates, and high job turnover. Arts economist Hans Abbing outlines this "exceptional economy," which is laden with historically rooted perceptions such as sacredness or scarcity. These social norms devalue the expected practices of commercial exchange found in other industries and confine their makers to the whims of the philanthropic-industrial complex. Often, attempting to earn a steady wage and establish a steady stream of work mystifies artists who do not have the privilege of wealthy social networks.[47] Another structural reason for not charging a fee is that the businesses are aware of the limited disposable incomes of their target audience and the competition for their consumption, especially if they are willing to locate the event in a majority non-Black space.

Alternatively, another monetization strategy is at work that shifts transaction costs (and benefits) to the organizers in the long run. As the music industry has done with the economics of streaming services and even corporate-sponsored festivals (e.g., the Jack Daniels Summer Series), advertising might be the most lucrative aspect of digital marketing businesses. Interlocutors and platform owners, then, can monetize *attention* by making physical presence a type of temporal and corporeal commodity. Perhaps they pitch these gatherings as having the competitive advantage of reaching a culturally influential niche set of consumers who are attuned to the pulse of Black culture. Many Black spectacular events (e.g., RnB Only) seemed to eschew being entirely free, but others may have added the low-cost or free option to further entice and inculcate an audience to create an ephemeral Black space: a status market.

Today's advanced stage of racial capitalism assumes modes even beyond what Cedric Robinson once articulated as the coevolution of racism and capitalism via the advent of European colonial slavery.[48] Racial capitalism also looks like what legal scholar Nancy Leong called the "revaluation" of racial identity itself as a type of "Marxian capital" through the commodification of nonwhite "diversity" as a benefit for white institutions, especially in workplaces and education.[49] However, BBLA operates in the realm of commerce and civic life. Unlike the pre-twentieth-century racist segregation of American public spaces, many twenty-first-century white-owned venues and cultural corridors hosting these nonwhite promotional events can see the benefits of having a "Black night" without having to lay claim to any permanent forms of belongingness.[50] Thus, BBLA benefits from this by engaging subversively with cultural commodification as a type of "potentially rebellious, liberatory, and transformative" praxis in the face of erasure.[51] Cultural commodification, when packaged and produced for and by a subaltern in-group, can provide a means of survival for the keepers of those traditions and practices under capitalist demands, but need not be profit-maximizing.

Whichever the case, psychosocial motivations for promoting culture while Black—whether as a marketing service provider or a goods-based service provider—are at work. As evidenced by this study, Black cultural economies illustrate some recursiveness and "nonrandom spatial clustering" that might be called "buzz" by cultural geographers or a "status market" by sociologists.[52] Previous geographic studies only used Getty Images as a data source that inherently focuses on elite entertainers and dominant culture; many Black-focused events are not status markets where Getty would send a photographer to cover and legitimize. Even Black-focused cultural sites that cover entertainment economies from a Black cultural lens (e.g., Bossip, the YBF, the Shade Room) tend to focus on celebrities. Further, they do not provide proprietary information as BBLA did for this study. At one point, Instagram was user-friendly to map location-based events, but it has gradually stripped away the application programming interface (API) access for nonpecuniary purposes.[53] Thus, this left an "elsewhere" and "no one knows" nature to the act of trying to map Black culture in the city with traditional geographic information systems (GIS) tools. Many of the events were self-promoted and user-generated on Facebook (now Meta circa 2022), Eventbrite, and specialized web development sites like SplashThat. Although BBLA provided a more readily available approach to map these diasporic geographies, more is needed.

Black Joy as a Distinctive Techno-Gravitational Draw

Postmodern urbanists of the 1980s and 1990s like Michael Dear and Steven Flusty framed LA as a Citistāt, the collective world city, that is a "both geographically corporeal and ageographically ethereal [place], in the sense that communication systems create a virtual space coordinating activities in physical space."[54] While their Citistāt rendering of reindustrialized urban structures reconstituted through the information technology revolutions was compelling, few have updated it with a twenty-first-century look at what digitally augmented life might mean for Black urbanites. This is crucial as new research fields such as "urban informatics" are being declared and technology is being further positioned *as* ideological governance itself.[55] Using their model, BBLA illustrated the existence of what one might call "commudities," the "commodified communities satisfying—and profiting from—the habitat preferences of the cybergeoisie."[56] However, since data on the BBLA attendees were not systematically collected, it is not clear whether they fit into the Dear and Flusty urbanist model based on binary socioeconomic categories of elite yuppie professionals or working-class proletarian millennials.

The mere promotion of Black people in BBLA's announcements implies a kind of missing element from the popularized leisure options. Specific modes of belonging (e.g., dialects, music, dance movements, informal advice, dialogues) are exchanged in these spaces. Observations at these events reinforced that Black millennials seek meaningful, culturally affirming engagement, which often manifests with other Black millennials. While this chapter did not collect experiential data from event goers to verify these feelings, I witnessed the effect of Black proximity at BBLA's 2017 mixer. There, I met fellow Black millennials with an eye for art and activism who changed my life and provided social opportunities to understand movements, to participate in public events, for play, and for reconnecting with family. The format of the event itself—games, discounted food, music, family picnic–style tables—was designed to do so.

In LA, I argue that this postintegration Black anxiety is what precipitates the existence of a digital service like BBLA, which was founded as a direct response to its public question, "Where all the Black people at?" The anxiety comes from the lack of shared understanding and predictability regarding where to find Black gatherings on an activity-driven and events-driven basis. Afrotech services are necessary to mitigate this cultural alienation. By fighting to liberate the various modes and forms in which Black culture and its prosumers manifest (e.g., across business and consumptive categories, inside/across/outside racialized neighborhood notions), the field of Black Geographies can manifest a capacious urbanism that makes liberation possible for similarly situated peoples (and possibly even nonhuman species) that face disbelonging in systematic ways. Afrotech services that take a critical approach to the notion of "buzz"—how to create it, for whom, and why—may be best positioned to turn this deficit into a "Black joy" value proposition. Buzz is generated among networks of like-minded individuals and network effects.

Like Afrofuturists, BBLA used digital technology to hack the psycho-geography of urban tourism and produce a network of Black joy. Afrotech can help expand racist technology and cities away from the fetishization of a posthuman future and toward that of a counterhumanist cartography. Given the Black roots of the internet technology with mathematician Philip Emeagwali and the Web 2.0 as we know it, forging a counterhumanist vision for Afrotech and its tectonics is not some linear Afrofuturist journey to an elsewhere untouched by Black hands. Arguably, Afrotechtonics could digitize the principle of Sankofa—meaning "go back and get it"—to reclaim lost and/or forgotten influence on the design of these ubiquitous technologies while also applying it to the contemporary interactional contexts.

Some Known Unknowns on This Approach

How does one make sense of the experience of a bar usually frequented by the largely mixed-race residents and older White workers of Hollywood that suddenly becomes awash in Black youth culture through a mere tweet? How does the etherealization of these culturally specific moments emplace Black belongingness while keeping it uncircumscribed and desegregated in a city whose Black population is historically cleaved by race and tethered by income? Do Black people filling these spaces take pride in occupying these social cleavages in zones with less than 10 percent of the residents who look like them? What do these centrally located and digitally augmented deviations *mean* in a metropolis that is economically expelling its Black population to exurban counties and whose remaining Black population is more transplanted than natively born? Many more questions remain than could be answered with this dataset alone.

This study was an attempt to make geographic sense out of a sociocultural phenomenon—the appeal of Black cultural events—and, thus, a variety of choices were made to quantifiably analyze and interpret these experiences. My choices carry some limitations. First, the BBLA dataset did not include attendee information; these details were the domain of the individual party promoters and event hosts, which this study did not aim to excavate. An assumption was made based around the digital engagement of BBLA's followers (e.g., comments, private spin-off groups like the BBLA Housing

FIGURE 9.1. Weeknight at a Hollywood-based bar frequented by Black Book LA attendees in 2017 and 2018. Photo by Matthew Jordan-Miller Kenyatta, 2021.

Network) and my personal experience attending the events (e.g., BBLA Link Up), which verified that the audience matched those advertised to.

Yet, there is an outstanding question: "Black joy for whom (besides me)?" Future Black geographic meditations can mind that gap by interviewing attendees to understand how Afrotech's services impacted them and whether the event truly offered a "Black joy" experience. Second, while the BBLA dataset included information on cost of entry, it provides no way of knowing where the attendees are coming from. Thus, this study did not ask about the cost of travel and transportation, which is a factor in terms of access to leisure.

Third, because the founders were informally interviewed, the study left unexplored the costs they shouldered to set up the infrastructure for the digital space: How "free" were their promotions? Email services, for example, that reach the range of the BBLA's subscribers—more than five thousand—currently can cost between $800 and $1,000 per year. Whether these costs plus any web hosting and social media advertisements may have been recovered and balanced by the paid advertisement placements of the companies is undetermined here.

To be clear, Afrotech alone does not perform the fullness of Black belongingness. Technology cannot emplace our beingness when the very ground on which technopower is designed and deployed needs shaking and shaping. Querying this necessary quaking might be called *Afrotechtonics*, defined here simply as ongoing engagement with the architectures and technologies of power shaping Afrodiasporic life. In this "postintegration" age, an Afrotechtonic agenda within Black geographies and allied fields could be to address the fact that Black consumers still need connectivity to physical Black space, perhaps more than ever. Urban alienation is understood as a socioeconomic phenomenon, but few studies offer insight on the spatial structure of Black taste as reflective of *cultural* alienation. This tends to be the privatized knowledge domain of marketers, who have understood since the 1960s how Blackness is a consumptive practice in collective identity formation.[57] Widely cited studies such as Karyn Lacy's work addressing Black class-based cultural interests sometimes paint them as posturing a "strategic assimilation" with white economies and culture through the banner of inclusion. Only a few studies have illustrated how these experiences might motivate responses from Black people to form their distinctive, celebratory "other" spaces: geocultural justice.[58] Thus, the interior worlds of Blackness in these digital corners are worth understanding independent of dominant gazes. Black discursive traditions persist through "pre-existing strategies like song, storytelling, and signifying" on digital corners, micro-publics that echo physical place-making strategies whenever Black people exercise spatial attachment.[59]

Toward Knowable (Cyber)Commons of Black Joy

"10 Fun Things for Black Millennials to Do in LA This Week!" "10 Ways to Put On for the Culture This Week!" "10 Dope Moves to Make This Week!" "In Search of Melanin This Weekend? Let's Link Up." "Where Are All the Black People in LA?" As these BBLA headlines gesture to the Black digital commons, this chapter aimed to illustrate that Black millennials have a distinct taste and voice with knowable space-time dimensions worth mapping—whether in Los Angeles or beyond. The project of "racing economic geography" must include an attentiveness to culture—how it is collectively consumed, produced, and "prosumed."[60] Given the lack of response from geographers to the questions of race—let alone Black experiences with it—Black geographies is an intellectual home for surfacing these complex relationships. As this chapter has shown, Black cultural space is a complex (e.g., distinctive), dynamic (e.g., nonbiogeographically determined), prosocial (i.e., subverting racial capitalism) phenomenon with distinctive patterns that continue to need surfacing. While there are challenges for Black digital start-ups to remain viable, the frame of Afrotechtonics may hold promise as one way to track and visualize how the Black digital commons can funnel the energies of Black public spheres into physical spaces, especially if we venture behind and beyond the apps.

If digital representations and banners of Black smiling faces were all that we needed to overcome alienation, the current project of Black geographies would hardly be necessary. Black joy still requires self-determined digital and/or physical space. In fact, the Afrotech company Blavity was founded on the idea of "Black Gravity," which is why its own portmanteau "Blavity" namesake combined these ideas. Proximity requires hitting the ground. Thus, using the philosophical notion of Black public spheres, I make conceptual interventions in Black studies to provide new language around Blackness, technology, and cultural geography. As indicated earlier, I define *Afrotech* as a neologism that broadly represents Black economic justice in technology industries, liberation for the Black digital commons, and cultural self-determination through Afrofuturism. This broader definition rescues Afrotech from the machinelike perception of technology by offering the realm of aesthetics. Black joy might be understood, then, as an oppositional practice or technology of Black love in the face of hegemonic injustice and racist disregard for the distinctive desires, dreams, and delimitations found within Afrodiasporic space. Last, I offer my own neologism, *Afrotechtonics*, to represent this ongoing engagement with making the architectures of technopower that shape Afrodiasporic life more legible across disciplines.

Notes

1   Dear and Flusty, "Iron Lotus," 63.

2   McKittrick and Woods, *Black Geographies and the Politics of Place*, 4.

3   Hunter and Robinson, "Sociology of Urban Black America," 385.

4   Wynter, "Unsettling the Coloniality of Being," 257–337.

5   Erasmus, "Sylvia Wynter's Theory of the Human," 47.

6   Lavender III, *Afrofuturism Rising*, 7; Dawson, "Black Public Sphere and Black Civil Society," 378; hamilton, hooks, and West, "Insurgent Black Intellectual Life," 2.

7   Quoted in Dent, "Black Pleasure, Black Joy," 1.

8   Dent, "Black Pleasure, Black Joy," 1.

9   Lu and Steele, "'Joy Is Resistance,'" 826.

10 Jackson, "Black Joy Project Creator."

11 Hunter et al., "Black Placemaking," 31.

12 Common, "The Corner," on *Be* (Geffen Records/GOOD Music, 2005).

13 Summers, *Black in Place*, 143–45.

14 Farley et al., "'Chocolate City, Vanilla Suburbs,'" 319–21.

15 Reardon and Bischoff, "Income Inequality and Income Segregation," 1092; Zuk et al., "Gentrification, Displacement and the Role of Public Investment," 6; Florida, *New Urban Crisis*.

16 Wei and Knox, "Neighborhood Change in Metropolitan America," 459.

17 Moore, "Gentrification in Black Face?," 118; Hyra, "Back-to-the City Movement," 1754.

18 Pratt, "Creative Cities," 107.

19 Dear and Flusty, "Postmodern Urbanism," 54.

20 Chapple, "From Central Avenue to Leimert Park."

21 Kern, "Rhythms of Gentrification," 441.

22 Pfeiffer, "African Americans' Search for 'More for Less,'" 64.

23 hooks, "Marginality as a Site of Resistance," 343; Hunter and Robinson, *Chocolate Cities*, 1–2.

24 DuCros, "'We Were Involved with the Club,'" 396.

25 Lee, "'Blowing Up' at Project Blowed," 113–39.

26 Azzara, "Grappling with the Impermanence of Place," 77.

27 Hunter and Winder, "Visibility Is Survival," 139.

28 Lu and Steele, "'Joy Is Resistance,'" 835.

29 Pardlo, "Colored People's Time," 361; Hunter, "Black Logics, Black Methods," 207.

30 Hibbing, Smith, and Alford, *Predisposed*.

31 Molotch, "Place in Product," 665.

32 Woods, *Development Drowned and Reborn*.

33 Zukin, Lindeman, and Hurson, "Omnivore's Neighborhood?," 2; Gottlieb, "'Dirty, Authentic…Delicious,'" 39; Glaeser, Kim, and Luca, "Nowcasting Gentrification," 77.

34 Brock, *Distributed Blackness*, 17.

35 Greer, *Represented*, 5.

36 White, "Afrotech and Outer Spaces," 90.

37 Squires, "Rethinking the Black Public Sphere," 446.

38 Benson, "Metasynthesis."

39 Coleman, "Race as Technology," 177; Chambliss, "Black Kirby Now"; Fluker, "Some Formal Remarks toward a Theory of Afrofuturism," 20.

40 Makiah Green, personal communication with author, January 2019.

41 For the purposes of this analysis, any vendor who promoted a specific donation amount (e.g., $15 suggested donation) was charging a price. At other times the cost of attendance would be waived if one became a member to ensure loyalty.

42 Lacy, "Black Spaces, Black Places," 908.

43 Bogan and Darity, "Culture and Entrepreneurship?," 1999; Association for Enterprise Opportunity, *Tapestry of Black Business Ownership in America*, 5.

44 Loukaitou-Sideris and Soureli, "Cultural Tourism as an Economic Development Strategy," 50.

45 Austin, "'Not Just for the Fun of It!'"

46 Lipsitz, *How Racism Takes Place*, 25–50.

47 Abbing, *Why Are Artists Poor?*, 34.

48 Robinson, *Black Marxism*, 2.

49 Leong, "Racial Capitalism," 2161, 2183.

50 Hunter and Winder, "Visibility Is Survival," 139.

51 Austin, "Commodifying Identities," 8.

52 Currid and Williams, "Geography of Buzz," 423.

53 "Social Media Data—Instagram Pulls Back on API Access," *Bright Planet*, January 5, 2017, https://brightplanet.com/2017/01/05/instagram-data/.

54 Dear and Flusty, "Postmodern Urbanism," 63.

55 Alvarez León and Rosen, "Technology as Ideology in Urban Governance," 497; Foth, Choi, and Satchell, "Urban Informatics," 4.

56 Dear and Flusty, "Iron Lotus," 160.

57 Lamont and Molnár, "How Blacks Use Consumption," 31.

58 Loukaitou-Sideris and Grodach, "Displaying and Celebrating the 'Other,'" 49; Banks, "Ethnicity, Class and Trusteeship," 97; Banks, "Cultural Socialization in Black Middle-Class Families," 61; Hunter et al., "Black Placemaking."

59 Lu and Steele, "Joy Is Resistance," 826.

60 Bonds, "Racing Economic Geography," 398; Zukin, Lindeman, and Hurson, "Omnivore's Neighborhood?," 3.

Bibliography

Abbing, Hans. *Why Are Artists Poor? The Exceptional Economy of the Arts.* Amsterdam: Amsterdam University Press, 2002. https://doi.org/10.1515/9789048503650.

Alvarez León, Luis F., and Jovanna Rosen. "Technology as Ideology in Urban Governance." *Annals of the American Association of Geographers* 110 (2020): 497–506.

Association for Enterprise Opportunity. *The Tapestry of Black Business Ownership in America: Untapped Opportunities for Success.* Washington, DC: Association for Enterprise Opportunity, 2017.

Austin, Regina. "Commodifying Identities: Kwanzaa and the Commodification of Black Culture." In *Rethinking Commodification: Cases and Readings in Law and Culture*, edited by Martha Ertman and Joan C. Williams, 178–90. New York: NYU Press, 2005. https://www.proquest.com/books/commodifying-identities -kwanzaa-commodification/docview/36499952/se-2?accountid=14707.

Austin, Regina. "'Not Just for the Fun of It!': Governmental Restraints on Black Leisure, Social Inequality, and the Privatization of Public Space." *Southern California Law Review* 71, no. 4 (1998): 667–714.

Azzara, Monique. "Grappling with the Impermanence of Place: A Black Baptist Congregation in South Los Angeles." *City and Society* 31, no. 1 (2019): 77–93. https://doi.org/10.1111/ciso.12203.

Banks, Patricia Ann. "Cultural Socialization in Black Middle-Class Families." *Cultural Sociology* 6, no. 1 (2012): 61–73. https://doi.org/10.1177/1749975511427646.

Banks, Patricia Ann. "Ethnicity, Class and Trusteeship at African-American and Mainstream Museums." *Cultural Sociology* 11, no. 1 (2017): 97–112. https://doi .org/10.1177/1749975516651288.

Benson, Samii Kennedy. "A Metasynthesis: Theory Used to Ground Research Concerning Black Women in Entrepreneurship." *Journal of Colorism Studies* 2 (2016): 1–8.

Bogan, Vicki, and William Darity. "Culture and Entrepreneurship? African American and Immigrant Self-Employment in the United States." *Journal of Socio-*

Economics 37, no. 5 (2008): 1999–2019. https://doi.org/10.1016/j.socec.2007.10
.010.

Bonds, Anne. "Racing Economic Geography: The Place of Race in Economic
Geography." *Geography Compass* 7, no. 6 (2013): 398–411. https://doi.org/10.1111
/gec3.12049.

Brock, Andre. *Distributed Blackness: African American Cybercultures*. New York: NYU
Press, 2020.

Chambliss, Julian. "Black Kirby Now: An Interview with John Jennings." *Pop
Matters*, February 20, 2014. http://www.popmatters.com/feature/179294-black
-kirby-now-an-interview-with-john-jennings/.

Chapple, Reginald. "From Central Avenue to Leimert Park: The Shifting Center of
Black Los Angeles." In *Black Los Angeles: American Dreams and Racial Reali-
ties*, edited by Darrell Hunt and Ana-Christina Ramon, 66–81. New York: NYU
Press, 2010.

Coleman, Beth. "Race as Technology." *Camera Obscura: Feminism, Culture, and
Media Studies* 24, no. 1 (2009): 177–207. https://doi.org/10.1215/02705346–2008
–018.

Currid, Elizabeth, and Sarah Williams. "The Geography of Buzz: Art, Culture and
the Social Milieu in Los Angeles and New York." *Journal of Economic Geography*
10, no. 3 (2010): 1–29. https://doi.org/10.1093/jeg/lbp032.

Dawson, Michael C. "The Black Public Sphere and Black Civil Society." In *The
Oxford Handbook of African American Citizenship, 1865–Present*, edited by Law-
rence D. Bobo, Lisa Crooms-Robinson, Linda Darling-Hammond, Michael C.
Dawson, Henry Louis Gates Jr., Gerald Jaynes, and Claude Steele, 374–99.
New York: Oxford University Press, 2012. https://doi.org/10.1093/oxfordhb
/9780195188059.013.0015.

Dear, Michael, and Steven Flusty. "The Iron Lotus: Los Angeles and Postmodern
Urbanism." *Annals of the American Academy of Political and Social Science* 551, no. 1
(1997): 151–63. https://doi.org/10.1177/0002716297551001011.

Dear, Michael, and Steven Flusty. "Postmodern Urbanism." *Annals of the Association
of American Geographers* 88, no. 1 (1998): 50–72. https://doi.org/10.1111/1467
-8306.00084.

Dent, Gina. "Black Pleasure, Black Joy: An Introduction." In *Black Popular Culture*,
edited by Gina Dent, 1–10. Seattle: Bay Press, 1992.

DuCros, Faustina M. "'We Were Involved with the Club': Louisiana Creole Social
Clubs, Los Angeles, and the Great Migration." *Southern California Quarterly* 101,
no. 4 (2019): 396–429. https://doi.org/10.1525/scq.2019.101.4.396.

Erasmus, Zimitri. "Sylvia Wynter's Theory of the Human: Counter-, Not Post-
Humanist." *Theory, Culture and Society* 37, no. 6 (2020): 47–65. https://doi.org/10
.1177/0263276420936333.

Farley, Reynolds, Howard Schuman, Suzanne Bianchi, Diane Colasanto, and Shirley Hatchett. "'Chocolate City, Vanilla Suburbs': Will the Trend toward Racially
Separate Communities Continue?" *Social Science Research* 7, no. 4 (1978): 319–44.
https://doi.org/10.1016/0049–089X(78)90017–0.

Florida, Richard L. *The New Urban Crisis: How Our Cities Are Increasing Inequality, Deepening Segregation, and Failing the Middle Class—and What We Can Do about It*. New York: Basic Books, 2017.

Fluker, Clinton R. "Some Formal Remarks toward a Theory of Afrofuturism: Designing Liberation Technologies in Black Speculative Fiction." *ProQuest Dissertations and Theses*. Ann Arbor, 2017. https://www.proquest.com /dissertations-theses/some-formal-remarks-toward-theory-afrofuturism /docview/1920473412.

Foth, Marcus, Jaz Hee-jeong Choi, and Christine Satchell. "Urban Informatics." *Proceedings of the ACM 2011 Conference on Computer Supported Cooperative Work—CSCW '11* (March 2011): 1–8. https://doi.org/10.1145/1958824.1958826.

Glaeser, Edward L., Hyunjin Kim, and Michael Luca. "Nowcasting Gentrification: Using Yelp Data to Quantify Neighborhood Change." *AEA Papers and Proceedings* 108 (May 2018): 77–82. https://doi.org/10.1257/pandp.20181034.

Gottlieb, Dylan. "'Dirty, Authentic…Delicious': Yelp, Mexican Restaurants, and the Appetites of Philadelphia's New Middle Class." *Gastronomica: The Journal of Critical Food Studies* 15, no. 2 (2015): 39–48. https://www.jstor.org/stable/10.1525 /gfc.2015.15.2.39.

Greer, Brenna Wynn. *Represented: The Black Imagemakers Who Reimagined African American Citizenship*. Philadelphia: University of Pennsylvania Press, 2019.

hamilton, amy, bell hooks, and Cornel West. 1993. "Insurgent Black Intellectual Life: bell hooks and Cornel West Break Bread." *Off Our Backs* 23, no. 7 (1993): 1–3. https://www.jstor.org/stable/20834484.

Hibbing, John R., Kevin B. Smith, and John R. Alford. *Predisposed: Liberals, Conservatives, and the Biology of Political Differences*. New York: Routledge, 2013. https://doi.org/10.4324/9780203112137.

hooks, bell. "Marginality as Site of Resistance." In *Out There: Marginalization and Contemporary Cultures*, edited by Russell Ferguson, Martha Gever, Trinh T. Minh-Ha, and Cornel West, 341–43. Cambridge, MA: MIT Press, 1990.

Hunter, Marcus Anthony. "Black Logics, Black Methods: Indigenous Timelines, Race, and Ethnography." *Sociological Perspectives* 61, no. 2 (2018): 207–21. https:// doi.org/10.1177/0731121418758646.

Hunter, Marcus Anthony, Mary Pattillo, Zandria F. Robinson, and Keeanga-Yamahtta Taylor. "Black Placemaking: Celebration, Play, and Poetry." *Theory, Culture and Society* 33, nos. 7–8 (2016): 31–56. https://doi.org/10.1177 /0263276416635259.

Hunter, Marcus Anthony, and Zandria F. Robinson. *Chocolate Cities: The Black Map of American Life*. Berkeley: University of California Press, 2018. https://doi.org /10.1177/2332649219827829.

Hunter, Marcus Anthony, and Zandria F. Robinson. "The Sociology of Urban Black America." *Annual Review of Sociology* 42, no. 1 (2016): 385–405. https:// doi.org/10.1146/annurev-soc-081715-074356.

Hunter, Marcus Anthony, and Terrell J. A. Winder. "Visibility Is Survival: The Chocolate Maps of Black Gay Life in Urban Ethnography." *Urban Ethnogra-*

phies: Legacies and Challenges 16 (2019): 131–42. https://doi.org/10.1108/s1047-00422019000016010.

Hyra, Derek. "The Back-to-the-City Movement: Neighbourhood Redevelopment and Processes of Political and Cultural Displacement." *Urban Studies* 52, no. 10 (2015): 1753–73. https://doi.org/10.1177/0042098014539403.

Jackson, Imani. "The Black Joy Project Creator Explains Why He Centers Black Joy in an Anti-Black World." Black Youth Project. December 11, 2017. http://blackyouthproject.com/black-joy-project-turned-two-creator-explains-centers-black-joy-anti-black-world/.

Kern, Leslie. "Rhythms of Gentrification: Eventfulness and Slow Violence in a Happening Neighbourhood." *Cultural Geographies* 23, no. 3 (2016): 441–57. https://doi.org/10.1177/1474474015591489.

Lacy, Karyn R. "Black Spaces, Black Places: Strategic Assimilation and Identity Construction in Middle-Class Suburbia." *Ethnic and Racial Studies* 27, no. 6 (2004): 908–30. https://doi.org/10.1080/0141987042000268521.

Lamont, Michèle, and Virág Molnár. "How Blacks Use Consumption to Shape Their Collective Identity." *Journal of Consumer Culture* 1, no. 1 (2001): 31–45. https://doi.org/10.1177/146954050100100103.

Lavender, Isiah, III. *Afrofuturism Rising: The Literary Prehistory of a Movement*. Columbus: Ohio State University Press, 2019.

Lee, Jooyoung. "'Blowing Up' at Project Blowed: Rap Dreams and Young Black Men." In *Black Los Angeles: American Dreams and Racial Realities*, edited by Darrell Hunt and Ana-Christina Ramon, 113–39. New York: NYU Press, 2010.

Leong, Nancy. "Racial Capitalism." *Harvard Law Review* 126, no. 8 (2013): 2151–226. https://heinonline.org/HOL/P?h=hein.journals/hlr126&i=2181.

Lipsitz, George. *How Racism Takes Place*. Philadelphia: Temple University Press, 2011.

Loukaitou-Sideris, Anastasia, and Carl Grodach. "Displaying and Celebrating the 'Other': A Study of the Mission, Scope, and Roles of Ethnic Museums in Los Angeles." *Public Historian* 26, no. 4 (2004): 49–71. https://doi.org/10.1525/tph.2004.26.4.49.

Loukaitou-Sideris, Anastasia, and Konstantina Soureli. "Cultural Tourism as an Economic Development Strategy for Ethnic Neighborhoods." *Economic Development Quarterly* 26, no. 1 (2011): 50–72. https://doi.org/10.1177/0891242411422902.

Lu, Jessica H., and Catherine Knight Steele. "'Joy Is Resistance': Cross-Platform Resilience and (Re)Invention of Black Oral Culture Online." *Information Communication and Society* 22, no. 6 (2019): 823–37. https://doi.org/10.1080/1369118X.2019.1575449.

McKittrick, Katherine, and Clyde Adrian Woods. *Black Geographies and the Politics of Place*. Boston: South End, 2007.

Molotch, Harvey. "Place in Product." *International Journal of Urban and Regional Research* 26, no. 4 (2002): 665–88. https://doi.org/10.1111/1468-2427.00410.

Moore, Kesha S. "Gentrification in Black Face? The Return of the Black Middle Class to Urban Neighborhoods." *Urban Geography* 30, no. 2 (2009): 118–42. https://doi.org/10.2747/0272-3638.30.2.118.

Pardlo, Gregory. "Colored People's Time." *Callaloo* 39, no. 2 (2016): 361–71. https://doi.org/10.1353/cal.2016.0035.

Pfeiffer, Deirdre. "African Americans' Search for 'More for Less' and 'Peace of Mind' on the Exurban Frontier." *Urban Geography* 33, no. 1 (2012): 64–90. https://doi.org/10.2747/0272–3638.33.1.64.

Pratt, Andy C. "Creative Cities: The Cultural Industries and the Creative Class." *Geografiska Annaler: Series B, Human Geography* 90, no. 2 (2008): 107–17. https://doi.org/10.1111/j.1468–0467.2008.00281.x.

Reardon, Sean F., and Kendra Bischoff. "Income Inequality and Income Segregation." *American Journal of Sociology* 116, no. 4 (2011): 1092–153. https://doi.org/10.1086/657114.

Robinson, Cedric J. *Black Marxism: The Making of the Black Radical Tradition.* Revised and Updated Third Edition. Chapel Hill: University of North Carolina Press, 2020.

Squires, Catherine R. "Rethinking the Black Public Sphere: An Alternative Vocabulary for Multiple Public Spheres." *Communication Theory* 12, no. 4 (2002): 446–68. https://doi.org/10.1111/j.1468–2885.2002.tb00278.x.

Summers, Brandi Thompson. *Black in Place: The Spatial Aesthetics of Race in a Post–chocolate City.* Chapel Hill: University of North Carolina Press, 2019. https://muse.jhu.edu/book/67915.

Wei, Fang, and Paul L. Knox. "Neighborhood Change in Metropolitan America, 1990 to 2010." *Urban Affairs Review* 50, no. 4 (2014): 459–89. https://doi.org/10.1177/1078087413501640.

White, Michelle-Lee. "Afrotech and Outer Spaces." *Art Journal* 60, no. 3 (2001): 90–91. https://doi.org/10.1080/00043249.2001.10792080.

Woods, Clyde. *Development Drowned and Reborn: The Blues and Bourbon Restorations in Post-Katrina New Orleans.* Edited by Jordan T. Camp and Laura Pulido. Athens: University of Georgia Press, 2017.

Wynter, Sylvia. "Unsettling the Coloniality of Being/Power/Truth/Freedom: Towards the Human, after Man, Its Overrepresentation—an Argument." *CR: The New Centennial Review* 3, no. 3 (2003): 257–337. https://doi.org/10.1353/ncr.2004.0015.

Zuk, Miriam, Ariel H. Bierbaum, Karen Chapple, Karolina Gorska, Anastasia Loukaitou-Sideris, Paul Ong, and Trevor Thomas. "Gentrification, Displacement and the Role of Public Investment: A Literature Review." Working Paper 2015-05. San Francisco: Federal Reserve Bank of San Francisco, 2015.

Zukin, Sharon, Scarlett Lindeman, and Laurie Hurson. "The Omnivore's Neighborhood? Online Restaurant Reviews, Race, and Gentrification." *Journal of Consumer Culture* 17, no. 3 (2015): 1–21. https://doi.org/10.1177/1469540515611203.

10

The San Francisco Blues

LINDSEY DILLON

Tell Me about San Francisco

A young Black man speaks into a microphone held to his lips by the famed author James Baldwin. The man's back is against a white concrete wall, somewhere in the San Francisco neighborhood of Hunters Point. "You want me to tell you about San Francisco, I'll tell you about San Francisco," he says. "The white man, he's not…killing you out in public like they're doing down in Birmingham. But he's killing you with that pencil and paper, brother."[1]

In going to Hunters Point, Baldwin hoped to show "the real situation" of Black life in the city, "as opposed to the image San Francisco would like to present." His listening tour in 1963 was documented by the local public broadcasting station, KQED, in a film titled *Take This Hammer*. The classic labor song, popularized by folk and blues musician Leadbelly and reinvented by Odetta, had become a ballad of the civil rights movement. Baldwin saw how this long-standing struggle for racial justice was unfolding in the hills of San Francisco. At the time of his visit, the San Francisco Redevelopment Agency was tearing up the Fillmore District (also called the Western Addition)—the center of Black political, cultural, and sonic life in the city. Adjacent to the growing financial district and coveted by business interests and pro-growth politicians, the run-down Fillmore was declared "blighted" by urban planners in 1948. The designation of "blight" marked the Fillmore, a neighborhood the poet Maya Angelou later called "San Francisco's Harlem," as an economic cancer, requiring surgery through demolition and urban renewal. *He's killing you with that pencil and paper.*

The neighborhood of Hunters Point, with a majority of Black residents, was far from downtown, on a hilly ridge in the southeastern corner of the city, bordering the Hunters Point Naval Shipyard. Most Black Hunters Point residents had migrated from the rural South at some point during the previous twenty years. Thousands still lived in temporary, barrack-style homes, built for military shipyard workers during World War II. By the time of Baldwin's visit in 1963, Hunters Point residents also faced the prospect of displacement through urban renewal. The California state legislature required cities to demolish World War II worker housing by 1970, and the San Francisco Redevelopment Agency had begun to draw up plans for Hunters Point. And yet, by 1970, Black Hunters Point residents had organized to control, rather than be subjected to, the urban renewal process. They aimed to replace the dilapidated, poorly maintained military housing with a "new Hunters Point," built by and for Black San Franciscans. Their efforts reflected and produced Black geographies, which Katherine McKittrick writes, are "material and imaginative ... critical of spatial inequalities, evidence of geopolitical struggles, and demonstrative of real and possible geographic alternatives."[2]

The effort to build decent, affordable housing and community infrastructure—including playgrounds and childcare centers—in Hunters Point stemmed from a branch of the "blues epistemology" Clyde Woods identified in the Mississippi Delta, as this epistemology was crafted and reworked through the landscape and politics of the US West.[3] The blues found a new, regional form in wartime boomtowns around the Bay Area—the "West Coast blues," with one of its centers across the bay from Hunters Point, near the shipyards of West Oakland. In the postwar decades, Black Hunters Point residents were left with the physical detritus of the war—namely, the untenable living conditions of war worker housing, made worse by municipal neglect. The efforts of Black residents to build a new Hunters Point represents one story of "how and to what end people make freedom provisionally, imperatively, as they imagine *home* against the disintegrating grind of partition and repartition through which racial capitalism perpetuates the means of its own valorization."[4] In this chapter I show how Hunters Point residents worked to make space for Black life in the city, in an alternately collaborative and critical relationship with state agencies.

Black Geographies and Indigenous Land in California

Before exploring working-class Black urban planning in San Francisco, it is important to begin by acknowledging these ongoing spatial politics take place on the unceded territory of the Ohlone people.[5] Before European colonists arrived in what we now call California, the region was the most populated area of North America, north of central Mexico.[6] Waves of colonization killed, displaced, and enslaved Indigenous Californians before the United States took the land in 1848. Beginning in the late seventeenth century, Spanish colonizers built Franciscan missions and military presidios up the coast of California, from the Baja Peninsula to the northern reaches of the San Francisco estuary. Colonization decimated Indigenous populations, especially along the coast: by the end of Spanish rule, the native population had dropped from 300,000 to 150,000 people; with US control following the gold rush in 1849, this number declined to around 30,000 people.[7] Californian Indians survived this attempted genocide by fleeing to inland California and by fighting back. A century later, between 1969 and 1971, Indigenous activists reclaimed Alcatraz Island, in the middle of the San Francisco Bay, for nineteen months. They sought to build a cultural center and a university, and their standoff with the federal government inaugurated the contemporary Red Power movement.[8]

The plantation is a key spatial category for understanding the origins and ongoing workings of racial capitalism. McKittrick writes that the plantation was "often defined as a 'town,' with a profitable economic system and local political and legal regulations."[9] This is important because "it compels us to think about the ways the plantation became key to transforming the lands of no one into the lands of someone" and how "the plantation spatializes early conceptions of urban life within the context of a racial economy."[10]

Spanish missions in California bore similarities with southern plantations in form and function: they included a complex of schools, convents, and ranches and were often linked to military fortresses (the presidio) and commercial trading posts (the pueblo). Just as the plantation economy thrived on the backs of enslaved African Americans, "nearly everything grown or manufactured in the missions, presidios, and pueblos resulted from the labor of Indians."[11] After Mexico gained independence from Spain in 1821, it transferred mission lands and other parts of California to individuals as private property (the "lands of someone"). Mexican ranchos continued to rely on Indigenous labor as they developed the region's hide and tallow industry and connected it with international markets.[12]

When the United States claimed California in 1848, at the end of the Mexican-American War, it reimagined the Pacific Coast as an imperial embarcadero. US military captain John Frémont named the narrow strait separating the San Francisco Bay from the Pacific Ocean, Chrysopylae (golden gate), referring to Byzantium's harbor, Chrysoceras (golden horn), which functioned as imperial Rome's gateway to Asia.[13] A year earlier, in 1847, a writer in the *California Star* asserted that San Francisco (still, at the time, Mexican territory) "is destined to become the great commercial emporium of the north Pacific coast. With the advantages of so fine a harbor, and the enterprise of so hardy and intelligent a race of pioneers, it can scarcely be otherwise."[14] These sentiments reflect how "in the middle of the nineteenth century a sense of [white] racial destiny permeated discussions of American progress and of future American world destiny."[15]

This sense of white racial destiny articulated with the emergence of industrial racial capitalism in the US West. In the 1850s, Dutch labor recruiters began transporting Chinese male workers to sugar plantations in Hawai'i and soon thereafter to California, where they worked in mining camps and on the transcontinental railroad. Like Black workers who cleared swamps for cotton and rice plantations in the US South, Chinese workers drained and dredged the malarial tule bogs of California's Central Valley, producing arable land and what would soon become one of the most productive agricultural regions in the world.[16] In the context of market expansion, a growing wage labor force, and periodic economic depressions in the second half of the nineteenth century, a white working-class consciousness developed in relation to a virulent and violent anti-Chinese racism.[17] Just as white planters reestablished their power in southern states following the Civil War by providing a "new unity through emphasizing the importance of race," the Democratic Party in California sutured trade unionism and "anticoolie clubs," rebuilding itself through a populist white nationalism that led to the federal Chinese Exclusion Act of 1882.[18]

This historical geography is important because it reveals how racial segregation and grassroots, Black urban planning in San Francisco are part of the "layered histories embedded in place,"[19] including the ways California was produced through multiple colonial projects and imperial routes. Moreover, the legacies of these historical geographies had spatial impacts for Black social and economic life. For example, the strength of white labor in San Francisco meant that, by the late nineteenth century, most unions excluded Black workers, who could find little work in the skilled trades or manufacturing sectors in the city.[20] On the eve of World War II, the Black population in San Francisco was relatively small—4,806 people; by then, most African Americans moving to California headed to Oakland or Los Angeles, where it was easier to find jobs. World War II industrialization changed these demographics: by 1950, 43,460 Black people lived in the city.[21] Most moved to the Fillmore District, where forced Japanese internment had left vacancies for wartime newcomers. Housing shortages led to overcrowding and hastily constructed buildings, as people, drawn to military jobs, tried to find a place to live. If they worked in the shipyards, Black wartime migrants could find homes in the new military housing in Hunters Point. In the postwar decades, urban renewal projects threatened to displace Black communities from both neighborhoods.

The West Coast Blues

In *Development Arrested*, Clyde Woods traces a history of social and economic crises and the violent reconstitution of plantation power in the Mississippi Delta region. White supremacists fought to maintain regional hegemony and ensure a stable regime of capital accumulation against an evolving, alternative development practice and mode of social explanation found within working-class Black consciousness in the Delta region: the blues. Woods describes the blues epistemology (way of knowing) and ontology (way of being; world-making) as "a system of explanation that informs ... daily life, organizational activity, culture, religion, and social movements."[22] He extends this notion of the blues to the scholarly disciplines of regional studies and critical human geography, arguing that the Delta white planter bloc maintained hegemony through successive sociospatial fixes, up to the present day. Woods's emphasis on the relational construction of regions and the spread of Delta blues to northern urban centers such as Chicago and Memphis invites scholars to consider the historical and geographic particularities of blues innovations and their relation to working-class Black consciousness, in and through other places.[23]

Urbanization shapes musical traditions. Military urbanization during the 1940s brought hundreds of thousands of people from across the country to work in the shipyards and defense-related industries that sprouted up around the Bay Area: Marinship, in Sausalito; Kaiser Shipyards, in Richmond; Moore Dry Docks, in Oakland; along with nearly two dozen military installations in the Bay Area region, including the Hunters Point Naval Shipyard in San Francisco. The tremendous investment by the Department of Defense in California cities at this time shifted the geography of the Second Great Migration, from routes that led to industrial centers in the North to wartime boomtowns along the West Coast. Most Black migrants to the San Francisco Bay Area during and after World War II came from Oklahoma, Louisiana, Arkansas, and Texas.[24] In the Bay Area, these new residents quickly organized against exclusions in employment and housing, with the shipyards as an important site of political activism (e.g., where Joseph James, a trained singer from Boston, led a successful Bay Area–wide strike against racially segregated unions).[25]

The shipyards were also sites of musical production, with gospel groups such as the Singing Shipbuilders Quartet, and where soon-to-be legendary blues composer and producer Bob Geddins auditioned blues and gospel singers—"right there in the [hull of the] ships."[26] Born on a plantation in Texas, Geddins moved to Los Angeles before settling in Oakland at the beginning of the war. He worked as a burner and welder at Kaiser Shipyards and had started his own record-pressing plant in West Oakland when he met Lowell Fulson (born in Oklahoma), who was stationed at the Alameda Naval Air Station. Fulson was one of the many blues singers Geddins worked with to produce a distinctive Oakland sound, rooted in Black musical traditions of Texas, Louisiana, and Arkansas.[27] According to Joshua Jelly-Shapiro: "Joining the feel and structure of Texas blues to the propulsive harmonies of swing jazz, the groups who played this style employed full horn sections rather than a lone harmonica, forging a music that at once recalled the rural past of ancestors brought to America in wooden slave boats and spoke to the urbane lifeways of people building steel warships in modern cities."[28] West Oakland became the postwar center of the blues in the San Francisco Bay Area. By the 1930s, a strong Black working-class consciousness had emerged in the city's flatlands, by the water, where workers at the Southern Pacific Railroad, the Pullman Company, and freight yards and warehouses found inexpensive housing and built communities.[29] The West Coast headquarters of the Brotherhood of Sleeping Car Porters and the Alameda County National Association for the Advancement of Colored People both located their offices in West Oakland, alongside a "substantial black commercial and professional district, principally along Seventh Street" (near Geddins's pressing plant).[30] A generation later, the Black Panther Party for Self-Defense emerged from this particular sociospatial milieu.[31]

San Francisco's Fillmore District was known as a music and entertainment district prior to World War II, but wartime Black migration transformed the neighborhood into a place that served, rather than excluded, Black San Franciscans and other minoritized groups.[32] The expanding number of clubs and music halls owned by Black Americans, Japanese Americans, and Filipinx Americans were soon filled with local talent and rising stars, such as Louisiana-born Saunders King (later dubbed "King of the Blues") and San Francisco–born Filipinx Black American Sugar Pie De Santo. Black musicians on national tour played to white crowds in San Francisco's downtown clubs and returned to the Fillmore, after hours, to play and socialize.[33] The Fillmore District "began to serve as a West Coast fulcrum for the era's jazz movements," but the music pouring out of neighborhood clubs was always a mixture of sounds.[34] The popular Blue Mirror, on Fillmore Street, run by Oklahoma-born Leola King, played mainly the blues; T-Bone Walker was a regular. According to De Santo, "If you wanted to hear the blues, you went down to the Blue Mirror."[35]

Urban renewal in the 1960s nearly destroyed the music scene in the Fillmore District. The Redevelopment Agency took some music establishments by eminent domain, while others closed down as their clientele were evicted or compelled to move elsewhere. When the agency took Leola King's Oklahoma King barbeque restaurant, she was forced to retroactively sell the property for less than market value. In 1962, the city shut down the Blue Mirror for violation of municipal codes; the building was soon demolished.[36] As the first phase urban renewal unfolded in the Fillmore, a growing civil rights movement in San Francisco energized anti-redevelopment organizing. Groups such as the Western Addition Community Organization used direct action, including lying down in front of bulldozers, and lawsuits to delay the second phase of urban renewal until 1969, also pressuring the city to adopt a relocation policy for evicted residents.[37]

"San Francisco would have sworn on the Golden Gate Bridge that racism was missing from the heart of their air-conditioned city. But they would have been sadly mistaken," reflected former Fillmore resident Maya Angelou in her memoir *I Know Why the Caged Bird Sings*.[38] Angelou peels back the dominant image of San Francisco as a progressive, inclusive city to reveal a liberal form of whiteness that worked through municipal code violations, redevelopment agencies, and "civil" society, with effects similar to what was going on "down in Birmingham."[39] Chester Himes, a novelist recognized by Clyde Woods as part of the "Blues School of Literature," explores the psychological effects of West Coast whiteness in *If He Hollers Let Him Go*, written during Himes's brief yet emotionally devastating stay in Los Angeles during World War II. The constant fears and anxieties of the novel's protagonist—Robert Jones, who works at a shipyard—are symptomatic of an emergent urban racial formation and its impact on Jones's sense of self and place. In Los Angeles, Jones experiences "that tight, crazy feeling of race as thick in the street as gas fumes. Every time I stepped outside I saw a challenge I had to accept or ignore."[40] These lines resonate with Himes's personal reflections, in his autobiography, in which he wrote that Los Angeles "hurt [him] racially as much as any city [he] have ever known—much more than any city [he] remembered from the South."[41] Blues producer Bob Geddins could be understood as grappling with similar feelings of hurt, suffocation, and exhaustion through his musical style, which, he once explained, had "a slow, draggier beat and a kinda mournful sound," and which music journalist Lee Hildebrand described as having "an extremely sad, almost doomed quality."[42] In 1948, Geddins recorded a song he composed (with the same title as a traditional hymn), "I'm Just a Stranger Here," that includes the lyrics: "Well I am going back home if I wear ninety-nine pair of shoes / They'll know I'll be welcome and I won't have to sing these blues."[43] As sung by recent Black migrants to the Bay Area, this longing to return home could be interpreted as expressing an experience of alienation in California.

The alienating experience of not having a secure place in the city was well known to Black Hunters Point residents in the early 1960s—trapped in poorly built, temporary wartime housing and facing the looming threat of eviction by the San Francisco Redevelopment Agency. In the next section, I show how Hunters Point residents navigated these forces by establishing community organizations to control urban renewal in their neighborhood.

Building a New Hunters Point

When James Baldwin visited Hunters Point in 1963, he would have seen 232 two-story wood-frame barrack-style buildings on the Hunters Point ridge, housing nearly 7,100 people. Built in the 1940s, these homes were officially "temporary dwelling units," funded by the Defense Housing and Community Services (Lanham) Act. As a response to a national housing shortage, the Lanham Act sought to avert a crisis in wartime labor by providing homes for war workers, yet the act required these units to be dismantled after the war. On the same ridge, 5,500 people lived in low-rent apartment units run by the San Francisco Housing Authority, which maintained a de facto segregation policy for the city's public housing stock. During the war, Hunters Point (often referred to as "the hill") was known as an integrated residential community, yet by 1960 demographic surveys characterized Hunters Point as 75 percent Black; in 1967 it was 97 percent Black, reflecting broader national patterns of white residential mobility and Black immobility, shaped by state policy and the real estate industry. There were four elementary schools, in poor condition, and limited recreation areas for children.[44]

Although Hunters Point residents despised the state of housing and infrastructural neglect of their neighborhood, they also distrusted the San Francisco Redevelopment Agency and were threatened by the prospect of urban renewal—across the country, the latter had become associated with Black removal. Still, the Redevelopment Agency had the power Hunters Point residents needed—to demolish old war housing and mobilize federal funds to rebuild their neighborhood. Community organizers navigated this difficult bind by forming their own housing and redevelopment organizations, with the goal of establishing community control over the urban renewal process. In September 1965, for example, Black residents met at Ridgepoint Church on Hilltop Road (where the Black Panther Party also ran a free breakfast program) and established the Bayview–Hunters Point Community Development Corporation (CDC), to provide an institutional structure to control, rather than be subjected to, large-scale redevelopment. The Bayview–Hunters Point CDC quickly got to work, hosting workshops on possible legal avenues for the new organization and conducting a community needs survey. Osceola Washington, who moved to San Francisco in 1944 from Little Rock, Arkansas, served as the Bayview–Hunters Point CDC's first chairperson.[45] According to the Black-run, Hunters Point–based newspaper the *Spokesman*, "Under the chairmanship of Mrs. Osceola Washington, residents were active in the Bayview–Hunters Point CDC efforts to see that outside speculators or Urban Renewal groups are not allowed to buy or lease the land without regard for the thousands of people who now live there."[46] The primary goal of the Bayview–Hunters Point CDC was to build community power to "buy land to build homes for the people of Hunters Point."[47] The Bayview–Hunters Point CDC sought to control the provision of new housing on the hill and ensure that it benefited rather than displaced existing residents.

A second organization—the Joint Housing Committee—worked more closely with the Redevelopment Agency on a master plan for Hunters Point. One of the ways the Joint Housing Committee sought to control the master plan was by moving the planning process to Hunters Point. For example, when the committee hired a primary consultant to oversee the development of five different housing sites, it stipulated that the company open a site office in the neighborhood and arrange for the daily involvement of community members. This would help ensure, in the words of Texas-born Joint Housing Committee chair Elouise Westbrook, that "the practical work for the development of a new community for the residents is not just a theoretical 'downtown' concept but a reality that is unfolding in Hunters Point itself."[48]

Plans for the new Hunters Point included clearing old World War II temporary barracks and building two thousand new homes for low- to moderate-income families. Residents of demolished housing would receive a "certificate of preference," giving them priority to purchase or rent the new homes (this was a legacy of anti-redevelopment organizing in the Fillmore). The broader neighborhood design included curvy, tree-lined streets surrounding a commercial center and new schools, four childcare centers, and two churches; new parks (including playgrounds located near laundry buildings, so that mothers could wash clothes and watch their children at the same time); new lighting and signage; and the burying of utility lines. Instead of the San Francisco Housing Authority or a private company, the five new housing developments would be managed by locally run, Hunters Point–based organizations—thus providing a form of community control over the provision of housing in the neighborhood. The Joint Housing Committee sought to hire Black architects—ultimately three of the five firms selected to design each new housing development was Black-owned—while the Labor and Industry Subcommittee ensured local residents were hired to construct the new housing.[49]

A calendar spanning the months October 1969 through September 1971 was distributed at the groundbreaking ceremony for the first phase of urban renewal in Hunters Point, on November 1, 1969.[50] Thick with text and images, the calendar describes the work of the Joint Housing Committee and includes landscape designs and new street layouts for each housing development. On the calendar itself, nearly every day of the week is marked by an important moment in US Black history. The dates emphasize Black Californian history, including the 1855 San Francisco–based movement for the rights of testimony in court and the birth of Mary Ellen Pleasant, a Black abolitionist who harbored fugitive enslaved people in her San Francisco home in the 1850s and helped fund John Brown's raid on Harper's Ferry in Virginia in 1859.[51] The redevelopment calendar merges Black histories with the physical landscape of Hunters Point and the visions of Black Hunters Point organizers, establishing the repair and rebuilding of Hunters Point as guided by a Black spatial imaginary.

The San Francisco Blues

Yet construction on the new Hunters Point moved slowly. The work of the Joint Housing Committee became increasingly oriented toward struggling against rollbacks of federal grants and social programs. Then, after his reelection in 1972, President Nixon began to dismantle many of the federal programs that had supported urban renewal in Hunters Point.[52] The Black-owned, Fillmore-based *Sun-Reporter* lamented these effects: "Located in a section of the City which decision makers seldom visit and usually never live in, Hunters Point has borne the burden of Nixon's cutbacks in domestic spending."[53] Still, Hunters Point residents continued their work of rebuilding the neighborhood. In a television interview in 1972, against a background of wood frames and the sound of hammering, Elouise Westbrook spoke about the importance of an industrial park along the Hunters Point waterfront—part of the master redevelopment plan—which would provide jobs for Black residents in Hunters Point. This, she told the reporter, would allow people to "live here for ever and ever."[54]

The experiences of Hunters Point residents working to make space for Black life in San Francisco during the 1960s and 1970s raise questions about a political strategy that relies on state agencies for sociospatial change. And yet, rebuilding Hunters Point required state power to accomplish large, capital-intensive redevelopment on the hill—demolishing thousands of wartime temporary dwellings and constructing an entirely new, modern neighborhood, with careful attention to the needs of mothers and the daily work of social reproduction. Residents worked with these constraints while maintaining a critical relationship with the state, aiming to leverage the state's resources to reshape the built environment in Hunters Point. This careful dance can be interpreted as similar to the improvisation techniques of the jazz music continuing to play in music halls in the Fillmore District.[55] If the 1969–71 calendar's landscape designs never fully materialized, it was not for Hunters Point residents' lack of effort or vision, but because what they desired placed them in a tense, asymmetrical relationship with the city agencies and with broader shifts in national politics. In *Development Arrested*, Woods finds the origins of an alternative, more just form of development in the Mississippi Delta region "among the scattered, misplaced and often forgotten movements, projects, and agendas of its African American communities and of other marginalized groups."[56] The work of the Bayview–Hunters Point CDC and the Joint Housing Committee represent one way Black San Franciscans responded to exclusionary forms of development and worked to build more just urban geographies.

> *Suitcase packed*
> *trunk's already gone.*
> *Going to San Francisco*
> *to make it my home.*
> *San Francisco,*
> *please make room for me.*

By the late 1980s, blues guitarist Lowell Fulson crooned a requiem to the city. "San Francisco," he sang, "please make room for me." His words lament the decline in Black population in San Francisco since 1970, in the context of ongoing urban renewal in Fillmore and post–Great Society era state abandonment in Hunters Point. And yet in the bars of Fulson's song, "The San Francisco Blues," might also be heard a paean to the people who worked to produce a more livable, humane sociospatial arrangement—to "make room," rather than exclude.[57] Hunters Point residents continue the work of Osceola Washington, Elouise Westbrook, and others today.[58]

Notes

1 Moore, *Take This Hammer*.

2 McKittrick, *Demonic Grounds*, 17.

3 Woods, *Development Arrested*.

4 Gilmore, "Abolition Geography and the Problem of Innocence," 238.

5 According to Field, "the ethnonym 'Ohlone' refers to a native group with a postcontact history shaped mainly by the demographic collapse caused by missionization and the subsequent regrouping during the Mexican period." Field, "Unacknowledged Tribes, Dangerous Knowledge," 86.

6 Anderson, Barbour, and Whitworth, "World of Balance and Plenty."

7 Madley, *American Genocide*; Hurtado, *Indian Survival on the California Frontier*; Lightfoot et al., "European Colonialism and the Anthropocene."

8 Estes, "America Fears the Past."

9 McKittrick, *Demonic Grounds*, 75.

10 McKittrick, "Plantation Futures," 8–9.

11 Hackel, "Land, Labor, and Production," 122.

12 Hornbeck, "Land Tenure and Rancho Expansion in Alta California."

13 Brechin, *Imperial San Francisco*.

14 Quoted in Mawn, "Framework for Destiny," 174.

15 Horsman, *Race and Manifest Destiny*, 1.

16 Chan, *This Bittersweet Soil*.

17 Saxton, *Indispensable Enemy*.

18 Du Bois, *Black Reconstruction in America*, 680; on anti-Chinese racism in San Francisco, see Saxton, *Indispensable Enemy*.

19 Hawthorne and Lewis, introduction to this volume.

20 Broussard, *Black San Francisco*.

21 Broussard, *Black San Francisco*.

22 Woods, *Development Arrested*, 16.

23 Woods writes, "Jazz can also be considered a blues-based movement if we examine the people who gave it birth, its blues elements, and the role it has played for successive generations." Woods, *Development Arrested*, 116.

24 Johnson, *Negro War Worker in San Francisco*.

25 Wollenberg, "James vs. Marinship."

26 Moore, *To Place Our Deeds*, 69.

27 Hildebrand, "Oakland Blues, Part I."

28 Jelly-Shapiro, "Hide Tide, Low Ebb," 62.

29 Murch, *Living for the City*; Self, *American Babylon*.

30 Self, *American Babylon*, 50.

31 Murch, *Living for the City*.

32 Pepin and Watts, *Harlem of the West.*

33 Jelly-Shapiro, "High Tide, Low Ebb."

34 Chapman, *Jazz Bubble*, 167.

35 Quoted in Pepin and Watts, *Harlem of the West*, 130.

36 Pepin and Watts, *Harlem of the West*; Chapman, *Jazz Bubble.*

37 Brahinsky, "'Hush Puppies,' Communualist Politics, and Demolition Governance"; Lai, "Racial Triangulation of Space."

38 Angelou, *I Know Why the Caged Bird Sings*, 213.

39 Here, I refer to David Theo Goldberg, writing about the violence of civil society: "The architecture of states embedded violence (individualized and institutionalized) rendered standardized relations and modes of violence regular even as they become regulated, structured *embedded*, in a word, civil." Goldberg, *Threat of Race*, 41.

40 Quoted in Carby, "Figuring the Future in Los(t) Angeles," 24.

41 Quoted in Carby, "Figuring the Future in Los(t) Angeles," 24.

42 Hildebrand, "Oakland Blues, Part I," 107.

43 Howey, "Oakland Blues."

44 On the Lanham Act, see Baranski, *Housing the City by the Bay*; on demographic change in Hunters Point, see Agee, *Streets of San Francisco*; for the description of Hunters Point, see M. Justin Herman to Harry Ross, July 3, 1961.

45 "Portrait of a Community Worker, Osceola Washington."

46 Residents Start Housing Co-op."

47 "Men Take Over."

48 Prime Consultant for the Development of the New Hunters Point Community.

49 Hunters Point & India Basin Industrial Park Calendar.

50 This phase included 652 units built under the Federal Housing Administration Section 236 program. Bayview–Hunters Point Joint Housing Committee Progress and Activity Report.

51 Papazoglakis, "Feminist, Gun-Toting Abolitionist with a Bankroll."

52 Mollenkopf, *Contested City.*

53 "Housing at Hunters Point." The announced closure of the Hunters Point Naval Shipyard—still an important source of income for many Hunters Point residents—in 1973 exacerbated the next phase of state abandonment.

54 "Eloise Westbrook on the New Look for Hunters Point."

55 On jazz and social improvisation, see Fischlin and Porter, *Playing for Keeps.*

56 Woods, *Development Arrested*, 3–4.

57 In writing the words "more livable, humane sociospatial arrangement," I am thinking of McKittrick, *Demonic Grounds.*

58 Allenworth, Hall, and McElroy, "(Dis)location/Black Exodus and the Anti-Eviction Mapping Project."

Bibliography

Agee, Christopher. *The Streets of San Francisco: Policing and the Creation of a Cosmopolitan Liberal Politics, 1950–1972*. Chicago: University of Chicago Press, 2014.

Allenworth, Ariana Faye, Adrienne Hall, and Erin McElroy. "(Dis)location/Black Exodus and the Anti-Eviction Mapping Project." *Abusable Past*, August 6, 2019. https://www.radicalhistoryreview.org/abusablepast/dislocation-black-exodus -and-the-anti-eviction-mapping-project/.

Anderson, M. Kat, Michael Barbour, and Valerie Whitworth. "A World of Balance and Plenty: Land, Plants, Animals, and Humans in a Pre-European California." In *Contested Eden: California before the Gold Rush*, edited by Ramón A. Gutiérrez and Richard J. Orsi, 12–47. Oakland: University of California Press, 1998.

Angelou, Maya. *I Know Why the Caged Bird Sings*. 1969. New York: Ballantine Books, 2003.

Baranski, John. *Housing the City by the Bay: Tenant Activism, Civil Rights, and Class Politics in San Francisco*. Palo Alto, CA: Stanford University Press, 2019.

Bayview–Hunters Point Joint Housing Committee Progress and Activity Report, September 16, 1966, to November 20, 1969. Box 14, Folder 41. Joseph L. Alioto Papers, 1958–1977. San Francisco Public Library, San Francisco.

Brahinsky, Rachel. "'Hush Puppies,' Communalist Politics, and Demolition Governance: The Rise and Fall of the Black Fillmore." In *Ten Years That Shook the City: San Francisco, 1968–1978*, edited by Chris Carlsson, 141–53. San Francisco: City Lights Books, 2011.

Brechin, Gray. *Imperial San Francisco: Urban Power, Earthly Ruin*. Berkeley: University of California Press, 2006.

Broussard, Albert S. *Black San Francisco: The Struggle for Racial Equality in the West, 1900–1954*. Lawrence: University Press of Kansas, 1993.

Carby, Hazel V. "Figuring the Future in Los(t) Angeles." *Comparative American Studies: An International Journal* 1, no. 1 (2003): 19–34.

Chan, Sucheng. *This Bittersweet Soil: The Chinese in California Agriculture, 1860–1910*. Berkeley: University of California Press, 1989.

Chapman, Dale. *The Jazz Bubble: Neoclassical Jazz in Neoliberal Culture*. Oakland: University of California Press, 2018.

Djedje, Jacqueline Cogdell, and Eddie S. Meadows. "Introduction." In *California Soul: Music of African Americans in the West*, edited by Jacqueline Cogdell Djedje and Eddie S. Meadows, 1–22. Berkeley: University of California Press, 1998.

Du Bois, W. E. B. *Black Reconstruction in America: An Essay toward a History of the Part Which Black Folk Played in the Attempt to Reconstruct Democracy in America, 1860–1880*. 1936. New York: Free Press, 1992.

"Eloise Westbrook on the New Look for Hunters Point." KPIX News, October 25, 1972. Bay Area Television Archive. https://diva.sfsu.edu/collections/sfbatv /bundles/217297.

Estes, Nick. "America Fears the Past." *The Nation*, November 4, 2019.

Field, Les W. "Unacknowledged Tribes, Dangerous Knowledge: The Muwekma Ohlone and How Indian Identities Are Known." *Wicazo Sa Review* 18, no. 2 (2003): 79–94.

Fischlin, Daniel, and Eric Porter, eds. *Playing for Keeps: Improvisation in the Aftermath*. Durham, NC: Duke University Press, 2020.

Gilmore, Ruth Wilson. "Abolition Geography and the Problem of Innocence." In *Futures of Black Radicalism*, edited by Gaye Theresa Johnson and Alex Lubin, 225–40. London: Verso, 2017.

Gilmore, Ruth Wilson. *Golden Gulag: Prisons, Surplus, Crisis, and Opposition in Globalizing California*. Berkeley: University of California Press, 2007.

Goldberg, David Theo. *The Threat of Race: Reflections on Racial Neoliberalism*. Malden, MA: Blackwell, 2009.

Hackel, Steven W. "Land, Labor, and Production: The Colonial Economy of Spanish and Mexican California." In *Contested Eden: California before the Gold Rush*, edited by Ramón A. Gutiérrez and Richard J. Orsi, 111–46. Berkeley: University of California Press, 1998.

Herman, M. Justin, to Harry Ross, July 3, 1961. Box 2, Folder 20. John F. "Jack" Shelley Papers, 1953–1967. San Francisco Public Library, San Francisco.

Hildebrand, Lee. "Oakland Blues, Part I: Essay." In *California Soul: Music of African Americans in the West*, edited by Jacqueline Cogdell Djedje and Eddie S. Meadows, 104–11. Berkeley: University of California Press, 1998.

Himes, Chester. *If He Hollers Let Him Go*. 1945. Philadelphia: Da Capo, 2002.

Hornbeck, David. "Land Tenure and Rancho Expansion in Alta California, 1784–1846." *Journal of Historical Geography* 4, no. 4 (1978): 371–90.

Horsman, Reginald. *Race and Manifest Destiny*. Cambridge, MA: Harvard University Press, 1981.

"Housing at Hunters Point: What Will Happen Next?" *Sun-Reporter*, November 16, 1973.

Howey, Brian. "The Oakland Blues." *Beats and Measures*. Podcast audio. September 21, 2018. https://www.beatsandmeasures.com/single-post/The-Harlem-of-the-West-Seventh-Street-and-the-Oakland-Blues.

Hunters Point & India Basin Industrial Park Calendar. Box 17. Joseph L. Alioto Papers, 1958–1977. San Francisco Public Library, San Francisco.

"Hunters Point: Community at Crossroads." *Sun-Reporter*, January 15, 1972.

Hurtado, Albert L. *Indian Survival on the California Frontier*. New Haven, CT: Yale University Press, 1988.

Jelly-Shapiro, Joshua. "High Tide, Low Ebb." In *Infinite City: A San Francisco Atlas*, edited by Rebecca Solnit, 57–67. Berkeley: University of California Press, 2010.

Johnson, Charles Spurgeon. *The Negro War Worker in San Francisco*. YWCA in connection with the Race Relations Program of the American Missionary Association, 1945. Bancroft Library, Berkeley, CA.

Lai, Clement. "The Racial Triangulation of Space: The Case of Urban Renewal in San Francisco's Fillmore District." *Annals of the Association of American Geographers* 102, no. 1 (2012): 151–70.

Lightfoot, Kent G., Lee M. Panich, Tsim D. Schneider, and Sara L. Gonzalez. "European Colonialism and the Anthropocene: A View from the Pacific Coast of North America." *Anthropocene* 4 (2013): 101–15.

Madley, Benjamin. *An American Genocide: The United States and the California Indian Catastrophe, 1846–1873*. New Haven, CT: Yale University Press, 2016.

Mawn, Geoffrey P. "Framework for Destiny: San Francisco, 1847." *California Historical Quarterly* 51, no. 2 (1972): 165–78.

McKittrick, Katherine. *Demonic Grounds: Black Women and the Cartographies of Struggle*. Minneapolis: University of Minnesota Press, 2006.

McKittrick, Katherine. "Plantation Futures." *Small Axe: A Caribbean Journal of Criticism* 17, no. 3 (42) (2013): 1–15.

"Men Take Over." *Spokesman*, December 10, 1966.

Minutes of Joint Housing Committee Executive Committee, September 29, 1969. Box 14, Folder 40. Joseph L. Alioto Papers, 1958–1977. San Francisco Public Library, San Francisco.

Mollenkopf, John. *The Contested City*. Princeton, NJ: Princeton University Press, 1983.

Moore, Richard O., dir. *Take This Hammer*. San Francisco, CA: KQED, 1964. Bay Area Television Archives. https://diva.sfsu.edu/collections/sfbatv/bundles/187041.

Moore, Shirley Ann Wilson. *To Place Our Deeds: The African American Community in Richmond, California, 1910–1963*. Berkeley: University of California Press, 2000.

Murch, Donna Jean. *Living for the City: Migration, Education, and the Rise of the Black Panther Party in Oakland, California*. Chapel Hill: University of North Carolina Press, 2010.

Papazoglakis, Sarah. "'Feminist, Gun-Toting Abolitionist with a Bankroll': The Black Radical Philanthropy of Mary Ellen Pleasant." *New Global Studies* 12, no. 2 (2018): 235–56.

Pepin, Elizabeth, and Lewis Watts. *Harlem of the West: The San Francisco Fillmore Jazz Era*. San Francisco: Chronicle Books, 2006.

"Portrait of a Community Worker, Osceola Washington." *Spokesman*, September 17, 1966.

Prime Consultant for the Development of the New Hunters Point Community, November 1, 1966. Carton 94, Folder 8. NAACP Region 1, Records, 1942–1986. Bancroft Library, Berkeley, CA.

"Residents Start Housing Co-op." *Spokesman*, September 2, 1965.

Saxton, Alexander. *The Indispensable Enemy: Labor and the Anti-Chinese Movement in California*. Berkeley: University of California Press, 1971.

Self, Robert. *American Babylon: Race and the Struggle for Postwar Oakland*. Princeton, NJ: Princeton University Press, 2005.

Shange, Savannah. *Progressive Dystopia: Abolition, Antiblackness, and Schooling in San Francisco*. Durham, NC: Duke University Press, 2019.

Wollenberg, Charles. "James vs. Marinship: Trouble on the New Black Frontier." *California History* 60, no. 3 (1981): 262–79.

Woods, Clyde Adrian. *Development Arrested: The Blues and Plantation Power in the Mississippi Delta.* London: Verso, 1998.

11

Today Like Yesterday, Tomorrow Like Today

Black Geographies in the Breaks of the Fourth Dimension

ANNA LIVIA BRAND

This is a moment that has never happened. . . .
This is a moment that is always happening.
—DAWN LOGSDON, LOLIS ERIC ELIE, LUCIE FAULKNOR, AND JONELL KENNEDY,
"Faubourg Treme: The Untold Story of Black New Orleans"

Prologue

On August 29, 2005, the levees protecting the city of New Orleans failed. In a moment, the city was inundated with water, homes and neighborhoods were torn from their foundations, and New Orleans was irrevocably changed. As the water receded, centuries of racial injustice and environmental vulnerability were reexposed. And as newly deepened geographies of destruction were laid bare by the receding water, percolating below the surface were the deep histories of white supremacist, anti-Black geographic formations that had shaped the city since its colonization and up until the moment of Katrina. In this post-Katrina moment, a rush to envision the city's future reactivated and folded in these longer histories. The rush toward envisioning a new future was infused by deep social and racial inequality, and environmental and developmental vulnerability. Indeed, as the waters receded, a deluge of images and visions detailing a more resilient, green, sustainable, and just city poured in. Steeped in rhetorical commitments to equity and environmental sustainability, the envisioned landscape of post-disaster justice instead fused and mobilized neoliberal concepts of race and environment into planning practice, policy decisions, and, over the last seventeen years, development decisions.[1] Having been exposed by the floodwaters, the lingering foundations of geographic racism were reassembled into contemporary, multifaceted, and multiscaled anti-Black geographic formations that increasingly intersect with neoliberal space-making and economic/environmental vulnerability. Despite commitments to a diverse and equitable future city, New Orleans's new geography reveals the harmful and violent spatial imaginary of white supremacism in the twenty-first century.[2] Brought to life in the wake of the storm, new modes of Black dispossession dominate the city's reemergence.

The "post-Katrina moment," many argued, was a time for reimagining the city, for rethinking how to attend to the racial injustices laid bare by the storm and to attend to the city's increasing environmental vulnerability. Metrics of erosion and soil subsidence were utilized to provide a foundation for envisioning future environmentally sustainable and resilient settlement patterns. Yet these measurements of mud and muck codified centuries of development steeped in racial capitalism. Post-Katrina analyses that rationalized clearance and abandonment based on metrics of topography and historical development were abstracted from the social and historical workings of race, racism, and resistance in and across the city. Indeed, the blank slate that many leaders protracted as the post-Katrina moment was not blank; it was saturated by racialized imaginings and a Cartesian spatial logic steeped in whiteness. The blank slate from which planners, city officials, and policymakers imagined the new New Orleans was therefore selectively blank. It erased Black voices and centuries of Black place-making. It included data that would sediment and expand the ongoing (spatial) lives of white supremacism and concretize the (spatial) foundations of whiteness while simultaneously problematizing Black geographic temporalities and formations.[3] Its metrics were abstracted from and assigned a rational distance from what has been, is, and would be a deeply racialized (re)contouring of land.

To be certain, a cacophony of visions for the future of the city abounded in the wake of the storm—erupting from within and outside of the city, from policymakers and scholars, and from residents themselves. Envisioning the future city through the discipline of urban planning quickly became the critical foundation for how federal funding and new development might be deployed to the city. It became a framework through which residents' competing ideas of equity and visions for the future were articulated and a way that residents claimed a space in the future of the city.[4] As such, urban planning and landscape architecture became critical venues for anticipating, imagining and enacting new futures.

Futurity is one of the roots of planning and design thought, though its formations are problematically assumed from within practices that calcify and delineate racial processes and racial oppression within a framework that itself lacks culpability. Planning has largely lost its institutional praxis of discerning between and among claims on the state made via the planning process itself. As many planning scholars argue, it has, to a large degree, embraced the logics of neoliberalism.[5] As the planning and redevelopment process unfolded in New Orleans, the dominant visions of recovery proffered by urban planning silenced the simultaneous and complex black geographic epistemologies long characterized by deep social belonging and practices of care, mutual aid, love and life. The planning process sundered connections between futurity and Blackness. As New Orleans has redeveloped, this distancing between Black geographic formations and the future of the city has had diasporic repercussions, leading to a drastically whiter city supported by new (and continuing) logics of Black dispossession. Despite Black residents shouting from the rooftops, as Clyde Woods describes, racially just visions for the city's future, these visions were partially subsumed by neoliberal and anti-Black rhetoric that came to cement white supremacism into the very fabric of New Orleans's reemergence.[6] The "whereness" of Black residents' lives was well documented in post-disaster urban planning processes.[7] However, broader understandings and analyses of racial capitalism and racial geographic formation, that arguably should have informed future imaginaries of the city, were absent from much of city- and planning-led visioning of the city's future. At this moment, then, Black geographies across the city became newly vulnerable to the neoliberal development epistemology and a selectively colorblind racism within which recovery visions would be situated. At this moment, the pace of the long durée of racial geographic formation would pick up; and instantly futurity, at least from within urban planning, was set within a series of contradictory assumptions about race, racism, and racial futures.[8]

> We come to a moment that is one that has never happened before, and that is always happening.
>
> —WYNTON MARSALIS, quoted in Logsdon et al., "Faubourg Treme"

New Orleans had never before experienced this level of flooding and devastation. Yet the city has, for over three hundred years, been implicated in other forms of devastation, originating from white supremacy and its geographic lives—land theft, colonization, slavery, plantationism, segregation, and violence. The city is built on a plantation geography that haunts but does not delineate or circumscribe freedom geographies and their endless, present possibilities. Racial capitalism has ordered the geometry of streets—the radial arpent that emplaced the commerce of racism and a hierarchy in the built environment. These spatial logics, which render rationality, positivism, and abstraction geographically, were not washed away in the flood. Black communities in New Orleans experience multiple forces of devastation that intersect with their daily lives and across generations, back toward ancestral lives, up toward future visions of settlement. The ongoing half-lives of past devastation meet new iterations of anti-Black geographic and human violence in the wake of events like Katrina. White supremacism is unfolding new forms of displacement that legitimate and normalize geographic moments up to the present, echoing them into the future.

We can enumerate many dimensions of black dispossession in New Orleans.[9] Displacement is evidenced at multiple scales: from the lack of electricity in the Lower Ninth Ward that lasted months after the water receded to the racialized conceptualizations of a limited return of the city; from the near abandonment of the Lower Nine to the increased pace of development pressures on Tremé; from dispossession of Black-owned property to the co-optation of Black culture. But enumerations inherently carry with them a finality that eclipses deeper truths. As Katherine McKittrick and Clyde Woods warn us, they normalize and strip bare what Adam Bledsoe, Latoya Eaves, and Brian Williams argue is the always present work of Black place-making.[10] While enumerations of Black death delineate the contours and geographic workings of racism, it is Black life that propels geographic and temporal considerations of futures not hinged to systems of oppression.[11] Black life, as Woods and Robin D. G. Kelley tell us, is constantly making space outside of the confines, logics, and echoes of white supremacism.[12] Black life collapses space and time and recontours not only how we imagine the future but also what we imagine. Black life breaks the Cartesian logics of whiteness, shatters its orthogonality, and contests ways that it constructs a relationship between people and place: it connects freedom to spatial transformation.[13]

Enumerations are not the only way to understand Black lives and geographies. Residents' shouted in a cacophony from afar and within, from the rooftops and beneath an overpass, moving to a rhythm along a sidewalk and from a front stoop.[14] Taking up space—these reverberations cannot be enumerated or inventoried, and they defy the archive. Black residents in New Orleans have always folded into community spaces sociospatial epistemologies not originated in white supremacism or privilege. Sidewalks, streets, porches, neutral grounds, underpasses, bayous, and levees—the use and love of these spaces is not steeped in denigration. And while the bare foundations, the porches without a home that emerged from the flood, speak volumes about loss and absence, they also speak about wood and brick, worn steps and creaking porch furniture, the slope of a porch on settling land and walls of family photographs. They speak of home as a location that has magnitude and direction and whose position within a constellation of homes is linked to a complex, rich geographic expression that is multiscaled and multifaceted; that collapses moments of survival, resistance, loving, and being into the dimensions of a porch and the plain lettering on a "hand-lettered sign."[15] The "innovative practices of Black survival and resistance [that have] been inseparable from the production" of space are outside of the spatial and temporal logics of whiteness.[16]

Enumerations and Black life coexist, but they do not offer the same future. There is too much certainty, as McKittrick warns us, in mathematically tracing dispossession toward an echo of continued dispossession and displacement into the future.[17] The grid, the point, the line and the volume of Black death pinpoint only a system of oppression. Black geographic praxis reconceptualizes the temporality of imagining and the geography of love: time is collapsed, the past is simultaneous, resistant imaginaries are folded into the present, threading a new future of possibilities. The space|time of Black geographies, the fourth dimension, puts the present in conversation with the past, puts the future in conversation with complex and vibrant geographic understandings where time is folded and Blackness is presenced (not erased).

Black geographies,
here,
have magnitude and a multidirectional velocity.
They propel the possibility of liberation as a geographic project.

The Cartesian Coordinates of Disaster Time

In the wake of the storm, urban planning and post-disaster policy fused frozen concepts of race and racial subjects into a series of future imaginaries of the city. These projections into the future hinged, as many have noted, on neoliberal development practices and projections of a city on high ground that lives with water.[18] This city is stripped of its historically Black neighborhoods like the Lower Ninth Ward and Tremé, whose deeply resonant contexts of Black place-making that still echo(ed) across the landscape are absented.[19] At times the contours of future maps directly erased Black geographies. Both the 2006 recommendations of the Bring New Orleans Back Commission for a limited return of certain majority Black or racially mixed areas of the city and the New Orleans Water Plan's 2010 bird's-eye vision of a new wetland in the northern portion of the Lower Ninth Ward, where residents had already rebuilt homes, unambiguously proposed erasure. Other visions, such as the Claiborne Corridor Improvement Coalition's 2010 projection of a new Claiborne Avenue neutral ground where Tremé residents gather and have fought for (and fight for) place are implicitly erased by new programming, a streetcar lane, a bike/walking path, and a water retention area. Planners, landscape architects, and policy officials rationalized tacit and overt forms of erasure through a narrative that elicited environmental equity, protection, and diverse, multicultural futures. In this future, bike lanes and wetlands take the place of Black public space.[20]

Together, these iterations of anti-Blackness delineated a new city form fundamentally absent of its Black residents. This future city does not presence and hold space for Black lives. We can read in these imaginaries a new New Orleans that is no longer chocolate.[21] Both the diversification and the abandonment of Black strongholds are masked by seemingly neutral development projects such as tourist-centered infrastructural development, green gentrification, and high-ground development rationales and by seemingly rational or even environmentally just approaches to dealing with stormwater and environmental vulnerability in a sinking city.

Yet hidden behind these masks is a deeply erosive spatial logic of whiteness enacted through a future imaginary of the city. A "white spatial imaginary" informs future visions of investment and dispossession through exclusive, dispossessing, and racialized property valuations.[22] It is a racial formation projected forward into a future that leaps ahead from rationalized conceptions of space, which themselves elude the temporal workings of race.[23] The Cartesian blank space of the post-Katrina moment, an ideology that underlies the multiscaled erasure of Black geographies from new wetlands where former homes stood to a programmed, filled-up neutral ground devoid of gathering space, is full of incongruous measurements and indices that locate the moment of Katrina in a declining and depopulating city.[24] The depopulation metrics used in planning narratives themselves have hinged on a narrative of decline linked to white flight from the city in the wake of Black organizing for school desegregation and liberation and on Black displacement during Katrina. The notion of the blank slate has itself always been tied to modes of conquest in the United States, but white spaces are never blank. Thus the contradictions of whiteness work together: planners' visions of the future enumerated a limited return of Lower Ninth Ward residents, despite prohibitions on residents' return enabling these very numbers; defined as vulnerable a low-lying, Black topography and as valuable a low-lying white topography; and diversified Black (not white) cultural geographies.[25] This work enumerates black death rather than Black life.[26] These projected future landscapes are absented of Black bodies, labor, and histories.

Inherently, envisioning the future from a positivist, Cartesian imaginary does the underlying work of white supremacy through seemingly benign, rhetorical commitments to reducing vulnerability. Cartesianism itself is outside of time; it concretizes space and fixes identities. Epistemologically, Cartesianism and the spatial logics of positivism suggest a way of knowing that is both absolute and separate from interpretative knowledge systems. Cartesian knowledge is located within an atemporal coordinate system; it positions point, line, and volume with a common point of origin. Any point, any volume is positioned and delineated in relation to this point of origin. It is a system that seemingly naturalizes itself through rational metrics and a positionality seemingly outside of a multiplicity of perspectives and knowledge systems. Whiteness operates in the same way. Within the unfolding racial hierarchy in the United States, whiteness as a position and a knowledge system has a singular point of origin from which all others are measured and understood. This gives whiteness a vexing endurance. It is grounded in positivist and Cartesian conceptualizations that rationalize displacement and assume a neutral empiricism; it is singular, absolute. This outdated, disputed philosophy still frames our world.[27] It is, as Wynton Marsalis notes, a moment that is always happening.

The dimensions of a Cartesian coordinate system therefore describe relationships. They are thus tools of knowing, pinpointing and locating objects relative to one another. Rooted in Euclidean space, three values locate a known quantity in a Cartesian coordinate system that defines and depicts relative positionality and connects to unfolding white supremacist realities as a point of origin. In other words, in a Cartesian mode of thought, Black geographies would always be relative to white geographies. The spatial coordinates of different bodies (x, y, z) describe the distance between them, thus implying a known distance of conquest and colonization and the ability to be reduced to a specific value system outside of time. Thinking temporally, we see a stripping of time from the geographic coordinates of disaster—one that reduces environmental vulnerability to known (quantifiable) factors such as soil subsidence and topographic location relative to the height of water. Thinking topographically (and not temporally), we see the Cartesian impacts of disaster in these imaginaries and renderings, which depict a future without low-lying Black geographies. This orthogonality is inherently raced: all white geographies are given future life in the Cartesian imaginary.

Cartesian coordinates construct a way of seeing racism spatially. The coordinates of disaster construct spatial relationships between Black bodies, communities, and space in relation to the ways that white geographies are inherently valued. They project this value through enumerations and maps that codify and spatialize a future, conveying a future hybridity of white racial formation through a new geography of solidified color lines, erased Black geographies, and racially mixed, formerly Black communities.[28] These interlocking forms of displacement are new iterations of spatial traumatization.[29]

> The blank slate is full of whiteness.

Taken metaphorically, Cartesianism is the spatial logic of whiteness that renders, locates, defines (or attempts to define), limits interactions, limits multiplicity, eliminates time. In a map of the future drawn from this logic, time moves forward and space has no past. The map of the future forecloses questions about how race, racism, and white supremacy work geographically and temporally.

The intent of this chapter is not to focus on white supremacist spatial logics as much as it is to say that dominant modes of thinking in the post-Katrina moment reveal how this white spatial imaginary saturates and scales whiteness and its interlocking logics of white supremacy and privilege onto Black space in the future.[30] Drawing from collective Black community efforts to counter this spatial epistemology, I want to suggest that while whiteness relies on the absolutism and orthogonality of Euclidean thinking in such a way that it contours anti-Blackness and even racial diversity in specific ways, attempting to locate Black life within proposed erasure by wetland or programming highlights how the Cartesian coordinates of the post-disaster city are unable to account for a future where Black geographies are all geographies.

> White orthogonality: the making of a Cartesian map, the acceptance of its dimensions, scale, and erasures
> . . . What is left out?

Up toward and Down from Black Geographic Time: Into the Breaks of the Fourth Dimension

Her shape haunts the maps drawn by his hand. She implies a different spatial and temporal geography of tunnels and time warps. She herself is not fully legible to colonialism's eye and cannot be defined by its sciences nor described through its grammar of power.
—LA PAPERSON, "The Postcolonial Ghetto"

We can't always pinpoint when something begins.
—SUNNI PATTERSON, quoted in Alyssa Long, "Words Off the Page"

In January 2006, when the Bring New Orleans Back Commission publicly presented recommendations to shrink the city's footprint, residents stood up and protested the erasure of Black geographies inherent in the generalizations and rationalizations of environmental protection.

Residents confronted the imaginary of a future city without them by presencing Black life:

WE ARE HOME.

Residents shifted the imaginary of absence by using the walls of their homes to make their lives visible:

FIGURE 11.1. Anna Livia Brand, *We Are Home*, 2022. Mixed media on canvas, 40 × 30 inches.

HOME, THIS WAS HOME.

Residents pressed and are pressing upon the city through development imaginaries of their own making. They have reclaimed and built spaces where city officials, planners, and designers said they could not go.

They have imagined a future made by themselves.[31]

Clyde Woods and Robin D. G. Kelley tell us that the moment from which alternative futures might leap ahead is present and has always been present within Black geographic imaginings and makings of place.[32] Read this way, the rationalized maps displacing Black residents from future geographies are disrupted by evoking not just a right to place and to home but a right to a future in the city. The moment of Katrina was devastating, but it did not disrupt Black place-making or resistance to erasure. The prohibitions on return and all iterations of Black human and geographic erasure, before and since, are themselves haunted by ongoing imaginaries and work to make place, whether through contesting the right to be in the future city, rebuilding a home, sitting on a porch, or gathering in a Lower Ninth Ward Walgreens turned church to shape a collective imaginary of the future. Though erased from the maps drawn by and from a white spatial imaginary, Black life implies a dynamic system, a dynamic logic within which positions are relative to but not defined by white supremacy.[33]

Black geographies not only saturate abstracted, Cartesian coordinates of space with life but also cast a critical lens on the spatial and empirical construction(s) of whiteness. By casting a shadow on white orthogonality, they expose how its coordinates not only are devoid of longer temporalities but also assume transparency and legibility.[34] In contrast to Cartesian space, Blacklife conceptualizations of space|time theorize the nonstatic, thick with ancestral temporalities and geographies, and scale the fourth dimension. The fourth dimension locates space temporally; its dimensions and axes are relative to the always present work of making freedom geographically, drawing out intergenerational possibilities, collapsing static notions and linearity.

> Space is always when;
> always located forward or backward in and across time.

The vectors of space|time therefore describe relationships that are dynamic and complex.

Quantities (bodies, homes, geographies of Blackness) are located within a continuum of where|when—they have both magnitude and direction. In other words, theorizing the where|when dimensions of Black geographies locates them not only physically but also temporally. Time is drawn into and confronts an anti-oppressive geography.

In its simplest form, this fusion of space and time allows us to think about how Black geographies and, for instance, Black residents in the Lower Ninth Ward and Tremé anticipate the future through a lens rooted in the fusion of where|when along a space|time continuum that is simultaneous with but not defined by time-abstracted notions of space and development (Cartesianism). Though simultaneous, the where|when continuum of Black geographies is a dynamic and complex collapse of the past into the present that asserts the inability to reduce history to enumerated or abstracted snapshots. Take residents' assertion of being home and seeing home in the wake of the flood, their assertion of the right to be human in a geography and a political economy that has disdained and oppressed. Take, for instance, the work of a porch, of sitting on a porch in the sun despite prohibitions to return. Take the countless acts of inhabiting the street in a second line along North Claiborne Avenue and through Tremé, filling the space with a brass band, Black life, Black movement. Take the Mardi Gras Indians defying words like *blight* and *abandonment* with the labor of costume, color, feathers and beadwork. These acts of being and Black life haunt the landscape despite all attempts to absent them in the future city.

This simultaneous fusion of space|time within each moment of the pre- and post-Katrina landscape is made through acts of resistance, critique, and dreams of freedom.[35] This understanding of space|time casts a shadow on Cartesian thought by situating it temporally as well as within the ongoing trajectory of racial capitalism and white supremacism.[36] Du Bois's double consciousness similarly centers this simultaneous duality by conceptualizing second sight and the ability to "see America in a way that white Americans cannot."[37] Second sight is not governed solely by white visual metrics or spatialities; it is a vector that dynamically connects time and space in a formula that equates the future with Black place-making now and in the past. And, yet, it is Elizabeth Alexander's reading of multiplicity and Michelle Wright's and Craig Wilkins's examinations of complexity that speak to the dynamic nature of the Blackness in the fourth dimension.[38] Moving temporally up toward and down from fluid notions of space|time allows us to locate Black geographies temporally, which in turn challenges notions of Blackness as relative only to whiteness or as monolithic, singular, and static.[39] It challenges the absolute collapse of time in Cartesian space by opening up the temporality of space, shedding light on white hegemony and the denigrating, geographic logics of white supremacy. Theorizing the where|when dislocates and simultaneously/energetically elongates the higher dimensions of Black geographic time. It provides, analytically, a way of bringing the past to bear on the present so that it can project more emancipatory configurations of space and settlement.

Black voices rose from the rooftops, in planning meetings, in community visioning meetings in once-empty Walgreens, in protests that confronted erasure in City Hall and in the act of rebuilding home.[40] This cacophonous vibration contested the simultaneous projections of the future that hinged on Black death and sought to solidify Black absence in the future of the city. Black residents make life by re-visioning North Claiborne Avenue with Black-owned market spaces that make room for second lines.[41] They make life in and across the geographies of the city through the watching of children playing on the sidewalk, the ride to work offered, the food offered to someone struggling to pay bills, the echo of laughter down the street, the stopping by to talk to neighbors. They shape space by building a platform to reconnect residents with the local environment, by using homes, businesses, churches and porches as gathering spaces. The ontological scope of Black life—the cacophony of words, imaginings, and the built environment—counters the ways through which whiteness is projected into and onto the future city, simultaneously drawing attention to and resisting the mathematical enumerations and absolute locating of Black lives inherent in the aforementioned maps.[42]

Maps of Black life, such as those explored by Marcus Hunter and Zandria Robinson, recontour possible futures by refusing absence and presencing Black life.[43] Black life is mapped by a Lower Ninth Ward resident who traces a network of porches to visit on her daily walks. Black life is mapped in the routes of second lines under and along the North Claiborne overpass. A map of Black life includes Lower Ninth Ward residents' work to reclaim their neighborhood through everyday acts of building and inhabiting space in the wake of Katrina. It includes residents' continued protests of de facto and de jure oppression that spans slavery, Jim Crow, school desegregation, environmental racism, and post-Katrina racial capitalism and prohibitions on return. Taken together and collapsed into present knowledge, this expanded temporality eclipses abstracted notions of space.

> Here,
> the moment of Katrina is expanded backward,
> through re-membering Black life.[44]
> Here,
> the moment of Katrina is expanded forward,
> through imagining Black life.

It reframes what is brought to bear on the present and thus the future; the distance between forms of resistance and being human is collapsed into the present. A map made up toward or down from Black geographic epistemologies and toward emancipatory futures necessarily expands the moment of post-Katrina back toward slavery, the Middle Passage, and beyond—bringing long histories of protest, resistance, and place-making into present truth and knowledge and ways of imagining and depicting the future city.[45]

> Perhaps I like Louis Armstrong because he's made poetry out of being invisible. I think it must be because he's unaware that he is invisible. And my own grasp of invisibility aids me to understand his music. . . . Invisibility, let me explain, gives one a slightly different sense of time, you're never quite on the beat. Sometimes you're ahead and sometimes behind. Instead of the swift and imperceptible flowing of time, you are aware of its nodes, those points where time stands still or from which

it leaps ahead. And you slip into the breaks and look around. That's what you hear vaguely in Louis's music.

—RALPH ELLISON, *Invisible Man*

In their work on the blues epistemology and freedom dreams, both Woods and Kelley explore nodes in black geographic thought and place-making.[46] Slipping into the nodes, as Ellison notes, allows you to hear through and beyond the invisibility of Blackness and into a world not solely defined by whiteness or even the duality of resistance and simultaneity. The nodes—the breaks—allow different locations of Blackness to emerge, allow for and center emancipatory geographic formations by bringing life to bear on the present|future imaginary. Slipping into the nodes opens up the possibility of future geographies in which Blackness is not considered the problem.[47]

These geographies escape the ongoing lives of the 1930s redlining maps and their continuities with the 2006 prohibitions on return, the 2010 wetlands, and the 2010 North Claiborne neutral ground by articulating a timeline that evades closure or linearity. This imaginary insists that Blackness cannot be erased, cannot be absented, cannot be silenced.

> Each moment is a break,
> each resistant act denotes a way of moving forward.
> Blackness has a velocity.

We could see Black residents as willful in the way that Ahmed considers feminists as willful. Ahmed defines being willful as "an act of self-description"; it is the connective tissue between and across generations, geographies, and temporalities.[48] This willfulness can also be seen in McKittrick's use of Édouard Glissant's "poetics of landscape" that "awakens language" and "unapparent histories" to chart new relationships between land and life.[49]

Slipping into the breaks of the fourth dimension therefore describes geographies not as abandoned and denigrated but as beautiful. It defines a frequency of seeing space and Black geographies that cannot be solely contoured by metrics and indices of blight or abandonment. Slipping into the breaks plants "the flesh of black experience" onto the plot of a single-family home, the space of a porch, a folding chair in a former Walgreens, a platform built over a corrugated steel levee to reconnect the Lower Ninth Ward with its larger environment, murals of oak trees and Black residents on the North Claiborne underpass, a design for the future neutral ground that celebrates Black life all the way toward the future.[50]

Black residents in New Orleans are willful of Black life in the past, present, and future city. This imaginary cannot be marked on or by abstracted coordinates and relative positionalities. A map of Black life would resound with a cacophony of voices that speak to and about making place, the materiality of a wood bench on a porch, the curve of a handrail on front porch steps, the solidity of a concrete stoop. They would dream from the long history of second lines and their derivation from Social Aid and Pleasure Clubs. They would render Black life back into the imagination of the future, insisting on its ever-present geographic formations. This imaginary would press upon the future in all its fullness—life that could not be invisibilized.

Thinking in the breaks of the fourth dimension premises a spatial logic of Blackness that is neither relative to whiteness nor orthogonal to its spatial logics. Black geographies cannot be mapped by a logic that fundamentally erases and absents Black life and history.

> This is a geography, a velocity, a space|time of love.

It is a city, as Hunter notes, where every neighborhood has "their orbits and timeline indigenous to their own localized emergence, thriving, surviving, and disappearance or death."[51]

Drawing Black geographies and analytically grounding them would refute the dimensionality of a topographic map or a way of knowing that delineates and abstracts. A collage of Black life would saturate and collapse space|time, would grow from a landscape rooted in love, in mutuality and multiplicity. A rendering of Black geographies—the nodes of the fourth dimension—might be drawn from the perspective of the porch, from the perspective of a child second-lining, the temporal collapse of a mural of the Black-owned business and the business itself. Renderings of Black geographic life would echo with the desire of each geography opened up to more life, more love, more joy.

> Those who dwell in the fourth dimension know that the universe includes something anterior, a world of feeling and understanding that has been relegated to another order of time or being.
> —NANCY BENTLEY, "The Fourth Dimension"

If planning is inherently about futurity, then planning in the fourth dimension would inherently incorporate the temporality of Black geographies; the velocity of moving toward a future would be inundated with a deluge of images, indices, accounts, and ideas from Black residents themselves.

It would be fundamentally imagined back from a future where all Black lives were present and all geographies were Black. It would be imagined back toward and across generations, across moments of life, voice, joy, love, protest. It would encompass the unfettered, the longing and light of hope, the brisk sparkle of the cusp of time where anything can happen.[52] The borders and topographies would be configured through a new language and a new imaginary through which development and land and Blackness are not synonymous with color lines and displacement or an "architecture of confinement," but are synonymous with the space|time arc of love.[53]

Coda: Today Like Yesterday, Tomorrow Like Today

love, find me in the morning.
Find me in the morning,
before the day has done its work on us.
While I'm un-punched, limber, in line with the
stars. Potassium. Closer to the bed of the
universe. Find me travelled; while I can still
hear my mother's voice, while my fear is
upside down and I am petal, I am unfettered,
silver-soft and I hear singing. Find me at the
top of light while I am exchanging with
my ancestors; far from the terror of
everything else. Find me open souled,
travelled, dense with hope. Find me.
—YRSA DALEY-WARD, "Notes"

return to the past to build the future
—"The African Burial Ground: Return to the Past to Build the Future," as quoted in
McKittrick, "Plantation Futures"

On August 29, 2005, the levees protecting the city of New Orleans failed.

On August 29, 2006, residents in the Lower Ninth Ward mourned one year since the levees failed, since lives and homes were lost. This day, on the bridge over the Industrial Canal that separates the Lower Ninth Ward from the city, one man held aloft, over the heads of residents and mourners, a sign that read,

OUR ROOTS RUN DEEP HERE.

It is true that Lower Nine residents' roots run deep into the fertile soil sloping back from the Mississippi River levee and toward Bayou Bienvenue. This is the high slope of a levee where residents can see "the most beautiful view of the sky."[54] This was the bayou where residents once hunted and fished before the railroad separated residents from their own environment. This is the bayou where residents have built a viewing platform that reconnects them to the water. This is living with water.

Lower Nine residents have fought for home and against that which threatens their homes. It was here that residents desegregated the public schools. It is here that residents have continued to fight against environmental racism and imagined—in the wake of slavery, in the wake of segregation, in the wake of developmental abandonment, in the wake of human abandonment, in the wake of erasure—a system of land connected to family, a network of porches and talking with neighbors whose power exceeds the dimensions of limitation and locating oneself relative to oppression, whose power is informed by but not defined, limited, determined, or confined by oppression.

> This is a limber, silver-soft, travelled, far from the terror
> constellation of places, meaning, hope, love.
> —YRSA DALEY-WARD, "Notes"

The idea that Black residents' roots run deep in the fertile soil of the Lower Nine counters an imaginary that no residents and no homes existed in the plots of land laid bare by the levee failure and floodwaters. This imaginary suggests that beyond measuring subsidence, the soil and foundations of the Lower Nine must be understood outside of denigrating systems, languages, and visions of oppression. Roots like these are not eliminated by green dots or wetlands. Roots like these speak to residents' ongoing work, from August 29, 2005, forward and backward, to imagine Black life in the city, on these streets, on these porches. This is the substance of growth, the amalgamation of organic remains that have been broken down over time but are still present, still give life to new possibilities.

> Today like yesterday
> Tomorrow like today;
> The drip, drip, drip,
> Of monotony
> Is wearing my life away;
> Today like yesterday,
> Tomorrow like today
> —LANGSTON HUGHES, "Monotony"

We can read Langston Hughes's poem "Monotony" as a condemnation of the monotony of whiteness and the way it wears down efforts toward justice and equality. We can also read his poem as an entry point for moving between dimensions—time and place, here and the diaspora, here and then—to imagine a series of points from which we might leap ahead toward a future unhinged from plantationism and its ongoing lives. The fourth dimension not only introduces time into Cartesian spatial logics but also theoretically allows for nonlinearity and simultaneous positionality to inform developmental frameworks. By collapsing past time into the present, choices made in the wake of each moment can be understood relative to their systems of liberation.[55] This simultaneity fundamentally challenges the hegemony of systems of oppression by presenting resistance and other possible imaginaries for the future at every possible moment. Understood this way, "Monotony" is about cultivating and presencing ways of looking at the world from which we might anticipate plantation futures, counter their spatial logics, and project different landscape formulations. If today is like yesterday and tomorrow is like today, then the moments of resistance and liberation could saturate any attempt to erase Black life.

What happens when we take Black life in the past, present, and future to press upon how we envision and manifest the future? What might this necessitate in terms of Black geographies and their future formations? One point is that this framework would challenge the methodological workings of positivist social sciences. The data points would be situated relative to their systems of oppression or liberation. Simultaneous positionalities not only would be brought into the fold of understanding the present as an accumulation of the past but also would provide a new array of choices. Mapping would become different. The metrics to rationalize abandonment could not be calculated outside of logics of oppression and, instead, would inform a re-presentation of the future hinged on Black life. Dispossession would be countered by the ongoing work of possession and place-making. Words that linked dispossession to blank-slate development approaches could be countered by words that imagined Black presence (repossession, return, reparation, restitution). Repossession would surface as a possibility not only because it always had been a possibility but also because it would be necessitated by a spatial and temporal logic of racial justice.

Read this way, a simple rendering of erasure, such as mapping the absence of Black bodies or even mapping the post-Katrina building footprint of the Lower Ninth Ward, would include stories, residents, diaspora, desire, imaginary, history, and presence. The past would be collapsed into representations of Black spaces so that twinned logics would both illuminate white supremacy and present alternatives.

While understandings of race are contingent and framed around a set of social, cultural, and political structures, race is grounded in a particular kind of static knowing and logic of locating and interpreting the landscape. Whiteness has long been conditioned on and reflective of a need to statically ground identity in place, out of the fluidity of time. To know one's place in society is, for Black residents in New Orleans, a matter of life and death. Yet to ground racial formation in a spatial epistemology focused on the way whiteness orders, categorizes, and uses space renders invisible the tacit and cacophonous, subtle and overt, but always present and multiple ways Black residents in New Orleans appropriate, use, and destabilize the very foundations of a white sociospatial reality. Thinking in the fourth dimension encounters the dialectical interplay between oppression and resistance with the incommensurate ways Black geographies come and can come to settle the landscape.

> The ongoing lives of Black geographies lay claim on the future
> and the fourth dimension opens up the possibility that is folded into
>   each moment.
> the nodes of the fourth dimension
> are travelled,
> yet unfettered.
>
> They are "dense with hope"
> because freedom, as bell hooks notes,
> is linked to transforming space.[56]

Notes

1   Johnson, *Neoliberal Deluge.*

2   Melamed, "Spirit of Neoliberalism"; Mele, "Neoliberalism, Race and the Redefining of Urban Redevelopment."

3   McKittrick, "Plantation Futures"; Bhandar, *Colonial Lives of Property*; Harris, "Whiteness as Property"; Brand, "Sedimentation of Whiteness as Landscape."

4   Brand, "Politics of Defining and Building Equity."

5   Fainstein, *The Just City*; Brenner and Theodore, *Spaces of Neoliberalism.*

6   Woods, "Response from the Author."

7 McKittrick and Woods, "No One Knows the Mysteries at the Bottom of the Ocean."

8 Woods, *Development Drowned and Reborn*.

9 McKittrick and Woods, "No One Knows the Mysteries at the Bottom of the Ocean"; Tuck, "Suspending Damage."

10 McKittrick and Woods, "No One Knows the Mysteries at the Bottom of the Ocean"; Bledsoe, Eaves, and Williams, "Introduction: Black Geographies."

11 McKittrick and Woods, "No One Knows the Mysteries at the Bottom of the Ocean."

12 Woods, *Development Drowned and Reborn*; Kelley, *Freedom Dreams*.

13 hooks, "Art on My Mind."

14 Woods, "Response from the Author."

15 Alexander, "Praise Song for the Day."

16 Bledsoe, Eaves, and Williams, "Introduction: Black Geographies," 7; Hunter, "Black Logics, Black Methods."

17 McKittrick, "Mathematics Black Life."

18 Johnson, *Neoliberal Deluge*.

19 Bledsoe, Eaves, and Williams, "Introduction: Black Geographies."

20 Melamed, "Spirit of Neoliberalism"; Mele, "Neoliberalism, Race and the Redefining of Urban Redevelopment."

21 Hunter and Robinson, *Chocolate Cities*.

22 Lipsitz, *How Racism Takes Place*.

23 Ellison, *Invisible Man*.

24 City of New Orleans, "Plan for the 21st Century."

25 Brand, "Sedimentation of Whiteness as Landscape."

26 McKittrick, "Mathematics Black Life"; Woods, "Life after Death."

27 Wright, *Physics of Blackness*.

28 On the solidification of color lines, see Du Bois, *Souls of Black Folk*; on the erasure of Black geographies, see Fullilove, *Root Shock*.

29 Fullilove, *Root Shock*.

30 Lipsitz, *How Racism Takes Place*.

31 W. E. B. Du Bois, quoted in Meier, "W. E. B. Du Bois's Modernist Data Visualizations of Black Life."

32 Woods, *Development Drowned and Reborn*; Kelley, *Freedom Dreams*.

33 Paperson, "Postcolonial Ghetto"; Hunter, "Black Logics, Black Methods."

34 See McKittrick, "'Black and 'Cause I'm Black I'm Blue.'"

35 Kelley, *Freedom Dreams*.

36 Omi and Winant, *Racial Formation in the United States*.

37 Du Bois, "Criteria of Negro Art," n.p.; on Du Bois's double consciousness, see Du Bois, *Souls of Black Folk*.

38 Alexander, *Collage*; Wright, *Physics of Blackness*; Wilkins, *Aesthetics of Equity*.

39 Hinton, *New Era of Thought*; Wright, *Physics of Blackness*; McKittrick, "'Black and 'Cause I'm Black I'm Blue.'"

40 On voices rising from the rooftops, see Woods, "Response from the Author."

41 See Claiborne Corridor Cultural Innovation District, https://www.cidnola online.com.

42 McKittrick, "Mathematics Black Life."

43 Hunter and Robinson, *Chocolate Cities*.

44 Brand, "Black Mecca Futures"; Savoy, *Trace*.

45 Bledsoe, Eaves, and Williams, "Introduction: Black Geographies."

46 Woods, *Development Drowned and Reborn*; Kelley, *Freedom Dreams*.

47 Du Bois, *Souls of Black Folk*.

48 Ahmed, "Living a Feminist Life," 78–79.

49 McKittrick, *Demonic Grounds*, xxii.

50 Wilson, "Critically Understanding Race-Connected Practices."

51 Hunter, "Black Logics, Black Methods," 218.

52 Daley-Ward, "Notes"; Alexander, "Praise Song for the Day."

53 On color lines, see Du Bois, *Souls of Black Folk*; on displacement, see Fullilove, *Root Shock*; on an "architecture of confinement," see Shabazz, *Spatializing Blackness*.

54 Lower Ninth Ward resident.

55 Sharpe, *In the Wake*.

56 Daley-Ward, "Notes"; hooks, "Art on My Mind," 65.

Bibliography

Ahmed, Sara. *Living a Feminist Life*. Durham, NC: Duke University Press, 2017.

Alexander, Elizabeth. "Collage: An Approach to Reading African-American Women's Literature." PhD diss., University of Pennsylvania, 1992.

Alexander, Elizabeth. "Praise Song for the Day." Poetry Foundation. September 27, 2019. https://www.poetryfoundation.org/poems/52141/praise-song-for-the-day.

Bentley, Nancy. "The Fourth Dimension: Kinlessness and African American Narrative." *Critical Inquiry* 35, no. 2 (2009): 270–92.

Bhandar, Brenna. *Colonial Lives of Property: Law, Land, and Racial Regimes of Ownership*. Durham, NC: Duke University Press, 2018.

Bledsoe, Adam, Latoya E. Eaves, and Brian Williams. "Introduction: Black Geographies in and of the United States South." *Southeastern Geographer* 57, no. 1 (2017): 6–11. https://doi.org/10.1353/sgo.2017.0002.

Brand, Anna Livia. "Black Mecca Futures: Re-membering New Orleans's Claiborne Avenue." *Journal of Urban Affairs* 44 (2021): 1–14.

Brand, Anna Livia. "The Duality of Space: The Built World of Du Bois' Double-Consciousness." *Environment and Planning D: Society and Space* 36, no. 1 (2018): 3–22.

Brand, Anna Livia. "The Politics of Defining and Building Equity in the Twenty-First Century." *Journal of Planning Education and Research* 35, no. 3 (2015): 249–64.

Brand, Anna Livia. "The Sedimentation of Whiteness as Landscape." *Environment and Planning D: Society and Space* 40, no. 2 (2022): 276–91. https://doi.org/10 .1177/02637758211031565.

Brenner, Neil, and Nik Theodore. *Spaces of Neoliberalism: Urban Restructuring in North America and Western Europe*. Vol. 4. Malden, MA: Blackwell, 2003.

City of New Orleans. "Plan for the 21st Century." 2010. Accessed September 19, 2019. https://www.nola.gov/city-planning/master-plan/.

Daley-Ward, Yrsa. "Notes." Instagram. Accessed December 10, 2019. https://www .instagram.com/yrsadaleyward/.

Du Bois, W. E. B. "Criteria of Negro Art." *Crisis* 32, no. 6 (1926): 290–97.

Du Bois, W. E. B. *The Souls of Black Folk*. New York: Routledge, 2015.

Ellison, Ralph. *Invisible Man*. New York: Random House, 1952.

Fainstein, Susan S. *The Just City*. Ithaca, NY: Cornell University Press, 2010.

Fullilove, Mindy Thompson. *Root Shock: How Tearing Up City Neighborhoods Hurts America, and What We Can Do about It*. New York: Ballantine Books, 2005.

Harris, Cheryl I. "Whiteness as Property." *Harvard Law Review* 106, no. 8 (1993): 1707–91.

Hinton, Charles Howard. *A New Era of Thought*. London: Sonnenschein and Company, 1888.

hooks, bell. *Art on My Mind: Visual Politics.* New York: New Press, 1996.

Hunter, Marcus Anthony. "Black Logics, Black Methods: Indigenous Timelines, Race, and Ethnography." *Sociological Perspectives* 61, no. 2 (2018): 207–21. https:// doi.org/10.1177/0731121418758646.

Hunter, Marcus Anthony, and Zandria Robinson. *Chocolate Cities: The Black Map of American Life*. Oakland: University of California Press, 2018.

Johnson, Cedric. *The Neoliberal Deluge: Hurricane Katrina, Late Capitalism, and the Remaking of New Orleans*. Minneapolis: University of Minnesota Press, 2011.

Kelley, Robin D. G. *Freedom Dreams: The Black Radical Imagination*. Boston: Beacon, 2002.

Lipsitz, George. *How Racism Takes Place*. Philadelphia: Temple University Press, 2011.

Logsdon, Dawn, Lolis Eric Elie, Lucie Faulknor, and JoNell Kennedy. "Faubourg Treme: The Untold Story of Black New Orleans." San Francisco: Louisiana Public Broadcasting, WYES-TV, California Newsreel, 2008.

Long, Alyssa. "Words Off the Page: New Orleans Poet Sunni Patterson." UC Santa Barbara, Humanities and Fine Arts. May 17, 2019. https://www.hfa.ucsb.edu /news-entries/2019/5/17/finding-art-in-life-new-orleans-poet-sunni-patterson.

McKittrick, Katherine. "'Black and 'Cause I'm Black I'm Blue': Transverse Racial Geographies in Toni Morrison's *The Bluest Eye*." *Gender, Place and Culture: A Journal of Feminist Geography* 7, no. 2 (2000): 125–42.

McKittrick, Katherine. *Demonic Grounds: Black Women and the Cartographies of Struggle*. Minneapolis: University of Minnesota Press, 2006.

McKittrick, Katherine. "Mathematics Black Life." *Black Scholar* 44, no. 2 (2014): 16–28.

McKittrick, Katherine. "Plantation Futures." *Small Axe* 17, no. 3 (2013): 1–15.

McKittrick, Katherine, and Clyde Woods. "No One Knows the Mysteries at the Bottom of the Ocean." In *Black Geographies and the Politics of Place*, edited by Katherine McKittrick and Clyde Woods, 1–13. Toronto: Between the Lines, 2007.

Meier, Allison. "W. E. B. Du Bois's Modernist Data Visualizations of Black Life." *Hyperallergic*, July 4, 2016. http://hyperallergic.com/306559/w-e-b-du-boiss-modernist-data-visualizations-of-black-life/.

Melamed, Jodi. "The Spirit of Neoliberalism: From Racial Liberalism to Neoliberal Multiculturalism." *Social Text* 24, no. 4 (89) (2006): 1–24.

Mele, Christopher. "Neoliberalism, Race and the Redefining of Urban Redevelopment." *International Journal of Urban and Regional Research* 37, no. 2 (2013): 598–617.

Omi, Michael, and Howard Winant. *Racial Formation in the United States*. 3rd ed. New York: Routledge, 2015.

Paperson, La. "The Postcolonial Ghetto: Seeing Her Shape and His Hand." *Berkeley Review of Education* 1, no. 1 (2010): 5–34.

Savoy, Lauret. *Trace: Memory, History, Race, and the American Landscape*. Berkeley, CA: Counterpoint, 2015.

Shabazz, Rashad. *Spatializing Blackness: Architectures of Confinement and Black Masculinity in Chicago*. Urbana: University of Illinois Press, 2015. https://muse.jhu.edu/book/41570.

Sharpe, Christina. *In the Wake: On Blackness and Being*. Durham, NC: Duke University Press, 2016.

Tuck, Eve. "Suspending Damage: A Letter to Communities." *Harvard Educational Review* 79, no. 3 (2009): 409–28.

Wilkins, Craig L. *The Aesthetics of Equity*. Minneapolis: University of Minnesota Press, 2007.

Wilson, Bobby M. "Critically Understanding Race-Connected Practices: A Reading of W. E. B. Du Bois and Richard Wright." *Professional Geographer* 54, no. 1 (2002): 31–41.

Woods, Clyde. *Development Drowned and Reborn: The Blues and Bourbon Restorations in Post-Katrina New Orleans*. Athens: University of Georgia Press, 2017. https://muse.jhu.edu/book/52490.

Woods, Clyde. "Life after Death." *Professional Geographer* 54, no. 1 (2002): 62–66.

Woods, Clyde. "Response from the Author." *Journal of Planning History* 3, no. 3 (2004): 256–60.

Wright, Michelle M. *Physics of Blackness: Beyond the Middle Passage Epistemology*. Minneapolis: University of Minnesota Press, 2015.

12

A Black Geographic Reverie & Reckoning in Ink and Form

SHARITA TOWNE

"Ya'll gotta quit fearin' the deep water…"

Howard Sr.'s voice rolls out to his five-year-old daughter splashing in the shallow water along the banks of an Oregon river; she takes up the picture frame. His voice, captured in 1990 by his wife through a camcorder, now plays from gallery headphones at the 2019 Portland Biennial.

In the following pages, I'll try'n break down what that installation was, and what it continues to become, and share my "Ongoing Visual Index." I hope not to impose too much coherence. I hope to keep it real, good God! Art sometimes allows for that. Artspeak sure doesn't.

We'll start with the "close read" anyway.

photo by Mario Galluci

Surrounded by black walls and accented with a black loveseat, a brass reading lamp, and a custom black and brass book lectern, the installation consisted of three artworks—a print, book, and video. The large print, shown horizontally below a black barn light, intentionally casts a stark shadow on the concrete floor below. The print's title, *Black Life & Black Spatial Imaginaries, Glimpses across Time & Space: A Visual Bibliography, 2018–2019*, reflects its origins. It was born of the work Dr. Lisa K. Bates and I did in our three-year "art and research think tank," the Black Life Experiential Research Group (BLERG), where we coded the writings of George Lipsitz and Clyde Woods, among others, into public art interventions, print, video, and community vision. I call it the Black Life print for short.

The Black Life print is accompanied by an artist book, *Alluvium* (its shortened name), which contains written contributions from Alexis Pauline Gumbs, Derrais Carter, Katherine McKittrick, LaShandra Sullivan, Shana griffin, and Treva C. Ellison and "ends" with an "Ongoing Visual Index" where I (incompletely) cite the visual and nonvisual source material combined and remixed to make the collages in the print.

It was a rich time. I open the book with the following note and acknowledgments:

a note

I asked friends and scholars, whose work I heavily rely on and admire, to contribute to a book I'd pair with a three-by-four foot print that turned our collective bibliographies and citations into form. Images from archives, books, and maps.
I've called the print an atlas, a blueprint, a visual bibliography.
I've called it and understood it as many things.

It has been these folks' body of work—essays, poems, books—their conversation or friendship, and their gratitude for the lives and work of others that swept me up in rumination and reverie. That rumination and reverie asked to be given form.

I waded through archive streams. I held images up like river rocks. Read. Dreamed.
I was led back to my family, our life and movement following the harvest throughout the Lower Mississippi Alluvial Plains and then moving westward.

This is a delta—of scholarship, of art, of families.
Alluvial thought running within us, the land,
along waterways, roadways, on and off the page.
Black alluvial, fertile ground.

I'm humbled to share this work.

The undercurrents flowing
beneath and above and
through

Black Life & Black Spatial Imaginaries,
Glimpses across Time & Space

ACKNOWLEDGMENTS

This work was deeply informed by attending the symposium "Black Geographies: Insurgent Knowledge, Spatial Poetics, and the Politics of Blackness," at the University of California at Berkeley in the fall of 2017. I'd like to thank all the graduate students who put together such an amazing lineup of presenters, including some of the contributors to this book. Sitting in the Fannie Lou Hamer Center at my alma mater and hearing Katherine McKittrick's keynote lecture titled "Footnotes, Books, and Papers Scattered About the Floor," with pieces from her forthcoming book *Dear Science and Other Stories*, and hearing the collective "hmms" was breathtaking.

I'd like to thank Lisa K. Bates for staring at a four-foot, five-hundred-gram piece of paper until the aha! moment came: "What if it was a visual bibliography?" Thank you for immediately saying, "Yes. McKittrick." And before that introducing me to Clyde Woods, Kevin Young, Pruitt Igoe, the Mississippi River Gulf River Outlet Canal. And . . . and, and. I owe so much growth and creativity to the time we got to work together. Thank you.

Special thanks to the printmakers in the Watershed Center for Fine Art Publishing and Research, supported through the Print Media program at the Pacific Northwest College of Art for your work on *Black Life & Black Spatial Imaginaries, Glimpses across Time & Space*. It was a wild ride screen-printing five rainbow rolls, gluing down gampi paper, gold foiling, the litho, the digital. It still takes my breath away to stand before it and know all the work we put in to it. Thank you.

Thank you to Derrais (d.a.) Carter for dreaming with me.

And thank you to all the contributors in *Alluvium*. Thank you for your thinking, writing, feeling, and Blacking in this artist book and in the world.

I'd like to thank all my family, but name three women here: my sister Shadya Towne, my cousin Nicholl Helms, and my aunt Clara Harris (Aunt Cissy). I'm constantly in awe of what you provide and inspire in people. I thank you and love you.

—S.T.

In the Black Life print, there are five collages, or "clusters," as I call them, that are composed of black-and-white photography, book scans, maps, and round gradients meant to represent Black imagination and the skies and ethers that Black people move through, their steps gilding the waterways and roadways that run on and off the page. The round shapes are also meant to act as telescopes that collapse the past and present of Black place.

The "east" side of the print begins with St. Louis directly under the title, more specifically, archival images of Pruitt-Igoe, known by some as the biggest catastrophe of urban planning in the twentieth century. Starting under the foot of a small boy, an 1868 map of the Lower Mississippi River connects St. Louis to the largest cluster on the print, a stretch from the Mississippi Delta to New Orleans. Interstate 10 connects a "resting" cotton worker's elbow to the fingertips of a New Orleans–born performer, pictured both picketing and ready for the stage in Los Angeles. From there, the I-5 connects LA to the Black spatial imaginaries of Portland, where a house awaiting demolition, taken through eminent domain to build a hospital, sits atop a smiling woman's head like a church hat. Then finally on to Seattle, where a father carries his son on his shoulders on a leisurely walk beneath Mount Rainier, their shadow splitting a redlined Central District map. These places were chosen for a number of reasons—contrasts in urban and rural landscapes and altitudes, and the blending of familial and aspirational intellectual connection to Black thinkers that braid familial and activist histories.

The artist book *Alluvium* flows through the writing, thinking, and unseen relationships that inform the Black Life print. I asked for writing from Katherine McKittrick, whose lecture, as I mentioned in the book's acknowledgments, informed this work. *Alluvium* then moves into Derrais Carter's short Midwest family road trip essay, "Black Traces"; Shana griffin's independent research on Black women organizing in New Orleans public housing; Treva C. Ellison's "Un/geographies of Los Angeles," which depicts people, events, and places that animated the gay liberation movement in LA, alongside hot spots for anti-queer policing in the 1960s as well as Ellison's oral history work with Black and gender nonconforming activist and artist Sir Lady Java (pictured in the Black Life print); and an oracle incantation written in footnotes by Alexis Pauline Gumbs after Jamaica Kincaid's "Blackness" from her book *At the Bottom of the River*. It ends with LaShandra Sullivan's piece "Holding On," which divulges her modes of thinking as she moves through the space of her family home, which presents immense collections and accumulations of things.

BLACK LIFE
& BLACK SPATIAL IMAGINARIES
GLIMPSES ACROSS TIME & SPACE

The artist book is offset print on paper meant to mimic the spectrum of light, between gold-foiled black linen covers, with Galaxy Gold, Cosmic Orange, Rocket Red, Outrageous Orchid, Celestial Blue, Terrestrial Teal, Terra Green, Astrobright papers. Each color marks a shift in book signature and the transition from one writer to another. It is an exposed smyth-bound book, so you can see the resulting gradient that forms the book's spine, showing that all the writers' contributions have been sewn and braided together by thick, wheat-colored thread.

And, finally, the video, *5th Street Imaginary: A Family, a Geography*. The late 1980s/early 1990s family shown in the video is my own, captured by my Aunt Cissy (Clara Harris, née Helms) in Salem, Oregon. The video sets the scene for my cousin Quentin's Fourth of July birthday and then switches to a river trip five days later. The video was installed on the ground directly under the Black Life print, in its shadow, as a nod to the concept of shadow archives introduced to me by Lisa K. Bates from Kevin Young's *Gray Album: On the Blackness of Blackness*.

It's *also* on the ground as evocation and excavation in the place that I was born and currently live—the only US state in the Union to have racially exclusionary language written into its constitution, this place where families like mine migrated from Arizona, by way of Arkansas, among others. We bury our dead here. *And we live!* These two video clips were unedited, selected from digitized VHS segments as is, and together make eight minutes and forty-four seconds. They come from my Aunt Cissy's collection of VHS tapes, some of which dip in and out of precious and everyday family moments, before being interrupted by a football or basketball game that my *somebody* (let's not name names) sat at the VCR to record cable TV over it all.

While my art is *all right*, my Aunt Cissy's cinematography *is really the show here*. Take these time-coded stills to the left that sandwich a one-minute exchange of four siblings speaking of a fifth not present. Allow me to stretch this minute out.

Cissy/Clara: [approaches with camera to the grill area] *What you say, Fred?*
Fred: I said it's almost ready.
Shanika: Hamburger! You guys are cooking hamburgers!
Darlene: [inaudible]
Fred: Come get a picture of this meat. We need something to say, this how it look.

Cissy: [laughter] *So we can show Sol!*

Fred: Stay back now!

Lee: I wanna see it…

Cissy: [laughing]

Fred: …wait…wait…

Cissy: [hyping up her little brother, lifting the napkin to reveal]

Woooo get a close-up of that… OH MY LORD JESUS. It's done by the chef—

Fred: Y'all just call me the colonel.

Cissy: [laughs]

Lee: I hope they put some barbecue on that mush he ate this morning.

[pops chip in his mouth and walks off]

So. Who's missing here? Uncle Sol—the grillmaster. He's in jail. Hence my Dad's joke. When I watched the clip with Aunt Cissy, she remembered. My Dad and Uncle Sol were famous for avoiding jail time, so she laughs a bit when she tells me. It's good to see how *good* everyone looks. When my sister Shadya (the funniest person in the world) drove up from Sacramento to see this work exhibited, who like Gramma Parthenia is not a hugger, she just stretched out her arms to me and cried. "We were a family," she said into my ear. I'm guarded of this video—I've declined captioning it when I've shown it in the "white cube," even though I caption all of my work. And the uncaptioned points me to the unsaid—about how we lost Uncle Fred, my Dad Lee, Aunt Darlene, and all the things my oldest sister Shanika has lost—she's young enough here to cheer "*Hamburgers!*" (ain't nobody excited about the hamburgers, dearheart, the grillmaster would have a good laugh at all this meat sitting in the sun. *Ha!*)—and the unsaid points me to the unknowability of Black life.

Minutes stretch like this often, in what I suppose forms my "artistic process"—equally a Black geographic one. I hovered above this piece of paper for hours, every week, for *well* over a year, as it sat on the work table or drying rack and I ruminated between the ink layers of dawn and dusk. In that hovering, there's a juxtaposition of some real nerdy moments that I can recall. When I started reading Clyde Woods's *Development Arrested*, the map in its opening pages coaxed me to immediately start scouring Mississippi and (eventually South Carolina) census records for the first time for my own family's migration story. To hover over the Black Life print also means some heartwarming/heartbreaking moments, like what may have been the first (and what would become the last) time I met my Uncle David shortly after he got out of prison and shared my catfish with him at a Pappadeux restaurant in Houston. He told me my dad was the funniest person he ever knew—so much so, they used to sit and dream up ways of sending him from their tiny cotton-clearing town in Arizona to the Apollo.

As noted in the "Ongoing Visual Index" from *Alluvium*, reprinted in the following pages, the *Development Arrested* map is juxtaposed onto the hands of a cotton worker, Lonnie Fair. But I'm telling you here—it's *also* Vincent Fair, my Uncle David's older brother, who in a Houston garage before we headed out to eat, after a week of landscaping work, put on too much lotion. Dry hands still run in our family, so I grabbed his hands, and we worked in all the excess lotion together. And it's reflecting on moments like these now that I realize there's no "juxtaposition" of nerd versus heartwarming versus heartbreaking moments in the cracked Black geographic maps of me and Uncle Vincent's eczema-etched hands—they are one in the same.

The coded moments in the clusters of the Black Life print feel *endless*. A collapse of past, present, the body, the page, life, death, reverie, and reckoning. A counteratlas quilt hanging in the window. The Black Life print is literally and figuratively a heavy paper, a shroud and shadow archive *for so much*. And yet it's still *light*—a bird's-eye view flying over in Black geographic reverie. The video beneath reminds us that in addition to Black geographies being a verb, it can be through our own families that we gain an expansive subterranean view—like digging down from below to examine an unearthed palimpsest, to reread histories and place. *Alluvium* keeps reminding me of the ways friend-scholarship as praxis means Black thought on and off the page, a Black collective harvest of knowing and unknowing, an act of re-re-reading, also endlessly. As an artist/researcher and Parthenia Regina Fair's grandchild, I'm humbled to keep re-digging, re-asking, and re-infusing Black life and citation into form.

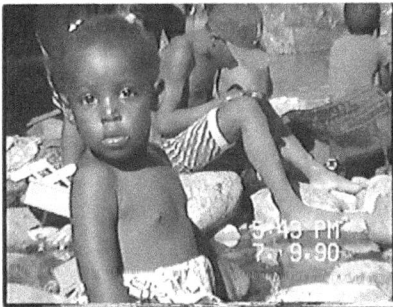

To view images in full color, see the e-book for *The Black Geographic: Praxis, Resistance, Futurity* at https://read.dukeupress.edu/. To watch the *5th Street Imaginary*, see https://vimeo.com/sharita/5thstreet.

An Ongoing Visual Index
a running bibliography and works cited for *Black Life*
& Black Spatial Imaginaries

[flowing footnotes &
alluvial excerpts]

Glimpses across Time & Space[1]

---

1 I'm singing "Voices Inside (Everything Is Everything)" by Donny Hathaway, somewhere between his version and a bright funeral dirge of my own making, the dappled shade from northeast Portland trees moves across my face, as I bike down Going Street:

> *I hear voices, I see people*
> *I hear voices of many people*
>
> *Everything is everything*
> *Everything is everything*
> *Everything is everything*
> *Everything is everything*

ST. LOUIS
AT
PRUITT-IGOE [2]

It was like another world.
Everybody had a bed.
My mom had her own
bed, and I was so happy to
see her just in a room to
herself, with a door.

Before we moved into Pruitt-Igoe,
the welfare department came to our home,
they talked with my mother about moving
into the housing project, but the stipulation was that my father could not be with
us. They would put us into the housing project only if he left the state. My mother
and father discussed it, and they decided that it was best for the twelve children for
the father to leave the home, and that's how we got into the projects.

We're giving you money.
We want to be able to control you.
We're giving you money, so we have
the right to make stipulations as to
how you use it and what you use it for.
There were so many restrictions.
We couldn't have a telephone.
We couldn't have a television.
We were really left at the mercy of
the system.

And then my mother got a letter that we could
have a TV. [...] I was always interested in the
family programs. Programs with fathers. "My
Little Margie" did not live that way. And I
never questioned, I never wondered why, I just
figured this is how it is, where the father was so
involved with his daughter.

[...] When I looked at those
sitcoms, I just felt like this is the
way white people live because
Black people, from my experience,
did not live that way. And I never
questioned, I never wondered why,
I just figured this is how it is.[3]

2 All images and excerpts come from *The Pruitt-Igoe Myth*, directed by Chad Freidrichs (Unicorn Stencil Documentary Films, 2011), kanopy.com.
3 Jacquelyn Williams, interview, *The Pruitt-Igoe Myth*.

In 2005, columnist Sylvester Brown began a series of articles on the Pruitt-Igoe public housing development, where he once resided as a child.[4]

I like people,
I like neighborhoods,
I like driving, and
I like to hear music,
I like to see people
on their front porches,
I like to see kids
playing in parks,
I like to see schools,
I like to see libraries,
I like to see ...
you know ...
and at one time,
Pruitt-Igoe had that.
It had this, this life,
this engaging, electric life.

I was driving down Jefferson Avenue, and I happened to notice the trees. And I've driven by Pruitt-Igoe before, but I really never paid attention to it. There were full-grown trees and the question hit me, "How long does it take to grow a tree?" So, I pulled over and I just looked at those trees, and there were so many, many, many trees, and I thought, "Wow, you know, it's been at least thirty years since I been in there." And I was supposed to get a police escort, and I said, "Eh, I'm not gonna do all that." I wanted my first revisit to Pruitt-Igoe to be alone. It was like a little, mini forest. There was tall grass, white-tip weeds, trees all over the place. And I followed this dusty, little path and I walked up this path and I sat on this big mound of concrete and dirt. I just sat there and I reflected and the sun was goin' down. I remembered it as a child, looking out my tenth-story window and watching the sun go down. So the memories started to come back. And as I was sitting there, I heard this ... and I looked across and there was this black dog just running. I started runnin' out of there and I had this idea that this slobbery dog's gonna jump on my back. But I made it out of there and I remember sitting outside there, panting, and being afraid and I was afraid again. Feeling this fear I felt when I was six years old, the danger of being at Pruitt-Igoe.

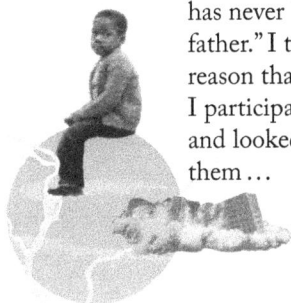

I remember, vividly, my mother telling us, "If white people come to the house and ask you guys questions, tell them that your father is not here. Tell them that your father has never been here, you have not seen your father." I trusted her, I knew there was a reason that we had to do this charade and I participated in the charade, I sat there and looked those people in the eye and told them ...

With pure earnestness that "No, I have not seen my father and no, my daddy does not live here," and, um ... but I knew that I was lyin' and that made me wonder, "Who are these people and how do they have the power to make my mother lie?"[5]

4 *The Pruitt-Igoe Myth.*
5 Sylvester Brown, interview, *The Pruitt-Igoe Myth.*

We have our home here and if the colored move in and run real estate values down it's bound to create tension, and you will have, well, I think their aim is mixed marriages and becoming equal with the whites. I just could not live beside them. I don't feel that they should be oppressed, but I moved here … one of the main reasons was because it was a white community, and that's the only place I intend to live.[6]

Almost from day one, these buildings were undermaintained. There was never an adequate provision for the maintenance, which was so important to these very complex structures. Government paid for building them, but the maintenance had to come out of money from the rents of the tenants. And the tenants couldn't afford the very highly skilled maintenance people to keep these buildings operating. So, in this very basic way, I think the public sector failed the people who were living in these buildings.[7]

The bigger story is in fact of the decline of the city overall. What happened to St. Louis was tragic. It's kind of a slow-motion Katrina in a way. St. Louis lost half its population and had a devastated tax base and a drained economy over the course of fifty years from World War II even to the present. It's no wonder Pruitt-Igoe declined in those circumstances. I mean, it'd be hard to imagine a public housing project surviving under those conditions.[8]

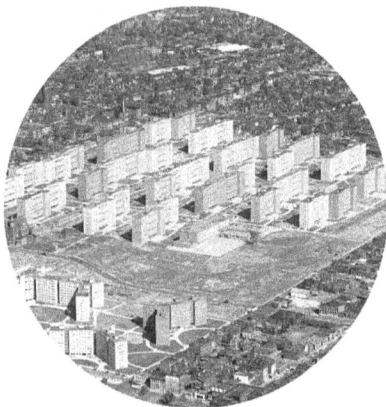

Public housing in St. Louis was always used as a segregation tool. The city did everything in its power to prevent what was called "negro deconcentration"—that is, African Americans moving out of particular neighborhoods. Every project is imagined as a white or Black project, solely, and they're actually placed on the map in St. Louis in ways that deepen the pockets of segregation in one place or the other. It's a way to really radically separate whites from Blacks in ways that no other kind of legislation or other tool had ever been able to do. Pruitt was settled in 1954, right after the *Brown v. Board of Education* decision, and so, very quickly the projects had to be desegregated. And what happens is that whites actually just leave in droves and it in effect becomes an all-Black project, almost immediately. So, by the time you get to the Pruitt-Igoe moment, you have a city that is hypersegregated, in fact, in a region that's hypersegregated.[9]

In the project, it seemed to be strategically planned to create an environment that people felt isolated, that people felt, uh, restricted, that people felt, you know, inhuman almost. "You're bad, we have to restrain you, we have to curtail what you're doing." It was void of humanity. It was void of caring. It seemed more like a prison environment that you have to escape from.[10]

6 Unnamed interviewee, archival footage from local news channel, *The Pruitt–Igoe Myth*.
7 Robert Fishman, interview, *The Pruitt–Igoe Myth*.
8 Joseph Heatchcollt, interview, *The Pruitt–Igoe Myth*.
9 Heatchcollt, interview.
10 Brian King, interview, *The Pruitt–Igoe Myth*.
11 King, interview.
12 Ruby Russel, interview, *The Pruitt–Igoe Myth*.

In February 1969, St. Louis public housing residents began a rent strike, the first of its kind in the history of public housing.

The air of violence and anger […] what I would do is go across away from the projects, and there were fields over there, there was vacant lots with … with weeds. And I had this fascination with insects. What a spider would do to this insect, praying mantises, how they ate other insects. You felt empowered to be able to outthink these insects or be quick enough to catch a grasshopper, so it gave me a sense of control. It gave me a sense of power. That would be my escape. I would be maybe a hundred feet from the projects, but it was like I was a world away in a world all my own. Right across the street, on the other hand, it seemed like it was an environment created by people that didn't like these people. They didn't like me. They didn't like the other people that lived there. The one thing you always ask yourself is why? Why is it like this? Why do I live here? What did I do wrong?[11]

So, handbills were passed out, meetings were held. Senior citizens, handicapped people, young people walking the streets saying, "Don't pay the rent." Well, we're gonna keep rent strikin' until they do something because we know that somebody can do something. They're saying that they're bankrupt—we are, too. They're saying they can't do any more—we can't either. The tenants don't have any money, so I'm tellin' the people to eat and damn the rent. They cannot pay this kind of rent and eat, too, so I'm tellin' the people to eat and damn the rent.[12]

The implosion footage was so shocking just because there was still in people's minds the idea that this had been the solution. It was a very painful moment of truth to see that failure. And that's why, in many ways, Pruitt-Igoe is not just the national and even the world's symbol for the failure of American public housing; it's also been a symbol for the perceived failure of well-intentioned government policies in general. And that's why I think it's so important to look beyond those famous pictures of the towers being destroyed and really try to understand what failed and why. In some ways, Pruitt-Igoe failed because housing alone couldn't deal with the most basic issues that were troubling the American city. There was just no way to build your way out of that tragedy.[13]

In 1972, three buildings of Pruitt-Igoe were imploded with dynamite, the first of which was nationally televised.

I was one of the people that they had to come up with to be able to watch it. It's almost like losin' a child. You hated to see it occur. You hated to see it occur. Here I'm saying again it all depends on how you felt when you went into Pruitt and Igoe, and what it did for you. With me, I was excited about gettin' my first apartment. I was excited about gettin' my poor man's penthouse. It had its ups and downs. It had its crimes, it had its prostitutes, it had its dope pushers. It had everything that everybody else had, but that didn't stop me from caring for it. And when they blowed the building down, yeah, I . . . I hated that very much. And that may not be what people wanna hear, but that's a fact. Some people loved Pruitt-Igoe. Some people hated Pruitt-Igoe. People today, there are people today you meet, they'll tell you, "Don't tell nobody I came from Pruitt and Igoe." They're ashamed . . . I don't know what affected their lives, how it affected their lives. I don't know. I don't know that.[14]

13 Fishman, interview.
14 Russel, interview.
15 Joyce Ladner, interview, *The Pruitt-Igoe Myth*.
16 Valerie Sills, interview, *The Pruitt-Igoe Myth*.

My relationship with Pruitt-Igoe was that of a research assistant. I went to Washington University, to graduate school in 1964. I was working on a National Institute of Mental Health–funded study on social problems in public housing. My role was to study women and girls in Pruitt-Igoe. I was twenty years old, I had just gotten out of college. Some of the girls were eighteen years old and I was two years older, but yet, my life was vastly different. As time passed, I did wonder, would my life have been similar to that of the girls had my parents migrated from Mississippi to St. Louis? Would my opportunities have been different? I guess to put it bluntly, I never saw the people in Pruitt-Igoe as that different from the lives of poor people I had grown up with in Mississippi, except for one thing. The strong, tightly knit communities and families in which I grew up had begun to shatter around the people who were displaced in a northern city with few supports, and the policy of the housing authority was to move the poorest of the poor, the most dependent families, to Pruitt-Igoe.[15]

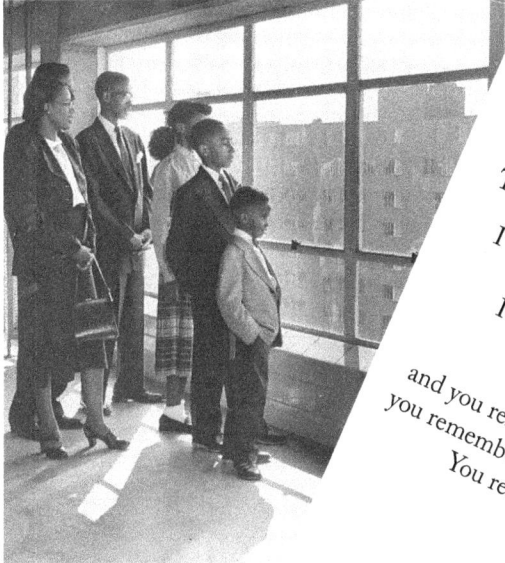

To go to church, I have to come down Cass Avenue. When I hit Cass Avenue, the library is right there and there's a white building on the left-hand side. That's where Pruitt and Igoe started. I look at Pruitt and Igoe in my mind's eye. I try not to think of the bad times. I like to think about the good times. I can see it. It's like when you're a kid and you remember your first Christmas, you ... you remember everything about that Christmas. You remember every toy you got.

I remember Pruitt and Igoe.
  I remember the Christmas lights, I remember the snow.
    I remember the rain, I remember the people, I remember people gettin' beat up,
      I remember people havin' parties, I remember dancin' in the streets,
        I remember ridin' my bike.
          I remember we raced up and down the hills.
            It was our home. It was a good thing.

Nobody could tell me that anybody that made that made it for a bad thing.
And if they did, God blessed us.

          He gave us good things in there, he gave us really good memories.
                And, um ... I ain't gonna never forget it.
        When I feel bad, I don't intend to, but I dream about Pruitt and Igoe.
      And I always see myself standin' in the window, lookin' out the window.[16]

What Happens to a Dream Arrested?

The Lower Mississippi Delta region became arrested during these changes . . .
and is presently chained by the bonds of illiteracy, poverty and prejudice.
     Dr Jocelyn Elders, director of the Arkansas Department of Health, 1988[1]

Dear Mr President:

The Lower Mississippi Delta Development Commission was established . . .
in October 1988 as a result of legislation introduced by a bipartisan group of
senators and congressmen representing the Lower Mississippi Delta region
. . . 214 of the poorest and most depressed counties in Arkansas, Louisiana,
Mississippi, Missouri, Illinois, Tennessee and Kentucky.
     . . . Our goal is ambitious but simple—*to make the Delta and its people a
full partner in America's future*. That means giving every person in the Delta
the chance to be a part of the American Dream.
     America as a whole faces difficult challenges as it attempts to compete in
the global marketplace. By any objective economic, educational and social
measurement, the 8.3 million people in the Delta region are the least prepared
to participate in and to contribute to the nation's effort to succeed in the
world economy.
     Governor Bill Clinton of Arkansas, chairman of the Lower Mississippi Delta
          Development Commission, to President George Bush, 15 October, 1989[2]

The establishment of the Lower Mississippi Delta Development Commission
(LMDDC) marked the beginning of a new era for the poorest and most heavily
African American region in the United States. The official goal of the commission was to design a ten-year development plan to eliminate the most profound
features of economic exhaustion and human desperation. Yet the social origins,
organizational practices, and public polices of the LMDDC ensured that the
people of the seven-state Delta region would remain mired in a seemingly
bottomless state of crisis. Led by the then Governor of Arkansas and future
President, Bill Clinton, the LMDDC concerned itself with stabilizing the
region's dominant plantation leadership while simultaneously silencing the
century-old African American vision of human development. Consequently, a
development agenda based on social justice and economic sustainability fell
before one based upon the relentless expansion of social inequality.

MISSISSIPPI DELTA TO NEW ORLEANS

In a larger sense, the LMDDC was part of a new international movement led by numerous regional alliances to respond to the devastating consequences of global economic restructuring. The goal of the dominant alliances or blocs is to restore and reproduce their profitability and power. Conversely, the ethnic and working-class communities still trapped in the previous structures of regional inequality are mobilizing in unprecedented numbers to create new and fundamentally transformed societies.

The intellectual traditions and the social conditions that led to the creation of the LMDDC can best be understood by examining the development history of the Mississippi Delta. In 1990, some 60 percent of the nearly half-million people living in these eighteen northwestern Mississippi counties were African Americans (see Figure 1). Although small in size this region is known nationally and internationally as a center of tragedy and schism; of extreme levels of poverty and wealth; and of historic movements of repression and freedom; and as the center of both plantation culture and the African American working-class culture known as the blues.

In order to understand the traditions of development thought that shaped the LMDDC, in this book I examine the Commission as part of the twelfth transformation of the Mississippi Delta's plantation regime. As analyzed in successive chapters, each transformation involved an economic and social crisis; a mobilization by the dominant plantation bloc; a shift in the form of social explanation; the establishment of a new stable regime of accumulation; and a new transformative crisis generated by the countermobilizations of the region's African American, Native American, and poor White communities. Successive Delta mobilizations and countermobilizations have defined and redefined the nation's identity.

17 Clyde Woods, *Development Arrested: The Blues and Plantation Power in the Mississippi Delta* (New York: Verso, 2017), 1–2.

Clyde Adrian Woods's extensive archive is at the Southern California Library for Social Studies and Research in Los Angeles. The archive is enormous. I think he never met a piece of paper he didn't like. But as he demonstrates in *Development Arrested*, we might better encounter archives as proposals rather than proofs. If proposals are evidence of struggle, they indicate, as Woods consistently argues, the perpetual presence of alternatives, neither lost nor in hidden transcripts, but rather out in the open, repeatable, simultaneously syncopating other worlds. In its capaciousness, the blues epistemology employs dialectics as method without reducing consciousness to experience, even though experience matters. I was fortunate to have known this man, to have danced with him (I can't dance), sung with him (I can carry a sea lion better than I can carry a tune), and argued late into the night with him and others (like Bobby M. Wilson) for whom the purpose of what we do is to be able to depend on each other in pleasure and struggle, loss and joy. Clyde Adrian Woods, *presente*.

Ruth Wilson Gilmore, Lisbon, 23 June 2016

18 Ruth Wilson Gilmore, "Introduction," in Woods, *Development Arrested*, xiv.

21 Ben Cosgrove, "Under a Mississippi Sun: Portraits of Depression-Era Sharecroppers," *Money*, October 23, 2014, www .money.com/money/3525476/under -a-mississippi-sun-portraits-of - depression-era-sharecroppers/.

Eisenstaedt's pictures chronicle the lives—at work, at worship, at rest, at play—of sharecroppers on "the world's largest staple cotton plantation," near Greenville, Mississippi.

These photos show Lonnie Fair and his family. My family, same last name, also worked surrounding areas. The girl in this photo shares the same name as my great-aunt, Viola Fair.

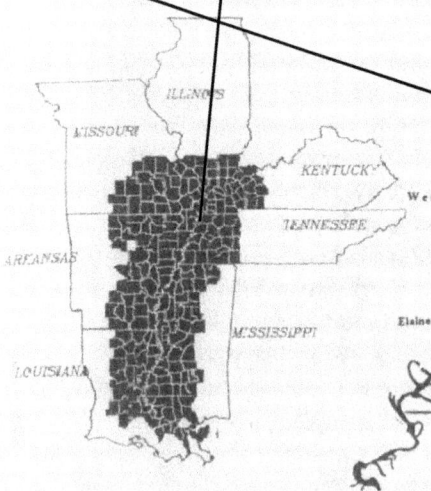

19 Clyde Woods, map on page 3.
pointing to Mississippi County, Arkansas, one of the 214 counties in the LMDCC, and where grandmother, Parthenia Regina Fair, was born.

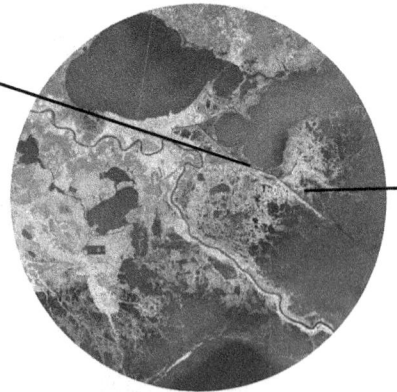

20 Image screenshot from the National Oceanic and Atmospheric Administration's data viewer, May 14, 2018, www.coast.noaa.gov25

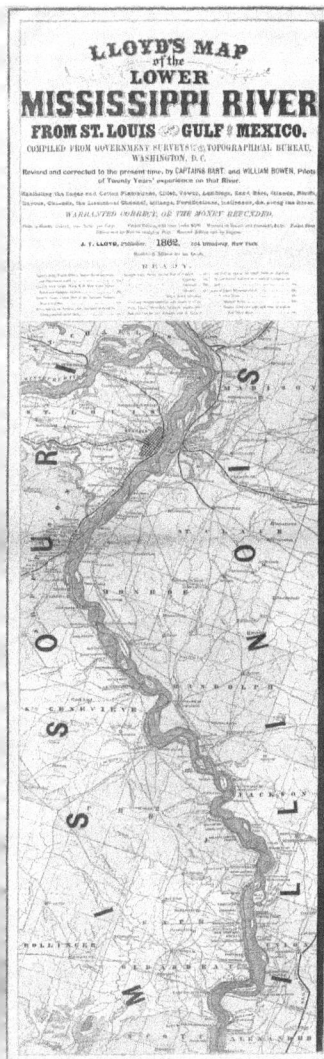

LLOYD'S MAP
of the
LOWER
MISSISSIPPI RIVER
FROM ST. LOUIS TO GULF OF MEXICO.

[Map] exhibiting the sugar and cotton plantations, cities, towns, landings, sandbars, islands, bluffs, bayous, cut-offs, the steamboat channel, mileage, fortifications, railroads along the river.[22]

The Mississippi River Gulf Outlet (MRGO; commonly pronounced "Mister Go") is a seventy-six-mile-long channel that was built to provide a navigation shortcut from the Gulf of Mexico to the heart of New Orleans. Authorized by Congress in 1956 and completed by the U.S. Army Corps of Engineers (the Corps) in 1968, the MRGO originally was 650 feet wide at the top and at least 36 feet deep. More earth was dredged to construct the MRGO than was moved to construct the Panama Canal. [. . .] Prior to construction of the MRGO, the coastal wetlands provided economic opportunities, helped clean water, and provided natural storm surge protection to urban communities like the Lower Ninth Ward, New Orleans East, Chalmette, and Arabi. St. Bernard Parish locals had long called for the closure of the meagerly utilized MRGO, but the exaggerated value of the outlet to the navigation industry perpetuated the channel.[23]

Hurricane Katrina makes landfall in Louisiana on August 29, 2005 with storm surges causing 53 breaches in the federal levee systems protecting New Orleans, flooding 80% of the city. Over 135,000 housing units, approximately 72% of all occupied units, suffer damage and subsequent flooding. Racially- and economically-segregated communities bear the brunt of the disaster, with more than 75% of heavily low-income black neighborhoods flooding. The Lower 9th Ward, the neighborhood with the highest concentration of black homeowners, is devastated by storm surges generated by the Mississippi River Gulf Outlet (MRGO) and by the failed federal levee system.

--

September 28, 2005, Alphonso Jackson, Secretary of HUD, states New Orleans "is not going to be as black as it was for a long time, if ever again."[24]

---

22 James T. Lloyd and Millard Fillmore, Map of the Lower Mississippi River from St. Louis to the Gulf of Mexico; compiled from Government surveys in the Topographical Bureau, Washington, DC (New York, 1862). Retrieved from the Library of Congress, www.loc.gov/item/98688409/.
23 "MRGO'S History and Its Impacts," MRGO Must Go, www.mrgomustgo.org/history-of-the-mrgo-channel-impacts/
24 Shana griffin, "DISPLACED. New Orleans: An Abbreviated Timeline," 2017.

LOS ANGELES

West Hollywood

The second location of the Gay Community Services Center (now the LA LGBT Center). This property was purchased in 1975.

This was listed as the mailing address for GCA, although they also held meetings at the Metropolitan Community Church

Site of Sir Lady Java's ongoing struggle against the LAPD over Rule No. 9, December 1966 - November 1967

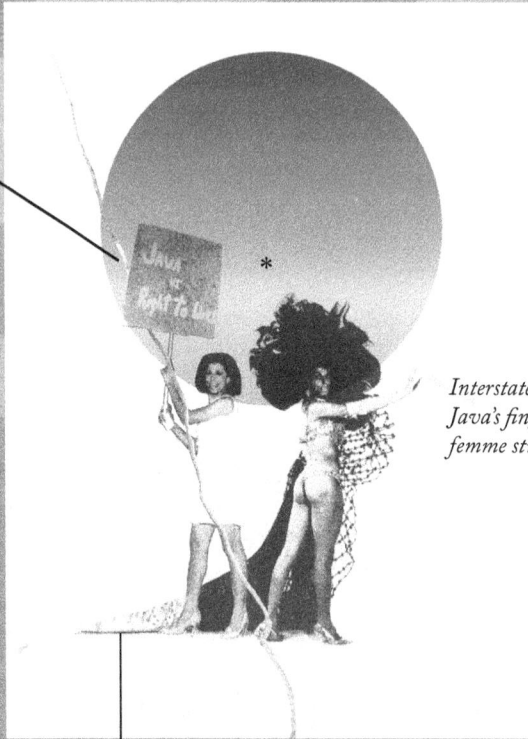

Interstate 10, traced in gold foil, runs from Sir Lady Java's fingertips. As lightning and conduit for the Black femme strategy she brought from New Orleans to LA.

On January 27, 1950 an LAPD officer saw three young black women exiting a theater restroom. The officer approached them assuming they were "pickpockets" and upon booking "discovered" that they were not cis-gender women and then arrested them for masquerading. It is not clear if there was any evidence substantiating the pickpocket accusations.

US Mission is a gay religious charity organization that provided shelter, meal, and job placement services throughout the 1970s. They were also actve in the Effland and Turner mobilizations

The Black Cat is a site of one of three pre-Stonewall melees between police and LGBTQ people

Silver Lake

This is where GLF - LA listed as their mailing address and office. For the firt year of its existence, Transgender Action Organization, founded by Angela Douglas, shared office space with GLF-LA

Map Description

—"Un/geographies of Los Angeles" depicts people, events, and places that animated the gay liberation movement in Los Angeles alongside hot spots for anti-queer and anti–sex worker policing in the decade of the 1960. The "hot spots" are the translucent shaded areas and represent the LAPD districts in which the average yearly arrest rate for charges of sex work and lewd conduct exceed two hundred during the decade of the 1960s. The map is underlaid with the neighborhood ratings established by the Homeowners' Loan Corporation in the late 1940s that rated Residential Security on a scale of First Grade (green) to Fourth Grade (red). Often a rating of Fourth Grade (also termed Hazardous) could be given to a neighborhood simply for having a presence of nonwhite and/or foreign-born residents. My goal with this map is to show how the racialization of space is the unacknowledged logic that guides both LGBTQ criminalization and LGBTQ social movements and mobilizations in Los Angeles.

—Treva C. Ellison

This is the first location of the Gay Community Services Center, which is now known as the LA LGBT Center. The GCSC rented property at several addresses in this area to house the at least 13 survival programs that the center spearheaded from its inception. These programs were modeled off of the survival programs of the Black Panther Party

One of the early homophile / gay liberation era organizations that arose and played in active role in the mobilizations around Effland and Turner's murders

SANTA MONICA BLVD

MELROSE AVE

W 6TH

Alvarado Terrace

South Park

Finan Distr

Fash Distr

W ADAMS BLVD

PORTLAND & OREGON

Interstate 5 runs up from Sir Lady Java in LA, as she once came to Portland and performed at Geneva's Lounge.[25]

NOV 15 1962

Negroes

NET MIGRATION of Negroes from the South to the North and West averaged about 12,000 monthly in the 1950s, a pace which continues.

"Around 1962, when I was living in Spokane, Washington, I looked in the bank one day and realized I had saved this bunch of money. So I thought it's time for me to go buy a nightclub," recalls Paul Knauls, a longtime leader in Portland's African-American community. [...] "The Cotton Club was the spot to be, because we ran a good operation, with the best music, best food, and great camaraderie. [...] All the celebrities who came to Portland in those years ended up at Cotton Club," Knauls recalls. "When Joe Louis came to town, he hauled in there; the Mamas and the Papas, the Kingston Trio—they all came because they wanted to hear our rhythm and blues and jazz." [...] "We bought another club, at 4228 N Williams, which we called Geneva's. So now there were five clubs this side of town, and Geneva and I owned three of them. Two were basically Black clubs, and the Cotton Club served both white and Black clientele." Things remained good for the Knauls until April 4, 1968, the day Dr. Martin Luther King Jr was assassinated. [...] "I closed all my businesses during the time of the riots," Knaul recalls, referring to the racial tensions that led to demonstrations along Union Avenue, now Martin Luther King Jr. Boulevard. "You don't want alcohol involved in all that."

"After the riots, I could tell right away a big change was coming, because I knew the whites wouldn't come anymore. [...] Business at the Cotton Club fell off right away." [...] "In the 1970s, when Emanuel Hospital bought so many houses and businesses along Williams, most of our people moved to Parkrose out on Sandy Blvd. [...] Now, if you go block by block, there's probably not four businesses owned by African-Americans in the same block."[27]

---

25 Kellen Lambert-Vail, "Intersectional Women's Day: Amazing Transwomen," *Tomboy X*, March 7, 2019, https://tomboyx.com/blogs/news/intersectional-womens-day-amazing-transwomen.
26 *Oregon Journal* clipping, November 15, 1962, courtesy of Sharita Towne.
27 Judy Blankenship, interview with Paul Knauls, in "Intersections: Trimet Interstate MAX Light Rail Community History Project," 2003, Portland, OR.

PDC
PORTLAND
DEVELOPMENT
COMMISSION

4

ADOPTED AUGUST 2000

As Amended on June 13, 2001

I. INTRODUCTION

The Interstate Corridor Urban Renewal Area includes a diverse collection of historic communities in north and northeast Portland. It comprises a variety of older residential neighborhoods, interconnected by commercial corridors, with large scale industrial centers lying on its western and northern edges. It also incorporates parts of such regional features as the I-5 freeway, the Willamette River, and the Columbia Slough.

The changes occurring in north and northeast Portland, and the potential benefits of urban renewal, promise reinvestment in the area. At the same time, these investments represent a source of serious concern to many, particularly lower income families, individuals, and small businesses which are potentially threatened by the revitalization of the Corridor.

People are the backbone of this community – those who live, work, learn, play, and worship in the neighborhoods within the Corridor. To a large extent, the future success of urban renewal efforts within the Interstate Corridor must be measured in terms of how they benefit the people in this community. This is especially important given the past experience of many in the Corridor. Past large scale public projects have been harmful to many, particularly members of the African-American community, entailing the involuntary displacement of residents and businesses for projects such as Memorial Coliseum, the I-5 freeway, and Emanuel Hospital. The negative legacy of urban renewal, and of these other large scale public projects in this community, still lingers.

"People were displaced—life investments and achievements were disrupted with no chance to rebuild. All people who were affected by condemnation had a difficult time re-establishing their lives. African Americans had an especially hard time achieving their goals—they faced discrimination, red-lining, and the perception that they were considered a bad risk for the programs that were supposedly designed to assist them."--Pauline Bradford

"There has been a lot of displacement, a lot of promises that were not kept, a lot of things that were promised, following on the heels of programs that never happened."--Cathy Galbraith

---

Interstate Corridor Urban Renewal Plan

Page 1

---

28 (*Opposite, photo collage*) House on northwest corner of North Stanton and Commercial looking northwest. Area about to be demolished. Emanuel Hospital building site. December 20, 1960. Photo courtesy of Thomas Robinson.

29 (*Right*) Voter registration drive at the McDonald's, Union and Fremont, president of United Minority Workers Nate Proby administering oath to voter Francis Newman, April 18, 1972. Photo courtesy of Thomas Robinson.

30 Interstate URA Plan, 2000, 1, accessed August 17, 2019, prosperportland.us/wp-content/uploads/2016/07/Interstate -URA-plan.pdf.

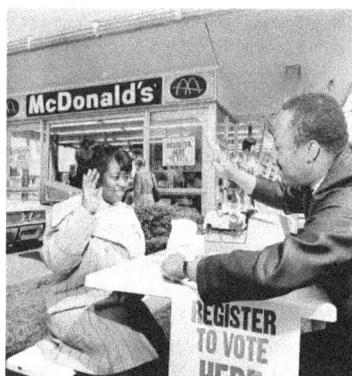

Interstate Alliance to End Displacement

Our purpose is

To increase the power of low-income residents and residents of color in the Interstate neighborhoods to demand real change and to win concrete victories in order to prevent further forced housing displacement and to preserve affordable housing.

We are

Individuals and organizations that are acting as allies to low-income residents and residents of color in the Interstate neighborhoods.

To get involved

- Sign the attached "Interstate Declaration of Rights",
  fill out the coupon on the back and mail or fax to CAT
- Ask your organization and friends to sign the "Declaration"
- Attend the next action or meeting
- Volunteer your time and skills – Call Tomás Garduño at CAT at 503.460.9702

Organizations that comprise the Interstate Alliance to End Displacement

Community Alliance of Tenants– Community Development Network– Coalition for a Livable Future – Fair Housing Council of Oregon– Portland Community Land Trust – Elders in Action – Park Terrace Tenants Council - Augustana Lutheran Church - Democratic Socialists of America, Oregon - Peninsula CDC - Rondel Court Residence Council - Portland Community Reinvestment Initiatives Inc. - Environmental Justice Action Group – League of Women Voters – Open Hand
Portland New Party – Portland Radical Women – Growing Gardens - People's Food Co-op
Hayden Island Mobile Home Owners and Renters Association – POWER! – Portland Jobs with Justice
Portland Industrial Workers of the World – Sisters In Action For Power – Oregon Food Bank – Poverty Action Team Hacienda CDC – Workers' Organizing Committee – Northwest Housing Alternatives - the Latino Network - 1000 Friends of Oregon - Black Youth Political Action Committee - Better People - Bicycle Transportation Alliance - Laughing Horse Books-City Repair Project – Portland Gray Panthers
Seattle Tenants Union and the Mission Anti-Displacement Coalition (San Francisco, CA)

The big deal about Forced Displacement

What is forced displacement?

It is the forced movement of people out of and away from their neighborhoods because of the rising costs of housing. Forced displacement has historically been known to create an almost complete cultural and identity shift of a neighborhood and its residents. It moves poor, working poor, working class residents, and often people of color, immigrants and elderly out, while moving an influx of wealthier, often white, residents in.

Who is at risk for forced displacement in Interstate?

The vast majority of people at risk are *renters*, most of who are *people of color* and *long-time residents who cannot afford rent increases or moving costs*.

*People working in low-paying service jobs • People who are unemployed or underemployed
Single parent families • People with disabilities who cannot work
Elderly and others on limited and fixed incomes • Recent immigrants
Families with high medical or childcare costs • Young families who grew up in the area*

What causes forced displacement?

- *Forced displacement* happens when rents and property values rise faster than incomes. Renters' incomes don't keep pace with rent increases, nor with the costs of moving when their homes are sold out from under them, and they are forced to find a new home outside of their neighborhoods.

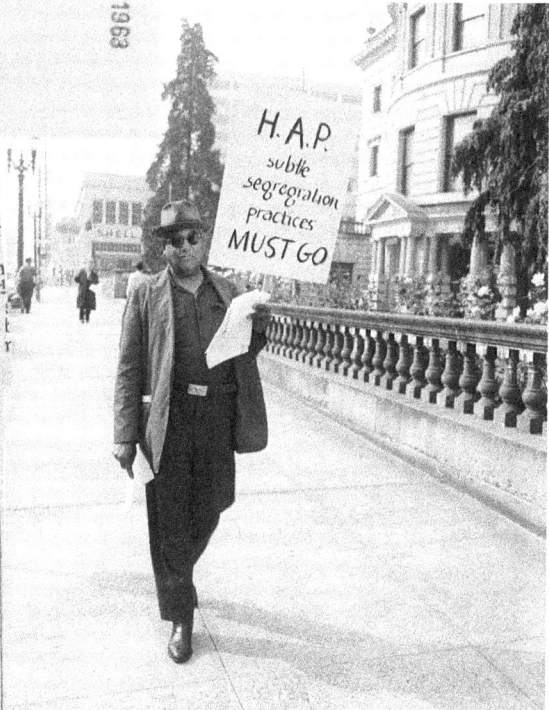

Picketing Here Rips HAP 'Bias'

Negroes–

A dozen pickets from NAACP marched around City Hall Monday morning calling for the removal of all officials of the Portland Housing Authority.

The pickets carried placards and handed out pamphlets in which they accused HAP of racial discrimination.

THERE WAS no disorder. Two policemen stood watch, but passersby gave the pickets only a curious glance.

Several pickets were white.

Particularly singled out for attack were two of the authority's top officials, Executive Director Gene Rossman and Chairman Roy Renoud.

"They're running the whole show," said Mayfield Webb, local president of the NAACP.

Webb found Mayor Terry D. Schrunk presiding over a council chamber meeting with a 19-member Japanese study team. Webb had made no appointment, and unable to see the mayor he left a letter in Schrunk's office. Signed by Webb, it read:

The Portland branch NAACP through action of its executive committee and membership calls for the removal of the chairman and executive director of the Housing Authority of Portland . . ." Attached was a mimeographed list of "complaints" against the housing body.

Later Schrunk set up an afternoon meeting in his office with Webb, to discuss the matter.

The pamphlets also charge the Housing Authority with attempting in 1961 and 1963 to build a project in the Albina district, mainly for Negroes.

The storm over Northwest Tower blew up again recently when HAP advised President Kennedy not to come to Portland to dedicate the project because of threatened NAACP picketing.

WEBB SAID the NAACP

31 (*Opposite*) Interstate Alliance to End Displacement handout, 2002, courtesy of Lisa K. Bates.

32 (*Above*) *Oregon Journal* clipping, September 30, 1963, courtesy of Sharita Towne.

33 (*Above, right*) NAACP picketing City Hall, Portland, Oregon, photographed by Hugh Ackroyd, September 30, 1963, www.theskanner.com/photo-gallery /news-events/racing-to-change.

SEATTLE

When my father, Al Smith, was given a Kodak camera as a preteen, he fell in love with photography. From then on, he always had his camera. It was like a universal key that opened doors and gave him license to go anywhere. My father prided himself in knowing Seattle's streets and what was happening around town and in the black community. He seemed to know everyone.

The son of Jamaican immigrant parents, Al was born in 1916 and grew up in the Central District around 14th Avenue and Madison Street. […]

Shouldering his camera seemed to give him a certain confidence as he ventured into the crowded jazz clubs. He usually didn't ask people's permission to take pictures. Everyone just assumed he was supposed to be there. He would get right onstage to photograph the jazz greats.

During my parents' 50th wedding anniversary celebration in June 1991, my father made the only speech I ever heard him make, saying, "I would like to introduce you to someone who has been with me most of my life … my camera."[34]

34 Al "Butch" Smith Jr., "My Father and His Camera," in *Seattle on the Spot: The Photographs of Al Smith* (Seattle: Museum of History and Industry, 2017), 35.

35 Linda Holden Givens, "Oscar William Holden: Seattle's Patriarch of Jazz through the Eyes of a Granddaughter," *History Link*, June 2, 2015, www.historylink.org/File/11074.

36 *Seattle on the Spot: The Photographs of Al Smith*, 61.

37 (*Opposite, photo collage*) Al's brother-in-law Dr. Donald Phelps during a family picnic to Mount Rainier National Park, around 1955. Dr. Phelps was a prominent educator who later became the chancellor of Seattle Central Community College. *Seattle on the Spot: The Photographs of Al Smith*, 45.

38, 39 (*Opposite, above*) E. G. Wendland, "Commercial Map of Greater Seattle," Kroll Map Company, via Home Owners' Loan Corporation, January 10, 1936.

Robert K. Nelson and Edward L. Ayers, "Mapping Inequality," *American Panorama*, accessed August 20, 2019, https://dsl.richmond.edu/panorama/ redlining/#loc=4/36.71/-96.93 &text=intro.

Oscar Holden Sr. at his home in 1952. […] Five of his children became musicians.[36]

COMMERCIAL MAP OF
GREATER SEATTLE
Published by
KROLL MAP COMPANY, INC.
Seattle

Scale

Elliott Bay

GRADE OF SECURITY:
A. BEST.
B. STILL DESIRABLE.
C. DEFINITELY DECLINING.
D. HAZARDOUS.
E. BUSINESS.
E. INDUSTRIAL.

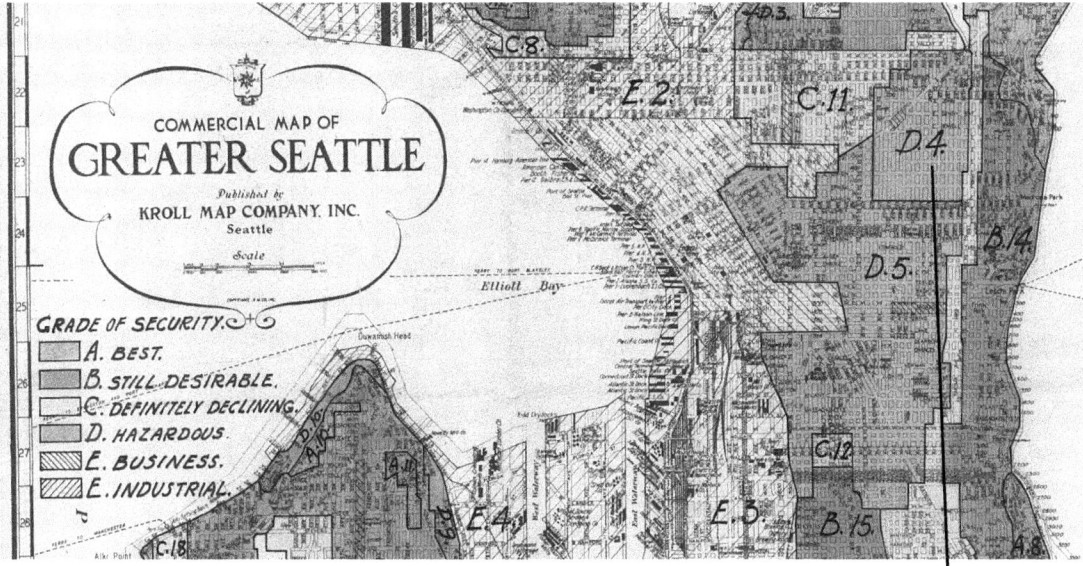

D-4 Area:
This is the Negro area of Seattle.

D-5 Area:
This district is composed of various mixed nationalities.   Homes
are occupied by tenants in a vast majority.   Homes generally old
and obsolete in need of extensive repairs.

I was fortunate enough to have spent time with my grandfather from when I was born. My family had been living in Los Angeles for two years when my grandfather passed in 1969. A quiet man, he never discussed his past with us and I never asked questions at that young age. My mother Sandra Browne made sure we had some kind of relationship with our grandfather. She said he would hug and kiss us every time we were all together. He was proud of his grandchildren. We loved him as grandchildren love their grandfather. My memories are vague but distinctive: He would call my mother to take us to Mount Rainier or local parks or to watch parachutes in Issaquah. My mother would cook and take food to him. If I knew what I know today, I would have spent more quality time with him. Wouldn't you know it, my grandfather turns out to be a well-known and well respected musical genius of a man and many musicians call him the "Patriarch of Seattle Jazz," a legend, a leader, influential, and a premium pianist.[35]

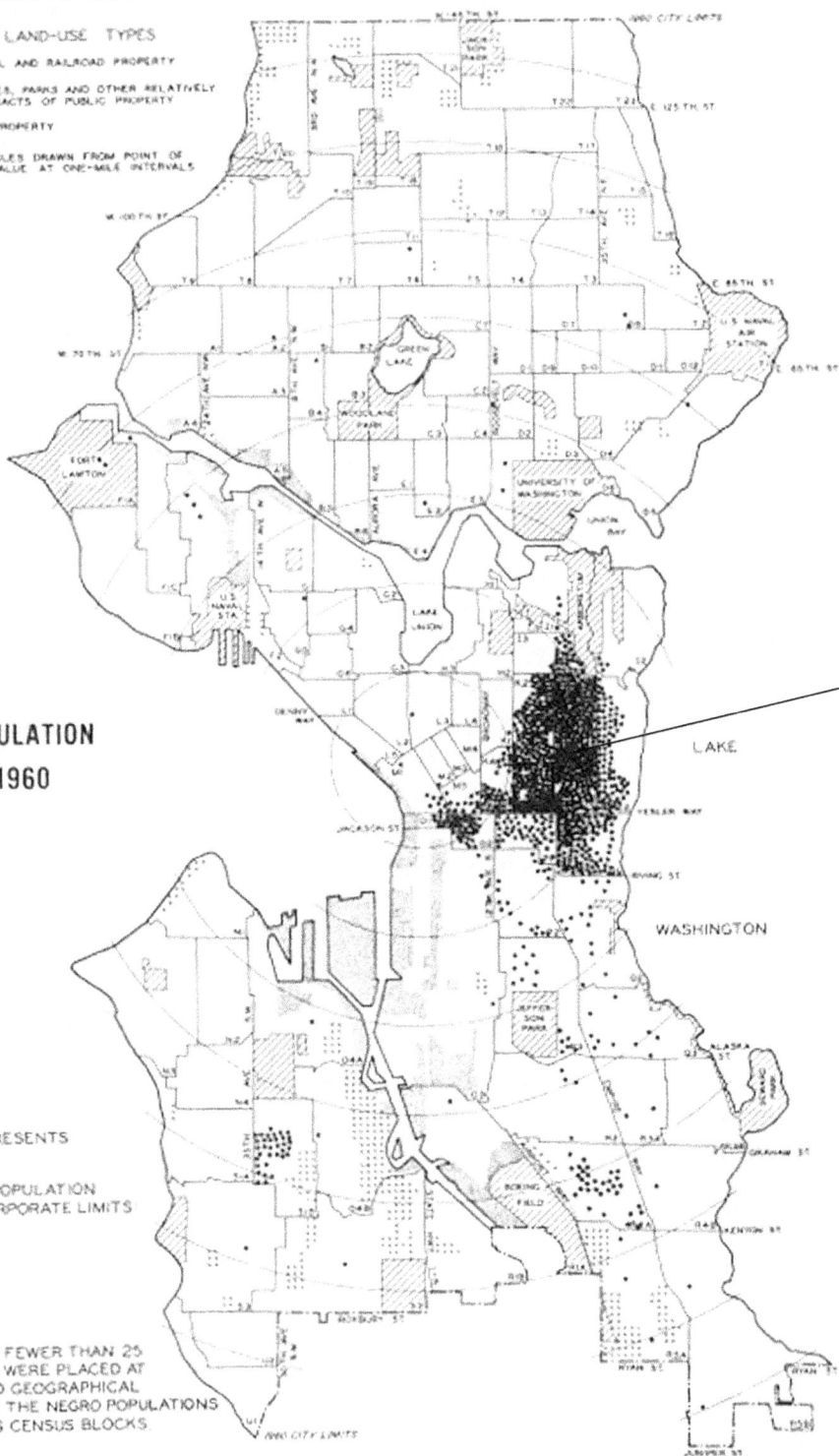

GENERALIZED LAND-USE TYPES

INDUSTRIAL AND RAILROAD PROPERTY

CEMETERIES, PARKS AND OTHER RELATIVELY
LARGE TRACTS OF PUBLIC PROPERTY

VACANT PROPERTY

CONCENTRIC CIRCLES DRAWN FROM POINT OF
HIGHEST LAND VALUE AT ONE-MILE INTERVALS

NEGRO POPULATION
SEATTLE: 1960

EACH DOT REPRESENTS
25 PEOPLE

TOTAL NEGRO POPULATION
WITHIN 1960 CORPORATE LIMITS
26,901

IN AREAS WITH FEWER THAN 25
NEGROES, DOTS WERE PLACED AT
THE ESTIMATED GEOGRAPHICAL
MEAN POINT OF THE NEGRO POPULATIONS
OF CONTIGUOUS CENSUS BLOCKS

LAKE

WASHINGTON

In this rapidly gentrifying neighborhood, the deliberate decision to hold on to the family home and create a Black-centric space is a powerful symbol.

Making Wa Na Wari a home for Black art and community is a way to "signal, both to my family members and my broader community, that their presence is recognized and valued. That they're welcome here," Wokoma says. However, he adds, creating a Black home for art in [the Central District] is not a comeback: "I never left."

"Keeping this space Black in this neighborhood is a reclaiming of space," Johnson points out. Making a home for Black art, Black stories and Black connection, she says, is a political, radical act. That's why the team is planning to host big, joyous parties later this spring and summer. "Black folks are not interested in telling their pain all the time. We're interested in the joy part of our story. A house party can act as an anti-gentrification proclamation."[42]

---

40 (*Opposite*) Calvin F. Schmid and Wayne William McVey, *Growth and Distribution of Minority Races in Seattle Washington* (Seattle: Seattle Public Schools, 1964), figure 1:6.

41 (*Above*) Wa Na Wari, photograph by Matt McKnight, courtesy of Elisheba Johnson.

42 Margo Vansynghel, "Turning a Central District House into a Home for Black Artists," Crosscut.com, March 26, 2019, www.crosscut.com/2019/03/turning-central-district-house-home-black-artists.

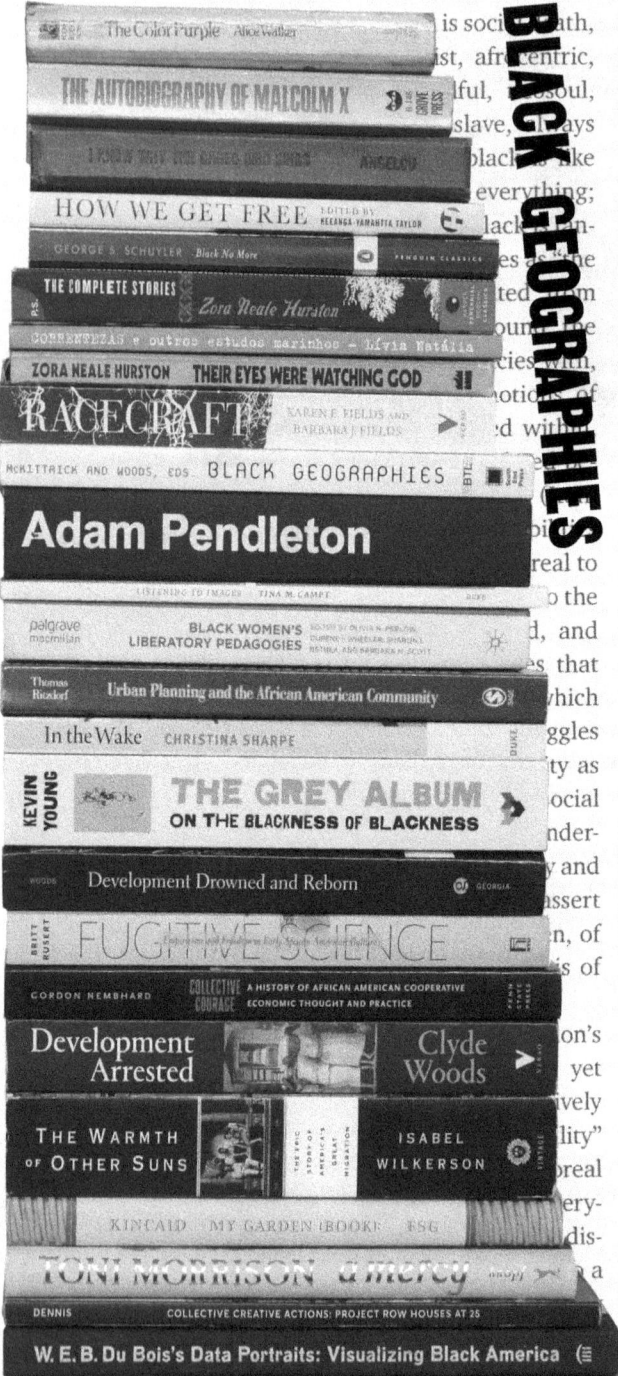

BLACK GEOGRAPHIES

The Color Purple · Alice Walker

THE AUTOBIOGRAPHY OF MALCOLM X · Grove Press

I KNOW WHY THE CAGED BIRD SINGS · ANGELOU

HOW WE GET FREE · EDITED BY KEEANGA-YAMAHTTA TAYLOR

GEORGE S. SCHUYLER · Black No More · PENGUIN CLASSICS

THE COMPLETE STORIES · Zora Neale Hurston

CORRENTEZAS e outros estudos marinhos · Lívia Natália

ZORA NEALE HURSTON · THEIR EYES WERE WATCHING GOD

RACECRAFT · KAREN E. FIELDS and BARBARA J. FIELDS

MCKITTRICK AND WOODS, EDS · BLACK GEOGRAPHIES

Adam Pendleton

LISTENING TO IMAGES · TINA M. CAMPT

palgrave macmillan · BLACK WOMEN'S LIBERATORY PEDAGOGIES

Thomas Rozdof · Urban Planning and the African American Community

In the Wake · CHRISTINA SHARPE

KEVIN YOUNG · THE GREY ALBUM · ON THE BLACKNESS OF BLACKNESS

WOODS · Development Drowned and Reborn · GEORGIA

BRITT RUSERT · FUGITIVE SCIENCE

GORDON NEMBHARD · COLLECTIVE COURAGE · A HISTORY OF AFRICAN AMERICAN COOPERATIVE ECONOMIC THOUGHT AND PRACTICE

Development Arrested · Clyde Woods

THE WARMTH OF OTHER SUNS · ISABEL WILKERSON

KINCAID · MY GARDEN (BOOK) · FSG

TONI MORRISON · a mercy

DENNIS · COLLECTIVE CREATIVE ACTIONS: PROJECT ROW HOUSES AT 25

W. E. B. Du Bois's Data Portraits: Visualizing Black America

So, to return to Brand (2002). She writes: "places and indeed those who inhabit them are fictions" (18). She writes: "Everyone thinks that a city is full of hope, but it isn't. Sometimes it is the end of imagination" (110). She writes: "water is another country" (56). She writes: "in the diaspora, as in bad dreams, you are constantly overwhelmed by the persistence of the spectre of captivity" (29). She writes: "The road knows that wherever you find yourself you are" (152). The puzzle I am trying to work out is: how do we think about black impossibility in relation to geography and black geographies? If there is no *from*, where are we? What do we do with the profoundly disturbing impossibility of black geographies that unfold into prisons, north stars, apartheids, and swaths of premature death?

It is worth repeating here some of my signposts: the terrible discursive burden, the brutal unforgetting, the fantastic and impossible, the corporeal predicaments, the profoundly disturbing door of no return – the nowhere of black life. What I want to propose is that the nowhere of black life is one of many useful analytics through which to orient our political vision of black geographies.

The project of black studies, which has long worked through the monumental workings of corporeal dispossession, has also consequently conceptualized liberation and modernity as tied to multi-scalar spatial processes that cannot easily replicate the prevailing order of geographic knowledge. This is to say that the profoundly disturbing nowhere of black life, in fact, provides a template to imagine the production of space not through patriarchal and colonial project trappings (e.g. we want our own space, and to own space, on your (anti-black colonial) terms, give us a place in your system) but instead as a project that, to borrow from Glissant (1997), engenders relations of uncertainty (e.g. space is relational to praxis of black human life, black geographies are therefore not nouns but rather are verbs that are ongoing and never resolved). The corporeal predicament – the body weighed down by an unforgettable history – is there, but it is not knowable as a suffering object that reinforces the global web of anti-blackness. So, in this conceptualization of black geographies, the nowhere of blackness is not rendered non-existent, rather fosters an *outlook* that is structured by, but not necessarily beholden to, crass positivist cartographies.

This kind of analytics, I hope, does something new to the black body – dislodging it as the only source of black knowledge (and therefore liberation), while also honoring it as the location through which black anti-colonial praxis emerges. The geographic puzzle, then, becomes one of cautiously reordering our methodological approach to anti-blackness, so that the question of liberation is not tied to already existing analytical cosmogonies that refuse black life. This is a brutal unforgetting that wants a different future for the unforgettable.

What I have learned from black studies about black geographies is that we might be joyous about the impossibility of wholly institutionalizing black knowledge. This is not about forgetting black queer, feminist, trans, or other insurgent voices, it is about knowing them differently, outside the institutional structures that crudely spatialize the black body – not black people, not black humanity – as only usefully captive and unfree and crudely demarcated as disconnected to other genres of being human. Prevailing geographic

systems prop up this logic: there is a reason a certain analytics of flesh (rather than humanity) is academic currency. I don't want this anymore. I want to forget this. Or, I want to know black life differently. When I wrote *Demonic Grounds* the work of Sylvia Wynter allowed me to think black life differently. I want to remember this, and to remember the radical geographic work of black studies, where the fantastic nowhere of black life allows us to puzzle out new and unexpected – and undisciplined and unacceptable – modes of being human.

44

43 (*Left*) image by Sharita Towne.
44 Katherine McKittrick, "Commentary: Worn Out," *Southeastern Geographer* 57, no. 1 (2017): 98–99, www.jstor.org /stable/26367645.

Anna Livia Brand's research focuses on the historical development and contemporary planning and landscape design challenges in Black mecca neighborhoods in the American North and South. She is investigating how redevelopment paradigms in the twenty-first century reflect ongoing racialization, and her work interrogates the gendered, racialized, and resistant constructions of the built environment over time. Her work on post-Katrina New Orleans examines how racial geographies have been reconstructed after the storm through disciplines like urban planning. Her comparative work on Black mecca neighborhoods traces historical and contemporary productions of racial landscapes and resistance to these constructions in New Orleans, Chicago, and Washington, DC. Brand received her PhD in urban planning from MIT and is currently an assistant professor in the Department of Landscape Architecture and Environmental Planning at Berkeley College of Environmental Design.

C.N.E. Corbin is an assistant professor at Portland State University in the Toulan School of Urban Studies and Planning and serves on the Portland Parks Board. Corbin studies the relationships between society and nature within the built environment by investigating the concept of the green city within the United States. As an environmentalist and urban political ecologist, she focuses on public green spaces and how urban "sustainable development" initiatives and environmental policies and practices impact and shape land uses and public park access.

Lindsey Dillon is an assistant professor of Sociology at UC Santa Cruz. She received her PhD in geography from UC Berkeley and held a postdoctoral fellowship in American studies at UC Davis. Her research focuses on environmental justice in US cities, drawing from environmental history, urban geography, and critical race and ethnic studies. She is finishing a book manuscript on redevelopment and environmental repair in San Francisco. Her publications include articles in *Antipode*, *Environment and Planning D*, the *American Journal of Public Health*, and other journals.

Chiyuma Elliott is an associate professor of African American studies at UC Berkeley. She is the author of four books of poetry and is at work on a monograph tentatively titled "The Rural Harlem Renaissance."

Ampson Hagan is the 2022–23 Dean's Research Associate Postdoctoral Fellow in the Department of Anthropology at Michigan State University. Hagan completed his PhD in sociocultural anthropology at the University of North Carolina at Chapel Hill in 2022. His work examines the alignment of humanitarianism with policing in West Africa, as both target African migrants as objects of concern.

Camilla Hawthorne received her PhD from the Department of Geography at UC Berkeley in 2018. She currently serves as an associate professor in the Department of Sociology at UC Santa Cruz. She is the author of *Contesting Race and Citizenship: Youth Politics in the Black Mediterranean* (2022), which explores the politics of Blackness and citizenship in Italy.

Matthew Jordan-Miller Kenyatta, PhD (or "Dr. Matt"), is a geographer, storyteller, and planning scholar who works at the intersection of place, taste, and urban change from Black speculative and queer perspectives. His academic scholarship focuses on cultural and economic geographies of Black joy, the urban design of public space (especially in commercial corridors), and preserving diasporic heritage through digital humanities and world-building practices. Since 2018, he has been a researcher and lecturer at the University of Pennsylvania Stuart Weitzman School of Design's departments of City Planning and Architecture. His work has been published as articles in *Planning Theory and Practice* and as book chapters in *Just Urban Design: The Struggle for a Public City* (2022).

Jovan Scott Lewis is an associate professor and chair of the Department of Geography at UC Berkeley. He is the author of *Scammer's Yard: The Crime of Black Repair in Jamaica* (2020) and *Violent Utopia: Dispossession and Black Restoration in Tulsa* (Duke University Press, 2022).

Judith Madera specializes in African American and Caribbean literatures from the eighteenth century to the present. At Wake Forest University she teaches classes on the topics of race, critical place studies, and Pan-American intellectual history. She regularly offers seminars in contemporary environmental movements. Madera is the author of *Black Atlas: Geography and Flow in Nineteenth-Century African American Literature* (Duke University Press, 2015) and is completing a long-arc study of Black emancipatory politics and the radical geographic record that emerged through the abolition epoch. She received her PhD in English from the City University of New York Graduate Center, where she was awarded the Melvin Dixon Prize for African American Studies.

Jordanna Matlon is an assistant professor at the School of International Service at American University. Prior to that, she was a postdoctoral fellow at the Institute for Advanced Study in Toulouse. She received her PhD in sociology from UC Berkeley. Matlon is an urban sociologist interested in questions of race and belonging in Africa and the African diaspora, and the ways "Blackness" operates as a signifier, intersects with gender norms, manifests in popular culture, and illuminates our understanding of political economy. In her forthcoming book, *A Man among Other Men: The Crisis of Black Masculinity in Racial Capitalism*, she investigates the relationship between masculinity, work, and globalization in Abidjan, Côte d'Ivoire.

Solange Muñoz is an assistant professor in the Department of Geography at the University of Tennessee. She is an urban geographer and Latin Americanist whose research interests include urban inequality and the ways that marginalized communities access fundamental resources and services, with a particular focus on housing.

Diana Negrín is a geographer, educator, and curator with a focus on race, space, and social movements in Latin America and the United States. Her teaching and writing bridge human and cultural geography, decolonial theory, and environmental justice. Since 2003 she has conducted ethnographic and archival research in Wixarika Indigenous territory in the Mexican states of Jalisco, Nayarit, and San Luis Potosí. She is the author of *Racial Alterity, Wixarika Youth Activism, and the Right to the Mexican City* (2019).

Danielle Purifoy is an assistant professor of geography at the University of North Carolina at Chapel Hill. She earned a JD from Harvard Law School and a PhD in environmental policy and African American studies from Duke University. Her research focuses on the racial politics and law of development in Black towns and communities. Her research has been supported by the Temple Hoyne Buell Center for the Study of American Architecture at Columbia University, the US Environmental Protection Agency, and the Ford Foundation. Purifoy serves on the board of *Inside Climate News*; is the former board chair of the North Carolina Environmental Justice Network; and is also the former Race and Place editor of *Scalawag*, a media organization devoted to southern storytelling, journalism, and the arts.

Sharita Towne is a multidisciplinary artist and educator based in Portland, Oregon. She was born and raised on the West Coast of the United States along Interstate 5 from Salem, Oregon, to Tacoma, Washington, and down to Sacramento, California. She is most interested in engaging local and global Black geographies, histories, and possibilities. In her work, a shared art penetrates and binds people—artists, audience, organizers, civic structures, sisters, cousins, and landscape—in collective catharsis, grief, and joy. Towne holds a BA from UC Berkeley and an MFA from Portland State University. Her work has received support from organizations including Creative Capital, the Fulbright Association, Art Matters, and the Ford Family Foundation. Most recently, Towne was awarded the Fields Artist Fellowship by Oregon Humanities and the Oregon Community Foundation.

Note: Page numbers in italics indicate figures and tables.

www.ingramcontent.com/pod-product-compliance
Lightning Source LLC
Chambersburg PA
CBHW080042280326

41935CB00014B/1762